Lecture Notes in Computer Science 12556

More information about this subseries at http://www.springer.com/series/7410

Mikael Asplund · Simin Nadjm-Tehrani (Eds.)

Secure IT Systems

25th Nordic Conference, NordSec 2020
Virtual Event, November 23–24, 2020
Proceedings

 Springer

Editors
Mikael Asplund [ID]
Linköping University
Linköping, Sweden

Simin Nadjm-Tehrani [ID]
Linköping University
Linköping, Sweden

ISSN 0302-9743 ISSN 1611-3349 (electronic)
Lecture Notes in Computer Science
ISBN 978-3-030-70851-1 ISBN 978-3-030-70852-8 (eBook)
https://doi.org/10.1007/978-3-030-70852-8

LNCS Sublibrary: SL4 – Security and Cryptology

This Springer imprint is published by the registered company Springer Nature Switzerland AG
The registered company address is: Gewerbestrasse 11, 6330 Cham, Switzerland

Preface

This volume contains the proceedings of the 25th Nordic Conference on Secure IT Systems (NordSec 2020) organised at Linköping University, Linköping, Sweden during 23–24th November 2020. It was organised by the Department of Computer and Information Science with support from the national Research Centre on Resilient Information and Control Systems (RICS) financed by the Swedish Civil Contingencies Agency (MSB).

The conference, originally expected to be a physical gathering of researchers, practitioners, and policy makers from Nordic countries, has in the past few years become attractive to many European researchers. This year, the COVID-19 pandemic created an exceptional situation whereby it became clear that the conference had to be held virtually. This obviously impacted the ability of the attending presenters to engage in networking outside the presentation sessions. However, the conference program also reached a wider circle of presenters from across the globe who were able to attend and present.

The conference attracted 45 full paper submissions of which 15 were accepted to be presented and included in the proceedings. All papers were subject to at least 3 reviews by the 39 members of the program committee, to whom we would like to extend our warmest thanks. Altogether, participants from nine countries co-authored the papers in the conference, from as far away places as New Zealand and China.

The program for NordSec 2020 included two outstanding keynote lectures, one from academia, and one from the European Agency for Cyberecurity (ENISA). They discussed security issues and research in the context of future networks and applications, as well as policy issues of importance to society and decision makers, as follows:

- "Security, Privacy and Safety in the IoT", by Prof. Elisa Bertino, Samuel D. Conte Professor of Computer Science, Purdue University, USA
- "Cybersecurity breach reporting in the EU", by Dr. Marnix Dekker, Cybersecurity Expert, ENISA

The organisers of the conference are grateful for the time and effort allocated by the keynote speakers and their excellent talks as a contribution to the program.

The technical papers presented at the conference were organised in 5 sessions: Malware and attacks, Formal analysis, Applied cryptography, Security mechanisms and training, and Applications and privacy. One poster session with discussions around a setup created for education of students in a hacking environment was also organised. Without the timely preparations by the authors and the flexibility of presenters to make the necessary adjustments to do virtual presentations the conference would not have been the successful forum for discussions it became.

In addition to the reviewers and members of the program committee, there was a small group of local organisers essential for the conference to take place in this on-line setting. We gratefully acknowledge the help by Felipe Boeira and Lene Rosell in preparations for the conference and for being prepared to hold the conference in its original physical shape right until September when the decision to go virtual was made.

We do expect that lessons learnt in 2020 can enrich the forthcoming instances of the conference, and more than ever look forward to the possibility of meeting our colleagues in person in some Nordic country every year.

January 2021   Simin Nadjm-Tehrani
                                                    Mikael Asplund

Organization

General Chair

Mikael Asplund   Linköping University, Sweden

Program Committee Chairs

Simin Nadjm-Tehrani   Linköping University, Sweden
Mikael Asplund   Linköping University, Sweden

Steering Committee

Audun Jøsang (Chair)   University of Oslo, Norway
Luca Aceto   Reykjavik University, Iceland
Aslan Askarov   Aarhus University, Denmark
Mikael Asplund   Linköping University, Sweden
Tuomas Aura   Aalto University, Finland
Karin Bernsmed   SINTEF Digital, Norway
Billy Brumley   Tampere University, Finland
Sonja Buchegger   KTH Royal Institute of Technology, Sweden
Bengt Carlsson   Blekinge Institute of Technology, Sweden
Mads Dam   KTH Royal Institute of Technology, Sweden
Simone Fischer-Hübner   Karlstad University, Sweden
Dieter Gollmann   Hamburg University of Technology, Germany
Nils Gruschka   University of Oslo, Norway
Peeter Laud   Cybernetica, Estonia
Helger Lipmaa   Simula UiB, Norway
Katerina Mitrokotsa   Chalmers University of Technology, Sweden
Simin Nadjm-Tehrani   Linköping University, Sweden
Hanne Riis Nielson   DTU, Denmark
René Rydhof Hansen   Aalborg University, Denmark
Juha Röning   University of Oulu, Finland
Andrei Sabelfeld   Chalmers University of Technology, Sweden
Erland Jonsson (Founder)   Chalmers University of Technology, Sweden

Technical Program Committee

Magnus Almgren   Chalmers University of Technology, Sweden
Tuomas Aura   Aalto University, Finland
Stefan Axelsson   Stockholm University, Sweden
Musard Balliu   KTH Royal Institute of Technology, Sweden
Billy Brumley   Tampere University, Finland

Sonja Buchegger	KTH Royal Institute of Technology, Sweden
György Dán	KTH Royal Institute of Technology, Sweden
Christian Damsgaard Jensen	DTU, Denmark
Nicola Dragoni	Technical University of Denmark, Denmark
Mathias Ekstedt	KTH Royal Institute of Technology, Sweden
Katrin Franke	NTNU, Norway
Ulrik Franke	RISE, Sweden
Martin Gilje Jaatun	SINTEF Digital, Norway
Nils Gruschka	University of Oslo, Norway
Meiko Jensen	Kiel University of Applied Sciences, Germany
Thomas Johansson	Lund University, Sweden
Kristian Gjøsteen	NTNU, Norway
Dieter Gollmann	Hamburg University of Technology, Germany
Kimmo Halunen	VTT, Finland
René Rydhof Hansen	Aalborg University, Denmark
Tor Helleseth	University of Bergen, Norway
Audun Jøsang	University of Oslo, Norway
Marcel Kyas	Reykjavik University, Iceland
Martin Hell	Lund University, Sweden
Luigi Lo Iacono	Cologne University of Applied Sciences, Germany
Ville Leppänen	University of Turku, Finland
Stefan Lindskog	Karlstad University, Sweden and SINTEF Digital, Norway
Olaf Maennel	Tallinn University of Technology, Estonia
Raimundas Matulevičius	University of Tartu, Estonia
Per Håkon Meland	SINTEF Digital, Norway
Nils Nordbotten	FFI, Norway
Tomas Olovsson	Chalmers University of Technology, Sweden
Hans P. Reiser	University of Passau, Germany
Mohit Sethi	Aalto University, Finland
Einar Snekkenes	NTNU, Norway
Teodor Sommestad	FOI, Sweden
Emmanouil Vasilomanolakis	Aalborg University, Denmark
Stephen Wolthusen	NTNU, Norway
Øyvind Ytrehus	University of Bergen, Norway

Poster Committee

Felipe Boeira (Chair)	Linköping University
Mohammad Hamad	Technical University of Munich
Ulf Kargén	Linköping University

Additional Reviewers

Abasi-Amefon Affia
Annika Andreasson
Anton Christensen
Jacob Dexe
Edlira Dushku
Alberto Giaretta

Andreas Viktor Hess
Juha Nurmi
Shreyas Srinivasa
Koen Tange
Benjamin Taubmann
Markku Vajaranta

Contents

Security Mechanisms and Training

Applications and Privacy

Malware and Attacks

Persistence in Linux-Based IoT Malware

Calvin Brierley$^{(\boxtimes)}$, Jamie Pont, Budi Arief, David J. Barnes,
and Julio Hernandez-Castro

School of Computing, University of Kent, Canterbury, England
{C.R.Brierley,J.Pont,B.Arief,D.J.Barnes,jch27}@kent.ac.uk

Abstract. The Internet of Things (IoT) is a rapidly growing collection of "smart" devices capable of communicating over the Internet. Being connected to the Internet brings new features and convenience, but it also poses new security threats, such as IoT malware. IoT malware has shown similar growth, making IoT devices highly vulnerable to remote compromise. However, most IoT malware variants do not exhibit the ability to gain *persistence*, as they typically lose control over the compromised device when the device is restarted. This paper investigates how persistence for various IoT devices can be implemented by attackers, such that they retain control even after the device has been rebooted. Having persistence would make it harder to remove IoT malware. We investigated methods that could be used by an attacker to gain persistence on a variety of IoT devices, and compiled the requirements and potential issues faced by these methods, in order to understand how best to combat this future threat. We successfully used these methods to gain persistence on four vulnerable IoT devices with differing designs, features and architectures. We also identified ways to counter them. This work highlights the enormous risk that persistence poses to potentially billions of IoT devices, and we hope our results and study will encourage manufacturers and developers to consider implementing our proposed countermeasures or create new techniques to combat this nascent threat.

Keywords: IoT · Security · Malware · Persistence · Attack · Proof of concept

1 Introduction

A standard piece of advice typically given to affected users for removing malware from an Internet of Things (IoT) device is to restart it, as most forms of IoT malware lack the ability to maintain *persistence* [3,4]. This is because, in general, IoT malware is stored and executed from within temporary filesystems that reside in Random-Access Memory (RAM) [32]. As this type of memory is volatile, the stored programs and data are lost when the device loses power, including any changes that the attacker may have made to the filesystem.

However, there have been some families of IoT malware that are able to maintain persistence in some form [15,27]. If persistent IoT malware becomes

© Springer Nature Switzerland AG 2021
M. Asplund and S. Nadjm-Tehrani (Eds.): NordSec 2020, LNCS 12556, pp. 3–19, 2021.
https://doi.org/10.1007/978-3-030-70852-8_1

more prevalent, many IoT devices will not be recoverable at all once they have been infected. Therefore, it is increasingly crucial for IoT developers both *to understand their devices' potential vulnerabilities to persistence* and *to implement preventative measures to prohibit attackers from exploiting them*. These two aims serve as the motivation for our work.

Contributions. The key contributions of this paper are:

- We summarise IoT persistence and its role in IoT based malware.
- We explain the challenges currently preventing IoT malware from establishing persistence.
- We outline methods that could be used by IoT malware to gain persistence.
- Finally, we explore how this will change the approach of IoT malware and how attackers could achieve and use persistence to perform new and previously infeasible attacks, and what can be done to counter this threat.

The rest of the paper is organised as follows. Section 2 provides some background on Linux malware, IoT based malware and persistence. We also highlight previous research and some of the challenges attackers may encounter when attempting to gain persistence on IoT devices. Section 3 describes several methods that could be used by attackers to gain persistence on various types of IoT device, along with their requirements and limitations. Section 4 shows the results of attempting to gain persistence on four vulnerable IoT devices using these methods. Section 5 discusses some potential countermeasures that could be implemented to prevent an attacker from gaining persistence on an IoT device. Section 6 covers our conclusions and defines some recommended further work.

2   Background

Various families of malware have increasingly attacked IoT devices. Popular botnets such as Bashlite and Mirai have infected hundreds of thousands of devices and have been responsible for one of the largest DDoS attacks in history [11,33]. Fortunately, this type of IoT malware is relatively simple to remove. By restarting the device, the malware will be unloaded from volatile memory, removing the infection from the device when it reboots [3,4].

However, some malware (such as Mirai) often exhibits worm-like behaviour [5] and after hijacking a device, it will scan the Internet for more victims to infect. While users would sometimes restart their devices (either deliberately or coincidentally) and clear the infection, it would not remove the underlying issue. The devices could easily be reinfected, possibly within minutes [3].

In effect, this behaviour has led to competitions between botnet authors, each seeking to maximise their share of the limited number of vulnerable IoT devices. Some malware even exhibited security features to remove competing malware. Mirai, for instance, would search for strings present in competing malware, kill any associated running processes and close any potentially vulnerable services running on specific ports to prevent any further attacks by competitors [5]. However, as these changes were not persistent they were removed when the device was reset.

2.1   Persistent IoT Malware

IoT malware capable of making persistent changes that secure its presence would be able to maintain control over the device through reboots, both removing the requirement to reinfect the equipment and helping towards keeping competitors at bay. The ability to secure persistence would also allow significant changes to the device to persist after rebooting, allowing for more creative types of malware and attacks, such as ransomware [10] or long term spyware. This would also provide a means for the malware operator to install additional malicious features, such as modules that can attack other devices on the infected device's network.

Currently, restarting an infected device will remove the majority of IoT malware, but with persistence, the user would have to modify the flash memory of the device to remove the infection. This is something not usually readily available nor practical to an average user. If the malware can also prevent updates or factory resets, specialist equipment or access to a debug/programming interface may be required to clear the infection. This is considered too complicated for most IoT users to perform and may lead to IoT devices being discarded, or worse, knowingly left in an infected state.

2.2   Challenges with Gaining Persistence

There are two key challenges currently faced by IoT attackers when attempting to gain persistence on IoT devices:

- **Read-Only**. IoT devices often have data that is set to read-only for various reasons, such as to prevent accidental modifications due to programmer error. This feature may also prevent attackers from making the necessary modifications to the stored data or filesystems in order to gain persistence.
- **Variance**. Each device is likely to have different hardware, update mechanisms, software, architecture and filesystem types. Fortunately for IoT developers, the variation in IoT devices makes it quite difficult for attackers to create a universal method for gaining persistence. However, if an attacker were to develop a method that affects a large number of devices with similar implementation, it could reduce the required time investment immensely, leading to persistent IoT Malware becoming more common.

2.3   Previous Persistent IoT Malware and Related Work

After identifying an increase in the presence of Linux based malware, researchers analysed 10,548 samples over a year to gain a better understanding of the techniques used by malware authors [12]. They highlighted the quick development and deployment of insecure IoT devices as a potential motive for attackers to target Linux for malware development.

As part of this analysis, they found that 21.10% (1,644) of the analysed samples implemented persistence methods. Some of these methods can be applied to IoT devices, but the attacker must be able to modify the filesystem. As mentioned previously, IoT devices often set certain data as read only, which would prevent these methods from working.

Some variants of IoT malware have achieved persistence, but these are less common and they rely on the device having a writeable filesystem, which may reduce the applicability of this approach. We examine two examples of persistent IoT malware below.

Torii is a variant of Mirai that adds several features, most notably the introduction of six techniques to gain persistence [15]. Each technique modifies files on the infected device which are executed as part of the boot process, such as:

- `.bashrc`, which is executed whenever an interactive bash session is started;
- `initab`, which is used to determine which processes should be ran during the Linux boot process at certain runlevels;
- `crontab`, which is used to execute files at a certain time or interval.

Modifications to these files would allow the attacker to set particular programs or shell scripts to be run when the device boots.

VPNFilter is a complex IoT malware which affects a large number of routers [30]. It is believed to have been developed by "Fancy Bear", a Russian based hacker group [31]. Its modular structure allows many features to be implemented, ranging from man-in-the-middle attacks to SCADA sniffing. Additionally, VPNFilter seems to include a section of code to erase and rewrite Memory Technology Devices (MTDs)[1], which could potentially be used to brick the device by wiping segments of the device's storage [28]. VPNFilter modifies the `/etc./config/crontab` file, which will run the malware (which has presumably already been written to memory) every 5 min [27,29], even when the device is rebooted.

3   Methods for Gaining Persistence

Due to the challenges described in Sect. 2.2, no universal methods to gain persistence on IoT devices have yet been identified. Instead, our approach is to use a *collection* of methods to gain persistence on *certain subsets* of IoT devices.

We have identified several viable methods that could be used by an attacker to gain persistence on a variety of IoT devices. A summary of these methods can be found in Table 1 and a detailed overview of each is provided in the following subsections. The description of each method includes a list of *requirements* for its applicability, its *feasibility*, and any *potential issues* that may prevent it from working effectively. A malware writer could perform reconnaissance to ascertain which method should be used, or simply attempt each method sequentially until they gain persistence. Some methods could be used in conjunction with others to improve their chances of success.

The techniques described assume that the attacker has gained access to the shell (such as via a guessable telnet password), and can run arbitrary commands.

---

[1] Memory Technology Devices (MTD) are commonly used to communicate with flash devices to manage storage on IoT devices.

Ideally, the attacker should be able to determine the storage capabilities of the device and identify the device model. Many of these techniques also require the identification and modification of filesystems and partitions in flash memory. The /proc/mtd file contains the partition definition and a name set by the developer via MTD, which may indicate its purpose. These partitions can be accessed by using the files /dev/mtd$X$ or /dev/mtdblock$X$ where X is the partition index. The attacker can also find a list of mount points and their filesystem types in the /proc/mounts file, or use analytic tools such as Binwalk [25] to identify recognisable file headers and metadata.

Table 1. IoT Persistence Methods

ID	Method	Modified Partition	Ease of Use
A	Modifying Writeable Filesystems	Filesystem	Easy
B	Recreating Read-Only Filesystems	Filesystem	Medium
C	Initrd/Initramfs Modification	Kernel	Hard
D	"Set Writeable Flag" Kernel Module	N/A	Hard
E	Update Process Exploitation	Filesystem/Kernel	Device Dependent*
F	UbootKit	Bootloader	Hard

*Device update processes differ, so the complexity of exploits will vary.

3.1 Modifying Writable Filesystems

When an IoT device has a writeable filesystem by default, the attacker should be able to modify the filesystem directly via the shell, allowing them to edit important files that run on startup.

Requirements: The device must use a writable filesystem (e.g. yaffs2/ jffs2). The MTD filesystem partitions must be writeable. The attacker must be able to modify the startup scripts.

Feasibility: This is the simplest method and does not require any additional tools. If the filesystem is writeable by default, the attacker can copy their malware to a known location on the device, then modify the startup scripts so that it is executed when the device is rebooted. This is similar to the technique used by VPNFilter and Torii, as described in Sect. 2.1.

Potential Issues: The attacker must be able to obtain write permissions for the files they are attempting to modify, which is dependent on the privileges held by the exploited application or compromised account used by the attacker.

Furthermore, the writable filesystem must store files that can lead to the execution of arbitrary code on startup. Otherwise, while the attacker may be able to store malware permanently, they will not be able to set it to run when the device is booted. The filesystem may also be mounted as read only, so additional steps may be required to remount it as writeable.

3.2   Recreating Read-Only Filesystems

If the device is using a compressed read-only filesystem, the attacker will not be able to modify its files directly. Instead, the attacker can use specialised tools to recreate the filesystem.

Requirements: The device must use a compressed read-only filesystem (such as `cramfs`/`squashfs`). The attacker must be able to modify the flash partition which contains the read-only filesystem. The attacker must have the required software to recreate the filesystem.

Feasibility: While it is not possible to modify files *within* compressed read-only filesystems, it is possible to replace the entire filesystem in flash memory with a modified version. To create a new version of the filesystem the attacker must first obtain the compressed version, which resides in flash memory.

Once the attacker has identified the partition that holds the filesystem, they can use the MTD subsystem to read it from flash to a file, which can then be extracted and modified to their requirements. The attacker can then re-pack it in the correct format. For `squashfs` and `cramfs` filesystems, this requires using the `mksquashfs` and `mkcramfs` utilities respectively. The old version stored in the filesystem partition can then be overwritten via the MTD files in `/dev`.

Potential Issues: Filesystems can vary significantly, even those of the same format. If the replacement filesystem type is different from what is expected by the device, it might not be interpreted correctly, which will lead to a failure during the boot process. For this approach to be practical, the attacker must match the used filesystem as closely as possible.

Read-only filesystems may prove challenging to modify, as it is unlikely that the tools used to build a new filesystem will be included on the exploited device. For device updates, it would be expected that another machine would generate a new filesystem that is then transferred to the device itself. To follow this same philosophy, the attacker would need to copy the filesystem from the infected device to an external computer, then modify it using the required tools. It would then need to be uploaded back to the device for writing. Filesystems are likely to be much larger than the average malware upload, and as they will need to be uploaded to each infected device; this might not scale well if used for a large number of devices.

Alternatively, attackers could compile and upload the required tools for use on the devices themselves. However, as there are likely to be many different filesystem types and device architectures, this may be not easy to manage.

3.3   Initrd and Initramfs Modification

As part of its booting processes, the Linux kernel may utilise an appended `initrd` or `initramfs` filesystem [18]. This is an initial filesystem which allows some setup of the device to be performed before mounting the real filesystem.

Requirements: The device must use an `initrd` or `initramfs` filesystem. The attacker must be able to modify the flash partition that contains the kernel.

Feasibility: First, the attacker must identify the MTD partition that contains the Linux kernel. Once the correct partition has been identified, the attacker must analyse it and determine the offset of the filesystem that is appended to the kernel. After carving out the relevant data, they must save the original kernel and filesystem separately. The attacker can then extract and modify the filesystem to include their required malware. Typically, an `initramfs` filesystem will be contained in a CPIO archive, which will likely also be compressed, and as such, this may require multiple extraction steps. The extraction process must then be reversed, and the resulting filesystem can then be appended to the original kernel. Finally, this data can be used to overwrite the original kernel flash partition.

Potential Issues: The kernel may be stored on the flash chip as an image for use with a chosen bootloader. This may require the attacker to take additional steps to recreate the image and maintain compatibility with the bootloader, such as the inclusion of image headers that the bootloader may use to boot from the partition effectively. As with Method B: unless the filesystem modifications are performed locally, large amounts of data may need to be transferred via the Internet, which might not scale well.

3.4   "Set Writeable Flag" Kernel Module

MTD can be used to manage partitions of flash memory. Developers may unset the `MTD_WRITEABLE` flag for partitions that are unlikely to need modification, which may also prevent attackers from making modifications that would allow them to gain persistence. This method allows an attacker to re-enable the `MTD_WRITEABLE` flag from within userspace if the requirements are met. While this method may not allow an attacker to gain persistence on its own, it may allow other methods to circumvent the read-only protections that were put in place by the developers.

Requirements: The Linux kernel must support loadable modules. Access to a device's kernel header files or source tree will improve the kernel module's odds of being compatible.

Feasibility: The `MTD_WRITEABLE` partition flag can be difficult to modify from userspace at runtime. However, by using a Loadable Kernel Module (LKM), an attacker could force this flag to be set from kernel space. There are existing kernel modules that have been created to implement this [16,19].

Kernel modules typically need to be compiled against the targeted kernel source to be compatible. This is normally achieved by having access to either the kernel's headers or source tree [1]. If IoT developers use modified software that falls under the GNU Public License (GPL), they may be required to make the corresponding source code available [26]. The attacker can use this to compile the kernel module for the targeted device.

After compiling and uploading the LKM to the target device, the attacker can use the `insmod` utility to insert the module into the kernel. Once inserted, the module is able to set all MTD partitions to be writeable, after which the attacker can use one of the other techniques to gain persistence.

Potential Issues: If the device's kernel header and source code are unavailable, it may be difficult to compile the LKM such that it remains compatible. However, a defensive IoT tool "HADES-IoT" demonstrated that loadable kernel modules could be compiled without the support of the original developer [9].

The developer may be able to prevent this method from being used by configuring the Linux kernel to verify the signature of kernel modules when they are loaded [2]. The attacker will not be able to forge a signature for kernel modules if they do not have access to the developer's cryptographic keys.

3.5   Update Process Exploitation

Most devices are expected to receive updates over their lifetime, either to provide new user features or patches for security issues. However, vulnerable update implementations can potentially be used to attack the device and gain persistence.

Requirements: The device must implement a vulnerable update function, such that the attacker can forge fake updates. The attacker must be able to access the update function.

Feasibility: If an attacker gains access to a vulnerable update function, they may be able to provide a false firmware update which is accepted by the device. For example, researchers found vulnerabilities in devices produced by Disney [8] and Netgear [7], which allowed them to upload modified firmware. An attacker could use these modified updates to include malware and configuration files such that arbitrary code is run each time the device is booted.

Potential Issues: The requirements for this method are quite niche. It not only requires that the attacker has access to the update process (for which they will likely need to be authorised), but the process itself must also be vulnerable in such a way that the updates are not verified before being implemented.

As the update process will differ from device to device, what may work for one is very unlikely to work on another. The attacker will need to reverse engineer the required format of the update for each targeted device's update process. If the forged update is incorrectly formatted, the update process may be halted, preventing the attacker from gaining persistence.

The attacker could attempt to modify the filesystem of an existing firmware file provided by the developer, but the update process may also need to interpret metadata defined by the developer. As such, the attacker will be expected to recreate the metadata, such as file sizes or checksums. Some tools are available that may assist in this process, such as the "Firmware Mod Kit" [24]. This will not work for all update formats, especially if the developer has obfuscated, encrypted or signed the firmware they make available.

3.6   Ubootkit

Das U-Boot (Normally shortened to U-Boot), is a universal bootloader designed for use with a variety of embedded devices [14]. It is commonly used in IoT devices to manage the booting process into the main operating system.

Requirements: The device must implement U-Boot as its bootloader. The attacker must be able to modify the bootloader flash partition.

Feasibility: Researchers have produced an attack that demonstrates the creation of persistent root-level access in IoT devices, dubbed "UbootKit" [35].

If the filesystem MTD partition is marked as read-only, it may prevent some of the other methods from being used. UbootKit, however, targets the bootloader partition. If the bootloader partition is writeable, UbootKit can modify U-Boot in such a way that when the device is next booted, it will run arbitrary code written by the attacker. UbootKit will use this vulnerability to corrupt subsequent boot stages and modify startup scripts during Linux's boot sequence, gaining the ability to make persistent changes.

Potential Issues: The authors of Ubootkit state that it can be applied to other devices and architectures than those used in the demonstration [35], but that it would require modification. This technique relies on patching the bootloader and kernel of the device with new shellcode at specific offsets. As the bootloader and kernel will differ slightly on each targeted device model and version, determining the correct shellcode modifications may be time-consuming.

Table 2. Device persistence methods exploits

Device	Persistence method(s)	Exploit
Netgear R6250 Router	Recreate Read-Only Filesystem & "Set Writeable Flag" Kernel Module	Command Injection CVE-2016-6277 [21]
D-Link DCS-932L	Initrd/Initramfs Modification	Buffer Overflow CVE-2019-10999 [22]
Yealink SIP-T38G	Modify Writeable Filesystem	Command Injection CVE-2013-5758 [20]
WiPG-1000	Modify Writeable Filesystem	Command Injection CVE-2019-3929 [23]

4   Experimental Proof of Concepts and Results

To test the viability of the techniques described in the previous section, we applied them to a range of IoT devices. We chose these devices as they have been known to be vulnerable, with publicly available exploits. Some had also been previously targeted by IoT malware. For persistence to be considered a viable and realistic attack method, the following two constraints were applied:

– No physical access to the device must be required during the process. Persistence must be achievable remotely, preferably over the Internet.
– The method of persistence must allow an attacker to force the device to run a custom application when the device is rebooted.

During our testing, we examined some local files on the device that are commonly found on Linux based systems to gather information about the device, such as /proc/mtd to identify partitions and /proc/mounts to identify filesystems. These would help determine the best technique to apply when attempting to gain persistence on that device.

4.1   Netgear R6250 Router (Using Methods B and D)

The Netgear R6250 router is one of many routers that had a command injection vulnerability present in their web server [17,21]. We used this vulnerability to gain access to the shell and begin reconnaissance.

First, we read the /proc/mounts file and found that the router used both a jffs2 and squashfs filesystem. We initially targeted the jffs2 filesystem as it was writeable by default and would have been the easiest to modify. However, it was mounted to /tmp/openvpn and only contained configuration files, so while we were able to make persistent modifications to the directory, it would not cause any arbitrary execution when the device was rebooted.

We instead decided to target the squashfs filesystem as it was mounted as the root directory. We read /proc/mtd and identified a partition named "rootfs", which was most likely the root filesystem. We read the partition and found it was using squashfs version 4.0, with xz compression.

Gaining Persistence. After extracting the files, we modified the result to include a file named testfile in /bin, then re-created the filesystem using the mksquashfs utility. We then uploaded the generated filesystem to the temporary memory of the router. We overwrote the existing filesystem by writing our modified version to /dev/mtdblock15. When we rebooted the device, the testfile was readable, indicating a persistent edit.

Read-Only MTD Partitions. During our exploitation of the device, we found that some of the partitions, notably the bootloader, had been marked as read-only via MTD. We were able to compile the Netgear's mtd-rw kernel module against the firmware's GPL source (https://kb.netgear.com/2649/NETGEAR-Open-Source-Code-for-Programmers-GPL) and confirmed that inserting the module would allow attackers to set MTD partitions as writeable from userspace.

4.2 D-Link DCS-932L (Using Method C)

The DCS-932L is a web-connected camera for both indoor and outdoor use. Customers can access the camera remotely via a web browser or linked application.

This camera has a buffer overflow vulnerability that allows an attacker to gain access to the shell and run arbitrary commands [22]. We used this to gain access to the device and investigate how it manages its storage. We read the `mounts` file and found only temporary and pseudo filesystems were being used, leading us to believe that it was using `rootfs` as its main filesystem, which should be appended to the end of the kernel. For this device, we used Method C, modifying the `initramfs` so that a custom filesystem would be loaded.

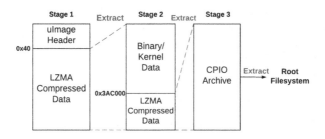

Fig. 1. Extracting the DCS-932L's root filesystem from the kernel partition

We read the `/proc/mtd` file and identified an MTD partition named "kernel" which we copied to a host machine to analyse. Using Binwalk [25], we found that the filesystem could be extracted in three stages, as shown in Fig. 1.

1. Stage one was the raw data of the partition as it was stored on the flash chip. It was made up of a 64-bit uImage Header, and LZMA compressed data. The uImage header contained metadata that the U-Boot bootloader can use to boot the kernel contained in the LZMA payload. We extracted the LZMA compressed data in preparation for stage two.
2. Stage two consisted of the kernel and some further LZMA compressed data. We identified that the LZMA data began at the offset `0x3AC000`, so we carved the data from this offset to the end of the file. We then decompressed this data into stage three.
3. After extracting the LZMA data, we were left with a CPIO archive, which we could then extract or mount to view the root filesystem of the device.

Gaining Persistence. To gain persistence on this device, we needed to modify the kernel partition in such a way that the device would be able to boot and mount it correctly. To test our process, we changed the root filesystem to contain a file named `testfile` in the `/bin` directory, then began to reverse the process we used to extract it. First, we compressed the filesystem into a CPIO archive. We then needed to compress the CPIO archive using LZMA. However, the compression used by the device was non-streamed. To recreate this as best as possible, we used an old version of "LZMA utils" (https://tukaani.org/lzma/). We then prepended the original binary/kernel data and compressed it using LZMA. Finally, we had to add a new uImage header. As uImage headers include checksums to check the integrity of the image contents and the header itself [13], we could not simply prepend the original, as the checksums would fail to match when the device starts, causing a fault. Instead, we created a new header with the `mkimage` utility. The arguments to recreate the metadata, such as the architecture, load address and firmware name, were found by referring to the previous header. We uploaded the new image to the device in temporary memory. As the kernel flash partition was writeable, we could copy it from temporary memory to flash memory via the MTD subsystem.

After restarting the device, we found our `testfile` was present in `/bin`, indicating a successful persistent modification. Attackers could use this technique to modify various startup scripts to perform malicious actions or even run applications included in the new filesystem.

4.3   Yealink SIP-T38G (Using Method A)

The SIP-T38G is an Internet-connected VoIP desk phone, allowing users to manage multiple calls and messages. We gained control of the device using an adaptation of an existing exploit for previous versions of the phone [20], which allowed us to investigate the device further.

We read the `/proc/mounts` file and found that the device used `yaffs2` filesystems mounted to multiple locations, including the root (`/`), `/boot`, `/phone`, `/data`, `/config` and `/etc`. directories.

As `yaffs2` is a writeable filesystem with an MTD user module, we wrote to the filesystem via the shell. The `/etc`. directory held scripts that are run at boot-time, which we could modify to run custom shell commands or applications when the system next boots.

4.4   WiPG-1000 (Using Method A)

The WiPG-1000 is a presenter that allows users to stream their screen from other devices on the same network. We used a command injection vulnerability [6,23] to start a `telnet` daemon, which we used to interact with the device via the shell remotely.

After connecting via `telnet`, we read `/proc/mounts` to identify the root mount. We found that the presenter used two types of storage, a flash chip and an Embedded Multi Media Card (eMMC). The eMMC used an `ext2` filesystem, which was mounted to the root directory as read only. We were able to remount it as write enabled with the `mount` utility, after which we were able to easily modify the filesystem via shell commands, which persisted through reboots.

4.5   Results Summary

There were significant variations in the structure of the devices we sought to exploit, with the different types of storage implementations requiring a variety of methods to be applied. However, we were able to gain persistence on every device by applying the described techniques.

While the implementation of these tests was performed manually for this paper, aspects of these techniques could be automated. As device reconnaissance for selecting the correct method was very time-consuming, automation of this step would be essential for large scale attacks. Hard coding the appropriate method when a specific model of the device is detected is a possibility, but this would require manually identifying the best method for *each* device. Alternatively, method identification could be performed when a device is exploited, but this may be quite complicated to implement without generating false positives. If performed incorrectly, this could also lead to the device being bricked.

We have created a process graph to show the best method for gaining persistence, by prioritising on those which require the lower complexity to be implemented. This graph can be seen in Fig. 2.

5   Countermeasures

We propose several countermeasures that could be used to mitigate the risk or prevent the threat caused by these persistence methods. Due to the variance of IoT devices, there are no "perfect" countermeasures, but those that are implemented will frustrate attackers in their attempt to gain persistence. As a consequence, these countermeasures will make the device a less appealing target.

- **Data Signing.** The use of signatures allows verification that the data contained on the flash chip has not been modified, which can prevent an attacker from gaining persistence. For example, uBoot has a "trusted boot" feature that can check whether an image is correctly signed before continuing the boot process [34]. By cryptographically signing each stage of the booting process – including the bootloader(s), operating system and filesystem – each step can verify the signature of the next, creating a chain of trust. If a stage has been modified, its signature will not be valid, and the device will fail to boot. Immutable memory should be used to bootstrap the process, so that an attacker cannot modify the chain of trust at the very first stage. As the attacker should not have the developer's cryptographic keys, they would not be able to forge a signature for any modifications they might have made to the protected stages.
- **Principle of Least Privilege.** All of these methods require an attacker to modify data on the device. By running potentially exploitable applications at a lower privilege level and only allowing certain privileged accounts to interact with the storage device or make persistent changes to important files, attackers would not be able to make modifications to gain persistence.

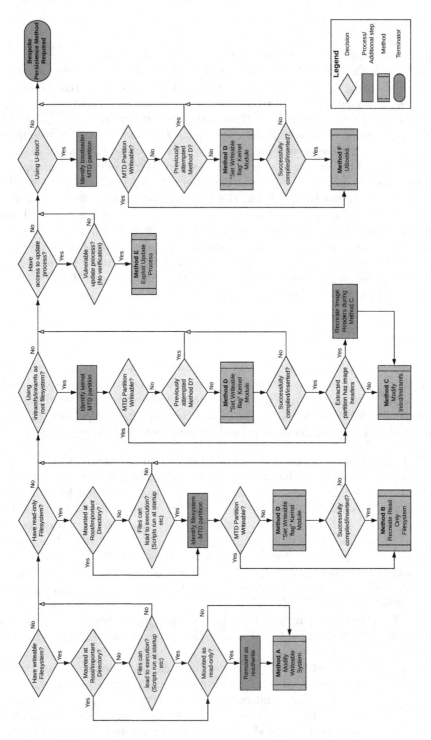

Fig. 2. Process to gain persistence

- **HADES-IoT.** HADES-IoT is a system designed for use on IoT devices, which provides a process whitelisting feature [9]. HADES-IoT records a hash of benign executables that are run in an uninfected state during a "profiling" stage. When a new process is spawned, HADES-IoT can compare it against its list of known benign executable hashes, preventing unknown processes from being created. This can frustrate attackers attempting to gain persistence and prevent uploaded malware from running.
- **Device Updates.** The methods outlined in our paper assume that an attacker has shell access. Users can prevent attackers from abusing these methods by regularly updating their device to patch vulnerabilities and prevent exploitation that would provide a shell access to the attacker.
- **Effective Factory Resetting.** IoT devices often include a "factory reset" feature that can be used to restore corrupted partitions to their original state. This could be used by victims to remove malware from the device if the process can reset partitions that have been modified by an attacker.

6 Conclusions and Future Work

In this work, we have discussed the increasing threat of persistence in IoT malware. We outlined the challenges that currently prevent IoT persistence from being easily achieved. We then detailed techniques that attackers could use to gain persistence on IoT devices, describing their requirements, what methodology they can use and which potential issues they might encounter. We demonstrated our ability to achieve true persistence in a wide range of different IoT devices. Based on our findings, we outlined a potential process to identify the best method of obtaining persistence. Finally, we listed several possible countermeasures that can be used to hinder attackers from getting persistence on vulnerable IoT devices.

Whilst we were able to gain persistence on all of our targeted devices, the variations on device structure and implementation meant that it was a time-consuming process that involved significant manual work. An attacker would almost certainly want to automate this for massive-scale attacks. One possible approach is to search for or remotely fingerprint vulnerable devices and then launch the method appropriate for that model.

Additionally, whilst it was straightforward to gain persistence on some of the devices we tested, others required more sophisticated methods that were time-consuming to discover and implement. Attackers may soon look towards automating both the discovery and the implementation of these more involved methods for abusing them in large scale operations.

Finally, further research should be performed to discover new countermeasures against persistence attack on IoT devices, for example through novel network intrusion detection systems that are effective for IoT scenarios.

References

1. Building external modules. https://www.kernel.org/doc/html/latest/kbuild/modules.html. Accessed Aug 2020
2. Kernel module signing facility. https://www.kernel.org/doc/html/v4.15/admin-guide/module-signing.html. Accessed Aug 2020
3. What is the mirai botnet? https://www.cloudflare.com/learning/ddos/glossary/mirai-botnet/. Accessed Aug 2020
4. What's a mirai botnet doing with my router? (2016). https://blog.f-secure.com/whats-a-mirai-botnet-doing-with-my-router/. Accessed Aug 2020
5. Antonakakis, M., et al.: Understanding the mirai botnet. In: 26th {USENIX} security symposium ({USENIX} Security 17), pp. 1093–1110 (2017)
6. Baines, J.: Crestron am/barco wepresent wipg/extron sharelink/teq av it/sharp pn-l703wa/optoma wps-pro/blackbox hd wps/infocus liteshow - remote command injection (2019). https://www.exploit-db.com/exploits/46786 Accessed Aug 2020
7. Birngruber, S., Hehenberger, F., Gründlinger, P., Zeilinger, M., Vymazal, D.: Netgear nighthawk firmware update vulnerability (2017), https://iot-lab-fh-ooe.github.io/netgear_update_vulnerability/. Accessed Aug 2020
8. Bozzato, C., Wyatt, L.: Circle with disney firmware update signature check bypass vulnerability (2017). https://talosintelligence.com/vulnerability_reports/TALOS-2017-0405. Accessed Aug 2020
9. Breitenbacher, D., Homoliak, I., Aung, Y.L., Tippenhauer, N.O., Elovici, Y.: Hades-IoT: a practical host-based anomaly detection system for IoT devices. In: Proceedings of the 2019 ACM Asia Conference on Computer and Communications Security, pp. 479–484 (2019)
10. Brierley, C., Pont, J., Arief, B., Barnes, D.J., Hernandez-Castro, J.: Paperw8: an IoT bricking ransomware proof of concept. In: Proceedings of the 15th International Conference on Availability, Reliability and Security, pp. 1–10 (2020)
11. Cloudflare: Famous ddos attacks — the largest ddos attacks of all time, https://www.cloudflare.com/learning/ddos/famous-ddos-attacks/ [Accessed: August 2020]
12. Cozzi, E., Graziano, M., Fratantonio, Y., Balzarotti, D.: Understanding linux malware. In: 2018 Symposium on Security and Privacy (SP), pp. 161–175. IEEE (2018)
13. Denk, W.: u-boot/image.h (2020). https://github.com/u-boot/u-boot/blob/master/include/image.h. Accessed Aug 2020
14. Glass, S.: Das u-boot - the universal boot loader (2020). http://www.denx.de/wiki/U-Boot. Accessed Aug 2020
15. Ilascu, I.: New IoT botnet torii uses six methods for persistence, has no clear purpose (2018). https://www.bleepingcomputer.com/news/security/new-iot-botnet-torii-uses-six-methods-for-persistence-has-no-clear-purpose/. Accessed Aug 2020
16. jclehner: mtd-rw: Write-enabler for MTD partitions (2016). https://github.com/jclehner/mtd-rw. Accessed Aug 2020
17. Land, J.: Multiple netgear routers are vulnerable to arbitrary command injection (2016). https://www.kb.cert.org/vuls/id/582384/. Accessed Aug 2020
18. Landley, R.: ramfs, rootfs and initramfs (2005). https://www.kernel.org/doc/Documentation/filesystems/ramfs-rootfs-initramfs.txt. Accessed Aug 2020
19. mwarning: mtdrw (2019). https://github.com/mwarning/mtdRW. Accessed Aug 2020
20. NIST: Yealink voip phone sip-t38g - remote command execution (2014). https://nvd.nist.gov/vuln/detail/CVE-2013-5758. Accessed Aug 2020

21. NIST: Cve-2016-6277 detail (2017). https://nvd.nist.gov/vuln/detail/CVE-2016-6277. Accessed Aug 2020
22. NIST: Cve-2019-10999 (2019). https://nvd.nist.gov/vuln/detail/CVE-2019-10999. Accessed Aug 2020
23. NIST: Cve-2019-3929 detail (2019). https://nvd.nist.gov/vuln/detail/CVE-2019-3929. Accessed Aug 2020
24. rampageX: firmware-mod-kit (2019). https://github.com/rampageX/firmware-mod-kit. Accessed Aug 2020
25. ReFirmLabs: Binwalk (2019). https://github.com/ReFirmLabs/binwalk. Accessed Aug 2020
26. Smith, B.: A quick guide to gplv3. Free Software Foundation, Inc. (2007). http://www.gnu.org/licenses/quick-guide-gplv3.html. Accessed 4 2008
27. Sophos: Vpnfilter botnet (2018). https://news.sophos.com/en-us/2018/05/24/vpnfilter-botnet-a-sophoslabs-analysis/. Accessed Aug 2020
28. Sophos: Vpnfilter botnet: a sophoslabs analysis: part 2 (2018). https://news.sophos.com/en-us/2018/05/27/vpnfilter-botnet-a-sophoslabs-analysis-part-2/. Accessed Aug 2020
29. Talos Intelligence: New vpnfilter malware targets at least 500k networking devices worldwide (2018). https://blog.talosintelligence.com/2018/05/VPNFilter.html. Accessed Aug 2020
30. Talos Intelligence: Vpnfilter update: Vpnfilter exploits endpoints, targets new devices (2018). https://blog.talosintelligence.com/2018/06/vpnfilter-update.html. Accessed Aug 2020
31. Tung, L.: Fbi to all router users: Reboot now to neuter russia's vpnfilter malware (2018). https://www.zdnet.com/article/fbi-to-all-router-users-reboot-now-to-neuter-russias-vpnfilter-malware/. Accessed Aug 2020
32. Vignau, B., Khoury, R., Hallé, S.: 10 years of IoT malware: a feature-based taxonomy. In: 2019 IEEE 19th International Conference on Software Quality, Reliability and Security Companion (QRS-C), pp. 458–465. IEEE (2019)
33. Woolf, N.: DDoS attack that disrupted internet was largest of its kind in history, experts say (2016). https://www.theguardian.com/technology/2016/oct/26/ddos-attack-dyn-mirai-botnet. Accessed Aug 2020
34. Yamada, M.: verified-boot.txt (2017). https://github.com/u-boot/u-boot/blob/master/doc/uImage.FIT/verified-boot.txt. Accessed Aug 2020
35. Yang, J., et al.: Ubootkit: A Worm Attack for the Bootloader of IoT Devices. BlackHat Asia (2019)

Real-Time Triggering of Android Memory Dumps for Stealthy Attack Investigation

Jennifer Bellizzi[1(✉)][iD], Mark Vella[1][iD], Christian Colombo[1][iD],
and Julio Hernandez-Castro[2][iD]

[1] Department of Computer Science, University of Malta, Msida, Malta
{jennifer.bellizzi,mark.vella,christian.colombo}@um.edu.mt
[2] School of Computing, Cornwallis South, University of Kent, Canterbury, UK
jch27@kent.ac.uk

Abstract. Attackers regularly target Android phones and come up with new ways to bypass detection mechanisms to achieve long-term stealth on a victim's phone. One way attackers do this is by leveraging critical benign app functionality to carry out specific attacks.

In this paper, we present a novel generalised framework, JIT-MF (*Just-in-time Memory Forensics*), which aims to address the problem of timely collection of short-lived evidence in volatile memory to solve the stealthiest of Android attacks. The main components of this framework are i) Identification of critical data objects in memory linked with critical *benign* application steps that may be misused by an attacker; and ii) Careful selection of trigger points, which identify when memory dumps should be taken during benign app execution.

The effectiveness and cost of trigger point selection, a cornerstone of this framework, are evaluated in a preliminary qualitative study using Telegram and Pushbullet as the victim apps targeted by stealthy malware. Our study identifies that JIT-MF is successful in dumping critical data objects on time, providing evidence that eludes all other forensic sources. Experimentation offers insight into identifying categories of trigger points that can strike a balance between the effort required for selection and the resulting effectiveness and storage costs. Several optimisation measures for the JIT-MF tools are presented, considering the typical resource constraints of Android devices.

Keywords: Memory forensics · Android security · Digital forensics · Incident response · Accessibility attacks

1 Introduction

Android has established itself as a leader in the mobile OS market [14], making it a primary target for malware. Whereas several detection mechanisms exist in the Google Play Protect suite [7], both to hinder the availability of malicious apps as well as to provide on-device detection, evasion techniques are still widely used, from obfuscation to stealthy execution.

M. Asplund and S. Nadjm-Tehrani (Eds.): NordSec 2020, LNCS 12556, pp. 20–36, 2021.
https://doi.org/10.1007/978-3-030-70852-8_2

Accessibility services misuse in Android has emerged as a predominant stealth technique in recent years, primarily adopted by accessibility trojans pulling off phishing attacks in a particularly stealthy manner [2,3,6]. While initially proposed as a way to maliciously interact with victim apps in a stealthy way requiring only accessibility and overlay-related permissions [12], more recent work suggested that the level of stealth can be increased further by offloading most or all of the attack steps to benign apps [22]. In this setting, any classifier-based malware detector is fooled since critical attack steps are executed solely via white-listed victim apps. For instance, in the case of a messaging hijack attack, whereby an attacker aims to hide behind a victim's identity to send a message, or intercept conversations from the victim's phone, a malware may simply request accessibility permission and leverage other existing (or secretly installed) apps on the phone to read or send messages through that benign app.

Once the detection layer is breached, mitigation responsibility is shifted to incident response, where the use of digital forensics tools is central. In the case of such stealthy attacks, it becomes paramount to recreate the intrusion scenario by identifying the main attack steps. In the case of messaging hijacks, these comprise legitimate message sending or receiving/reading functionality, this time attacker-controlled. Evidence uncovering the critical attack steps is akin to an application logging its primary functionality. However, the absence of such fine-grained audit trails, which is usually the case, leaves investigators with no evidence in non-volatile storage to work with. Evidence collected from volatile memory becomes essential. While forensics tools that operate similarly have shown promise within very narrow domains, one cannot underestimate the significant challenge of dealing with short-lived evidence [15,21,22].

In this work, we aim to harmonise the approach taken by these individual tools into a generalised framework, focusing specifically on the challenge of timely memory dumps from benign victim apps through the careful selection of trigger points. While we present the *Just-in-Time Memory Forensics* (JIT-MF) framework within an accessibility misuse messaging hijack setting, the proposed concept extends to the general case of attacks carried out largely through benign apps. JIT-MF's underpinning principles that distinguish it from state-of-the-art memory forensics tools are: i) Real-time collection of critical *data objects in volatile memory* related to the critical attack steps from victim apps; and, ii) The timely dumping of specific fragments of process memory as specified by *trigger points*. Notably, in contrast to malware detection and forensics tools, JIT-MF tools focus on the collection of evidence from misused benign victim apps (rather than malware).

Evidence objects and trigger points are specific to investigation scenario-victim app pairs, as defined within *JIT-MF Drivers*. Four real-world case studies presented in this paper provide further insight into how to proceed from framework to tool implementation. This mainly revolves around the creation of

JIT-MF drivers. All cases concern messaging hijacks involving Pushbullet[1] and Telegram[2], covering SMS and instant messaging (IM).

Experimentation results from these case studies show that evidence object identification should focus on those data structures related to app functionality that are most likely to serve as critical attack steps. As for trigger points, we identified different candidate categories, ranging from those requiring general knowledge of the Android framework to ones requiring more in-depth knowledge of specific apps. Yet, results show that those requiring only Android framework knowledge are sufficiently effective. Furthermore, experimentation that focuses on the optimised implementation of JIT-MF tools shows that storage is a valid concern, especially for devices with limited resources and propose an approach to collect the specific objects through interactions with the Android's runtime Garbage Collector. The key contributions of our work are:

- We introduce the concept of JIT-MF as a generic framework for memory forensic tools concerning Android attacks that offload their critical steps to benign apps.
- Provide insight into trigger point selection, a fundamental aspect to JIT-MF.
- Experimentation using four case studies that provide insight into developing practical JIT-MF tools.

2 Background and Motivation

2.1 Stealthy Android Accessibility Attacks

The misuse of accessibility services is on the increase in Android malware. Early instances [2] demonstrated how through phishing and the misuse of accessibility features, a malicious app could steal a victim's credentials and attack other benign apps and services by interacting with them without the user's consent. In the case of Gustuff [2] this was done to perform banking transactions. More recently, however, with malware such as Eventbot [6] and BlackRock [5], this misuse has shifted from being leveraged to perform the actual attack to being used to maintain stealth. In the case of both Eventbot and BlackRock, the only permission requested upon installation is that of accessibility. The rest of the permissions required to perform the attack are obtained through the accessibility permission granted by the user. Malware developers can also exploit accessibility to leverage critical benign app functionality that coincides with the features they need. For instance, attackers who are motivated to create a malicious app to send SMSs via another phone to hide their identity (SMS crime-proxy), may exploit accessibility to silently install a benign legitimate SMSonPC app, e.g. Pushbullet [22], whose normal usage involves proxying sent/received SMSs through a remote PC. By signing up with phished credentials, as part of the setting up (step 1 of Fig. 1b) on the installed app, attackers gain full control over every SMS that is received and can send SMS remotely through a benign app, hiding its tracks and increasing the stealth level of the attackers' subsequent steps.

---

[1] https://www.pushbullet.com.
[2] https://telegram.org.

(a) SMS hijack attack using accessibility to attack default SMS app.

(b) SMS hijack attack using accessibility to install an SMSonPC app that legitimately interacts with the default SMS app.

Fig. 1. Misusing accessibility in different ways to carry out an SMS hijack attack.

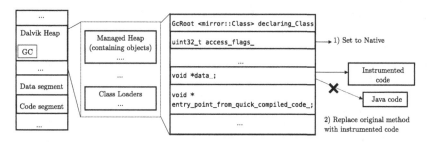

Fig. 2. Instrumenting code via `ArtMethod` entry point.

2.2   Evidence Collection

Android Runtime (ART) has been the main managed runtime used by applications on Android [4] since it was released with Android KitKat in 2013 [23]. Similar to how JVM operates, ART uses two separate memory spaces to store application data; the stack and the heap [20]. Short-lived data objects of a running app, critical to attack steps, are found in volatile memory within the application's heap, managed by the Android Runtime.

Out of the box, ART provides functionality through which developers can dump heap data in the standard format of an `hprof` file, mainly for debugging purposes. The Java API equivalent for this is `Debug.dumpHprofData`[3]. A typical heap dump is semantically rich, containing information about an app's memory contents at the time the dump was taken. Most importantly, in our case, it includes information on the objects used and created by the app [4].

Another feature of ART is that of garbage collection. Figure 2 shows how ART provides a managed memory environment which enables the Garbage Collector (GC) to keep track of objects in memory, to reclaim heap space once those are no longer in use [4]. To do so, the GC uses a function exported by ART's binary module (`libart.so`), `Heap::GetInstances`, which has an object type filter, allowing the GC to filter on specific objects in memory. While convenient

---

[3] https://developer.android.com/reference/android/os/Debug#dumpHprofData.

for selective evidence collection, the downside is that this function is not part of the public API and therefore may change unexpectedly between versions.

2.3 Android App Instrumentation

The Android OS uses APKs (Android Package Kit) as a package file format for distributing and installing mobile apps. The typical make up of an apk file consists of: an Android Manifest file providing essential information about the app, Dalvik (managed) bytecode in `classes.dex`, a `lib` directory for native code (e.g. ARM instructions), and other resources such as images/files required by the app. Native code can access the Android framework through the Java Native Interface (JNI), which enables the switching between native code and Dalvik bytecode. Therefore, since native code also calls into the Android framework, by using this framework to facilitate interception, we would also be able to intercept native code that calls into it.

ART uses specific C++ classes to mirror Java classes, their methods and associated instances, specifically using `Class`, `Object` and `ArtMethod` data structures respectively, as shown in Fig. 2 [10]. The `ArtMethod` data structure contains all the information about a particular Java method (method descriptors), such as the modifier, the class in which it is declared and the entry address of the method's code. Figure 2 shows how method hooking can be attained through `ArtMethod` patching, by first setting the method as native (Step 1), followed by entry point patching (Step 2), completing control-flow re-direction to instrumentation code.

3 JIT-MF

We assume the context of an investigation scenario whereby the device owner is not a perpetrator but a victim of a potential accessibility misuse attack targeting stealth. This may be the case with high-ranking government officials, or even high-profile business owners, as was the case in a report published earlier on this year [8]. In such cases, victims are expected to collaborate with forensic investigators to obtain critical evidence in the case of such an attack.

Our main aim is to obtain evidence, in the form of data objects, corresponding to critical application functionality from volatile memory which otherwise won't be made available by other sources of evidence. Due to their ephemerality, which is typical of app-level data objects, timely collection of such objects becomes critical. The primary goal behind the concept of Just-in-Time Memory Forensics (JIT-MF) is to extend the notion of memory forensics. We refer specifically to the kind that is carried out in real-time, over live process memory, capturing evidence associated with critical benign app misuse steps in a just-in-time fashion.

While the identification of evidence object(s) revolves around critical app functionality central to the threat in question, their timely collection requires the selection of *trigger points* which is a concept that is somewhat novel to our approach and requires more insight. These trigger points are events that occur during the app's runtime at which JIT-MF will invoke a partial memory dump. If the selected trigger points do not coincide with the invocation of misused app functionality, critical attack evidence may be lost.

Figure 3 gives an overview of the steps involved when implementing a tool based on the JIT-MF framework. Once a benign app is identified as having critical application steps which can be misused by an attacker, the app is extracted from the device (using `adb`). The app is instrumented, possibly using a combination of static and dynamic tools (depending on whether the device is rooted), to include code which uses the capabilities provided by ART to dump memory at the identified trigger points. Once repackaged, the app is re-installed and set up on the user's phone. The memory dumps collected over time would then be gathered by a forensic analyst to reconstruct the attack steps.

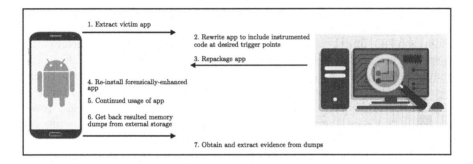

Fig. 3. JIT-MF steps.

3.1   Heuristic for Evidence Object and Trigger Point Selection

A typical memory dump contains all the objects created and/or being used by an app (both specific to the app as well as those specific to the Android API), at the point in time when this is performed. Not all of these objects are relevant to the critical attack steps. For instance, in the case of a messaging hijack attack, we are only after the message objects supporting the execution of messaging functionality and which may be hijacked during eventual attacks.

The selection of trigger points is specific to the following two aspects: i) The attack scenario for which we want evidence to be collected, and ii) How the app itself operates. Attempting to define a method for trigger point selection requires full knowledge of the specific app being analysed (and its version at the time). Given that the majority of the apps being analysed are expected to be third-party, assuming comprehensive knowledge of the app's codebase is not practical. Instead, we propose a heuristic which we have used across four case studies. Taking into account an attack scenario, corresponding target app functionality and the associated evidence objects, trigger points are selected based on the code that processes the said objects; specifically concerning: i) The **storing** and **loading** of the objects from storage; ii) The **transferring** of objects over the network (e.g. Wi-Fi, 4G, etc.); or else iii) Any **object transformation** of some sort (e.g. display on screen etc.).

In the case of a messaging hijack, evidence objects comprise precisely those that contain the messages themselves (as defined by an app-specific structure). In contrast, the operations related to these objects involve storing/loading messages from local content repositories and sending/receiving messages over communication networks. The latter provides the basis for trigger point selection.

Trigger Point Categories. Although the operations identified as candidate trigger points are all potentially valid, their degree of specificity to the app may differ. For instance when receiving a new instant message, one can safely assume that the source code in the app handling the data object of interest (evidence object) must have made use of underlying network functionality at some point. Otherwise, the message would not have been received. In this case generic network-related operations - such as `recv` system calls - are considered viable, generic trigger points requiring minimal app reverse engineering effort, since they can be derived without detailed knowledge of the app's codebase. However, such trigger points may not be as accurate as those selected with a more in-depth understanding of app functionality. The latter kind of trigger points encompasses app-specific methods, reflecting the precise invocation of the sought after functionality, e.g. displaying the message in an app-specific GUI grid on the device screen. Such trigger points are expected to be more accurate, both in terms of producing timely memory dumps and in not being triggered too frequently (over-execution). That said, there may be instances in which generic trigger points can have *filters* associated with them that decrease their invocation.

Overall, the varying degree of specificity of a trigger point reflects the amount of effort put into comprehending the codebase of an app. Therefore we categorise trigger points as follows, starting from the least specific (and require least reverse engineering effort) to the most specific, as described in Table 1. The first three categories are considered black-box, meaning they require the least knowledge of an app's codebase. The final category is considered white-box due to the need of having to peek inside an app's codebase for their identification. At first glance, the impact of this trade-off is not obvious. Therefore we dedicate significant experimentation effort on comparing trigger point categories as part of the case studies presented in Sect. 4, to provide the necessary insight into trigger point selection for eventual JIT-MF based tools.

Table 1. Trigger point categories.

Trigger point category	Classification	Description
Native Runtime (RT)	Black-box	Generic native runtime system calls
Device Events	Black-box	Generic events related to the device state
Android & 3rd party library APIs	Black-box	Android API calls
App specific APIs	White-box	API calls specific to the app

3.2   Offline Vs Online Evidence Collection Methods

Once triggered, memory dumps can comprise entire ART heap sections as in `hprof` dumps, with subsequent evidence collection happening *offline* using an `hprof` parser, e.g. Eclipse MAT. A more frugal approach leverages ART's Garbage Collector (GC) to dump solely the required/critical objects in memory. In this setting, evidence objects are collected during the dumping process itself in an *online* fashion. Both approaches are compatible with non-rooted devices.

While JIT-MF defines those common steps followed by every JIT-MF tool, those aspects that are specific to the investigation scenario/target app pair at hand are described, and eventually implemented, by JIT-MF drivers. Their implementation starts off the aforementioned evidence/trigger point selection heuristic along with any argument value restrictions identified and is completed with the selection of an appropriate evidence collection method. Figure 4 illustrates the involvement of these drivers in the JIT-MF framework.

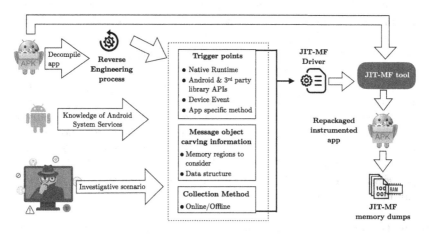

Fig. 4. JIT-MF drivers.

4 Experimentation

To evaluate the effectiveness and runtime overheads imposed on forensically enhanced devices, we conducted a series of experiments. These had the following objectives: i) Demonstrate that JIT-MF tools can collect evidence on stealthy accessibility attacks, effectively amplifying their forensic footprint; and ii) Perform a comparative analysis of the different trigger point categories, based on accurate memory dump triggers and their associated overheads.

4.1 Setup

Four messaging hijack case studies were set up for experimentation purposes, encompassing SMS and IM: 1) SMS Crime-proxy, 2) SMS Spying, 3) IM Crime-proxy and 4) IM Spying. A crime-proxy attack involves an attacker proxying messages through a victim's phone via a benign app. This could help to foil attribution of compromising communication, possibly even resulting in incorrect attribution to the device owner. Spying through unlawful message interception comprises of attackers spying on device owners' messages threatening their privacy, and possibly even their safety. SMS hijack case studies make use of Pushbullet, an SMSonPC app that provides remote access to a device's SMS functionality, and more. SMSonPC could be smuggled as part of an attack for stealth, or else could be the target of an attack in case a device owner is already making using of it. Telegram, on the other hand, is the app chosen for the IM setting due to its large userbase. In all case studies, we assume that accessibility malware has been installed and granted the accessibility permission by a non-suspecting device owner. We also carry out performance tests to analyse overhead storage and runtime costs incurred on legitimate user activity.

All four attacks were implemented as extensions to the Metasploit's Meterpreter for Android[4]. For SMS-related attacks, the accessibility malware typically first sets up a Pushbullet installation and signs in using phished credentials. The remaining attack steps to send messages make direct use of Pushbullet's web portal, automated using Selenium[5] whereas any incoming messages can be obtained from browser logs. Furthermore, after sending an SMS, the attack can delete the Pushbullet app for additional stealth. SMS conversations for interception were simulated using `adb emu send <number> <message>`. No message deletion ensued in this case. IM-related attacks required the malware's permanence, interacting with Telegram's IM sending and viewing functionality in a continuous manner. The malware makes use of overlays in order not to attract the device owner's attention. In Telegram's crime-proxy attack case study, all sent messages are deleted after sending. In contrast, in the spying case study, a new phone with a different SIM card was used to assume the role of the sender and `adb` input events were used to automate message sending and receiving.

The full setup comprises: Pushbullet v17.7.19; Telegram v6.1.1 instrumented with the trigger points described in Sect. 3.1; both installed on an Android 10 emulator equipped with Frida-server v12.8.20 for instrumentation. Both online and offline evidence collection methods are encoded within the instrumentation code as described in Sect. 3.2, leveraging Frida's `Java.choose()` and Android's API `Debug.dumpHprofData()` respectively. To measure runtime overheads, we analyse storage and execution time overheads of both apps during legitimate message sending and reading/retrieving activities. In the case of Pushbullet, we assume a legitimate user did the initial installation. To measure effectiveness we search for the proxied/stolen messages in the resulting memory dumps and take note of whether or not they were found. All attacks were repeated 10 times, since it sufficed to reach convergence for all measurements taken.

Trigger Points. Eight trigger points (TP) were chosen, per attack scenario, two for each category defined in Table 1, attempting to leverage all available candidate trigger points in terms of disk input/output, network send/receive and miscellaneous object transformations. The chosen TPs are listed in Table 2, where TP1 is either file/disk or object transformation-related, whereas TP2 is network-related.

---

[4] https://github.com/rapid7/metasploit-framework/tree/master/documentation/modules/payload/android.

[5] https://selenium-python.readthedocs.io/.

Where possible, we put filters on black-box trigger points, for better specificity. For instance, the app directory (in the case of device events) is specific to the app and obtained dynamically at runtime using `getApplication`
`Context().getFilesDir().getParent()` provided by the Android API (typ-
ically being `/data/data/pushbullet|telegram`). Incoming/outgoing network
statistics were obtained using Android's `TrafficStats` package to monitor an
increase in either, depending on the use case. Device event trigger point checks
are triggered based on their native category counterpart, so the instrumentation
checks for increased directory size, after a `write()` call is made. Native runtime
calls were restricted to trigger on specific scenarios by checking whether the type
of the file descriptor passed as an argument is a TCP socket or a file.

Table 2. Trigger points selected.

Case study	TP Category	TP #	Event selected
(SMS) Pushbullet - Crime-proxy	Native Runtime	TP 1	`write()` - to disk
		TP 2	`read()` - from socket
	Device Event	TP 1	Increase in app directory size
		TP 2	Increase in incoming network traffic
	Android & 3rd Party APIs	TP 1	`android.content.ContentResolver.insert`
		TP 2	`android.telephony.SmsManager.sendTextMessage`
	App specific APIs	TP 1	`com.pushbullet.android.sms.SmsSyncService.a`
		TP 2	`com.pushbullet.android.providers.syncables.SyncablesProvider.insert`
(SMS) Pushbullet - Spying	Native Runtime	TP 1	`read()` - from disk
		TP 2	`write()` - to TCP socket
	Device Event	TP 1	Increase in app directory size
		TP 2	Increase in outgoing network traffic
	Android & 3rd Party APIs	TP 1	`android.content.ContentResolver.registerContentObserver`
		TP 2	`com.google.android.gms.gcm.GcmReceiver.onReceive`
	App specific APIs	TP 1	`com.pushbullet.android.sms.SmsSyncService.a`
		TP 2	`com.pushbullet.android.gcm.GcmService.a`
(IM) Telegram - Crime-proxy	Native Runtime	TP 1	File open()
		TP 2	`send()` - to socket
	Device Event	TP 1	Increase in app directory size
		TP 2	Increase in outgoing network traffic
	Android & 3rd Party APIs	TP 1	`android.widget.EditText.setText`
		TP 2	`android.app.SharedPreferencesImpl$EditorImpl.commitToMemory`
	App specific APIs	TP 1	`org.telegram.tgnet.ConnectionsManager.native_sendRequest`
		TP 2	`org.telegram.messenger.SendMessagesHelper.performSendMessageRequest`
(IM) Telegram - Spying	Native Runtime	TP 1	File open()
		TP 2	`recv()` - from socket
	Device Event	TP 1	Increase in app directory size
		TP 2	Increase in incoming network traffic
	Android & 3rd Party APIs	TP 1	`android.view.ViewGroup.dispatchGetDisplayList`
		TP 2	`android.app.ContextImpl.sendBroadcast`
	App specific APIs	TP 1	`org.telegram.ui.Cells.DialogCell.update`
		TP 2	`org.telegram.messenger.MessagesStorage.putMessages`

4.2   Results

Effectiveness. Table 3 compares the trigger points based on accurately dumping
evidence objects related to the proxied or intercepted SMS/IM messages over
ten runs per attack. The first six rows are the results obtained for the black-box

trigger points, while the next two are for the white-box. The results presented show the effectiveness obtained by using both offline and online collection methods which, as can be observed from the table, have very similar results. Looking at the results column-wise, i.e. across trigger point categories, results show that the hypothesis that white-box trigger points are more accurate than their black-box counterparts does not hold. Having said that, when results are analysed row-wise, i.e. across attacks, in each case study there is at least one trigger point that returns a 100% accuracy. For both Pushbullet and Telegram case studies, the collected evidence contains the following metadata: i) The contents of the message sent/read; ii) The sender/recipient (for crime proxy and spying, respectively); and iii) The time at which the message was received/intercepted.

Overall, results from this small, albeit representative, number of case studies show that while identification of entirely accurate trigger points is possible, this is not at all straightforward. This, of course, merits further investigation since the timely dumping of evidence is central to JIT-MF. On the upside, it looks like selecting accurate trigger points could be possible solely within the black-box categories, which are those requiring minimal app-specific knowledge.

To further make a case for the JIT-MF framework, we compare the evidence obtained by the JIT-MF tool (highlighted in Table 3), with that returned by typical (baseline) logs which feature in classical forensic analysis. For every attack scenario in the experiment, we obtain a copy of logcat at the point in time when an attack has occurred, we analyse network traffic and get sqlite database files which are used for on-device storage for both apps.

In the case of logcat we did not observe any of the metadata acquired by JIT-MF in any of the logs for all four attack scenarios. For Telegram, it was possible to instrument the app to enable verbose logging in logcat dynamically. However, this did not make any difference with regards to critical metadata present in logcat. As for sqlite files, in the case of Pushbullet, we could only observe the received SMS messages, but no history of their access. For sent messages, one would have to root the phone to obtain Android's default message store `mmsms.db`. In the case of Telegram, being a cloud app, sqlite files only provide portions of cached data of received and sent messages. In the case that the attacker deletes the chat, no evidence of the sent messages is found at all. Furthermore, in the case of intercepted messages in Telegram, whereas there is a `state` field that indicates whether or not a particular message was read, it does not indicate the *time* at which the message was read. All network traffic related to Pushbullet and Telegram communication protocols was exchanged over HTTPS. Therefore while an initialised connection can be observed, none of the traffic is decipherable unless decryption keys are obtained.

Runtime overheads. Runtime overheads were obtained during normal usage of the app, by legitimately invoking events that would be misused by an attacker in the case of a messaging hijack attack. Figure 5 shows the storage requirements per trigger point category over the ten runs. Here we only consider the online collection method for the time being. Overall, storage requirements are tied to the number of times trigger points are hit per run. What is interesting to note is that the black-box categories can still be as frugal as their white-box counterparts, showing that the use of filters paid off. As for the hprof-based offline method, we note that while the average dump size required by online collection is around 143 kB, that required by the offline method is 203 MB (an order of magnitude *more* on average), per attack scenarios and trigger point chosen. Execution overheads associated with memory-dumping instrumentation code were negligible for both collection methods in Telegram's case, with an increase of 0.2 s at worst. For Pushbullet this value increases to 6s at worst (20% of the cases) however given that Pushbullet operates from a browser setting, this execution overhead does not incur any lag on the phone's main UI thread, enabling the user to continue using the phone normally.

4.3   Discussion

JIT-MF Amplifies the Forensic Footprint of Stealthy Attacks. Effectiveness results show that, while trigger point-dependent, key evidence related to stealthy messaging hijacks was only accessible through the JIT-MF approach. This is the central tenet of the approach. While at the code and network levels key evidence can be hidden through obfuscation and encryption, evidence linked to the key attack steps must be revealed in volatile memory, even if only for a brief time.

Table 3. Trigger point effectiveness: % accuracy over 10 runs.

Trigger point Category/Scenario		Crime-proxy - IM		Spying - IM		Crime-proxy - SMS		Spying - SMS	
		Online	Offline	Online	Offline	Online	Offline	Online	Offline
Native RT	TP 1	100	80	100	100	30	80	80	80
	TP 2	50	50	100	100	100	100	0	30
Device Event	TP 1	40	40	100	90	50	80	20	30
	TP 2	50	50	100	100	100	100	0	30
Android & 3rd Party APIs	TP 1	90	90	100	100	100	100	0	0
	TP 2	80	60	100	100	100	100	80	80
App specific APIs	TP 1	100	100	100	100	0	0	0	0
	TP 2	0	0	60	60	100	100	80	80

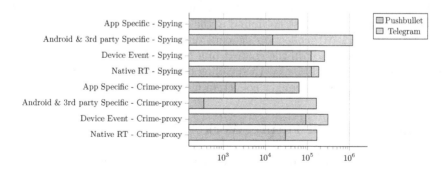

Fig. 5. Storage overhead in bytes, per trigger point category, attack scenario and app.

Black-Box Trigger Point Categories Show Promise. While results show that selecting the right, most accurate, trigger point can be an arduous task, the fact that black-box ones can be as effective and efficient as white-box ones is good news. Obviously, this observation requires substantial follow-up; however, this bodes well for efforts attempting to automate tasks related to JIT-MF driver implementation, of which trigger point selection is central. While both effectiveness and runtime overheads so far do not favour any of the three black-box categories, it seems that certain trigger point categories might be less resource-intensive for some apps, and more for others. This, however, merits more investigation.

Optimising on Storage Costs. Whilst results show that black-box trigger points do not necessarily incur higher storage costs, with online collected dumps requiring as little as 0.1 kB to be effective, these results must also be analysed in the context of practical JIT-MF tool deployment. When one considers that dumps are triggered per critical app functionality, which in our case studies corresponds to SMS/IM sending/viewing, dumps are expected to be very frequent. While perhaps SMS is of less concern nowadays, IM is an entirely different story. IM functionality could result in daily triggers on the order of hundreds to thousands. While 128GB smartphones are now the norm, users would rather use the space for smartphone functionality rather than to store forensic evidence.

In this respect, the suggested way-forward concerns enhancing the collection method as defined in JIT-MF drivers in two ways. Firstly, we propose to improve the collection method with a data transfer method. A transfer method should establish both the transport channel, e.g. SD card, adb, network etc., as well as the frequency of synchronisation points whenever applicable. Secondly, a sampling option should also be provided. Rather than collecting the entire evidence, successful incident response is possible even if only a subset of the attack steps are recorded. In the case of crime-proxy attack, for example, a fragment of a conversation could already provide sufficient clues pointing towards ongoing hijacks, full content disclosure would require further effort. Sampling may be carried out either periodically, e.g. sample maximum event objects per time-frame, or else on a rule basis, e.g. sample outgoing messaging objects based on their destination number, say those not found in the contact list. Ultimately, the right combination for JIT-MF collection depends on the sensitivity of the investigation context. For instance, in the context of a high-profile government agent, or Fortune 500 CEO, it could be worth spending extra money on high-spec devices to opt for a more resource-hungry collection method.

5   Limitations and Future Work

The primary contribution made by this early attempt to investigate stealthy Android attacks is a general framework, JIT-MF, upon which specific tools can be modelled. The four case studies presented here provide valuable insight concerning how to go about evidence object identification and trigger point selection. Therefore these results have to be understood within this limited scope. Moving on to a larger-scale empirical study is undoubtedly going to require some level of automation. The experience derived from the manual process undertaken so far, as guided by the heuristic described in Sect. 3.1, presents a solid foundation for this crucial next step.

A natural progression of this research also concerns developing complete JIT-MF tools, initially those targeting messaging hijack investigation scenarios. In this context, JIT-MF tool development can begin with those evidence object and trigger point combinations that were already shown to be sufficiently effective. The pending work concerns: i) Target app repackaging, compatible with non-rooted devices; ii) JIT-MF driver enhancement with an extension for the collection method as discussed; iii) Correlation with additional evidence, e.g. Call Data Record logs and cloud back-ups to provide additional context for the collected evidence objects, within a forensic timeline. Comprehensive timelines can help give investigators a complete picture of events, and thus assist in discerning between hijack activity and normal device usage with device owner consent. Additionally, it would be interesting to assess the difference JIT-MF evidence makes on forensic timeline richness as compared to those produced using only state-of-the-art evidence collection.

Ultimately JIT-MF is not intended as a comprehensive solution. JIT-MF tools also need to pull robust implementation, as well as addressing instrumentation issues related to apps that perform code integrity checks. Despite the assumption of the device owner's collaboration, privacy issues still abound and have to be taken care of. Finally, app instrumentation for memory dumping is incompatible with system apps on non-rooted phones.

6   Related Work

While our work focuses on the problem of accessibility misuse to aid stealthy attacks and builds on previous work in this regard [22], stealthy attacks aiming for persistence go beyond accessibility misuse. Other similar attack vectors include dual-instance apps [19] and stealthy persistent trojans like Triada [1] which evade common detection mechanisms.

Similar to monitors like REAPER [11] and MOSES [25], JIT-MF uses trigger points which, rather than being indicators for malicious events, such as permission misuse, are indicators of *benign* events that may be misused by an attacker. In contrast to typical monitors, JIT-MF dumps necessary memory contents for post-analysis at runtime, which is less costly than online analysis.

Saltaformaggio et al. [15–17] and Taubmann et al. [21] also developed tools which are after ephemeral data in memory, to reconstruct flows within an app's runtime which can be critical in a forensic investigation. They do so by reconstructing critical data structures from memory dumps. Rather than within a general concept, their ephemeral data is very specific (GUI elements for screen flows and TLS private keys respectively). DroidKex [21] acquires memory dumps upon *send* and *receive* functionality of an app, an indicator that TLS connections are being established, similar to JIT-MF's concept of trigger points.

Having a custom specification (JIT-MF driver) underpinning a generic framework is common in digital forensics tools. Frameworks such as Autopsy and

Volatility allow the addition of modules and plugins which enable them to cater for a broad range of investigation scenarios. The concept can be even applied to reconstructing timelines from specific log files using custom analysers [13].

Several works have tackled recovery and digital forensics of specific messaging apps, like Telegram [9,18,24]. The techniques mainly utilise disk images to retrieve valuable evidence. While stored data can be useful, it is up to app developers which metadata to store. Metadata critical to an investigative scenario may not be available at all from disk (as seen in the results). Even if it was, that may not be the case across versions. Furthermore, with the increase in popularity of cloud-based messaging apps, fewer data becomes available locally to retrieve.

7 Conclusions

Due to its ubiquitous presence, Android has become a significant target for malware. Recent studies show the existence and gradual increase of stealthy Android attacks that through accessibility, leverage benign app functionality to execute critical attack steps. Since such attacks offload the majority of their actions to benign apps, current techniques aimed at detecting malware based on the presence of malicious behaviour are rendered ineffective. Volatile memory remains the only place where evidence of such attacks may be found.

To address this problem, we introduce a framework called JIT-MF which, through carefully selected trigger points, forensically enhances apps to timely dump sections of memory that could contain critical data objects, as evidence. We evaluate this framework in the context of accessibility messaging hijack attacks, using widely deployed apps as victim apps. Results from four case studies show that: i) JIT-MF tools enhance the forensic footprint of stealthy attacks beyond the current baseline; ii) There is a category of trigger points that is both effective and only requires basic knowledge of the app; and iii) JIT-MF can be optimised for storage. In this paper, we shed light on the capabilities of JIT-MF in the context of messaging hijack attacks within Android. However, the framework can be extended to cater for other investigative scenarios and even operating systems, to capture evidence that would otherwise be irreparably lost.

Acknowledgement. This work is supported by the LOCARD Project under Grant H2020-SU-SEC-2018-832735.

References

1. Triada: organized crime on Android (2016). https://www.kaspersky.com/blog/triada-trojan/11481/
2. Gustuff: Weapon of Mass Infection (2019). https://www.group-ib.com/blog/gustuff
3. Year of the RAT (2020). https://www.threatfabric.com/blogs/2020_year_of_the_rat.html

4. Android Developer's Guide (2020). https://developer.android.com/
5. BlackRock - The Trojan that wanted to get them all (2020). https://www.threatfabric.com/blogs/blackrock_the_trojan_that_wanted_to_get_them_all.html
6. Eventbot: A new mobile banking trojan is born (2020). https://www.cybereason.com/blog/eventbot-a-new-mobile-banking-trojan-is-born
7. Google Play Protect (2020). https://www.android.com/play-protect/
8. Jeff Bezos hack: Saudi Arabia calls claim 'absurd' (2020). https://www.bbc.com/news/business-51171400
9. Azhar, M.A.H.B., Barton, T.E.A.: Forensic analysis of secure ephemeral messaging applications on android platforms. In: Jahankhani, H., et al. (eds.) ICGS3 2017. CCIS, vol. 630, pp. 27–41. Springer, Cham (2016). https://doi.org/10.1007/978-3-319-51064-4_3
10. Costamagna, V., Zheng, C.: ARTDroid: a virtual-method hooking framework on android art runtime. In: ESSoS, pp. 20–28. IMPS (2016)
11. Diamantaris, M., Papadopoulos, E., Markatos, E., Ioannidis, S., Polakis, J.: Reaper: real-time app analysis for augmenting the android permission system. In: CODASPY, pp. 37–48. ACM (2019)
12. Fratantonio, Y., Qian, C., Chung, S.P., Lee, W.: Cloak and dagger: from two permissions to complete control of the UI feedback loop. In: IEEE S&P, pp. 1041–1057. IEEE (2017)
13. Hargreaves, C., Patterson, J.: An automated timeline reconstruction approach for digital forensic investigations. Digital Invest. 9, S69–S79 (2012)
14. L., S.: Android - Statistics & Facts (2020). https://www.statista.com/topics/876/android/
15. Saltaformaggio, B., Bhatia, R., Gu, Z., Zhang, X., Xu, D.: GUITAR: Piecing together android app guis from memory images. In: CCS, pp. 120–132. ACM SIGSAC (2015)
16. Saltaformaggio, B., Bhatia, R., Gu, Z., Zhang, X., Xu, D.: VCR: app-agnostic recovery of photographic evidence from android device memory images. In: CCS, pp. 146–157. ACM SIGSAC (2015)
17. Saltaformaggio, B., Bhatia, R., Zhang, X., Xu, D., Richard, G.: Screen after previous screens: spatial-temporal recreation of android app displays from memory images. In: USENIX, pp. 1137–1151 (2016)
18. Satrya, G., Daely, P., Nugroho, M.: Digital forensic analysis of telegram messenger on android devices. In: ICTS, pp. 1–7. IEEE (2016)
19. Shi, L., Fu, J., Guo, Z., Ming, J.: "Jekyll and Hyde" is Risky: shared-everything threat mitigation in dual-instance apps. In: MobiSys, pp. 222–235. ACM (2019)
20. Surin, T.: Dealing with Large Memory Requirements on Android (2020). https://pspdfkit.com/blog/2019/android-large-memory-requirements/
21. Taubmann, B., Alabduljaleel, O., Reiser, H.: DroidKex: fast extraction of ephemeral TLS keys from the memory of android apps. Digital Invest. 26, S67–S76 (2018)
22. Vella, M., Rudramurthy, V.: Volatile memory-centric investigation of SMS-hijacked phones: a Pushbullet case study. In: FedCSIS, pp. 607–616. IEEE (2018)
23. Vitas, M.: ART vs Dalvik Introducing the New Android Runtime in KitKat (2020). https://infinum.com/the-capsized-eight/art-vs-dalvik-introducing-the-new-android-runtime-in-kit-kat
24. Zhang, L., Yu, F., Ji, Q.: The forensic analysis of WeChat message. In: IMCCC, pp. 500–503. IEEE (2016)
25. Zhauniarovich, Y., Russello, G., Conti, M., Crispo, B., Fernandes, E.: Moses: supporting and enforcing security profiles on smartphones. IEEE TDSC 11(3), 211–223 (2014)

Using Features of Encrypted Network Traffic to Detect Malware

Zeeshan Afzal[1,2(✉)], Anna Brunstrom[2], and Stefan Lindskog[2,3]

[1] KTH Royal Institute of Technology, Stockholm, Sweden
zafzal@kth.se
[2] Karlstad University, Karlstad, Sweden
[3] SINTEF Digital, Trondheim, Norway

Abstract. Encryption on the Internet is as pervasive as ever. This has protected communications and enhanced the privacy of users. Unfortunately, at the same time malware is also increasingly using encryption to hide its operation. The detection of such encrypted malware is crucial, but the traditional detection solutions assume access to payload data. To overcome this limitation, such solutions employ traffic decryption strategies that have severe drawbacks. This paper studies the usage of encryption for malicious and benign purposes using large datasets and proposes a machine learning based solution to detect malware using connection and TLS metadata without any decryption. The classification is shown to be highly accurate with high precision and recall rates by using a small number of features. Furthermore, we consider the deployment aspects of the solution and discuss different strategies to reduce the false positive rate.

1 Introduction

The Internet is moving towards ubiquitous encryption with more than 80% of enterprises encrypting their web traffic today [5]. Moreover, with over 93% of web traffic across Google being encrypted [8] and nearly 80% of web pages loaded by Firefox using HTTPS [5], this trend will only move in one direction. It is clear that encryption is a net gain for the security of both the Internet and society in general. However, it seems that encryption is interesting for threat actors too. They are leveraging these same benefits of encryption to evade detection and to secure their malicious activities. The situation is important as already over half of malware attacks carried out in 2019 use encryption [5]. It is expected that more than 70% of malware will use encryption to hide its operation in 2020 and alarmingly 60% of organizations will have no means to detect such threats [5].

Traditional network security infrastructure such as security middleboxes normally detect malicious events by scanning the payload part of the traffic. The problem is that, with encrypted traffic, this is not possible. One alternate approach to solve this problem depends on decrypting the encrypted traffic in the middle to detect malicious activity, but it has multiple drawbacks. First, such

© Springer Nature Switzerland AG 2021
M. Asplund and S. Nadjm-Tehrani (Eds.): NordSec 2020, LNCS 12556, pp. 37–53, 2021.
https://doi.org/10.1007/978-3-030-70852-8_3

a solution breaks the end-to-end security principle [17] and thus weakens the privacy of users. Second, it is not always practical as it depends on end-point cooperation. The biggest problem, however, is that it will be almost impossible to use such an approach with newer versions of encryption protocols, such as TLS 1.3. Moving forward, only the solutions that accept encrypted traffic as it is and do not suggest any decryption to detect malicious activity in encrypted traffic will sustain.

Research has shown that it is possible to detect non-benign usage of encryption without requiring decryption [1]. Using the potential of machine learning, traffic metadata and communication behavior can be used in a way to reliably distinguish between benign usage of encryption and a malware using encryption to hide itself. In this paper, we further explore this possibility. We analyze a large number of malware flows using our acquired dataset and study their communication behavior. We compare this to the behavior of benign usage of encryption using a benign dataset and extract features that can be used to identify instances of malware using encryption. The extracted features are evaluated for their discriminatory power using a number of binary machine learning classifiers. Our evaluation concludes that it is possible to detect encrypted malware with high accuracy and precision by using a small number of features.

The rest of the paper is structured as follows. Section 2 provides the necessary background and summarizes related work. Section 3 describes the datasets used in this work and analyzes them. Section 4 describes the classification experiments and presents the results. Finally, Sect. 5 summarizes the work presented and provides concluding remarks.

2   Background and Related Work

Transport Layer Security (TLS) [14] is a popular protocol that is increasingly being implemented on top of TCP to encrypt protocols such as HTTP for web browsing or SMTP for email transmission. It enhances privacy of applications by encrypting application data and is considered to be an important tool in the security landscape. One side effect of encryption is that it takes away network visibility. This is a concern considering that a lot of security infrastructure still relies on the traditional assumption of visibility into the network traffic. As a response to TLS, network operators and enterprises that need network visibility to perform important security functions developed solutions to perform traffic decryption. One approach employed, known as passive out-of-band decryption, is based on a static private key used to decrypt captured encrypted traffic when necessary [3]. Other solutions use a man-in-the-middle (MITM) approach to analyze encrypted communications [3]. All traffic traversing a middlebox is decrypted to gain required visibility to perform security functionality. To achieve this, a middlebox generates a local root certificate that is installed on all devices for which the TLS traffic needs to be inspected. During a subsequent TLS handshake by the inspected device, the middlebox modifies the certificate provided by the server and signs it with its own private key from the root certificate, allowing it visibility into all further exchanges on that TLS session. Despite the ethical questions and the degraded end-to-end security [6] that arises as a result of TLS inspection by decryption, the approach enables many use-cases [3] and is utilized massively. However, the latest version of TLS (version 1.3) mandates the use of dynamic(ephemeral) keys and encrypts more TLS handshake messages (everything after the second message), among other changes. These changes will make most TLS decryption approaches impossible.

Hence, as decryption of encrypted traffic is not a viable solution, there is only one way forward. Encryption needs to be accepted as it is and, instead of relying on traditional approaches to perform security functions, novel approaches that do not suggest decryption need to be investigated. Anderson and McGrew [1] contributed a landmark work in this area. They suggested a "data omnia" approach that uses over 25 features from the TLS handshake, connection metadata, DNS, and HTTP, to train a machine learning classifier that can accurately detect malware in encrypted traffic without decryption. In another work [2], they showed how such features can also be used to accurately attribute malware flows to a specific malware family. The work in [19] follows a similar approach and uses nearly 30 features. Other works [4,10] aim to achieve similar goals. However, both studies are only concerned with older versions of encryption protocols i.e., TLS 1.2 or earlier versions. Interestingly, a number of features used in these works, especially those based on data from TLS handshake, DNS, and HTTP, are either hard or impossible to obtain with TLS 1.3. Few other works [12,16,20–22] have proposed ways to classify unencrypted traffic based on flow metadata for the purpose of application identification or malware detection. BotHunter [9] aims to detect the process of a successful malware infection by focusing on the communication patterns of a host and using a state-based model. Overall, detection of malware in encrypted traffic without decryption has not been extensively studied. The proposals that do so are based on limited datasets (500,000 flows or lower) and suggest the use of a large number of features, some of which are only possible with TLS 1.2 or earlier versions. To this end, this paper further explores the idea of detecting malware using features of encrypted network traffic in a machine learning approach. Our study is based on relatively large datasets (over 2 million flows) and focuses on using a small set of features that are also available with TLS 1.3. In addition, we consider the deployment aspects of such a detection set-up and propose different strategies to reduce the number of false positives.

3   Datasets

The size and correctness of a dataset have a direct impact on the quality of research. There are not many publicly available datasets for encrypted malware and benign traffic in comparison to datasets for other fields such as image recognition and classification. One reason for this is that capturing malware traffic is not a simple task. It requires access to a large number of malware binaries where each binary, after a successful injection, can take a long time (weeks or months) until it generates traffic. Moreover, not all malware uses encryption, so this further reduces the possibility of collecting encrypted malware flows on a large scale. Collection of benign traffic can be manually done on a small scale, but a large dataset of benign encrypted traffic is hard to collect and then share in the public domain for privacy reasons. Despite these challenges, we have managed to acquire relatively large datasets for both malware and benign flows. Below, we describe these datasets in detail.

3.1 Malware

We considered a number of malware datasets for this work. However, we found that there is only one dataset that can provide us with a large volume of encrypted malware flows. The malicious dataset considered in this paper was collected at the Stratosphere Malware Capture Facility Project (MCFP) in the Czech Republic [7]. The dataset referred to as MCFP consists of over 400 malware files (pcaps) captured over eight years from 2011 to 2018. The dataset includes some malware communication over a real network but the majority of malware captures are collected after infecting virtual machines with malicious binaries. Thus, it is expected that only a small quantity of background traffic in the form of OS updates is also part of the dataset. The dataset has a readme file for each capture that provides details about the traffic labels and occasionally extra information about how the traffic was collected. As shown in Table 1, the dataset consists of millions of malware flows. The number of malware flows using encryption are over 2.2 million in total. The TLS ratio refers to the fraction of malware flows using encryption in each year. As the majority of the malware flows are not captured in the wild, these numbers can not be used to make any inferences about the increasing usage of encryption by malware.

Table 1. Statistics of malware data by year.

Year	Total flows	TLS malware flows	TLS ratio
2011/2012	33,632,712	565	0.00%
2013	166,305,676	434,726	0.26%
2014	10,811,159	121,976	1.12%
2015	60,308,666	274,254	0.45%
2016	72,094,904	93,915	0.13%
2017	151,961,617	1,230,292	0.80%
2018	40,630,858	136,630	0.33%
Total	**535,745,592**	**2,292,358**	**0.42%**

3.2 Benign

Our efforts to acquire a considerable dataset that represents real world benign usage of encryption led us to three different sources. The first source is a benign dataset from the MCFP project [7]. This data is a collection of Windows 7 users browsing a number of common websites to mimic the benign usage of encryption. This part of the dataset consists of 147,779 benign TLS flows. The second source is the CICIDS-2017 [18] dataset from the University of Brunswick. The dataset captures benign human activities based on HTTPS, SSH, and SMTPS. It contains 96,500 TLS flows. The combination of these two sources still did not provide us with enough data as compared to the malware data. This was resolved by convincing an enterprise to collect benign TLS flows from their demilitarized zone (DMZ). Instead of gaining access to the traffic itself, we gained access only to the requested features of the traffic. An ethical review was conducted by the ethical advisers at Karlstad University to assess the data we gained from the enterprise, and it was decided that ethical approval is not needed as the data have no sensitive or personally identifiable information. This private part of our benign dataset is based on flows collected during November 2019. The data provides us with information of around 626,120 benign TLS flows. In total, as shown in Table 2, the combination of these three sources provides us with either raw flows or features, of around 870,399 TLS flows. Of these flows, only 784,712 flows were used for this work as they contained all the required data. It is assumed that all benign flows are truly benign with no malware in them. We believe that although the volume of benign flows is small compared to the malware flows, it still provides a reasonable representation of encrypted benign flows.

Table 2. Statistics of benign datasets.

Source	Benign TLS flows
MCFP	147,779
CICIDS-2017	96,500
Enterprise Network (only features)	626,120
Total	**870,399**

3.3 Data Exploration

This section explores our malware and benign datasets and provides details about the data features employed in this work. We use joy [11], a tool developed by Cisco, to process the malware and benign pcap files from the datasets. It generates JSON files as output where each line in an output file corresponds to a TLS flow with its metadata nicely summarized as keys and objects. Joy allows for a number of data features related to, e.g., connection, TLS, HTTP, and DNS to be calculated and added to the output file. Our hypothesis in this work is that it should be possible to capture malware's behavior with only a minimum number of features as a detection method that depends on too many features is hard to deploy. In addition, only the features that are available in the long term should be considered. For example, with TLS 1.3, features based on certificates are going to be useless as only the initial two messages in the handshake are in plaintext. To this end, this work focuses on using only five features of encrypted flows. Four of these features are based on connection metadata, i.e., bytes out, bytes in, packets out, and packets in. The last feature is based on the first unencrypted TLS handshake message, i.e., "ClientHello" which contains the client offered list of cipher-suites. We considered additional TLS-based features such as the order of advertised cipher-suites and extensions, and the server selected cipher-suite but they did not improve the detection performance.

Connection Metadata Features. A histogram analysis is performed on the benign and malware datasets to explore the distribution of four selected connection metadata features. Figure 1 compares the normalized distribution of outgoing and incoming bytes among the malware and benign data flows, revealing some interesting patterns. It can be seen that most of the malware flows have less than 800 outgoing bytes and that most normal flows have a higher number of total outgoing bytes between 800 to 2,000. Moreover, over 60% of benign flows have more than 14,000 incoming bytes whereas the majority of malware flows have an initial spike at around 0–200 bytes and then relatively smaller spikes between 1,500 and 4,500 bytes. These spikes can be explained by considering that the malware, after a successful injection, normally contacts its command and control (C&C) server and downloads configuration files and additional binaries. We expected more malware flows to send a large amount of data outside than what was observed. One explanation for this can be that malware, after settling down, waits for further commands from the server to send the data outside, and those commands do not arrive in the malware capture time window.

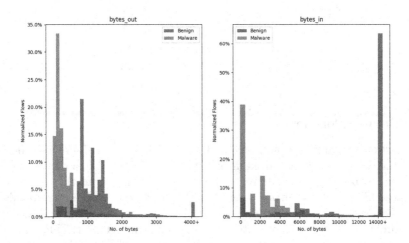

Fig. 1. Histogram comparing bytes distribution.

Hence the lack of a large amount of bytes going out in the malware flows. Figure 2 shows the distribution comparison in terms of packets. The plots reveal that the majority of malware flows send and receive between 0 and 10 packets whereas more benign flows have a higher number of incoming packets than outgoing packets. Considering the large volume of malware flows, it can be established that this is how malware in our dataset operates. However, to verify that the observations about benign flows are actually true and not dependent on the dataset, we performed additional comparisons between the data obtained from three sources and found that they show similar communication behavior. This indicated that the benign dataset used in this work appropriately represents benign encrypted flows as they come from three different sources and are collected at different times. The inferences we are able to make as a result of these comparisons hint at a distinct malware communication behavior that should allow for accurate models to be built.

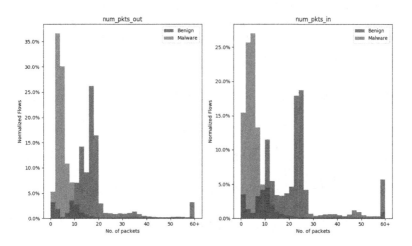

Fig. 2. Histogram comparing packets distribution.

TLS Features. Previous work on encrypted malware detection [1] has suggested the use of a large set of TLS features. However, only a few of those features are possible to obtain with TLS 1.3. We performed a TLS analysis on our benign and malware datasets focusing only on the initial message in the TLS handshake. Figure 3 shows a comparison between malware and normal flows from our datasets. The same coding of cipher-suites as suggested in the RFC for TLS 1.2 [15] is used to ensure accurate comparisons. It can be seen that some cipher-suites such as TLS_RSA_WITH_AES_128_CBC_SHA (0x002f) and TLS_RSA_WITH_AES_256_CBC_SHA (0x0035) are advertised by both malware and benign flows. However, certain weaker cipher-suites are almost exclu-

sively used by malware flows, e.g., TLS_DHE_RSA_WITH_AES_256_CBC_SHA
256 (0x006b), TLS_RSA_WITH_RC4_128_MD5 (0x0004), and TLS_RSA_WITH_
RC4_128_SHA (0x0005). On the other hand, benign flows are likely to prefer stronger cipher-suites, e.g., TLS_ECDHE_ECDSA_WITH_AES_128_GCM_
SHA256 (0xc02b) and TLS_ECDHE_RSA_WITH_AES_128_GCM_SHA256
(0xc02f). These observations point towards infected machines advertising TLS
cipher-suites in an identifiable fashion that can be captured by our fifth feature
based on advertised TLS cipher-suites.

4 Classification

In this section, we provide details about the machine learning experiments performed to classify encrypted malware traffic. The problem presented is a binary
classification as we are only interested in predicting whether an encrypted flow is
benign or malware. We use the two datasets discussed in the previous section for
this task. The evaluation is performed in two stages. To begin with, a basic evaluation is presented. Later, a deployment focused evaluation is presented where
we consider different strategies to improve the classification performance.

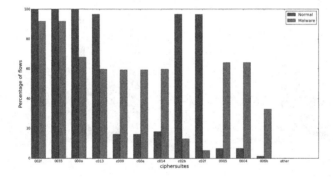

Fig. 3. Client offered TLS cipher-suites between benign and malware datasets.

4.1 Classifier Selection

To get a better understanding of the type of binary classifiers that are best suited
for this task, we compare the performance of multiple supervised machine learning classifiers available in the scikit-learn library [13]. The number of flows used
for cross-validation (CV) are 784,712 benign flows and 2,159,432 malware flows
(2,944,144 samples in total) where only 80% (2,355,315) of the total samples
are used for the first phase of classifier selection. Joy provides five features for
each of these samples and we assign a label of either malware or benign to each
sample. Table 3 details the result of evaluating multiple models in terms of their
estimated accuracy, i.e., how successfully a classifier learns from the training
data based on given features. A 10-fold cross-validation is utilized to estimate
the accuracy, and the data used by each classifier is kept the same. From the

table it can be seen that the tree based algorithms perform best for this problem. In particular, decision tree and random forest have the largest percentage of estimated accuracy and exhibit minimum variance in terms of training accuracy across the runs. This indicates that the decision boundaries of the data are more accurately separable using non-linear and non-parametric models that make no assumption about the distribution of data. As random forest utilizes an ensemble method to provide more accurate results, we conclude that random forest provides the best balance between accuracy and interpretability for this problem.

4.2   Model Evaluation

On the basis of the cross-validation results, we focus on classification with random forest from this point. We train a random forest model with 80% (2,355,315) of the total samples in our dataset and reserve the remaining 20% (588,829 samples) for validation by using the trained model to make predictions on these unseen samples. The same distribution of classes as the original dataset is maintained in the training and test subsets using the "stratified" parameter of scikit-learn. All other model parameters were set to default during the training process.

Table 3. Cross-validation results for different classification models.

Classifier	Mean cross-validation accuracy	Standard deviation (SD)
Logistic Regression	88.02%	0.079%
Linear Discrimination	87.61%	0.079%
K-nearest Neighbors	98.57%	0.037%
Decision Tree	98.88%	0.013%
Random Forest	98.94%	0.011%
Gradient Boosting	96.33%	0.074%
Naives-Bayes	87.06%	0.089%
Multi-layer Neural Network	96.97%	0.067%

Using Connection Features. The first set of experiments was conducted using only the four connection features and no TLS information. A random forest classifier is trained accordingly and then asked to make predictions on unseen data. Table 4 shows the classification report of predictions by the trained random forest model. The numbers demonstrate a good prediction accuracy by the model. However, as the training samples contain an unequal class distribution (more malware than benign), the accuracy can be misleading. The precision score shows that 99.11% of samples predicted as malware by the classifier were actually malware. The recall score (also known as sensitivity) demonstrates that 99.50% of malware was correctly detected. The F1-score is just a harmonic mean of precision and recall scores. Table 5 shows a confusion matrix to further diagnose the performance of the model and the type of errors it encountered. The matrix shows that 153,114 benign samples were correctly classified as benign (true negatives) but 3,828 benign samples were incorrectly classified as malware (false positives). Moreover, 429,751 malware samples were correctly predicted as malware (true positives) but 2,136 malware samples were incorrectly classified as benign (false negatives).

It is important for a classifier to show a good balance between precision and recall. A high recall but low precision will yield too many false positives with the advantage of not missing any malware. On the other hand, a high precision but low recall will ensure a low false positive rate but at the cost of missing some malware instances. Figure 4 plots the precision-recall (PR) curve from the classification results. We can see that our model only achieves perfect precision values up to a certain threshold of recall. After the threshold, to reach a higher recall, the precision of the model suffers. This trade-off between precision and recall is an important consideration for deployment in a real setting. Overall, the random forest classifier model shows decent, but not perfect, performance by using only four connection features.

Using Connection and TLS Features. The previous set of experiments was conducted using only the four connection features and no TLS information. Next we investigate the impact of adding the TLS feature on classification results. As the TLS feature is not based on a number but a text, we used one-hot encoding to encode this feature into a number. Dummy variables (either one or zero) are created for each cipher-suite where a one is assigned to a sample if it has a particular cipher-suite and zero if it does not. This allows a random forest model to be trained with both the four connection features and the fifth TLS feature. After training, the model makes predictions on unseen data. Table 6 shows the classification results. We can see that these results are a big improvement over the results obtained by only using connection features. The model now achieves a precision of 99.92% and a recall of 99.88% with an overall accuracy of 99.85%. The confusion matrix in Table 7 also shows better results, with reduced false

Table 4. Random forest classification results with connection features.

Features	Model	Accuracy	Precision	Recall	F1-score
Connection	Random forest	98.79%	99.11%	99.50%	99.31%

Table 5. Confusion matrix with connection features.

Actual labels	Predicted labels	
	Benign	Malware
Benign	153114	3828
Malware	2136	429751

positives of 364 and false negatives of 405. The precision-recall curve in Fig. 5 now also shows near perfect behavior as it achieves a high precision and recall for different thresholds. It would have been interesting to take a deep look at why certain flows are miss-classified, however the lack of detailed readme files on the malware dataset did not allow that. Overall, the results show that adding TLS information is valuable for a classifier to improve its performance. Hence, all forthcoming experiments are based on using both the four connection based features and the fifth TLS feature.

Table 6. Random forest classification results with connection and TLS data.

Features	Model	Accuracy	Precision	Recall	F1-score
Connection + TLS	Random forest	99.85%	99.92%	99.88%	99.91%

Testing for Stability. The evaluation so far has employed a 10-fold cross validation strategy over a dataset collected over eight years. This implies an inherent assumption that neither the benign nor the malicious flows have changed during these years. To clarify this further, we performed two additional set of experiments. In the first set, we trained a random forest model on 80% of all flows from years 2011 to 2017 only. The trained model is then used to make predictions on another distinct subset (20%) of flows from the same time period. This gave us an estimated accuracy A1 of 99.92%. In the second set of experiments, we trained another random forest model on all flows from years 2011 to 2017 but tested the model on latest flows from years 2018 and 2019. The resulting estimated accuracy A2 was 98.36%. These experiments show that although A2 is lower than A1 i.e., the estimated accuracy reduces when the model is trained on

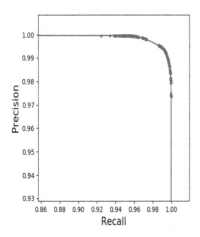

Fig. 4. PR-curve with 4 features.

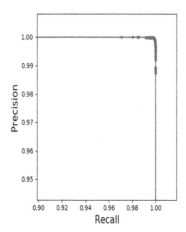

Fig. 5. PR-curve with 5 features.

Table 7. Confusion matrix with connection and TLS data.

Actual labels	Predicted labels	
	Benign	Malware
Benign	156578	364
Malware	405	431482

older flows and used to make predictions on latest flows, the stability of features over eight years still exists. This also bodes well for the long-term usability of the approach as it is possible to make future predictions based on training data from the past.

4.3 Deployment Considerations

This subsection focuses on deployment based considerations of the model. A model that is trained on an imbalanced dataset with a majority class of malware samples is likely to put more emphasis on detecting malware and thus have inherent bias. This can result in more false positives and fewer false negatives. Similarly, a model trained with a balanced weight of classes is likely to put equal emphasis on classifying malware as benign or benign as malware. Both of these training methods are not optimal, as the proposed random forest model is expected to be deployed in a real network where the appearance frequency of benign traffic is much higher than malware. It is important to consider the cost of different mistakes (false positives vs false negatives) and the base rate. Clearly, in the case of malware detection in a real network, it is likely that there will be more occasions for false alarms (false positives) than true positives. Such false alarms can swamp the correct predictions and make the task of detection useless from a cost/benefit perspective. It is therefore crucial to detect malware only when the model has extra confidence in its prediction (optimize precision) even if doing so comes at the cost of missing some malware instances. To this end, we explore two different approaches to undertake the task of optimizing the precision of a random forest model. This also provides insights into tuning the model to find the right balance between false positives and false negatives.

Class Weights. The first approach is based on cost and operates at the model level. In scikit-learn, different class weights can be assigned to each class during the training phase of a random forest. The weight places a higher penalty or cost on miss-classifying the minority class so that, although the overall accuracy of the model suffers, the minority class has a greater chance of being correctly classified. In other words, a higher class weight means we want to give more importance to a particular class. For our use-case, class weights can be exploited to assign a higher weight to the benign class (which is actually the minority class in our dataset) with an expectation that this will put more emphasis on its accurate classification. Table 8 shows the results when higher weights are assigned to the benign class while the weight for the malware class is kept at 1. A weight fraction of 1:10 means that the benign class has been assigned 10 times the weight of the malware class. For each combination of class weights, 10-fold cross-validation is performed using the entire dataset of 2,944,144 samples. Scores for precision, recall, and accuracy are calculated in each fold and averaged to get mean performance metrics over all folds. Confusion matrices from all folds are summed up to form a cumulative matrix that is presented in the table. It can be seen from the table that, as the class weight for benign samples increases, the precision of the model increases and the number of false positives decreases. However, the recall of the model suffers because a higher weight of benign class causes more false negatives. The class weight fraction of 1:2.75 represents the case when the classes are equally balanced and the results at fraction 1:1 are relatable to the results reported earlier in Table 6. Moving on, at a weight of 10 to 1 in favor of the benign class, the number of false positives (FPs) is reduced by almost three times from 1,581 to 543 at the cost of more than doubling the number of false negatives (FNs) from 2,141 to 5,155. The number of true positives (TPs) also reduces and the number of true negatives (TNs) rises. Increasing the benign class weight further only reduces the number of false positives by a small amount and at the cost of missing a large number of malware instances. We deduce that altering class weights can improve the classification of malware in a deployment scenario by reducing the FPs. However, even after training the model with a benign class weight set to one million times the weight of the malware class, the FPs do not reduce at the same rate and the cost of reducing a FP in terms of extra FNs is too big.

Table 8. CV evaluation results with different class weights.

Weight fraction	Accuracy	Precision	Recall	FPs	FNs	TPs	TNs
1:1	99.87%	99.92%	99.90%	1,581	2,141	2,157,291	783,131
1:2.75	99.86%	99.95%	99.85%	951	3,095	2,156,337	783,761
1:10	99.80%	99.97%	99.76%	543	5,155	2,154,277	784,169
1:10^2	99.68%	99.97%	99.59%	437	8,841	2,150,591	784,275
1:10^3	99.07%	99.98%	98.75%	393	26,874	2,132,558	784,319
1:10^4	98.92%	99.98%	98.55%	398	31,187	2,128,245	784,314
1:10^5	98.21%	99.98%	97.58%	390	52,048	2,107,384	784,322
1:10^6	98.17%	99.98%	97.52%	311	53,503	2,105,929	784,401

Adjust Decision Cutoff. In a random forest model, there are many individual decision trees all of which make their own class prediction in the form of a vote for each sample in the testing phase. The final decision of a random forest is the class that has the most votes. So, for example, if we have ten decision trees and a sample gets four votes for negative class (benign) and six votes for positive class (malware), then the final decision for that sample will be positive class as it has more votes (more than 50%). By default, this decision threshold or cutoff probability is set to 0.5. Anything above 0.5 is predicted to be positive and anything below 0.5 is predicted to be negative. Another possible way to increase the prediction accuracy of the malware class samples is to adjust these cutoffs for the predicted probabilities. A higher cutoff than 0.5 can ensure that positive predictions are based on more votes (less chance of FPs) while accepting the possibility of miss-classifying some malware samples as benign (FNs).

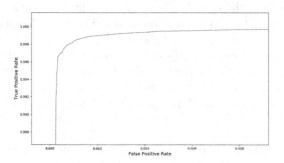

Fig. 6. ROC curve for different thresholds.

The best approach to determine a better cutoff for predictions and thus a better balance between TP rate (TPR) and FP rate (FPR) is to use a receiver operating characteristic (ROC) curve. Figure 6 shows the ROC curve for the random forest model described in Sect. 4.2. We observe that there lies a cutoff point on this curve such that, if the model operates there, it can ensure a high TPR while keeping FPR low. Table 9 shows the effect of moving the cutoff point from 0.5 to 0.99 on different performance scores. For each cutoff value, scores for precision, recall, and accuracy are calculated for different folds using 10-fold cross validation and averaged to get mean performance metrics over all folds. Confusion matrices from all folds are summed up to form a cumulative matrix that is presented in the table. It can be seen that, when a higher cutoff is selected, the number of FPs decreases at the cost of extra FNs. The precision of the model increases while the accuracy and recall decreases. At a cutoff point of 0.99, the model is able to achieve a precision of 99.99% and reduce the number of FPs (as compared to the default cutoff) by more than nineteen times from 1,522 to 77 while increasing FNs from 1,763 to 10745. We believe that this approach of adjusting the decision cutoff gives a better balance between FPR and FNR for the use-case of malware detection as compared to the earlier presented class weight approach. To complement the cutoff approach in a deployment scenario, a confidence score can also be added to all the generated alarms where a higher confidence score indicates that more decision trees voted in favor of generating an alarm.

Table 9. CV evaluation results at different cutoffs.

Cutoff	Accuracy	Precision	Recall	FPs	FNs	TPs	TNs
0.5	99.88%	99.92%	99.91%	1,522	1,763	2,157,669	783,190
0.6	99.88%	99.95%	99.89%	1,000	2,340	2,157,092	783,712
0.7	99.87%	99.96%	99.86%	712	2,881	2,156,551	784,000
0.8	99.86%	99.97%	99.84%	576	3,300	2,156,132	784,136
0.9	99.80%	99.98%	99.74%	234	5,415	2,154,017	784,478
0.91	99.78%	99.98%	99.72%	226	5,989	2,153,443	784,486
0.92	99.78%	99.98%	99.71%	223	6,061	2,153,371	784,489
0.93	99.78%	99.98%	99.71%	218	6,149	2,153,283	784,494
0.94	99.77%	99.99%	99.69%	188	6,490	2,152,942	784,524
0.95	99.76%	99.99%	99.68%	164	6,884	2,152,548	784,548
0.96	99.75%	99.99%	99.66%	152	7,130	2,152,302	784,560
0.97	99.72%	99.99%	99.63%	126	7,975	2,151,457	784,586
0.98	99.68%	99.99%	99.58%	100	9,067	2,150,365	784,612
0.99	99.63%	99.99%	99.50%	77	10,745	2,148,687	784,635

5 Concluding Remarks

The paper proposed a method to detect malware in encrypted traffic using a machine learning approach that does not require any decryption. Our hypothesis before conducting the machine learning experiments was that it should be possible to capture the behavior of encrypted malware flows using a small set of features. The work complements earlier work done in this area by focusing on relatively large datasets and a small number of features. The classification results show that by only using five connection and TLS-based features, it is possible to perform the detection and achieve a high precision (over 99%) and recall and a relatively low number of false positives and negatives. The detection method also depicts resilience against time as shown in earlier experiments. However, the possibility of a clever adversary to evade the detection method by modifying malware's communication pattern still exists. This limitation extends to the majority of machine learning based detection approaches as the models are trained on known communication patterns. All in all, using network traffic is just one way to detect malware. A robust detection approach should complement this with other information or indicators such as the local disk activity of a machine. In the paper, we have also considered the real world deployment aspects of the detection method and showed two different approaches to further reduce the false positive rate. The results of these experiments show a potential for deployment, but an implementation will require further tuning. This tuning will depend on a number of factors including the exact needs of the deployment environment and the observed base rate. It should be noted that our experiments are based on a single source of encrypted malware dataset. It is worth exploring in the future whether the general communication behavior of malware that we have observed is consistent with other malware, if such a dataset becomes available. We also envision to go one step further from the binary classification method used in this paper and attempt to predict the family or name of a malware.

Acknowledgment. The work was carried out in the High Quality Networked Services in a Mobile World project funded partly by the Knowledge Foundation of Sweden. The authors are grateful to František Střasák for his help with the understanding and processing of the malware dataset. We would also like to acknowledge Johan Garcia and Topi Korhonen for their feedback on the experiments.

References

1. Anderson, B., McGrew, D.A.: Identifying encrypted malware traffic with contextual flow data. In: Proceedings of the ACM Workshop on Artificial Intelligence and Security, Vienna, Austria, 28 October 2016, pp. 35–46 (2016)
2. Anderson, B., Paul, S., McGrew, D.A.: Deciphering malware's use of TLS (without decryption). J. Comput. Virol. Hacking Tech. **14**(3), 195–211 (2018)
3. Andreasen, F., Wang, E.: TLS 1.3 impact on network-based security. Internet-draft, RFC Editor, July 2019. https://tools.ietf.org/html/draft-camwinget-tls-use-cases-05
4. Bazuhair, W., Lee, W.: Detecting malign encrypted network traffic using Perlin noise and convolutional neural network. In: 10th Annual Computing and Communication Workshop and Conference, CCWC 2020, Las Vegas, NV, USA, 6–8 January 2020, pp. 200–206. IEEE (2020)
5. Cisco: Cisco encrypted traffic analytics (2019). https://www.cisco.com/c/en/us/solutions/collateral/enterprise-networks/enterprise-network-security/nb-09-encrytd-traf-anlytcs-wp-cte-en.html
6. Durumeric, Z., et al.: The security impact of HTTPS interception. In: Proceedings of the 24th Annual Network and Distributed System Security Symposium, NDSS San Diego, California, USA, 26 February–1 March 2017 (2017)
7. Erquiaga, M.J.: Malware capture facility project MCFP (2019). https://www.stratosphereips.org/datasets-malware
8. Google: HTTPS encryption on the web. https://transparencyreport.google.com/https/overview. Accessed 29 October 2019
9. Gu, G., Porras, P.A., Yegneswaran, V., Fong, M.W.: Bothunter: detecting malware infection through IDS-driven dialog correlation. In: Proceedings of the 16th USENIX Security Symposium, Boston, MA, USA, 6–10 August (2007)
10. Liu, J., Zeng, Y., Shi, J., Yang, Y., Wang, R., He, L.: Maldetect: a structure of encrypted malware traffic detection. Comput. Mat. Continua **60**(2), 721–739 (2019)
11. McGrew, D., Anderson, B., Perricone, P., Hudson, B.: Joy (2019). https://github.com/cisco/joy
12. Moore, A.W., Zuev, D.: Internet traffic classification using Bayesian analysis techniques. In: Proceedings of the International Conference on Measurements and Modeling of Computer Systems, SIGMETRICS, Alberta, Canada, pp. 50–60 (2005)
13. Pedregosa, F., et al.: Scikit-learn: machine learning in Python. J. Mach. Learn. Res. **12**, 2825–2830 (2011)

14. Rescorla, E.: The Transport Layer Security (TLS) Protocol Version 1.3. RFC 8446, RFC Editor, August 2018. https://rfc-editor.org/rfc/rfc8446.txt
15. Rescorla, E., Dierks, T.: The Transport Layer Security (TLS) Protocol Version 1.2. RFC 5246, RFC Editor, August 2008. https://rfc-editor.org/rfc/rfc5246.txt
16. Rieck, K., Holz, T., Willems, C., Düssel, P., Laskov, P.: Learning and classification of malware behavior. In: Proceedings of the Detection of Intrusions and Malware, and Vulnerability Assessment DIMVA, Paris, France, pp. 108–125 (2008)
17. Saltzer, J.H., Reed, D.P., Clark, D.D.: End-to-end arguments in system design. In: Proceedings of the 2nd International Conference on Distributed Computing Systems, Paris, France, 1981. pp. 509–512. IEEE Computer Society (1981)
18. Sharafaldin, I., Lashkari, A.H., Ghorbani, A.A.: Toward generating a new intrusion detection dataset and intrusion traffic characterization. In: Proceedings of the 4th International Conference on Information Systems Security and Privacy, ICISSP, Funchal, Madeira - Portugal, 22–24 January 2018, pp. 108–116 (2018)
19. Střasák, F.: Detection of HTTPS malware traffic. https://dspace.cvut.cz/bitstream/handle/10467/68528/F3-BP-2017-Strasak-Frantisek-strasak_thesis_2017.pdf (2017)
20. Tegeler, F., Fu, X., Vigna, G., Kruegel, C.: BotFinder: finding bots in network traffic without deep packet inspection. In: Proceedings of the Conference on emerging Networking Experiments and Technologies, CoNEXT 2012, Nice, France, 10–13 December, pp. 349–360 (2012)
21. Wurzinger, P., Bilge, L., Holz, T., Goebel, J., Kruegel, C., Kirda, E.: Automatically generating models for botnet detection. In: Proceedings of the 14th European Symposium on Research in Computer Security ESORICS, Saint-Malo, France, 21–23 September, pp. 232–249 (2009)
22. Zander, S., Nguyen, T., Armitage, G.: Automated traffic classification and application identification using machine learning. In: Proceedings of the 30th Annual IEEE Conference on Local Computer Networks (LCN), 15–17 November Sydney, Australia, pp. 250–257 (2005)

Formal Analysis

Machine-Checking the Universal Verifiability of ElectionGuard

Thomas Haines[1]([⊠]), Rajeev Goré[2], and Jack Stodart[2]

[1] Norwegian University of Science and Technology, Trondheim, Norway
thomas.haines@ntnu.no
[2] The Australian National University, Canberra, Australia
{rajeev.gore,jack.stodart}@anu.edu.au

Abstract. ElectionGuard is an open source set of software components and specifications from Microsoft designed to allow the modification of a number of different e-voting protocols and products to produce public evidence (transcripts) which anyone can verify. The software uses ElGamal, homomorphic tallying and sigma protocols to enable public scrutiny without adversely affecting privacy. Some components have been formally verified (machine-checked) to be free of certain software bugs but there was no formal verification of their cryptographic security.

Here, we present a machine-checked proof of the verifiability guarantees of the transcripts produced according to the ElectionGuard specification. We have also extracted an executable version of the verifier specification, which we proved to be secure, and used it to verify election transcripts produced by ElectionGuard. Our results show that our implementation is of similar efficiency to existing implementations.

Keywords: Verifiable e-voting · Interactive theorem provers · Code extraction

1 Introduction

Electronic voting has been in use for at least the last fifty years; however, the nature of elections makes it very hard to verify whether the electronic components are behaving as they should. Current best practice is to ensure that each software component creates publicly verifiable evidence that its output is correct with respect to certain criteria. A cascade of such processes then guarantees that the whole process is end-to-end-verifiable [1]. Such systems invariably require using increasingly complicated cryptographic techniques.

A particular group of techniques for adding verifiability to electronic voting is homomorphic tallying in which each vote is encrypted under a homomorphic encryption scheme to produce a ciphertext with all ciphertexts publicly tallied (without decrypting them) to produce an encryption of the tally. The tally ciphertext is then decrypted by the authorities. Zero-knowledge proofs can be used to prove publicly that the encrypted ballots are well-formed and that the tally was decrypted correctly. This does not suffice for overall verifiability since we do not know whether the collected ballots contain the votes

© Springer Nature Switzerland AG 2021
M. Asplund and S. Nadjm-Tehrani (Eds.): NordSec 2020, LNCS 12556, pp. 57–73, 2021.
https://doi.org/10.1007/978-3-030-70852-8_4

intended by the eligible voters but is rather evidence that the collected ballots are counted correctly. There are various ways to extend homomorphic tallying to have end-to-end verifiability, so that the counted ballots are guaranteed to be the intended ballots of the eligible voters, which we omit for brevity. The most famous deployed e-voting scheme using homomorphic tallying is surely the online voting system Helios [2], which is used by the International Association for Cryptologic Research.

ElectionGuard is a set of open-source software components and specifications released by Microsoft in 2019 [3]. It is designed to quickly allow ballot-collecting devices (such as ballot-marking devices and optical scanners) to work with trustees (so called because they are trusted to maintain privacy) to produce public evidence. Specifically, to allow such devices to produce evidence that the encrypted ballots are well-formed, that the ballots were correctly tallied, and that the announced result was correct with respect to the tally. All references to ElectionGuard in this document are to version 0.85.[1]

An election in the context considered by ElectionGuard is a protocol involving Election Officials, Trustees, Voters, and Interested Citizens. The Trustees are responsible for generating the required cryptographic keys and then decrypting the encrypted tally at the end of the election. The Election Officials have numerous responsibilities including providing the Ballot Marking Devices, Electronic Ballot Boxs, and Electronic Poll Books.

Prior to election day, the ballot style is determined by the Election Officials and the Trustees generate their cryptographic keys (including what threshold is required to decrypt); for brevity we elide much of the other preparation and refer the reader to the ElectionGuard documentation.[2] In the booth, the Voter selects her candidates using the Ballot Marking Device. The Ballot Marking Device then creates both a paper ballot and an electronic Cast Vote Record (CVR). It assigns the ballot a unique ID number, encrypts the CVR and constructs a non-interactive zero-knowledge proof that the ballot is well-formed. In addition to the paper ballot, the voter is also provided with a tracker which contains a human-comparable hash of the encrypted ballot. The voter is then given the option to cast or spoil the ballot. If the ballot is cast, the paper ballot is added to the ballot box and the CVR is added to the Electronic Ballot Box. If the ballot is spoiled the Ballot Marking Device must prove to the voter that it correctly encrypted the voter's selection (and the voter must create another ballot).

After the election, the encrypted ballots are homomorphically aggregated; the paper ballots are also tallied. Prior to tallying, the zero-knowledge proofs should be checked by trustees to ensure that we tally only well-formed ballots. The Trustees then decrypt the aggregated ciphertexts containing the election result. Voters need not check the result, however a diligent voter should check that any ballots (cast or spoiled) which match the trackers they posses appear

---

[1] https://github.com/microsoft/electionguard/wiki/Informal/
ElectionGuardSpecificationV0.85.pdf.
[2] For simplicity, we describe a fairly narrow use case of ElectionGuard.

correctly on the bulletin board. Any observer can check the well-formedness of voter encryptions and correct tallying by running a computer program called a verifier over the published transcripts, and ElectionGuard includes a reference verifier. The goal of this process is to give the voters high confidence that their ballot was recorded correctly and that the collected ballots are correctly tallied. The security guarantees from voter-initiated checks ensure individual verifiability. The checks performed by any interested party ensure universal verifiability.

The checks that the voter needs to make are simple. But the checks that the verifier software must make are considerably more complicated. Indeed, ElectionGuard is useful only if we can be sure that a verifier that correctly implements the ElectionGuard verifier specification will indeed give the security guarantees claimed by ElectionGuard. As we point out next, this critical relationship between the specification and implementation is easy to break.

1.1 Implementation Issues in E-Voting Systems

The theoretical foundations of verifiable electronic voting has matured greatly. Simple schemes, such as ElectionGuard, using homomorphic tallying are well-known and theoretically easy to construct. Nevertheless, we are now seeing small but critical bugs in the implementation of such schemes. For instance, the Swiss Post system, while not itself using homomorphic tallying, contained many of the same components, many of which were broken despite extensive review [4]. This is the tip of the proverbial iceberg in terms of failures and issues in allegedly end-to-end verifiable systems; other examples have included the iVote system deployed in the Australian state of New South Wales [5], and the e-voting system used in national elections in Estonia [6]. In addition, many general issues have been discovered [7–9] which need to be carefully avoided in any implementation. Most of these issues were present in the Helios e-voting system [2]. Thus even simple systems are prone to critical software errors.

General software development aims at increasing security through a process of best practice which is not specific to the particular goal of that software. This kind of development avoids many kinds of errors, including but not limited to, division by zero, off-by-one errors, syntax errors, and resource errors. Various organisations offer services for checking that software is developed according to these standards and indeed this is commonly done for e-voting software. It is interesting, then, that the bugs mentioned previously occurred even though the software, in many cases, was certified according to these best practice standards.

The reason that the bugs slipped through is due to their nature. These bugs are not standard programming bugs which might be caught by standard best practice techniques. Rather, the code does not correctly capture the logical flow of the protocol, as required by the cryptographic primitives. Compounding these issues is that many of the bugs were present in the specification as well as the code. So, at present, the problem of securely deploying electronic voting does not appear to be primarily about improving theory or requiring more secure programming; rather, it appears to be improving our ability to check that the specification and implementation contain the logical flow they should.

A key observation here is that while end-to-end verifiability protects against bugs in the software running the elections, it transfers the correctness requirements to the software that checks (verifies) the produced evidence. This is an excellent trade since the software required to check the evidence is much simpler and multiple independent verifiers can be developed. However, the independence of the verifiers is normally only skin deep since they are implementations of a common specification which may itself be incorrect. (The common practice to have under-graduate computer science students implement the independent verifiers is unlikely to result in insightful detection of errors in the cryptographic specification.) Our work here can be viewed as a formal proof that the specification is cryptographically secure and that our extracted verifier tests that our encoding of the specification is compatible (interoperable) with the existing implementations, as well as being another independent verifier itself.

1.2   Contribution

We have formally verified the (universal) verifiability of the ElectionGuard specification: that is, we have encoded the specification in Coq and proved its cryptographic soundness. Specifically, we prove special soundness (that if any adversary is able to produce multiple accepting transcripts then the collected ballots must be counted correctly) which is known to imply soundness [10].

We extend previous work on formally verifying the verifier of Helios by:

- Creating a richer type system to allow the ballots to be encoded into Coq;
- Defining a stand-alone verifier for these ballots and the associated proofs;
- Proving this verifier to be correct; that is to have correctness, special soundness, and honest-verifier zero-knowledge.

This compares to prior work [11] where the various components of the verifier were defined and proven secure in Coq but then composed in the extracted version. The fact that the components should compose correctly is trivial (it amounts to saying that the logical conjunction of n statements is true if all the statements are true) but defining it formally in Coq results in complicated types.

These contributions allow us to extract our formally verified verifier into an executable verifier which is comparable in efficiency to existing implementations. We used this verifier to verify transcripts produced by ElectionGuard. We have not proved any privacy properties of the ElectionGuard system but we have proved the honest-verifier zero-knowledge of the verifier in Coq.

1.3   Interactive Theorem Provers

Interactive theorem provers are pieces of software that check that mathematical "proofs" are correct. A human encodes the mathematical theorem and (purported) proof within the language of the interactive theorem prover and the interactive theorem prover checks the proof using a given finite collection of proof-rules. Trust rests upon three pillars: first, the code base for interactive theorem provers is usually very small and has been scrutinised by many experts, typically over decades; second, most interactive theorem provers produce a machine-readable proof of the claimed theorem and these can be checked either by hand or by a different interactive theorem prover; third, interactive theorem provers typically enjoy extremely rigorous mathematical foundations, which have withstood decades of peer review. Many interactive theorem provers transliterate (extract) correct proofs into ML, Haskell, Scheme or OCaml programs.

The main impediment to using interactive theorem proving and code extraction is the rather steep learning curve involving exotic mathematical logic(s) and the associated proof-rules. Consequently, interactive theorem provers mostly remained in an academic setting [12,13], and were rarely considered for real life software-engineering. Recent debacles, such as heartbleed[3], have led companies and researchers to focus on avoiding bugs by using formal verification, to the point where it is now gaining momentum in mainstream development.

In this work, we used the interactive theorem prover Coq [14] to: encode specifications; verify (machine-check) that (functional) programs are correct with respect to these encoded specifications; and extract the code corresponding to the verified functional programs.

1.4   Verification and Code Extraction via Coq

We now explain how to use the interactive theorem prover called Coq [14] to: encode specifications; encode functional programs; and to verify them correct against these encoded specifications to finally extract corresponding code.

Below, we exemplify one way to produce verified programs via Coq using addition of two natural numbers. As in the sequel, we first give a natural language definition as might be found in a mathematics text, then its encoding into Coq, followed by an explanation of the encoding. Doing so is important as it helps to ensure that the encoding really does do the job we intend it to do.

Definition 1. *The set mynat is the smallest set formed from the clauses:*

1. *the term O is in mynat;*
2. *if the term n is in mynat then so is the term S n;*
3. *nothing else is in mynat.*

```
Inductive mynat : Set :=
  | O : mynat                (* O is a mynat *)
  | S : mynat -> mynat.      (* S of a mynat is a mynat *)
```

Here, the first line encodes that *mynat* is of type *Set* and the vertical bar separates the two subclauses of the encoding. The terms O and S are known as constructors and anything in between "(*" and "*)" are comments. The first subclause illustrates that the colon can also be read as set membership $\in$ while the second clause illustrates that the constructor S is actually a function that

---

[3] http://heartbleed.com/.

accepts a member from *mynat* and constructs another member of *mynat* by prefixing the given member with S. Thus the explicit mention of n in the natural language definition is elided. Clause (3) of the natural language definition is encoded by the declaration `Inductive`. Intuitively, the natural numbers are the terms $O, (S\ O), (S\ (S\ O)), \cdots$ corresponding to $0, 1, 2, \cdots$.

Definition 2 (Specification of addition). *Adding O to any natural number m gives m, and for all natural numbers n, m, and r, if adding n to m gives r then adding $(S\ n)$ to m gives $(S\ r)$.*

```
Inductive add: mynat -> mynat -> mynat -> Prop :=
| addO: forall m, (add O m m)
| addS: forall n m r, add n m r -> add (S n) m (S r).
```

Here, the notation *mynat* $\rightarrow$ *mynat* $\rightarrow$ *mynat* $\rightarrow$ *Prop* encodes that *add* is ternary and that it is a "Proposition" which returns either true or else false, but in intuitionistic logic rather than classical logic. Our specification of addition is encoded as a ternary predicate *add n m r* that is true iff "adding n to m gives r", based purely on the only two ways in which we can construct the first argument: either it is O, or it is of the form $(S\ \cdot)$. The "extraction" facilities of Coq allow us to produce actual code in OCaml, Haskell, or Scheme. The encoding below is our hand-crafted function *myplus* in which the "where" keyword allows an infix symbol $+$ for *myplus* and $\Rightarrow$ (not $\rightarrow$) indicates the return value of the function:

```
Fixpoint myplus (n m: mynat) : mynat :=
   match n with
   | O   => m
   | S p => S (p + m)
   end
   where "p + m" := (myplus p m).
```

Our function is correct if it implies the specification below.

Theorem 1. *For all natural numbers n, m, r, if $r = myplus\ n\ m$ then add n m r is true.*

```
Theorem myplus_correct:
   forall n m r: mynat, (r = myplus n m) -> (add n m r).
Proof.
   induction n. intro m. intro r. intro H. simpl in H.
   subst r. apply addO. intros m r H. rewrite H.
   simpl myplus1. apply addS. apply IHn. reflexivity.
Qed.
```

The text shown between the words `Proof` and `Qed` consists of commands typed in by the user to guide Coq to the proof of the theorem. That is, the user interacts with Coq to obtain the proof, with Coq checking each step to ensure that it is acceptable. The Coq extraction mechanism turns our function "myplus" into Ocaml, Haskell or Scheme code giving us a program which is provably correct with respect to our specification of addition.

We can also reason about our specification itself inside Coq. For example, the theorem below encodes that our definition of addition is commutative:

Theorem 2. *For all natural numbers n, m, r, if add n m r then add m n r*

```
Theorem add_commutative:
  forall n m r: mynat, (add n m r) -> (add m n r).
Proof.  ...  Qed.
```

In the sequel, we give all of our theorems in both plain text and in Coq to enable the reader to confirm that our encodings do indeed capture our intentions.

1.5   Protecting Against Flaws in Code and Specifications

Haines *et al.* [11] suggested combining techniques for verifiable e-voting and formal verification of software. The idea is that the key component, at least for integrity, in a verifiable e-voting system is not the e-voting software but the verifier that checks the public evidence produced by the e-voting software; if the verifier is correct (and used) then the properties it guarantees will hold regardless of any bugs present in the e-voting software. This is useful because the verifier is a far simpler and more self contained than the e-voting software. Rivest [1] called this "Software independence" but the term is perhaps slightly misleading because there is still a fundamental reliance on the software that implements a correct verifier.

If the verifier is the key entity to verify (machine-check), the next logical question is what properties of the verifier need to be checked? Specifically, Haines *et al.* argued that the logical properties of the verifier are what need to be checked. In the context of e-voting systems built largely upon zero-knowledge proofs, the key property of the verifier is soundness. That is, the verifier should not accept the transcript unless the statement is true, at least with overwhelming probability. Collectively, this means that the integrity of a deployed e-voting scheme can be reduced to the strong guarantees of correctness provided by interactive theorem provers rather than the new and understudied e-voting scheme.

Haines *et al.* demonstrated the feasibility of this approach by creating several machine-checked sub-verifiers for the Helios e-voting system which collectively sufficed for universal verifiability. They achieved this by providing the logical machinery to easily prove secure the sigma protocols used in e-voting; we reuse this machinery in our work. The similarities in ElectionGuard and Helios mean many of the underlying components (sub-verifiers) are similar but in our work we take care of the various differences and extend Haines *et al.*'s work to prove the completed verifier secure rather than the sub-verifiers.

1.6   Residual Trust Assumptions

The residual trust assumptions differ between the different aspects of our contribution. In general, the work in Coq has fairly low trust assumptions whereas the extracted verifier has higher trust assumptions.

The correctness of the work in Coq depends on the correctness of Coq but also that we have correctly defined verifiability and ElectionGuard. The definition of verifiability takes the well established form of special soundness. The soundness of the ElectionGuard definition is resolved by proving that it satisfies verifiability; the compatibility of the definition is demonstrated by showing that it can handle real ElectionGuard transcripts.

The extracted verifier incurs several additional trust assumptions and for this reason we suggest that our extracted verifier should be one of many. First, the extraction facility in Coq has not been formally verified and this could introduce errors. In addition, we replace some of the inefficient Coq arithmetic functions with significantly faster native OCaml functions. Finally, since deployed sigma protocols are made non-interactive via the Fiat-Shamir transform, this transform also needs to be checked for correctness to ensure the deployed elections are secure. This is not challenging to do manually despite the prevalence of careless implementations. It would be nice to prove the correctness of the Fiat-Shamir transform inside an interactive theorem prover but unfortunately this would involve rewinding random oracles which is not currently supported in any prover known to the authors.

2   Machine Checking the Verifiability of ElectionGuard

In this section we will introduce our Coq specification which encapsulates the relevant parts of ElectionGuard. We will aim to provide sufficient detail to give an overview of what we did without completely overwhelming readers who are unfamiliar with Coq. It is important to provide such details so that readers can check that our Coq encodings do actually capture what we claim we capture. For conciseness we will not provide details of the sigma protocols and interested readers may consult [11].

2.1   ElectionGuard Elections

An election in the context of ElectionGuard consists of a fixed number of contests with one or more candidates in each contest. This style of voting varies between plurality voting and approval voting depending on the number of candidates which are allowed for selection. We assume for simplicity that each voter is allowed to select exactly one candidate in each contest: this is easy to change but doing so unduly complicates the presentation. We use numContests as the number of contests in any given election.

ElectionGuard uses ElGamal in Schnorr groups. We abstract our verifier over any group G of prime order since the exact group does not matter for the security reduction. For a given group G, the ElGamal ciphertext space is the product group DG.G of G and G: a product group is the group-theoretic analogue of the Cartesian product where all operations are taken component-wise. In the Coq examples that follow G and DG.G will refer to the sets that underly these groups.

Running example: here we give a running example to show how we encode ballots into Coq using the digit 1 to signify "preferred candidate" and using 0 to signify "unpreferred candidate". Suppose we have an election with three contests with four candidates in the first contest, three candidates in the second contest, and two candidates in the third contest. To vote for a candidate in the first contest, a voter has to create a list of natural numbers of length <u>four</u> containing exactly one 1 with the others all 0. The list entries are then mapped into the group G (which is the message space of the encryption scheme) before being encrypted to give ciphertext members of DG.G so we use $E(1)$ and $E(0)$ to stand for "encryption of 1" and "encryption of 0" respectively. For example, the vector $[E(1), E(0), E(0), E(0)]$ of length <u>four</u> is a vote for the first candidate out of the <u>four</u> candidates in contest 1 where $E(1) \in$ DG.G and $E(0) \in$ DG.G. Suppose that the election has two cast ballots with the first ballot cast for candidates 1, 2, and 1 in the <u>three</u> respective contests and the second ballot cast for candidates 2, 1, 2. respectively, as shown below:

Contests	1	2	3
Ballot 1	$[E(1), E(0), E(0), E(0)]$	$[E(0), E(1), E(0)]$	$[E(1), E(0)]$
Ballot 2	$[E(0), E(1), E(0), E(0)]$	$[E(1), E(0), E(0]$	$[E(0), E(1)]$

We now describe how we encoded such ballots into Coq using vectors and product types.

2.2 Vector and Product Types

We assume that the reader is not an expert in Coq and therefore explain how we encoded ballots into Coq in some detail. There is nothing particularly original in our encoding but it may appear complicated to a naive reader.

We encode most of our information in vectors which are defined in Coq via the command **vector type length** where **type** is the type of the elements of the vector and **length** is the length of the vector: thus **vector int 3** encodes that the vector contains integers and is of length three. To maintain generality, the declaration **vector nat numContests** tells Coq that each vector is of length **numContests** and contains natural numbers **nat**. Our running example of an election with <u>three</u> contests with <u>four</u>, three, and two candidates, respectively, would be a vector called **numSel** = [4, 3, 2] of type **vector nat 3**. The functions **Vhead** and **VTail** are provided by Coq to allow us to split a vector (a list) into its components, so **Vhead [4,3,2]** would return 4 and **Vtail [4,3,2]** would return [3,2].

In Coq, if A and B are two arbitrary types, then the type **prod A B** contains all pairs (a, b) such that a is of type A and b is of type B. If A and B are of type Set then so is **prod A B**.

An (encrypted) ballot, such as Ballot 1 above, is an ordered tuple where each member of the tuple is itself a tuple of ciphertexts. We define it in Coq as shown below. The type of a ballot is a nested product of vectors of ciphertexts where the depth of the product is the number of contests and at each layer of the product it contains a vector of ciphertexts of length equal to the number of candidates in that contest. For example, continuing our previous example above, a ballot would be of type **vector DG.G 4 * vector DG.G 3 * vector DG.G 2**. It is easy to see that the ballots in our example, $([E(1), E(0), E(0), E(0)], [E(0), E(1), E(0)], [E(1), E(0)]$ and $([E(0), E(1), E(0), E(0)], [E(1), E(0), E(0], [E(0), E(1)])$, are of this type.

The type `ballot` is defined in Coq as a set of functions which accept a vector of natural numbers of length `numContests`. By making `ballot` depend upon the argument `numContests`, we tell Coq that the type of the vector input depends on `numContests`. The function also specifics that the type it outputs will be a set. The function `fun ...` consists of two clauses depending upon the value of the natural number `numContests`:

Base case: the first is for the base case when the number of contests is zero in which case we simply return the empty set.

Inductive case: the second is for when the number of contests is non-zero when we recursively define the result as the Cartesian product of two sets whose types are, respectively, `vector DG.G (Vhead v)` and `ballot (Vtail v)`. The first set has type `vector DG.G (Vhead v)` where `(Vhead v)` is the number of candidates in the first contest. The second set has type `ballot (Vtail v)` as returned by `ballot` on all remaining contests.

```
Fixpoint ballot (numContests : nat) :
    vector nat numContests -> Set :=
match numContests with
| 0%nat => fun _ => Empty_set
| _      => fun v => prod (vector DG.G (Vhead v)) (ballot (Vtail v))
end.
```

A ballot on its own may be ill formed and contain a large number of votes for each candidate. ElectionGuard, therefore, requires that each ballot come with a cryptographic proof that it is well formed. We define the type of the ballot proof as shown below.

```
Fixpoint ballotProof (numContests : nat) :
    vector nat numContests -> Type :=
match numContests with
| 0%nat => fun _ => Empty_set
| _     => fun v1 => prod (ProofTranscript (OneOfNSigma (Vhead v1)))
                         (ballotProof (Vtail v1))
end.
```

In essence, it is a nested tuple where each element in the tuple corresponds to the cryptographic proof, in the form of a sigma-protocol transcript, that the corresponding ciphertexts are all encryptions of zero or else one and that the summation of the ciphertexts is equal to one. That is, in this context, the votes for each candidate are either yes or no and exactly one candidate has a yes vote.

The sigma protocol transcript type is returned by the function `ProofTranscript` which takes a sigma protocol and returns the type of its transcripts. In this case, the sigma protocol is `OneOfNSigma` which takes a natural number n and returns a sigma protocol to check that n ciphertexts are all encryptions of one or else zero and the product of the ciphertexts is one.

Once all the ballots are homomorphically combined, the authorities decrypt the summation of all ballots. They do this by each using their share of the secret key to produce decryption factors. These decryption factors can then be publicly combined by anyone to decrypt the ciphertext. We define the type of the decryption factors as shown below.

Algorithm 1: Election Verifier

Data: numTrustees numCast numContests
Data: vector containing the number of selections in each contest numSel
Data: group generator g, public key shares pks
Data: castBallots ballotProofs decFactors decProofs
Result: *valid*
valid := true;
acc := Encryption of zero;
for *(ballot,proof)* ∈ *(castBallots,ballotProofs)* **do**
 if *proof of correct encryption for ballot are invalid* **then**
  valid := false;
 end
 acc := *acc* × ballot
end
if *If decProofs are invalid for decFactors with respect to acc* **then**
 valid := false;
end

Fig. 1. Algorithm of the verifier

```
Fixpoint decryptionFactors (numContests numTrustees : nat) :
  vector nat numContests -> Set :=
  match numContests with
  | 0%nat => fun _ => Empty_set
  | S n'  => fun v1 => prod (vector (vector G numTrustees) (Vhead v1))
                           (decryptionFactors numTrustees (Vtail v1))
  end.
```

Since we do not trust the authorities (trustees) to honestly decrypt the result, ElectionGuard uses sigma protocols to prove that the decryption factors are computed correctly. We define the type of these proofs as below.

```
Fixpoint decryptionProof (numContests numTrustees : nat) :
    vector nat numContests -> Type :=
  match numContests with
  | 0%nat => fun _ => Empty_set
  | S n'  => fun v1 => prod
        (ProofTranscript (BallotDecSigma (Vhead v1) numTrustees))
        (decryptionProof numTrustees (Vtail v1))
  end.
```

2.3 Verifier

We will largely skip over the details of our implementation of the verifier because we have proven its cryptographic soundness and have checked that it is compatible with ElectionGuard, and as such, the exact details are not particularly important.

At a high level, the verifier is defined in Fig. 1 (for simplicity we use parameters implicitly); it takes in the election parameters, the cast ballots and various cryptographic proofs and decryption factors. It then checks that the crypto-graphic proofs that the ballots are well formed are valid and that the cryto-graphic proofs of correct decryption for the summation of all the ballots are valid. The Coq variant is shown below. bVforall2 takes a predicate p on two values, and two vectors v, v' of the same length m and checks that $p(v[i], v'[i])$ is true for all i in 1 to m.

```
Definition Verifier
  (* Parameters *)
  (numTrustees numCast numContests : nat)
  (numSel : vector nat numContests)
  (g : G) (pks : vector G numTrustees)

  (* Cast ballots *)
  (castBallots : vector  (ballot numContests numSel) numCast)

  (* Proofs of correct encryption *)
  (ballotProofs : vector (ballotProof numContests numSel) numCast)
  (decFactors : decryptionFactors numTrustees numSel)
  (decProofs : decryptionProof numTrustees numSel) : bool :=
  let pk := (g, VG_prod pks) in
  let tally := Vfold_left (multBallots numContests numSel)
                          (zeroBallot numContests numSel) castBallots in
  (* Check proof of correct encryption *)
  (bVforall2 (BallotVerifier pk numContests numSel)) castBallots ballotProofs
  (* Checks proof of correct decryption *) &&
  DecryptionVerifier g pks numContests numSel tally decFactors decProofs.
```

We describe each component of the Coq definition:

numtrustees: is the number of election authorities participating in the election;
numCast: is the number of ballots cast in the election;
numContests: is the number of contests in the election;
numSel: is a vector containing the number of candidates in each contest;
g: is the generator of the underlying Schnorr group G for ElGamal;
pks: is the vector of length numtrustees containing elements from G ie the public keys of the authorities;
ballot numContests numSel: is the set of all ballots for numContests contests with numSel candidates in each contest.
castBallots: of type vector (ballot numContests numSel) numCast is then the vector of length numCast containing each ballot of type (ballot numSel);
multBallots numContests numSel: is a function which forms the multiplication of two ballots in ballot numContests numSel by multiplying the cipher-texts component-wise.

2.4   Machine Checked Verifiability

In this subsection we will present our main theorem about the validity of the verifier. We will present it first in more standard notation and then in Coq notation. A reader familiar with sigma protocols will notice that it takes the form of cryptographic special soundness.

Recall that a zero knowledge proof demonstrates that a statement s belongs to a particular language, and it is common to use R to denote the relationship between statements and witnesses. Special soundness says that if any adversary can produce two accepting transcripts for different challenges then it is possible to extract a witness w from those transcripts efficiently such that $(s, w) \in R$. Bellare and Goldreich give the standard definition of proofs of knowledge in their work "On Defining Proofs of Knowledge" [15]. They define knowledge error, which intuitively denotes the probability that the verifier accepts even when the prover does not know a witness. It has been shown that a sigma protocol satisfying special soundness is a proof of knowledge with negligible knowledge error in the length of the challenge, as stated next.

Theorem 3. *A sigma protocol $\mathcal{P}$ for relation $\mathcal{R}$ with challenge length t is a proof of knowledge with knowledge error 2^{-t}.*

The intuition for why special soundness implies soundness is straightforward. Special soundness says that, for any given commitment, if the adversary can answer for two different challenges then the adversary must know a witness for the statement. This implies that if no witness is known there must be at most one challenge for which the adversary could successfully respond. The chance of drawing the single challenge for which the adversary can successfully respond is negligable in the security parameter. (The formal argument in the case of a proof of knowledge is slightly different and can be found in [10].)

The reader may also find that the upcoming Theorem 5 has a slightly odd feel. The proofs of correct encryption and decryption intuitively have a temporal ordering, the protocol even specifies that the trustees should check the proofs of correct encryption before decrypting. However, since we are defining the verifier for the public information after the election is concluded, we can fold these proofs into one large proof for simplicity. Formally, we are allowed to do this because the properties of sigma protocol are invariant under parallel composition [10], which was proven to be true for the formalisation of Sigma protocols we use in [11].

Theorem 4. *For all number of trustess, number of cast ballots, number of contests, for all ballot formats, generators, public key shares, cast ballots, for all decryption factors, if there exists an adversary $\mathcal{A}$ which can produce accepting proofs for the verifier for two different challenges on the same commitment then the ballots are all correctly formed and the summation is correctly decrypted.*

The Coq theorem is stated slightly differently, we show that the existence of two accepting proofs with two different challenges on the same commitment implies that the ballots are all correctly formed and the summation is correctly decrypted. Since this holds for any two transcript of this form it clearly holds for any $\mathcal{A}$ producing transcripts of this form. We show this modified theorem in Theorem 5.

Theorem 5. *For all number of trustees, number of cast ballots, number of contests, for all ballot formats, generators, public key shares, cast ballots, for all decryption factors, for all pairs of accepting proof transcripts, if the pair of proof transcripts have two different challenges on the same commitment, then the ballots are all correctly formed and the summation is correctly decrypted.*

Theorem 5 is encoded into Coq as shown below.

```
Theorem VerifierCorrect :
forall
    (numTrustees numCast numContests : nat)
    (numSel : vector nat numContests)
    (g : G)(pks : vector G numTrustees)
    (* Cast ballots *)
    (castBallots : vector  (ballot numSel) numCast)
    (* Proofs of correct encryption *)
    (balProf1 balProf2 : vector (ballotProof numSel) numCast)
    (decFactors : decryptionFactors numTrustees numSel)
    (decProf1 decProf2 : decryptionProof numTrustees numSel)
    (result : tally numSel),

let pk := (g, VG_prod pks) in
let summation := Vfold_left (multBallots numSel) (zeroBallot numSel)
                           (castBallots) in

(* The tally and the decryption factors are consistent *)
ResultDecFactorsConsistent numTrustees g numSel summation result decFactors
-> Verifier numSel g pks castBallots balProf1 decFactors decProf1
-> (* Conditions for special soundness *)
    Verifier numSel g pks castBallots balProf2 decFactors decProf2 ->
    Vforall2 (ballotProofDis numSel) balProf1 balProf2 ->
    Vforall2 (ballotProofComEq numSel) balProf1 balProf2 ->
    decryptionProofDis numTrustees numSel decProf1 decProf2 ->
    decryptionProofComEq numTrustees numSel decProf1 decProf2 ->

Vforall (BallotCorrectlyFormed pk g numSel) castBallots /\
BallotCorrectlyDecrypted pk numSel summation result.
```

`Vfold_left` Takes a binary function, an initial value, and a vector and reduces the vector to a single value. In this case it multiplies all the encrypted ballots using the function `multBallots`. The proof of Theorem 5 follows from the soundness of the underlying sigma protocols; in essence we extract witness to all the underlying statements and show that they collectively imply that all the encrypted ballots are well-formed and the aggregation of all encrypted ballots is correctly decrypted.

3   Using the Extracted Verifier

Having defined the verifier we could use it inside Coq to check election transcripts, but unfortunately, this is prohibitively slow. Instead, we make use of the Coq extraction facility to produce OCaml code which matches the Coq specification. This extraction facility is the subject of the CertiCoq project [16] which aims to verify its correctness. Our verifier is proven secure for any Schnorr groups in the sense that the reductions and logical proofs hold for any such group; of course, if the decisional Diffie-Hellman problem is easy in the chosen group then privacy is lost. We note that our extracted verifier replaces the Coq implementation of arithmetic with the native OCaml implementation for efficiency.

We now encounter an issue, the reference verifier released with ElectionGuard[4] does not appear to be compatible with the parameters in the

---

[4] https://github.com/microsoft/electionguard-verifier.

ElectionGuard specification.[5] The reference verifier works for a limited set of safe prime groups whereas the specification requires a Schnorr group which is not a safe prime group. To test our verifier, we therefore changed the parameters from those in the specification to the 1536-bit group from the reference verifier. We produced test cases (in the form of JSON files) with the reference verifier; we then wrote code to parse this JSON and feed it into our verifier. Our verifier accepted on the test cases and rejected on the incorrect inputs we tried.

3.1 Efficiency

Our extracted verifier with some underlying Coq functions replaced by OCaml counterparts is twice as efficient as the reference verifier provided by ElectionGuard. The time to verify is dominated by the number of ciphertexts which is the total number of candidates in all contests multiplied by the number of voters. Our verifier takes about 50 s per 1000 ciphertexts, so for an election with one million ciphertexts, it would take roughly 14 h. This compares to the reference verifier which takes 110 s per 1000 ciphertexts. We were surprised that our verifier was faster; the OCaml implementation we use of the mathematics is faster by a factor of two which might explain the difference.

Note, our current encoding is a first attempt and mimicks the underlying mathematics as closely as possible to ensure that the encoding does not contain transliteration errors. Our encoding can be further optimised for speed and parallelised if required, but this requires further work.

The performance of our ElectionGuard verifier on the test cases, while comparable in efficiency to other implementations, is significantly slower than the machine-checked verifier for Helios created by Haines *et al.* [11]. This is due to the use of a safe prime group in the ElectionGuard reference verifier even though the specification requires a Schnorr group. If we replace that safe prime group with a Schnorr group of comparable security, as used by Helios, but with prime order of around 256 bits, our implementation would be ~6 times faster than it currently is, meaning that an election of one million ciphertexts would take only 2 h to verify. The ElectionGuard specification mandates a Schnorr group with a prime order of around 256 bits, so in a real election, our verifier would be faster than it was on tests produced by the reference implementation.

4   Conclusion

In this work we machine-checked the verifiability specification of ElectionGuard to be cryptographically sound. We achieved this by encoding the specification inside the interactive theorem prover Coq and then proving that it has cryptographic soundness. In addition, we proved the zero-knowledge properties of the verifier. We extracted an executable version of the verifier specification which is

---

[5] https://github.com/microsoft/electionguard/wiki/Informal/ElectionGuardSpecificationV0.85.pdf.

of comparable efficiency to existing implementations and used it to verify election transcriptions produced by the reference implementation of ElectionGuard.

Acknowledgments. This work was supported by the Luxembourg National Research Fund (FNR) and the Research Council of Norway for the joint project SURCVS.

A   Coq Source

Our code is available via the link below:

https://github.com/gerlion/secure-e-voting-with-coq.

References

1. Rivest, R.L.: On the notion of 'software independence' in voting systems. Philos. Trans. R. Soc. A: Math. Phys. Eng. Sci. **366**, 3759–3767 (2008)
2. Adida, B.: Helios: web-based open-audit voting. In: van Oorschot, P.C. (ed.) USENIX Security Symposium, pp. 335–348. USENIX Association (2008)
3. Microsoft: Electionguard (2019)
4. Haines, T., Lewis, S.J., Pereira, O., Teague, V.: How not to prove your election outcome. In Oprea, A., Shacham, H. (eds.) 2020 IEEE Symposium on Security and Privacy, SP 2020, San Jose, CA, USA, May 17–21, 2020, pp. 784–800. IEEE (2020)
5. Halderman, J.A., Teague, V.: The New South Wales iVote System: security failures and verification flaws in a live online election. In: Haenni, R., Koenig, R.E., Wikström, D. (eds.) VOTELID 2015. LNCS, vol. 9269, pp. 35–53. Springer, Cham (2015). https://doi.org/10.1007/978-3-319-22270-7_3
6. Springall, D., et al.: Security analysis of the Estonian internet voting system. In: Proceedings of the 2014 ACM SIGSAC Conference on Computer and Communications Security, pp. 703–715. ACM (2014)
7. Bernhard, D., Cortier, V., Pereira, O., Smyth, B., Warinschi, B.: Adapting Helios for provable ballot privacy. In: Atluri, V., Diaz, C. (eds.) ESORICS 2011. LNCS, vol. 6879, pp. 335–354. Springer, Heidelberg (2011). https://doi.org/10.1007/978-3-642-23822-2_19
8. Cortier, V., Smyth, B.: Attacking and fixing Helios: an analysis of ballot secrecy. J. Comput. Secur. **21**, 89–148 (2013)
9. Bernhard, D., Pereira, O., Warinschi, B.: How not to prove yourself: pitfalls of the fiat-Shamir heuristic and applications to Helios. In: Wang, X., Sako, K. (eds.) ASIACRYPT 2012. LNCS, vol. 7658, pp. 626–643. Springer, Heidelberg (2012). https://doi.org/10.1007/978-3-642-34961-4_38
10. Damgård, I.: On Σ-protocols (2002)
11. Haines, T., Goré, R., Tiwari, M.: Verified verifiers for verifying elections. In: ACM Conference on Computer and Communications Security, pp. 685–702. ACM (2019)
12. Gonthier, G.: The four colour theorem: engineering of a formal proof. In: Kapur, D. (ed.) ASCM 2007. LNCS (LNAI), vol. 5081, p. 333. Springer, Heidelberg (2008). https://doi.org/10.1007/978-3-540-87827-8_28
13. Geuvers, H., Wiedijk, F., Zwanenburg, J.: A constructive proof of the fundamental theorem of algebra without using the rationals. In: Callaghan, P., Luo, Z., McKinna, J., Pollack, R., Pollack, R. (eds.) TYPES 2000. LNCS, vol. 2277, pp. 96–111. Springer, Heidelberg (2002). https://doi.org/10.1007/3-540-45842-5_7

14. Bertot, Y., Castéran, P., Huet, G., Paulin-Mohring, C.: Interactive Theorem Proving and Program Development: Coq'Art: The Calculus of Inductive Constructions. Texts in Theoretical Computer Science. Springer, Heidelberg (2004). https://doi.org/10.1007/978-3-662-07964-5
15. Bellare, M., Goldreich, O.: On defining proofs of knowledge. In: Brickell, E.F. (ed.) CRYPTO 1992. LNCS, vol. 740, pp. 390–420. Springer, Heidelberg (1993). https://doi.org/10.1007/3-540-48071-4_28
16. Anand, A., et al.: CertiCoq: a verified compiler for Coq. In: The Third International Workshop on Coq for Programming Languages (CoqPL) (2017)

Information-Flow Control by Means of Security Wrappers for Active Object Languages with Futures

Farzane Karami[1](✉), Olaf Owe[1](✉), and Gerardo Schneider[2]

[1] Department of Informatics, University of Oslo, Oslo, Norway
{farzanka,olaf}@ifi.uio.no
[2] Department of Computer Science and Engineering, Chalmers University
of Technology, Gothenburg, Sweden
gerardo@cse.gu.se

Abstract. This paper introduces a run-time mechanism for preventing leakage of secure information in distributed systems. We consider a general concurrency language model where concurrent objects interact by asynchronous method calls and futures. The aim is to prevent leakage of secure information to low-level viewers. The approach is based on a notion of *security wrappers*, where a wrapper encloses an object or a component and controls its interactions with the environment. Our run-time system automatically adds a wrapper to an insecure component.The wrappers are invisible such that a wrapped component and its environment are not aware of it.

The security policies of a wrapper are formalized based on a notion of security levels. At run-time, future components will be wrapped upon need, and objects of unsafe classes will be wrapped, using static checking to limit the number of unsafe classes and thereby reducing run-time overhead. We define an operational semantics and sketch a proof of non-interference. A service provider may use wrappers to protect its services in an insecure environment, and vice-versa: a system platform may use wrappers to protect itself from insecure service providers.

Keywords: Active objects · Futures · Information-flow security · Non-interference · Language-based security · Distributed systems

1 Introduction

Given the large number of users and service providers involved in a distributed system, security is a critical concern. It is essential to analyze and control how confidential information propagates between nodes. When a program executes, it might leak secure information to public outputs or send it to malicious nodes. *Information-flow control* approaches track how information propagates during execution and prevent leakage of secure information [24]. Program variables are tagged typically with security levels; such as *high* and *low*, to indicate secure

© Springer Nature Switzerland AG 2021
M. Asplund and S. Nadjm-Tehrani (Eds.): NordSec 2020, LNCS 12556, pp. 74–91, 2021.
https://doi.org/10.1007/978-3-030-70852-8_5

and public data. In this setting, an "attacker" could be seen as a low-level object that is not supposed to see high information. The basic semantic notion of information-flow security is *non-interference* [10]. This means that in any two executions of a program, if high inputs are changed, but low inputs are the same, then the low outputs will be the same (at least for locally deterministic programs). This way, an attacker (a low object) cannot distinguish between observable behaviors of the two executions since low outputs are independent of the high inputs [12].

We will consider a high-level model for object-oriented distributed systems suited for service-oriented systems, namely the *active object model* Method interaction is implemented by message passing; moreover, most active object languages support a communication paradigm called *futures* [5]. A future is a component that is created by a remote method call and eventually will contain the corresponding return value [3]. Therefore, the caller does not need to block while waiting to get the return value: it can continue with other tasks and later get the value from the corresponding future. Futures can be passed to other objects, called *first-class futures*. In this case, any object that has a reference to a future can access its content, which may be a security threat if the future contains secure data. Futures offer a flexible way of communication and sharing results, but handling them appropriately in order to avoid security leakages requires run-time checking (described in Sect. 2.1).

Our goal is to design a permissive and precise security mechanism for controlling object communications in active object languages supporting first-class futures. Our security mechanism is inspired by the notion of *wrappers* in [21], where a wrapper encloses an object and enforces safety rules. In the present paper, we suggest a notion of *security wrapper*, which wraps an object or a future at run-time and performs security controls. Such wrappers are added by the operational semantics upon need, and a wrapped component and its environment are not aware of the presence of the wrapper. Security wrappers block object communications that lead to leakage of secure data to low objects. A future is wrapped if it contains a high value, and the wrapper blocks illegal access by low objects. The operational semantics of a wrapper is defined based on run-time security levels, resulting from a flow-sensitive information-flow enforcement [23]. We enrich the operational semantics with dynamic information-flow rules [23] where security levels of variables are allowed to change after an assignment. Therefore, our dynamic approach guarantees a degree of permissiveness and is precise since it deals with the exact run-time security levels.

The operational semantics of our security framework is provided in the style of Structured Operational Semantics (SOS). In order to minimize run-time overhead, we suggest static analysis to limit the number of classes where security checking and wrappers are needed since often only a few methods deal with secure information. In the resulting hybrid approach, the static analysis determines which classes cannot produce any high output, so-called *safe classes*, while the run-time system takes care of the precise security checking of objects of unsafe classes and futures created by such objects. Assuming a sound static analysis, we show that our proposed hybrid approach ensures the non-interference property.

In summary, our contributions are: i) a notion of security wrappers for enforcing noninterference and security control in object interactions (Sect. 4), ii) the use of static analysis to reduce the run-time overhead (Sect. 4.1), iii) defining the operational semantics for the dynamic information-flow enforcement with automatic deployment of wrappers (Sects. 4.2, 4.3) for our language (Sect. 4), and iv) an outline of the proof that our approach satisfies non-interference.

2   Background

Information-flow control approaches detect illegal flows. During program execution, there are two kinds of leakage of information, namely *explicit* and *implicit flows* [24]. For simplicity, we assume two security levels, L (low) and H (high). In the setting with observable and non-observable variables, an explicit flow happens when assigning a low variable (l) with a high value (h) by $l := h$. In the setting without observable variables, one may deal with this by letting the level of l be dynamically changed to H. In an implicit flow, there is an indirect flow due to control structures. For example, in the if statement: $l := 0$ if h then $l := 1$ fi, the guard h is high, and it affects the value of l indirectly. In order to avoid implicit flows, a program-counter label (pc) is introduced [24]. If the guard is high, then pc becomes high, indicating a high context. (In run-time analysis, one may use a stack to deal with nested control structures.)

Information-flow control approaches are divided into two categories, static and dynamic [23]. Static analysis is conservative [12]: to be sound, it over-approximates security levels of variables (for example, it over-approximates a formal parameter to high, while at run-time, a corresponding actual parameter can be low). This causes unnecessary rejections of programs, especially when the complete program is not statically known, as is usually the case in distributed systems. On the other hand, static analysis has less run-time overhead since security checks are performed before program execution [12]. *Dynamic information-flow* techniques perform security checks at run-time, and this introduces overhead. But they are more permissive and precise since they deal with the exact security levels instead of an over-approximation [12].

For example, consider the following method body:

{if *low_test* then $x := high\_exp$ else $x := low\_exp$ fi; return x}

where *low_test* and *low_exp* evaluate to low values, while *high_exp* evaluates to a high value. A sound static analysis will detect a high method result here since the value of *low_test* is not known; while at run-time, an execution of the method may give a low result (when *low_test* evaluates to *false*). The example shows that static analysis over-approximates the security level, in contrast to run-time analysis. Similarly, the parameter mechanism gives rise to static over-approximation. For a method $T\ triv(T\ x)\{return\ x\}$, where T is a type containing both high and low values, static analysis will detect a (potentially) high result, whereas for calls with a low input value, the result is detected as low at run-time. However, this could be handled by multiple static method profiles as in [19] (when low T values are reflected by a subtype of T). For first-class futures, the situation is worse: a get statement on a future is detached from the call statement and also from the method name. Therefore, the static analysis of a get statement must over-approximate the level of the possible future values, while the exact level is revealed during run-time. This means that static analysis of security levels in languages with first-class futures can easily lead to a high degree of over-approximation.

In what follows, we briefly explain some of the terminologies of information-flow security that we use in this paper:

Security Levels. Variables are tagged with security levels, organized by a partial order $\sqsubseteq$ and a join $\sqcup$ operator, such that $L \sqsubseteq H$ and $L \sqcup H = H$. The $\sqcup$ operator returns the least upper bound of two security levels. Inside a class, declarations of fields, class parameters, and formal parameters may have statically declared initial security levels. These levels may change with statements. We define a new syntax for object creation to assign security levels to objects.

Flow-Sensitivity. By a *dynamic flow-sensitive analysis*, security levels of variables propagate to other variables, and precise levels are evaluated during execution. Variables start with their declared security levels (the ones without levels are assumed as L), but levels may change after each statement. In an assignment, the left-hand-side level becomes high if pc is high, or there is a high variable on the right-hand-side. The left-hand-side level becomes low if pc is low, and there is no high variable on the right-hand-side [23]. Otherwise, the security level of a variable does not change. E.g., a flow-sensitive analysis accepts the program $h := 0$; if h then $l := 1$ fi; return l; since the level of h is updated to L after the first assignment, hence there is no leakage. In if statements, in order to avoid implicit flows, when the guard is high, the security levels of variables appearing on the left-hand side of assignments in the taken and untaken branches are raised to high [23]. E.g., considering an initial environment $\Gamma = \{h \mapsto H, l_1 \mapsto L, l_2 \mapsto L\}$ and the program: if h then $l_1 := 1$ else $l_2 := 0$ fi when the condition is true, Γ changes to $\Gamma = \{h \mapsto H, l_1 \mapsto H, l_2 \mapsto H\}$ for a sound flow-sensitive analysis [23]. In a dynamic approach, in order to have a sound flow-sensitive analysis, the assigned variables in the untaken branches should be given to the analysis, which can be provided by static analysis of the program code [4,23].

2.1 Active Object Languages

Active object languages are based on a combination of the *actor model* [1] and object-oriented features [5]. Some well-known active object languages are Rebeca [25,26], Scala/Akka [11,27], Creol [14], ABS [13], Encore [6], and ASP/ProActive [7,8]. In communication with futures, when a remote method call is made, a future object with a unique identity is created. Futures can be explicit with a specific type and access operations like in ABS or can be implicit with automatic creation and access [5]. E.g., in ABS, explicit futures are created as in $Fut[T]$ $f := o!m(\overline{e}); v := f.\texttt{get}$, where f is a future variable of type $Fut[T]$, and T is the type of the future value. The symbol "!" indicates an asynchronous

method call m of object o with actual parameters $\bar{e}$, and the future value is
retrieved with a **get** construct when needed. The variable f can be passed to
other objects as a parameter (first-class futures). The caller may continue with
other processes while the callee is computing the return value. The callee sends
back the return value to the corresponding future, and then the future is called
resolved. A synchronous call is denoted by $o.m(\bar{e})$, which blocks the caller until
the return value is retrieved.

Basic constructs	
$x := \mathbf{new}_{lev}\ c(\bar{e})$	object creation with the security level *lev*
return e	creating a method result/future value
if b **th** s [**el** s'] **fi**	if statement (b a Boolean condition)
$f := o!m(\bar{e})$	remote asynchronous call, future variable f
$x := f.\mathbf{get}$	blocking access operation on future f
$o!m(\bar{e})$	simple asynchronous remote call

Fig. 1. Statement syntax. Here $\bar{e}$ is an expression list. Brackets denote optional parts.

Information-Flow Security with Futures. Static analysis is in general difficult for programs with futures, where the result of a call is no longer syntacti-
cally connected to the call, compared to the call/return paradigm in languages
without futures [15]. For example, a future may be created in one module and
received as a parameter in another. Thus, a future may not statically correspond
to a unique call statement. One could overestimate all future values as high, but
this would severely restrict the set of acceptable programs. It would be better to
overestimate the set of possible call statements that corresponds to a given get
statement, but this requires access to the whole program, which is often problematic for distributed systems. Moreover, the return values of these overestimated
calls may have different security levels, which also results in overestimation.

A static analysis that assumes references as low, allows passing of future
references. However, the exact security level of a future value is revealed when it
becomes resolved, which goes beyond static analysis. For example, if a low-level
object performs $x := f.\mathbf{get}$, and f refers to a future with a high value, it is a
leakage of information. A dynamic approach is required to control access to a
future value at run-time when it is resolved, and if the value is high it needs
protection. The futures concept makes static checking less precise, and the need
for complementary run-time checking is greater, as provided in the present paper.

3   Our Core Language

In order to exemplify our security approach, the security semantics (in Sect. 4.2)
is embedded in a simple, high-level core language. All remote calls are made by
means of futures, where the method result is always returned to the corresponding future. Figure 1 gives the syntax of statements. The statement $f := o!m(\bar{e})$

is an asynchronous call with futures, and $o!m(\bar{e})$ is an asynchronous call without waiting for the result and associating a future. We define an extended syntax for object creation $\text{new}_{lev}\ c(\bar{e})$, where lev is the object's level (it can be L or H).

Figure 2 illustrates a health care service in our core language, involving futures for the sharing of secure medical records. Personnel and patients with lower-level access are not allowed to access medical records. High variables are emphasized based on user specifications, in this case reflecting patients' medical test results. The server, specified by the class *Service*, searches for a patient's test result, and the object *proxy* publishes the result to the patient and personnel. In Fig. 2, in line 10, a produce cycle is initiated between the *server* and *proxy*. In line 13, the server searches for the test result of a patient with the userId a by sending a remote asynchronous call to the laboratory $f := lab!search(a)$, where f is the future variable. In line 14, the server calls *proxy!publish(f, a, d)* and passes the future f, userId a, and personnelId d to the object *proxy*. Both *search* and *publish* are asynchronous calls, thus the server does not wait for the return values and is free to respond to any client request. In line 18, the object *proxy* waits for the test result and assigns the result to variable x by performing $x := f.\text{get}$. Then *proxy* sends x to the patient and personnel.

```
 1  data type Result = ... // definition of medical data
 2  interface ServiceI { Void produce() ... }
 3  interface ProxyI { Void publish(Fut[Result] q, PatientI a, List[PersonnelI] d) ... }
 4  interface LabI { Result_H search(PatientI a) ... }
 5  interface PatientI { Void send(Result_H r) ... }
 6  interface PersonnelI { Void send(Result_H r) ... }
 7  interface DataBase { ... }
 8  class Service(LabI lab, DataBase db) implements ServiceI {
 9    ProxyI proxy = new_H Proxy(this);
10    this!produce();   // initial action, starting a produce cycle
11    Void produce() { Fut[Result] f;  PatientI a;   List[PersonnelI] d = Nil;
12      ....      // finding a patient and the associated personnel in a database
13      f:=lab!search(a); // searching for the test result of patient a
14      proxy!publish(f, a, d); } } //sending the future f, not waiting for the result
15
16  class Proxy(ServiceI s) implements ProxyI{ Result_H x;
17    Void publish(Fut[Result] f, PatientI a, List[PersonnelI] d) {
18    x:=f.get;   // waiting for future and assigning the value to x. x becomes H
19    a!send(x);   // x is now H
20    d!send(x);   // multicasting, x is H
21    s!produce(); } }
```

Fig. 2. Example of sharing *high* patients' test results by means of futures

A static analysis over-approximates the security levels of test results as high, which leads to rejections of information passing. Note that the two *send* calls in the class *Proxy* would not be allowed if we only use static checking since we cannot tell which patients and personnel have a high enough level. A static analysis which considers references as low allows passing the future f to the object *proxy* (line 14), but later when it is resolved, the future value can be high, and the *proxy* compromises security by sending this value to other objects.

4   A Framework for Non-interference

Like Creol, our core language is equipped with interface encapsulation, which means that created objects are typed by interfaces, not classes [14]. As a result, remote access to fields or methods that are not declared in an interface is impossible. Therefore, observable behavior of an object is limited to its interactions through remote method calls. Illegal object interactions are the ones leading to an information-flow from high information to low level objects. An object can reveal confidential information in method calls by sending actual parameters with high security levels to low-level objects. If a future contains data with a high security level, low-level objects' access is illegal.

We exploit the notion of wrappers to perform dynamic checking for enforcing non-interference in object interactions. A wrapper blocks illegal interactions. Wrappers' security policies are based on run-time security levels. Inside an object, in order to compute the exact security levels of created messages or return values, the flow-sensitivity must be active. The operational semantics for the dynamic flow-sensitive analysis, is given in Sect. 4.2 and for wrappers, in Sect. 4.3.

We can be conservative and wrap all objects and correspondingly activate flow-sensitivity, but this will cost run-time overhead. In order to be more efficient at run-time, it is important to perform dynamic checking only for components where it is necessary. We benefit from static analysis to categorize a class definition as *safe* or *unsafe*. *A class is safe if it does not have any method calls with high actual parameters and return values. A class is unsafe if it has a method call with at least one high actual parameter or a high return value.* Objects created from unsafe classes are wrapped, and flow-sensitivity will be active inside these objects. Objects from safe classes do not need a wrapper or active flow-sensitivity. This will make the execution of objects of safe classes faster, as we avoid a potentially large number of run-time checks and wrappers.

4.1   Static Analysis

Our security approach can be combined with a sound static over-approximation for detecting security errors and safe classes, e.g., the one proposed in [20], which is more permissive (to classify a class as safe) than the static analysis indicated here, in that high communication is considered secure as long as the declared levels of parameters are respected. In a class, variables are declared with maximum security levels (the maximum level that can be assigned at run-time). The same for future variables at the time of declaration, for example, $Fut[T_H]$ x indicates that x is a high future variable. Local variables without a declared security level start with the level L (as default) but may change after each statement due to the flow-sensitivity. Dataflow typing rules inside an object

$$
\begin{array}{ll}
\textsf{config} & ::= \epsilon \mid \textsf{object} \mid \textsf{flowsen-obj} \mid \textsf{msg} \mid \textsf{future} \mid \textsf{wrapper} \mid \textsf{class} \mid \textsf{config config} \\
\textsf{object} & ::= ob(o, a, p, lev) \qquad\qquad\qquad\quad d ::= v \mid v_{lev} \\
\textsf{flowsen-obj} & ::= ob(o, a, p, lev, pcs) \qquad\qquad\quad p ::= (l, s) \mid idle \\
\textsf{msg} & ::= invc(f, m, \bar{d}, o)_{lev} \mid comp(d, f)_{lev} \\
\textsf{future} & ::= fut(f, d) \\
\textsf{wrapper} & ::= Wr\{wId, lev \mid \textsf{config} \} \\
\textsf{class} & ::= Cl(c \mid a', mm)_{lev}
\end{array}
$$

Fig. 3. The components of a configuration.

can be defined similar to [20]; however, we change the typing rules for method calls and return values to classify unsafe and safe classes. A class is defined as safe if the confidentiality of each method is satisfied. The confidentiality of a method is satisfied if the typing rules for its return value and actual parameters are satisfied. The typing rules check that each occurrence of an actual parameter and a return value are not high; then, the class is safe; otherwise, it is unsafe and needs dynamic checking. The typing rule for getting a future, checks that if a future variable is high, then the class is classified as unsafe. Alternatively, we could have used another sound static analysis, for instance (the relevant parts of) the static analysis defined for ABS in [22], and adapt it to our setting.

We categorize safe and unsafe classes for the example in Fig. 2. The interface laboratory *LabI* has a method with a high return value (*search*). Thus the object *lab* is unsafe and flow-sensitivity is active to compute the security level of the return value at run-time. The class *Proxy* is unsafe since it has at least one method call with a high actual parameter (*a!send(x)*), thus object *proxy* is active flow-sensitive and wrapped.

4.2 Security Semantics

We here discuss the operational semantics of our core language with the embedded notions of flow-sensitivity and security wrappers in Figs. 4, 5. The small-step operational semantics is defined by a set of rewrite rules [17]. In a rule, premises are above the line and one step rewrite is under the line. A rule is applied to a subset of a configuration if the premises are satisfied, and the subset is changed from the left-hand-side to the right-hand-side of the rewrite rule.

In Fig. 3, an execution state is modeled as a configuration **config**, which is a multiset of objects (with or without active flow-sensitivity), messages, futures, wrappers, and classes. (Classes are included in a configuration to provide static information about fields and methods.) An **object** is represented as: $ob(o, a, p, lev)$, where o is the object identity, a is the field state, p is the current *active process*, and *lev* is the object's level (*lev* $\in \{L, H\}$). An active process p is a pair (l, s), where l is the local variables state, and s is a list of statements, or it is *idle* representing an empty local state and no statements. A state is a mapping (substitution) binding variables to values. A **flowsen-obj** represents an flow-sensitive object with an extra field *pcs* that denotes a stack of context security levels inside an object, where *pcs* = *emp* denotes an empty stack.

A **class** is represented as: $Cl(c \mid a', mm)_{lev}$, where c is the class name, a' is the initial state of the class fields (attributes), mm is a multiset of method declarations (with local variables and code), and lev denotes the type of the class, i.e., if $lev = L$, the class is safe, and if $lev = H$, the class is unsafe. A **msg** represents an invocation message or a completion message. In an invocation message, f is the future identity, m is the method name, $\bar{d}$ is a list of actual parameters, and lev is a level attached to the message at time of creation. If a message is created in a high context, then $lev = H$; otherwise, $lev = L$. A completion message contains a return value d and a future identity f, and lev represents the context level. The notation d denotes a value v or a value with security level v_{lev}. The **future** component shows a resolved future with identity f and the value d, and $fut(f, \_)$ denotes an unresolved future. A **security wrapper** is represented as: $Wr\{wId, lev \mid config\}$, where wId is the wrapper's identity, lev is the level, and $config$ denotes the configuration inside the wrapper.

Auxiliary Functions. Let Γ be a mapping and $[x \mapsto d]$ be a binding, mapping x to d. The notation $\Gamma[x \mapsto d]$ represents the update of Γ with the binding. The look-up function is represented as $\Gamma(x)$, where $\Gamma[x \mapsto d](x) = d$. The map composition $a\#l$ indicates that the binding of a variable in the inner scope l shadows any binding of that variable in the outer scope a. Thus $a\#l(x)$ gives $l(x)$ when defined, otherwise $a(x)$. Consider an object with attribute state a and local state l. Then the composition $a\#l$ defines the *object state*. The notation $[\![e]\!]$ denotes the evaluation of expression e, where variables are evaluated according to the object state. The evaluation in $[\![e]\!]$ is strict in the sense that the resulting level is high if e contains variables that have a high security level. Other auxiliary functions are given as follows:

- The function $level(d)$ returns the security level of d, such that $level(v_{lev}) = lev$, and for an untagged value $level(v) = L$. If $\bar{e}$ is a list of expressions, then $[\![\bar{e}]\!] = \bar{d}$ returns a list of data, and $level(\bar{d}) = \sqcup\ level(d_i), \forall d_i \in \bar{d}$ (the join of all data in $\bar{d}$).
- The function $level(o)$ returns the level of the object o.
- The function $level(pcs)$ returns the join of security levels in pcs, where if $pcs = emp$, $level(pcs) = L$, and if $pcs \neq emp$, $level(pcs) = H$.
- The function $update_H(s)$ raises the security levels of variables appearing in the left-hand-side of assignments in s to high.
- The function $fresh()$ returns a unique identity for an object or a future.
- The function $bind(o, m, \bar{d}, f)$ returns a process, where the method m in the class of the object o is activated, and the method' parameters are bound to the actual ones ($\bar{d}$), and a reserved local variable $label$ is bound to f, denoting where to send the return value of the method [13].
- The function $bind(o, m, \bar{d})$ returns a process without the binding for the $label$, in case the method's result is not needed.
- The function $safe(Cl(c \mid a, mm)_{lev})$ returns true if $lev = L$ and false otherwise.

Figure 4 represents the flow-sensitivity semantics of objects. The NEW rule shows the command $x := \mathbf{new}_{lev} c'(\bar{e})$ in the active process of an object o, where

c' is an unsafe class. The rule creates an active flow-sensitive object o' and a wrapper and assigns o' to x. The active process of the new object o' is initially *idle*, denoting an empty active process. The level of o' is *lev* as it is specified in the command $\mathbf{new}_{lev}c'(\bar{e})$, if not, the level is assumed low. The stack of *pcs* is empty, denoted by *emp*. The wrapper has the same identity (o') and the level (*lev*) of the object o'. The semantics of the actual class parameters is treated like parameters of an asynchronous call $x!init(\bar{e})$ (creating an invocation message by the rule CALL), where *init* is the name of the initialization method of a class. Note that if $\bar{e}$ contains high security level data, the wrapper does not send the corresponding invocation message to the new object if the new object is low-level (see rule WR-INVC-ERROR in Fig. 5, which we explain later). The Rule ASSIGN-LOCAL shows an assignment $x := e$, where x is in the local state l, e is evaluated to $v_{lev'}$, and x is updated in l with the new value v and the level $lev' \sqcup level(pcs)$. Therefore, the level of x is updated with the right-hand-side level joined with that of *pcs*. In IF-LOW-TRUE, the guard's security level is low, and the guard is true ($true_L$), thus the corresponding branch s' is taken. While in IF-LOW-FALSE, since the guard is false, the else branch s'' is taken. In IF-HIGH-TRUE and IF-HIGH-FALSE, since the guard's security level is high, similar to the approach in [23], the security levels of variables appearing in assignments in both branches are raised to high to avoid implicit flows. In the rules, the guard's security level H is pushed to the *pcs* stack, resulting in a high security context, where all the messages created in a high context will have high security levels (see rules CALL-FUT, CALL). Moreover, assignments in the taken branch result in high security levels (see ASSIGN-LOCAL and ASSIGN-ATTRIBUTE). The added statement $endif(s'')$, where s'' is the untaken branch, marks the join point of the **if** structure and raises the assigned variables' levels in the untaken branch. In the ENDIF rule, the function $update_H(s'')$ raises the security levels of variables appearing in the left-hand-side of assignments in s'' to high, and these variables are updated in the local state. Moreover, the last element of *pcs* is removed ($pcs.pop()$), reflecting the previous context level.

In the rules, we do not cover local calls, which do not involve object interactions (therefore, less interesting here). The CALL-FUT rule deals with an asynchronous call $x := e!m(\bar{e})$, where x is a future variable, and e is the callee. The call generates a (not resolved) future with a unique identity f, where f is assigned to x, and an invocation message containing f, m, actual parameters $\bar{d}$, and the callee o'. The invocation message's level is $level(pcs)$, which is needed to avoid indirect leakage from the caller. The rule CALL shows an asynchronous call $e!m(\bar{e})$ without an associated future, where the method's result is not needed. The call creates an invocation message containing m, $\bar{d}$, and the callee o', and the message' level is $level(pcs)$. The START-FUT rule is applied when an object is *idle*, and there is an invocation message to the object. The object's active process is updated with p, which is the *bind*'s result, where method m is activated, formal parameters are bound to the actual ones ($\bar{d}$), and the local variable *label* is bound to the future identity (f) for sending the method's result to the future by a **return** statement. The level of the received message lev' is added

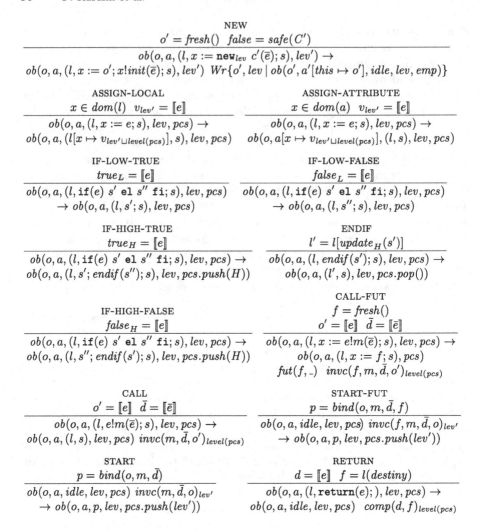

Fig. 4. Flow-sensitive operational semantics, $lev, lev' \in \{l, H\}$.

to the object's stack *pcs*. This avoids implicit leakage from the sender. In the START rule, the invocation message does not contain a future identity, and the object starts execution the corresponding method, which is activated by the *bind* function without the binding for the *label* variable. The RETURN rule interprets a **return** statement, which creates a completion message to the corresponding future, which is looked up in the local state ($l(label)$), and the object becomes *idle*. The security level of the completion message is $level(pcs)$ to avoid indirect leakage from the callee to the recipients of the future value. We assume that each method body ends with a **return** statement. The rules for objects without active flow-sensitivity are similar but without security levels, *pcs*, and wrappers.

4.3 Operational Semantics of Security Wrappers

In this section, we discuss the operational semantics of security wrappers. As mentioned, a wrapper for an object is created in the rule NEW in Fig. 4. A wrapper has the same identity as the wrapped component; thereby, the wrapper represents the component to the environment. Invocation messages generated by the CALL-FUT and CALL rules will first meet the object's wrapper for security checking before being sent to the callee. The WR-INVC rule in Fig. 5, represents a wrapper with an invocation message inside, which is produced by the object o. If the join ($\sqcup$) of the message's level lev' and the actual parameters' levels $level(\bar{d})$ is less than or equal to the destination object' level ($level(o')$), then the wrapper allows the message to go out. In WR-INVC-ERROR, since the recipient object's level is less than the message's level, the invocation message is deleted and the corresponding future value is replaced by an error value. This can be combined with an exception handling mechanism such that an exception is raised when a get operation tries to access an error value. However, as this is beyond the scope of this paper, we ignore the exception handling part. We simply indicate

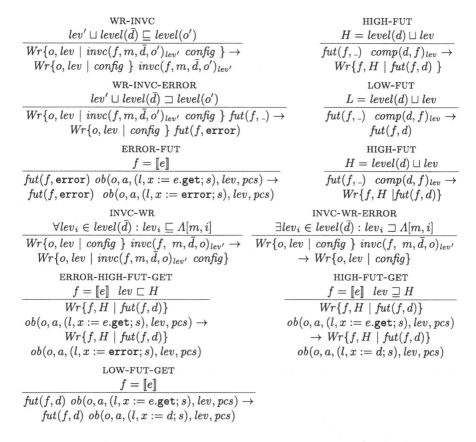

Fig. 5. Operational semantics involving wrappers, $lev, lev' \in \{l, H\}$.

exceptions by assignments with **error** in the right-hand-side. The ERROR-FUT rule represents the case where a future value is **error**; the object performing the get command $x := e.\text{get}$, where e refers to the future, assigns an error to x. The rule ASSIGN-ATTRIBUTE shows an assignment, where x is in the object's fields.

The INVC-WR rule represents a wrapper and an incoming invocation message to the object o. The notation $\Lambda[m, i]$ indicates the level of the ith formal parameter of the method m as declared in the class. If the security level of each actual parameter (lev_i) is less than or equal to the security level of the corresponding formal parameter, then the wrapper allows the message to go through and adds it to its configuration inside. Otherwise, the invocation message is deleted in INVC-WR-ERROR. In LOW-FUT, an unresolved future gets the corresponding completion message containing d, hence the future becomes resolved with d. The join of the message's level lev and $level(d)$ is low, thus no wrapper is created. In HIGH-FUT, $lev \sqcup level(d) = H$, thus the future becomes wrapped and resolved. Since the future is high, a wrapper is created to protect it, and the wrapper has the same identity and level as the future. The ERROR-HIGH-FUT-GET rule represents a wrapped future and an object that wants to get the future value. If the security level of the object (lev) asking for the value is less than the wrapper (H), then the wrapper sends an error value. In HIGH-FUT-GET, the object gets the value from the wrapped future since the object's level is greater than or equal to H. The LOW-FUT-GET rule shows that an object gets the value from an unwrapped future without security checking.

4.4   Non-interference

We show that our security framework satisfies non-interference. Non-interference considers the observable behavior of different executions. The *observable behavior* of an object consists of invocation messages and completion messages. Even the observable behavior of object creation, by the NEW rule in Fig. 4, is an asynchronous call $x!init(\bar{e})$, which creates an invocation message. Since object and future identities may change from execution to execution, we must compare executions relative to a correspondence of such identities in one execution to those in another execution. Corresponding objects must be of the same class.

A message is said to be low if it does not have a high tag nor contain any parameters with high tags. Two low messages are *indistinguishable*, $\simeq$, if the identities in the messages correspond to each other, and other values are equal. Two execution states of corresponding objects o and o' are said to be *indistinguishable* if the values of their local variables and attributes are indistinguishable and they have the same remaining statement lists, and also agree on other system variables, including flow sensitivity (with same values of pcs).

Definition 1. *Global non-interference means that for any two executions with corresponding objects and futures, such that the history of messages consumed or produced by an object in one execution state is indistinguishable from that of the corresponding object in a state of the other execution, and such that the next communication event of the first object is a low output, then the next low communication output event of the other object will be indistinguishable.*

Definition 2. _Local non-interference_ means that for two executions with corresponding objects o and o', and for execution states where o and o' are non-idle and where the execution states of o and o' are indistinguishable, the next execution states of these objects will also be indistinguishable when both have executed the next statement, and in case the statement gives an output, both make indistinguishable output (or neither makes no low output).

Note that our security approach includes termination aspects. We next prove that each object is _locally deterministic_, in the sense that the next state of a statement, other than idle and get, is deterministic, i.e., depending only on the prestate. The only source of non-determinism is get and the independent speed of the objects, which means that the ordering in the messages queues is in general non-deterministic. Thus only idle states and get cause local non-determinism.

Lemma 1. _In our security model, each object is locally deterministic._

Proof. According to our operational semantics, for each statement (other than idle and get) there is only one rule to apply, and for an `if` statement, the choice of the rule is given deterministically by testing the security level and value of the guard. There is no interleaving of processes inside an object as well.   □

Definition 3. _Low-to-low determinism_ means that any low part of a state or output resulting from a statement, other than get, is determined by the low part of the prestate and the statement, when ignoring states where pcs is high.

Lemma 2. _In our security model, each object is low-to-low deterministic._

Proof. This can be proved by case analysis on the statements. For an `if` with a high test, the taken branch does not result in low state changes nor low outputs. In particular, any invocation message made has label H, and the execution of that method invocation by the same or another object, will start in a high context (see the START-FUT and START rules), and so will a new object created from the branch. This ensures that there is no implicit leakage from a high branch. However, the choice of branch could depend on high information, and lead to distinguishable states, but this is compensated by $endif(s'')$, which raises the level of variables updated in the untaken branch s''. For an `if` with low test, the choice of branch is given by the low part of the prestate and the test. For an assignment, the level of the left-hand-side becomes low if the level of the right-hand-side is low and pcs is low. Otherwise, the left-hand-side' level becomes high after the assignment. The cases for the other statements are straightforward. □

Theorem 1. _Our security model guarantees local and global non-interference, and an attacker (i.e., a low object) will only receive low information._

Proof. Local non-interference can be proved by induction of the number of execution steps considering two executions of an object. The low part of each state and the low outputs must be the same by the two previous lemmas, using the fact that future values of corresponding futures will be indistinguishable, since these are given by earlier outputs, which are indistinguishable by the induction hypothesis. Global non-interference can be proved by induction on the number of steps considering two executions. It follows by local non-interference for all objects. Since an attacker is a low object, the wrappers will prevent it from receiving high inputs.   □

This theorem implies that an attacker will not be able to obtain high information explicitly or implicitly, nor observe difference of termination aspects.

5   Related Work

Starting with the work of Denning and Denning [9], a number of static techniques for lattice-based security information flow analysis have been suggested.

In [20], a secure type system has been suggested for Creol without futures to enforce noninterference in object interactions. Typing rules check that the security levels of variables respect the declared security levels in the interfaces. In [20], since the run-time security levels of objects, indicating the access rights, might not be available at static time, an if-test construct is added to check the security level of an object before sending data. Our approach is a dynamic technique, which is more permissive and precise and supports futures confidentiality. In [22], Pettai and Laud present a type system for ABS to ensure non-interference by means of over-approximation. E.g., a future's security level is the upper bound of the tasks' levels that the future refers to, while our run-time system does not use over-approximation (assuming the labels are exact). This work also deals with other concurrency features of ABS such as cogs and synchronization between tasks, where security issues are prevented by using the operational semantics and the type system. The cog feature of ABS is not relevant to our paper.

In [2], a dynamic information-flow control approach is performed for the ASP language. Security levels are assigned to activities and communicated data. The security levels do not change when they are assigned. Dynamic checks are performed at activity creations, requests, and replies. Since future references are not confidential, they are passed between activities without dynamic checking, but getting a future value is checked by a reply transmission rule. In [2], the security model guarantees data confidentiality for multi-level security (MLS) systems. Our approach adds flow-sensitivity, which allows security levels of variables to change during execution of an object. It makes our approach more permissive and a wrapper deals with run-time security levels. In addition to enforcing the non-interference property in object interactions, our approach guarantees that an object will be given access only to the information that it is allowed to handle.

In [18], Nair et al. implement and design a run-time system, named Trishul, to track the flow of information within the Java virtual machine (JVM). This paper focuses on implicit and explicit flows through the Java control flows and the architecture and does not enforce non-interference. Due to the Trishul's modular nature, our security wrappers can be deployed to prevent illegal flows.

Russo and Sabelfeld [23] prove that a sound flow-sensitive dynamic information-flow enforcement is more permissive than static analysis. In [16], the notion of wrappers is used to control the behavior of JavaScript programs and enforce security policies to protect web pages from malicious codes. A policy specifies under which conditions a page performs a specific action, and a wrapper grants, rejects, or modifies these actions. Moreover, the notion of wrappers has been developed for the safety of objects [21], where the programmer needs to specify which objects should have a wrapper and to program what each wrapper should do based on any input/output. In contrast, we apply wrappers to security analysis, letting the runtime system automatically decide which components should be wrapped, and also what the wrappers should do to prevent illegal flows.

6   Conclusion

We have proposed a framework for enforcing secure information-flow and non-interference in active object languages based on the notion of security wrappers. We have considered a high-level core language supporting asynchronous calls and futures. In our model, due to encapsulation, there is no need for information-flow restrictions inside an object. Wrappers perform security checks for object interactions (with methods and futures) at run-time. Furthermore, wrappers control the access to futures with high values. Security rules of wrappers are defined based on security levels of communicated messages. Inside an object, the security levels of variables might change at run-time due to flow-sensitivity. Wrappers on unsafe objects and future components protect exchange of confidential values to low objects. Wrappers on objects protect outgoing method calls and prevent leakage of information through outgoing parameters. The wrappers are created automatically by the run-time system without the involved parties being aware of it. Their behavior is also defined by the runtime system. We define non-interference for our language and outline a proof of it. By combining results from static analysis, we can improve run-time efficiency by avoiding wrappers when they are superfluous according to the over-approximation of levels given by the static analysis.

Acknowledgements. We thank Christian Johansen for useful interactions. The Norwegian Research Council has funded us by project *IoTSec* (no. 248113/O70).

References

1. Agha, G.A.: Actors: a model of concurrent computation in distributed systems. Technical report, Massachusetts Inst. of Tech, Cambridge Artificial Int. Lab. (1985)
2. Attali, I., Caromel, D., Henrio, L., Aguila, F.L.D.: Secured information flow for asynchronous sequential processes. Electron. Notes Theor. Comput. Sci. **180**(1), 17–34 (2007)
3. Baker Jr, H.C., Hewitt, C.: The incremental garbage collection of processes. ACM Sigplan Not. **12**(8), 55–59 (1977)
4. Balliu, M., Schoepe, D., Sabelfeld, A.: We are family: relating information-flow trackers. In: Foley, S.N., Gollmann, D., Snekkenes, E. (eds.) ESORICS 2017. LNCS, vol. 10492, pp. 124–145. Springer, Cham (2017). https://doi.org/10.1007/978-3-319-66402-6_9

5. De Boer, F., et al.: A survey of active object languages. ACM Comput. Surv. **50**(5), 76 (2017)
6. Brandauer, S., et al.: Parallel objects for multicores: a glimpse at the parallel language ENCORE. In: Bernardo, M., Johnsen, E.B. (eds.) SFM 2015. LNCS, vol. 9104, pp. 1–56. Springer, Cham (2015). https://doi.org/10.1007/978-3-319-18941-3_1
7. Caromel, D., Delbé, C., Di Costanzo, A., Leyton, M.: Proactive: an integrated platform for programming and running applications on grids and P2P systems. Comput. Methods Sci. Technol. **12**(1), 16 (2006)
8. Caromel, D., Henrio, L.: A Theory of Distributed Objects: Asynchrony-Mobility-Groups-Components. Springer, Heidelberg (2005). https://doi.org/10.1007/b138812
9. Denning, D.E., Denning, P.J.: Certification of programs for secure information flow. Commun. ACM **20**(7), 504–513 (1977)
10. Goguen, J.A., Meseguer, J.: Security policies and security models. In: 1982 IEEE Symposium on Security and Privacy, p. 11. IEEE (1982)
11. Haller, P., Odersky, M.: Scala actors: unifying thread-based and event-based programming. Theor. Comput. Sci. **410**, 202–220 (2009)
12. Hedin, D., Sabelfeld, A.: A perspective on information-flow control. Softw. Saf. Secur. **33**, 319–347 (2012)
13. Johnsen, E.B., Hähnle, R., Schäfer, J., Schlatte, R., Steffen, M.: ABS: a core language for abstract behavioral specification. In: Aichernig, B.K., de Boer, F.S., Bonsangue, M.M. (eds.) FMCO 2010. LNCS, vol. 6957, pp. 142–164. Springer, Heidelberg (2011). https://doi.org/10.1007/978-3-642-25271-6_8
14. Johnsen, E.B., Owe, O.: An asynchronous communication model for distributed concurrent objects. Softw. Syst. Model. **6**(1), 39–58 (2007)
15. Karami, F., Owe, O., Ramezanifarkhani, T.: An evaluation of interaction paradigms for active objects. J. Log. Algebr. Methods Program. **103**, 154–183 (2019)
16. Magazinius, J., Phung, P.H., Sands, D.: Safe wrappers and sane policies for self protecting JavaScript. In: Aura, T., Järvinen, K., Nyberg, K. (eds.) NordSec 2010. LNCS, vol. 7127, pp. 239–255. Springer, Heidelberg (2012). https://doi.org/10.1007/978-3-642-27937-9_17
17. Meseguer, J.: Conditional rewriting logic as a unified model of concurrency. Theor. Comput. Sci. **96**(1), 73–155 (1992)
18. Nair, S.K., Simpson, P.N.D., Crispo, B., Tanenbaum, A.S.: A virtual machine based information flow control system for policy enforcement. Electron. Notes Theor. Comput. Sci. **197**(1), 3–16 (2008)
19. Owe, O., Dahl, O.-J.: Generator induction in order sorted algebras. Form. Asp. Comput. **3**(1), 2–20 (1991)
20. Owe, O., Ramezanifarkhani, T.: Confidentiality of interactions in concurrent object-oriented systems. In: Garcia-Alfaro, J., Navarro-Arribas, G., Hartenstein, H., Herrera-Joancomartí, J. (eds.) ESORICS/DPM/CBT -2017. LNCS, vol. 10436, pp. 19–34. Springer, Cham (2017). https://doi.org/10.1007/978-3-319-67816-0_2
21. Owe, O., Schneider, G.: Wrap your objects safely. Electron. Notes Theor. Comput. Sci. **253**(1), 127–143 (2009)
22. Pettai, M., Laud, P.: Securing the future—an information flow analysis of a distributed OO language. In: Bieliková, M., Friedrich, G., Gottlob, G., Katzenbeisser, S., Turán, G. (eds.) SOFSEM 2012. LNCS, vol. 7147, pp. 576–587. Springer, Heidelberg (2012). https://doi.org/10.1007/978-3-642-27660-6_47

23. Russo, A., Sabelfeld, A.: Dynamic vs. static flow-sensitive security analysis. In: 2010 23rd IEEE Computer Security Foundations Symposium (CSF), pp. 186–199. IEEE (2010)
24. Sabelfeld, A., Myers, A.C.: Language-based information-flow security. IEEE J. Sel. Areas Commun. **21**(1), 5–19 (2003)
25. Sirjani, M., Movaghar, A., Mousavi, M.R.: Compositional verification of an object-based model for reactive systems. In: Proceedings of the Workshop on Automated Verification of Critical Systems (AVoCS 2001), Oxford, UK, pp. 114–118. Citeseer (2001)
26. Sirjani, M., Movaghar, A., Shali, A., De Boer, F.S.: Modeling and verification of reactive systems using Rebeca. Fundamenta Informaticae **63**(4), 385–410 (2004)
27. Wyatt, D.: Akka Concurrency. Artima Incorporation, USA (2013)

Efficient Mixing of Arbitrary Ballots with Everlasting Privacy: How to Verifiably Mix the PPATC Scheme

Kristian Gjøsteen, Thomas Haines, and Morten Rotvold Solberg[⊠]

Norwegian University of Science and Technology, Trondheim, Norway
{kristian.gjosteen,thomas.haines,mosolb}@ntnu.no

Abstract. The long term privacy of voting systems is of increasing concern as quantum computers come closer to reality. Everlasting privacy schemes offer the best way to manage these risks at present. While homomorphic tallying schemes with everlasting privacy are well developed, most national elections, using electronic voting, use mixnets. Currently the best candidate encryption scheme for making these kinds of elections everlastingly private is PPATC, but it has not been shown to work with any mixnet of comparable efficiency to the current ElGamal mixnets. In this work we give a paper proof, and a machine checked proof, that the variant of Wikström's mixnet commonly in use is safe for use with the PPATC encryption scheme.

Keywords: Everlasting privacy · E-voting · Verifiable shuffles · Coq

1 Introduction

Traditional paper-based and electronic voting has many good properties, but also limitations. A voter is not able to verify that her vote was counted as she cast it, and confidentiality of the votes relies heavily on trust in the election officials and procedures. In addition there are problems regarding for example counting errors and accessibility. Verifiable electronic voting systems can solve some of these issues. In particular, cryptographic techniques can be used to provide public verifiability of election results and raise each individual voter's confidence in the privacy and integrity of her vote.

To achieve verifiable elections, encrypted votes are often published on a public bulletin board, along with sophisticated cryptographic proofs that allow an individual voter to verify that their ballot was not only listed on the bulletin board, but also included correctly in the tally.

The votes are encrypted to provide confidentiality, which is usually considered essential for a fair vote. Confidentiality requires votes to remain private not only during the time of the election, but for all foreseeable future. However, due to computers and algorithms getting faster and the potential introduction of quantum computers, there is no way to safely predict how long it may take

© Springer Nature Switzerland AG 2021
M. Asplund and S. Nadjm-Tehrani (Eds.): NordSec 2020, LNCS 12556, pp. 92–107, 2021.
https://doi.org/10.1007/978-3-030-70852-8_6

before a ciphertext encrypted today is broken. Thus, the property of *everlasting privacy* has been introduced.

Everlasting privacy is a property of electronic voting schemes where the information released to the public perfectly (or information-theoretically) hides how each voter voted, up to the outcome of the election. This means that regardless of developments in practical computing power and algorithm design, individual votes cannot be recovered from the public record.

Everlasting privacy is a subtle concept. In all systems that are practical for large-scale voting, functional requirements mean that the voter will have to encrypt their ballot and transmit this encryption to some infrastructure. The subtlety is that this ciphertext is not part of the public record. This essentially assumes that the potential powerful *future* attacker did not record the network traffic, and is only working with the public record of the election. This is in many cases a reasonable assumption. We emphasize that it is only privacy against these potential future attackers that relies on this assumption. Computationally secure cryptography still protects against adversaries with greater network access. So schemes that provide everlasting privacy are no less secure than conventional cryptographic voting schemes, but they have greater security against future adversaries that work only from the public record.

There are various candidate constructions which achieve everlasting privacy while maintaining verifiability. Most of the schemes are inspired by Cramer *et al.*'s "Multi-Authority Secret-Ballot Elections with Linear Work" [3] and Moran and Naor's "Split-ballot voting: Everlasting privacy with distributed trust" [12]. In both cases perfectly hiding commitments are combined with zero knowledge proofs to provide verifiability without leaking any information. In this work we will focus on schemes in the style of [12] which are able to handle arbitrary ballots rather than the homomorphic tally supported by [3].

Before the authorities perform the tally, the encrypted ballots need to be decrypted. To ensure that privacy is preserved, the link between each ballot and the voter who submitted the ballot is destroyed by running the ballots through a mix net. Mix nets were first introduced by Chaum [2] and consist of a finite sequence of authorities (mixers), each of which permutes (shuffles) and hides the relationship between its inputs and its outputs. This style of schemes is less developed than the homomorphic schemes, but have greater practical implications since mixnet style schemes have been used in many of countries who have voted electronically (Australia, Estonia, Norway, and Switzerland), and where homomorphic counting is often hard to do.

The general idea in these schemes is to have a publicly verifiable part dealing only with commitments to ballots. We achieve everlasting privacy by using perfectly hiding commitments. However, somehow the ballots must be recovered by the infrastructure, and this is done in a private part, typically working on encrypted openings for the commitments. In this way, we get everlasting privacy. Note that we only get computational integrity.

There are two encryption schemes which are commonly suggested for use in this context, both involve first committing to the message and then encrypting the opening to the commitment. The schemes fit into a wider everlasting privacy scheme with the perfectly hiding commitments being publicly shuffled and then opened providing both verifiability and everlasting privacy; the encrypted openings are shuffled by the authorities and then publicly posted. The first is the MN encryption scheme from Moran and Naor [12] which is built on Paillier encryption [13] and Pedersen commitments [14]. The second is the PPATC encryption from Cuvelier *et al.* [4] which uses ElGamal and Abe *et al.*'s [1] commitment scheme. Since the latter encryption scheme can be instantiated on prime order elliptic curves, rather than the semi-prime RSA groups of the former, it is significantly faster.

Simple and efficient zero-knowledge proofs for correct encryption and decryption of both encryption schemes are known. An efficient mixnet for the MN encryption scheme was proven by Haines and Gritti [11], but at present the most efficient known mixnet for PPATC uses the general version of Terelius-Wikström proof of shuffle [15] which proves statements over the integers using Fujisaki-Okamoto commitments [6], based on an RSA modulus, which hampers the efficiency of the mixnet. The reason is that every operation must happen modulo the RSA modulus, which means that basic arithmetic is very slow. We will use pairing groups, but we arrange it so that most of the group arithmetic happens in a group where arithmetic is much faster, which means that Fujisaki-Okamoto commitments will be slow compared to most of our arithmetic. In practice everyone using the Terelius-Wikström proof of shuffle uses an optimised variant which avoids the use of Fujisaki-Okamoto commitments. It is folklore that the optimised variant of Terelius-Wikström works for wide class of encryption schemes but the precise variant for each encryption scheme should be proven.

1.1 Contribution

We prove a variation of the optimised Terelius-Wikström shuffle [15] for the PPATC encryption scheme [4]. This is essentially the optimised variation which is widely used, and which avoids the use of Fujisaki-Okamoto commitments. In addition we show how the Fiat-Shamir transform can be applied so that the public proofs of correct shuffling can be trivially derived from the private proofs of correct shuffling, nearly doubling the speed of mixing.

We provide a machine-checked proof using the interactive theorem prover Coq. The machine-checked proof relies on recent work which shows that any encryption scheme with certain properties works with the optimised Terelius-Wikström shuffle. For completeness and human understanding, we also give a straight-forward traditional paper proof.

2   Notation and Tools

We denote by $\mathbb{G}_1$ and $\mathbb{G}_2$ cyclic groups of large prime order q, and by $\mathbb{Z}_q$ the field of integers modulo q. Let A^n be the set of vectors of length n, with elements from the set A. We denote vectors in bold, e.g. **a**. We denote by a_i the ith element of the vector $\mathbf{a}$. Sometimes, we will work with vectors that have tuples as elements. In such cases, we also denote by a_i the ith element of $\mathbf{a}$, and by $a_{i,j}$ the jth element of the tuple a_i. Multiplication of tuples is elementwise multiplication, that is, $\mathbf{ab}$ is the tuple where the ith element is $a_i b_i$. We denote by $A^{n\times n}$ the set of $n \times n$-matrices with elements from the set A. Matrices will be denoted using capital letters, e.g. M. We denote by M_i the ith column of M, by $M_{i,*}$ the ith row of M, and by $M_{i,j}$ the element in row i and column j. A binary relation for a set S of statements and a set W of witnesses is a subset of $S \times W$ and is denoted by $\mathscr{R}$.

Matrix Commitments. We now describe how to commit to a matrix using a variation of Pedersen commitments [15]. We denote by $\mathsf{Com}_{\gamma,\gamma_1}(m,t)$ the Pedersen commitment of $m \in \mathbb{Z}_q$ with randomness $t \in \mathbb{Z}_q$, i.e. $\mathsf{Com}_{\gamma,\gamma_1}(m,t) = \gamma^t \gamma_1^m$ for group generators γ and γ_1. To commit to a vector $\mathbf{v} \in \mathbb{Z}_q^n$, we compute $u = \mathsf{Com}_{\gamma,\gamma_1,\cdots,\gamma_n}(\mathbf{v},t) = \gamma^t \prod_{i=1}^n \gamma_i^{v_i}$, where t is chosen at random from $\mathbb{Z}_q$, and the γs are random group generators. If the commitment parameters are omitted, it is implicit that they are $\gamma, \gamma_1, \cdots, \gamma_n$. An $n \times n$ matrix M is committed to column-wise. For a matrix $M \in \mathbb{Z}_q^{n\times n}$ and a vector $\mathbf{t}$ chosen at random from $\mathbb{Z}_q^n$, we compute the commitment $\mathbf{u}$ of M as

$$\mathbf{u} = \mathsf{Com}(M,\mathbf{t}) = \left(\gamma^{t_1} \Pi_{i=1}^n \gamma_i^{M_{i,1}}, \ldots, \gamma^{t_n} \Pi_{i=1}^n \gamma_i^{M_{i,n}}\right).$$

Abe Commitments. We now describe a perfectly hiding commitment scheme due to Abe *et al.* [1], that is used in a construction of the PPATC encryption scheme that we describe further down. Let $\Lambda_{sxdh} = (q, \mathbb{G}_1, \mathbb{G}_2, \mathbb{G}_T, e, g, h)$ be a description of bilinear groups, where g is a generator of $\mathbb{G}_1$, h is a generator of $\mathbb{G}_2$ and e is an efficient and non-degenerate bilinear map $e : \mathbb{G}_1 \times \mathbb{G}_2 \rightarrow \mathbb{G}_T$. We assume that the DDH problem is hard in both $\mathbb{G}_1$ and $\mathbb{G}_2$. In our notation, an Abe commitment to a message $m \in \mathbb{G}_1$ is the tuple $(h^{r_1} h_1^{r_2}, mg_1^{r_2})$, where r_1 and r_2 are random elements in $\mathbb{Z}_q$ and g_1 and h_1 are random elements of $\mathbb{G}_1$ and $\mathbb{G}_2$, respectively. An Abe commitment to m can be thought of as an ElGamal encryption of m where the first coordinate is hidden in a Pedersen commitment. An opening is of the form $(g_1^{r_1}, m)$ which is valid if $e(g, h^{r_1} h_1^{r_2}) = e(g_1^{r_1}, h)e(mg_1^{r_2}/m, h_1)$.

Polynomial Identity Testing. We will make use of the Schwartz-Zippel lemma to analyze the soundness of our protocol. The lemma gives an efficient method for testing whether a polynomial is equal to zero.

Lemma 1 (Schwartz-Zippel). *Let $f \in \mathbb{Z}_q[X_1, ..., X_n]$ be a non-zero polynomial of total degree $d \geq 0$ over $\mathbb{Z}_q$. Let $S \subseteq \mathbb{Z}_q$ and let $x_1, ..., x_n$ be chosen uniformly at random from S. Then $\Pr[f(x_1, ..., x_n) = 0] \leq d/|S|$.*

3   Commitment Consistent Encryption

We now describe *commitment consistent encryption* (CCE), as defined by Cuvelier *et al.* [4]. The idea is that for any ciphertext, one can derive a commitment to that ciphertext, and the secret key can be used to obtain an opening to that commitment. Furthermore, applied in a voting protocol, the idea is that the voters compute a CC encryption of their ballot, and the authorities derive a commitment to the ciphertext and post this commitment on a public bulletin board. If the commitments are perfectly hiding, they can be used to provide a perfectly private audit trail, which allows anyone to verify the correctness of the count, but does not contain any information about who submitted which ballots.

Definition 1 (CC Encryption [4]). *A commitment consistent encryption scheme Π is a tuple of six efficient algorithms (Gen, Enc, Dec, DeriveCom, Open, Verify), defined as follows:*

- *Gen(1^λ): on input a security parameter λ, output a triple (pp, pk, sk) of public parameters, public key and secret key. The public parameter pp is implicitly given as input to the rest of the algorithms.*
- *$Enc_{pk}(m)$: output a ciphertext c, which is an encryption of a message m in the plaintext space $\mathcal{M}$ (defined by pp) using public key pk.*
- *$Dec_{sk}(c)$: for a ciphertext c in the ciphertext space $\mathcal{C}$ (defined by pp), output a message m using secret key sk.*
- *$DeriveCom_{pk}(c)$: From a ciphertext c, output a commitment d using pk.*
- *$Open_{sk}(c)$: from a ciphertext c, output an auxiliary value a, that can be considered as part of an opening for a commitment d.*
- *$Verify_{pk}(d, m, a)$: On input a message m and a commitment d wrt. public key pk, and auxiliary value a, output a bit. The algorithm checks that the opening (m, a) is valid wrt. d and pk.*

Correctness. We expect that any commitment consistent encryption scheme satisfies the following correctness property: For any triple (pp, pk, sk) output by Gen, any message $m \in \mathcal{M}$ and any $c = Enc_{pk}(m)$, it holds with overwhelming probability in the security parameter that $Dec_{sk}(c) = m$ and $Verify_{pk}(DeriveCom_{pk}(c), Dec_{sk}(c), Open_{sk}(c)) = 1$.

The above definition does not guarantee that it is infeasible to create honest-looking CCE ciphertexts that are in fact not consistent. To address this issue, Cuvelier *et al.* [4] define the concept of *validity augmentation* (VA) for CCE schemes. A validity augmentation adds three new algorithms Expand, Valid and Strip to the scheme. The Expand algorithm augments the public key for use in the other algorithms. The Valid algorithm takes as input an augmented ciphertext c^{va} along with some proofs of validity. It then checks whether it is possible to derive a commitment and an encryption of an opening to that commitment. The Strip algorithm removes the proofs of validity.

Definition 2 (Validity Augmentation [4]). *A scheme $\Pi^{va} = ($ VA.Gen, VA.Enc, VA.Dec, VA.DeriveCom, VA.Open, VA.Verify, Expand, Strip, Valid) is a validity augmentation of the CCE scheme $\Pi = ($ Gen, Enc, Dec, DeriveCom, Open, Verify) if the following conditions are satisfied:*

- Augmentation: $VA.Gen$ *runs* Gen *to obtain* (pp, pk, sk) *and outputs an updated triple* $(pp^{va}, pk^{va}, sk^{va}) = (pp, Expand(pk), sk)$.
- Validity: $Valid_{pk^{va}}(c^{va}) = 1$ *for all honestly generated public keys and ciphertexts. In addition, for any PPT adversary* $\mathcal{A}$, *the following probability is negligible in* λ:

$$\Pr[Valid_{pk^{va}}(c^{va}) = 1 \wedge \neg Verify_{pk}(Strip_{pk^{va}}(c^{va})) = 1$$
$$\mid c \leftarrow \mathcal{A}(pp^{va}, pk^{va}); (pp^{va}, pk^{va}, sk^{va}) \leftarrow VA.Gen]$$

- Consistency: *The values* $Strip_{pk^{va}}(VA.enc_{pk^{va}}(m))$ *and* $Enc_{pk}(m)$ *are equally distributed for all* $m \in \mathcal{M}$, *i.e. it is possible to strip a validity augmented ciphertext into a "normal" one. In addition, it holds, for all ciphertexts and keys, that* $VA.Dec_{sk^{va}}(c^{va}) = Dec_{sk}(Strip_{pk^{va}}(c^{va}))$, *that* $VA.Open_{sk^{va}}(c^{va}) = Open_{sk}(Strip_{pk^{va}}(c^{va}))$ *and that* $VA.Verify_{pk^{va}}(c^{va}) = Verify_{pk}(Strip_{pk^{va}}(c^{va}))$. *In other words, the decryption, opening and verification for* Π^{va} *is consistent with those of* Π.

3.1   The PPATC Encryption System

We now describe an augmented CCE system called PPATC (Perfectly Private Audit Trail with Complex ballots). The system is defined as follows [4]:

- $VA.Gen(1^\lambda)$: Generate $\Lambda_{sxdh} = (q, \mathbb{G}_1, \mathbb{G}_2, \mathbb{G}_T, e, g, h)$ and random generators $g_1 = g^{x_1}, g_2 = g^{x_2} \in \mathbb{G}_1$ and $h_1 \in \mathbb{G}_2$. Now, $(pp, pk, sk) = ((\Lambda_{sxdh}, h_1), (g_1, g_2), (x_1, x_2))$. The augmented key $pk^{va} = Expand(pk)$ is computed by adding a description of a hash function $\mathcal{H}$ with range $\mathbb{Z}_q$ to the public key, resulting in the triple $(pp^{va} = pp, pk^{va}, sk^{va} = sk)$.
- $VA.Enc_{pk^{va}}(m; r)$: Compute the CCE ciphertext $c = Enc_{pk}(m; r)$ where $c = (c_1, c_2, c_3, d_1, d_2) = (g^{r_2}, g^{r_3}, g_1^{r_1} g_2^{r_3}, h^{r_1} h_1^{r_2}, m g_1^{r_2})$ and $r = (r_1, r_2, r_3) \in \mathbb{Z}_q^3$. Then compute the following validity proof. Select $s_1, s_2, s_3 \xleftarrow{r} \mathbb{Z}_q$ and compute $c' = (c_1', c_2', c_3', d_1') = (g^{s_2}, g^{s_3}, g_1^{s_1} g_2^{s_3}, h^{s_1} h_1^{s_2})$. Compute $\nu_{cc} = \mathcal{H}(pp^{va}, pk^{va}, c, c')$, $f_1 = s_1 + \nu_{cc} r_1$, $f_2 = s_2 + \nu_{cc} r_2$ and $f_3 = s_3 + \nu_{cc} r_3$. Let $\sigma_{cc} = (\nu_{cc}, f_1, f_2, f_3)$. The ciphertext is $c^{va} = (c, \sigma_{cc})$.
- $VA.Dec_{sk^{va}}(c^{va})$: Parse c^{va} as $(c_1, c_2, c_3, d_1, d_2, \sigma_{cc})$ and return $d_2/c_1^{x_1}$.
- $VA.DeriveCom_{pk^{va}}(c^{va})$: Parse c^{va} as $(c_1, c_2, c_3, d_1, d_2, \sigma_{cc})$ and return (d_1, d_2).
- $VA.Open_{sk^{va}}(c^{va})$: Parse c^{va} as $(c_1, c_2, c_3, d_1, d_2, \sigma_{cc})$ and return $a = c_3/c_2^{x_2}$.
- $VA.Verify_{pk^{va}}(d_1, d_2, m, a)$: Return 1 if $e(g, d_1) = e(a, h)e(d_2/m, h_1)$ and 0 otherwise.
- $Valid_{pk^{va}}(c^{va})$: Parse c^{va} as $(c_1, c_2, c_3, d_1, d_2, \nu_{cc}, f_1, f_2, f_3)$ and check if all elements of c^{va} are properly encoded. Compute $c_1' = g^{f_2}/c_1^{\nu_{cc}}$, $c_2' = g^{f_3}/c_2^{\nu_{cc}}$, $c_3' = g_1^{f_1} g_2^{f_3}/c_3^{\nu_{cc}}$ and $d_1' = h^{f_1} h_1^{f_2}/d_1^{\nu_{cc}}$. Return 1 only if

$$\nu_{cc} = \mathcal{H}(pp^{va}, pk^{va}, c_1, c_2, c_3, d_1, d_2, c_1', c_2', c_3', d_1', d_2').$$

- $Strip_{pk^{va}}(c^{va})$: Parse c^{va} as $(c_1, c_2, c_3, d_1, d_2, \sigma_{cc})$ and return the CCE ciphertext $c = (c_1, c_2, c_3, d_1, d_2)$ and the commitment $d = (d_1, d_2)$.

A CCE ciphertext $c = \mathsf{Enc}_{pk}(m; r) = (g^{r_2}, g^{r_3}, g_1^{r_1} g_2^{r_3}, h^{r_1} h_1^{r_1}, mg_1^{r_2})$ can be *re-encrypted*, by multiplying c with the encryption of 1 using randomness $r' = (r_1', r_2', r_3') \in \mathbb{Z}_q^3$. Thus, a ciphertext c', where

$$c' = c \cdot \mathsf{Enc}_{pk}(1; r') = (g^{r_2 + r_2'}, g^{r_3 + r_3'}, g_1^{r_1 + r_1'} g_2^{r_3 + r_3'}, h^{r_1 + r_1'} h_1^{r_2 + r_2'}, mg_1^{r_2 + r_2'}),$$

can be thought of as an encryption of m using randomness $r + r'$.

4 Shuffling Commitment Consistent Ciphertexts

In this section, we first describe how the PPATC can be used as a building block in a voting system. We then give concrete protocols for shuffling PPATC ciphertexts and their derived commitments, before describing how to apply the Fiat-Shamir heuristic to make the shuffles non-interactive.

4.1 Using the PPATC Scheme in a Voting System

A validity augmented CCE scheme can be applied in an election as follows [4]. First, a setup phase takes place, where the election authorities generate encryption and decryption keys, as well as two bulletin boards PB and SB. The public board PB will contain the public audit trail, while SB will contain encrypted votes, be kept secret by the authorities and will be used to compute the tally. To produce a ballot, each voter encrypts her vote using the PPATC scheme, and sends the resulting ciphertext to the authorities. The ciphertext is stored on SB and the derived commitment is stored on PB.

To preserve privacy, the link between voter and vote must be destroyed, the list of ciphertexts on SB is *shuffled*. A shuffle of a list $\mathbf{v}$ of ciphertexts is a new list $\mathbf{v}'$, such that for all $i = 1, \ldots, n$, $v_i' = v_{\pi(i)} \cdot \mathsf{Enc}_{pk}(1; r_{\pi(i)})$, where $\pi : \{1, \ldots, n\} \rightarrow \{1, \ldots, n\}$ is a randomly chosen permutation. Thus, the two lists $\mathbf{v}$ and $\mathbf{v}'$ contain encryptions of the same plaintexts in permuted order. To also provide verifiability, we keep track of the concordance between the ciphertexts on SB and the corresponding commitments on PB. To achieve this, the list of commitments on PB is also shuffled, using the same permutation as for SB.

The lists are shuffled several times, by a series of *mix servers*. It is necessary that each mix server provides a *proof of shuffle*, to prove that he follows the protocol, and that the lists of ciphertexts in fact decrypt to the same plaintexts. For our shuffle protocols we will use the optimised version of the Terelius-Wikström shuffle presented by Haenni *et al.* [8], where a proof of shuffle consists of proving knowledge of the permutation π and the random vector $\mathbf{r}$ used to re-encrypt the ciphertexts. Thus, the tally procedure will proceed as follows:

1. *Stripping*: Algorithms Valid and Strip are run on the ciphertexts stored on SB to obtain a vector $\mathbf{v}$ of n CCE ciphertexts and a vector $\mathbf{d}$ of the corresponding commitments.

2. *Performing the shuffles*: Each mix server selects a random permutation $\pi : \{1, \ldots, n\} \rightarrow \{1, \ldots, n\}$, also defining a permutation matrix M, and computes a commitment $\mathbf{u}$ on that permutation matrix, along with a proof of knowledge of the permutation. The mix server then selects a random vector $\mathbf{r} = ((r_{1,1}, r_{1,2}, r_{1,3}), \cdots, (r_{n,1}, r_{n,2}, r_{n,3}))$ and computes a new vector $\mathbf{v}'$ where $v_i' = v_{\pi(i)} \cdot \mathsf{Enc}_{pk}(1; r_{\pi(i)})$, and $r_{\pi(i)} = (r_{\pi(i),1}, r_{\pi(i),2}, r_{\pi(i),3})$. Let the last two components of each ciphertext v_i' form a vector $\mathbf{d}'$. This vector is posted on PB. Finally, the mix server computes two commitment consistent proofs of shuffle, showing that $\mathbf{v}'$ is a shuffle of $\mathbf{v}$ and $\mathbf{d}'$ is a shuffle of $\mathbf{d}$, with respect to the permutation π.

3. *Decryption of openings:* The authorities verify the proofs and perform a threshold decryption of the ciphertexts in $\mathbf{v}'$. In addition, they run the algorithm Open on these ciphertexts to obtain the auxiliary values for the commitments. The plaintexts and the auxiliary values are posted on PB.

4.2 Proof of Shuffle on the Private Board

We begin with the shuffle on the private board, i.e. the shuffle of the CCE ciphertexts. In the following, let $\mathscr{R}_{com}$ be a relation between the commitment parameters $\gamma, \gamma_1, \ldots, \gamma_n \in \mathbb{G}_1$, $\mathbf{m}, \mathbf{m}' \in \mathbb{Z}_q^n$ and $t, t' \in \mathbb{Z}_q$ which holds if and only if $\mathsf{Com}_{\gamma, \gamma_1, \ldots, \gamma_n}(\mathbf{m}, t) = \mathsf{Com}_{\gamma, \gamma_1, \ldots, \gamma_n}(\mathbf{m}', t')$ and $\mathbf{m} \neq \mathbf{m}'$. Let $\mathscr{R}_\pi$ be the relation between the commitment parameters $\gamma, \gamma_1, \ldots, \gamma_n$, a commitment $\mathbf{u} \in \mathbb{G}_1^n$, a permutation matrix $M \in \mathbb{Z}_q^{n \times n}$ and a randomness vector $\mathbf{t} \in \mathbb{Z}_q^n$ which holds only if $\mathbf{u} = \mathsf{Com}_{\gamma, \gamma_1, \ldots, \gamma_n}(M, \mathbf{t})$. Let $\mathscr{R}_{ReEnc}^{shuf}(pk, (v_1, \ldots, v_n), (v_1', \ldots, v_n'))(\pi, (r_1, \ldots, r_n))$, where π is a permutation of the set $\{1, \ldots, n\}$, be the relation which holds if and only if $v_i' = v_{\pi(i)} \cdot \mathsf{Enc}_{pk}(1; r_{\pi(i)})$ for all $i \in \{1, \ldots, n\}$.

Theorem 1. *Protocol 1 is a perfectly complete, 4-round special soundness, special honest-verifier zero-knowledge proof of knowledge of the relation $\mathscr{R}_{com} \vee (\mathscr{R}_\pi \wedge \mathscr{R}_{ReEnc}^{shuf})$.*

It is infeasible under the discrete log assumption to find a witness for $\mathscr{R}_{com}$, so Theorem 1 implies a proof of knowledge for $(\mathscr{R}_\pi \wedge \mathscr{R}_{ReEnc}^{shuf})$. To prove the theorem, we now demonstrate the completeness of the protocol, as well as the special soundness extractor and the special honest-verifier zero-knowledge simulator. For brevity we omit parts of the paper proof. The full proof can be found in the full version of our paper [7].

Special Soundness. We will follow the structure of Terelius and Wikström [15] and split the extractor in two parts. In the first part, the basic extractor, we show that for two accepting transcripts with the same $\mathbf{w}$ but different β, we can extract witnesses for certain sub-statements. In the second part, the extended extractor, we show that we can extract a witness to the main statement, given witnesses which hold for these sub-statements, for n different $\mathbf{w}$.

Protocol 1. Interactive ZK-Proof of Shuffle on Private Board

Common Input: A public key pk, a matrix commitment $\mathbf{u}$, commitment parameters $\gamma, \gamma_1, ..., \gamma_n$ and ciphertext vectors $\mathbf{v}, \mathbf{v}' \in (\mathbb{G}_1 \times \mathbb{G}_1 \times \mathbb{G}_1 \times \mathbb{G}_2 \times \mathbb{G}_1)^n$.

Private Input: Permutation matrix $M \in \mathbb{Z}_q^{n \times n}$ and randomness $\mathbf{t} \in \mathbb{Z}_q^n$ such that $\mathbf{u} = \mathsf{Com}(M, \mathbf{t})$. Randomness $\mathbf{r} \in (\mathbb{Z}_q \times \mathbb{Z}_q \times \mathbb{Z}_q)^n$ such that $v_i' = v_{\pi(i)} \cdot \mathsf{Enc}_{pk}(1; r_{\pi(i)})$ for $i = 1, ..., n$.

1: $\mathcal{V}$ chooses a random $\mathbf{w} \in \mathbb{Z}_q^n$ and sends $\mathbf{w}$ to $\mathcal{P}$.

2: $\mathcal{P}$ computes $\mathbf{w}' = (w_1', ..., w_n') = M\mathbf{w}$, and randomly chooses $\hat{\mathbf{t}} = (\hat{t}_1, ..., \hat{t}_n)$, $\hat{\mathbf{z}} = (\hat{z}_1, ..., \hat{z}_n)$, $\mathbf{z}' = (z_1', ..., z_n') \in \mathbb{Z}_q^n$, $z_1, z_2, z_3 \in \mathbb{Z}_q$ and $\tilde{\mathbf{z}} = (\tilde{z}_1, \tilde{z}_2, \tilde{z}_3) \in \mathbb{Z}_q^3$. $\mathcal{P}$ defines

$$\bar{t} = \langle \mathbf{1}, \mathbf{t} \rangle, \quad \tilde{t} = \langle \mathbf{t}, \mathbf{w} \rangle, \quad \hat{t} = \hat{t}_n + \sum_{i=1}^{n-1} \left(\hat{t}_i \prod_{j=i+1}^{n} w_j' \right) \quad \text{and}$$

$$\mathbf{r}' = \left(\sum_{i=1}^{n} r_{i,1} w_i, \sum_{i=1}^{n} r_{i,2} w_i, \sum_{i=1}^{n} r_{i,3} w_i \right),$$

and sends the following elements to $\mathcal{V}$ (for $i = 1, ..., n$):

$$\hat{u}_0 = \gamma_1 \qquad \hat{u}_i = \gamma^{\hat{t}_i} (\hat{u}_{i-1})^{w_i'} \qquad a_1 = \gamma^{z_1} \qquad a_2 = \gamma^{z_2}$$

$$a_3 = \gamma^{z_3} \Pi_{i=1}^{n} \gamma_i^{z_i'} \qquad a_4 = \mathsf{Enc}_{pk}(1; \tilde{\mathbf{z}}) \Pi_{i=1}^{n} (v_i')^{z_i'} \qquad \hat{a}_i = \gamma^{\hat{z}_i} (\hat{u}_{i-1})^{z_i'}.$$

3: $\mathcal{V}$ chooses a random challenge $\beta \in \mathbb{Z}_q$ and sends β to $\mathcal{P}$.

4: For $i \in \{1, ..., n\}$, $\mathcal{P}$ responds with

$$b_1 = z_1 + \beta \cdot \bar{t} \qquad b_2 = z_2 + \beta \cdot \hat{t} \qquad b_3 = z_3 + \beta \cdot \tilde{t}$$

$$\tilde{\mathbf{b}} = \tilde{\mathbf{z}} - \beta \cdot \mathbf{r}' \qquad \hat{b}_i = \hat{z}_i + \beta \cdot \hat{t}_i \qquad b_i' = z_i' + \beta \cdot w_i'.$$

5: $\mathcal{V}$ accepts if and only if, for $i \in \{1, ..., n\}$

$$a_1 = (\Pi_{i=1}^{n} u_i / \Pi_{i=1}^{n} \gamma_i)^{-\beta} \cdot \gamma^{b_1} \qquad a_2 = (\hat{u}_n / \gamma_1^{\Pi_{i=1}^{n} w_i})^{-\beta} \cdot \gamma^{b_2}$$

$$a_3 = (\Pi_{i=1}^{n} u_i^{w_i})^{-\beta} \cdot \gamma^{b_3} \cdot \Pi_{i=1}^{n} \gamma_i^{b_i'} \qquad a_4 = (\Pi_{i=1}^{n} v_i^{w_i})^{-\beta} \cdot \mathsf{Enc}_{pk}(1; \tilde{\mathbf{b}}) \cdot \Pi_{i=1}^{n} (v_i')^{b_i'}$$

$$\hat{a}_i = (\hat{u}_i)^{-\beta} \cdot \gamma^{\hat{b}_i} \cdot (\hat{u}_{i-1})^{b_i'}$$

Basic Extractor. Given two accepting transcripts

$$(\mathbf{w}, \hat{\mathbf{u}}, a_1, a_2, a_3, a_4, \hat{\mathbf{a}}, \beta, b_1, b_2, b_3, \tilde{\mathbf{b}}, \hat{\mathbf{b}}, \mathbf{b}')$$

$$(\mathbf{w}, \hat{\mathbf{u}}, a_1, a_2, a_3, a_4, \hat{\mathbf{a}}, \beta^*, b_1^*, b_2^*, b_3^*, \tilde{\mathbf{b}}^*, \hat{\mathbf{b}}^*, \mathbf{b}'^*)$$

where $\beta \neq \beta^*$, the basic extractor computes

$$\bar{t} = (b_1 - b_1^*)/(\beta - \beta^*) \qquad \hat{t} = (b_2 - b_2^*)/(\beta - \beta^*) \qquad \tilde{t} = (b_3 - b_3^*)/(\beta - \beta^*)$$

$$\hat{\mathbf{t}}' = (\hat{\mathbf{b}} - \hat{\mathbf{b}}^*)/(\beta - \beta^*) \qquad \mathbf{w}' = (\mathbf{b}' - \mathbf{b}'^*)/(\beta - \beta^*) \qquad \mathbf{r}' = (\tilde{\mathbf{b}} - \tilde{\mathbf{b}}^*)/(\beta - \beta^*)$$

We will prove that

$$\Pi_{i=1}^{n} u_i = \mathsf{Com}(\mathbf{1}, \tilde{t}), \quad \Pi_{i=1}^{n} u_i^{w_i} = \mathsf{Com}(\mathbf{w}', \tilde{t}), \quad \Pi_{i=1}^{n} v_i^{w_i} = \Pi_{i=1}^{n} (v_i')^{w_i'} \cdot \mathsf{Enc}_{pk}(1; -\mathbf{r}'),$$

$$\hat{u}_i = \mathsf{Com}_{\gamma, \hat{u}_{i-1}}(w_i', \hat{t}_i') \quad \text{and} \quad \hat{u}_n = \mathsf{Com}_{\gamma, \gamma_1}\left(\Pi_{i=1}^{n} w_i, \hat{t}\right).$$

The proof consists of algebraic manipulations:

$$\Pi_{i=1}^{n} u_i = \left(\frac{(\Pi_{i=1}^{n} u_i)^{\beta} \cdot a_1}{(\Pi_{i=1}^{n} u_i)^{\beta^*} \cdot a_1}\right)^{\frac{1}{\beta - \beta^*}} = \gamma^{\frac{b_1 - b_1^*}{\beta - \beta^*}} \cdot \Pi_{i=1}^{n} \gamma_i = \mathsf{Com}(\mathbf{1}, \tilde{t}).$$

$$\Pi_{i=1}^{n} u_i^{w_i} = \left(\frac{(\Pi_{i=1}^{n} u_i^{w_i})^{\beta} \cdot a_3}{(\Pi_{i=1}^{n} u_i^{w_i})^{\beta^*} \cdot a_3}\right)^{\frac{1}{\beta - \beta^*}} = \gamma^{\frac{b_3 - b_3^*}{\beta - \beta^*}} \cdot \Pi_{i=1}^{n} \gamma_i^{\frac{b_i' - b_i'^*}{\beta - \beta^*}} = \mathsf{Com}(\mathbf{w}', \tilde{t}).$$

$$\Pi_{i=1}^{n} v_i^{w_i} = \left(\frac{(\Pi_{i=1}^{n} v_i^{w_i})^{\beta} \cdot a_4}{(\Pi_{i=1}^{n} v_i^{w_i})^{\beta^*} \cdot a_4}\right)^{\frac{1}{\beta - \beta^*}} = \Pi_{i=1}^{n} (v_i')^{\frac{b_i' - b_i'^*}{\beta - \beta^*}} \cdot \mathsf{Enc}_{pk}\left(1; \frac{\tilde{\mathbf{b}} - \tilde{\mathbf{b}}^*}{\beta - \beta^*}\right)$$

$$= \Pi_{i=1}^{n} (v_i')^{w_i'} \cdot \mathsf{Enc}_{pk}(1; -\mathbf{r}').$$

$$\hat{u}_i = \gamma^{\frac{\hat{b}_i - \hat{b}_i^*}{\beta - \beta^*}} \cdot (\hat{u}_{i-1})^{\frac{b_i' - b_i'^*}{\beta - \beta^*}} = \gamma^{\hat{t}_i'} \cdot (\hat{u}_{i-1})^{w_i'} = \mathsf{Com}_{\gamma, \hat{u}_{i-1}}(w_i', \hat{t}_i').$$

$$\hat{u}_n = \gamma^{\frac{b_2 - b_2^*}{\beta - \beta^*}} \cdot \gamma_1^{\Pi_{i=1}^{n} w_i} = \gamma^{\hat{t}} \cdot \gamma_1^{\Pi_{i=1}^{n} w_i} = \mathsf{Com}_{\gamma, \gamma_1}\left(\Pi_{i=1}^{n} w_i; \hat{t}\right).$$

Thus, all the equations are satisfied.

Extended Extractor. The extended extractor takes, for one statement, n different witnesses extracted by the basic extractor, and produces a witness for the main statement. Let $\bar{\mathbf{t}}, \hat{\mathbf{t}}, \tilde{\mathbf{t}} \in \mathbb{Z}_q^n$, $\mathbf{r}' \in (\mathbb{Z}_q \times \mathbb{Z}_q \times \mathbb{Z}_q)^n$ and $\hat{T}', W' \in \mathbb{Z}_q^{n \times n}$ be the collective output from the n runs of the basic extractor, extracted from challenges $W \in \mathbb{Z}_q^{n \times n}$. Let W_j be the jth column of W, i.e. the challenge vector from the jth run of the basic extractor. The challenge vectors are sampled from a uniform distribution, but since the cheating prover may not succeed with uniform probability for all challenge vectors, the final distribution of challenge vectors is non-uniform. However, since the adversary has a significant probability of success, any set of challenge vectors with a significant success probability must be much larger than the set of non-invertible matrices. It follows that the columns of W will be linearly independent with overwhelming probability.

Thus, W will, with overwhelming probability, have an inverse. We call this inverse A. For such matrix A, we have that $W A_k$ is the kth standard unit vector in $\mathbb{Z}_q^n$, where A_k is the kth column of A. We see that

$$u_k = \Pi_{i=1}^{n} u_i^{W A_k} = \Pi_{i=1}^{n} \left(\Pi_{j=1}^{n} u_i^{W_{i,j} A_{j,k}}\right) = \Pi_{j=1}^{n} \mathsf{Com}(W_j', \tilde{t}_j)^{A_{j,k}}$$

$$= \Pi_{j=1}^{n} \mathsf{Com}(W_j' A_{j,k}, \tilde{t}_j A_{j,k}) = \mathsf{Com}(W' A_k, \langle \tilde{\mathbf{t}}, A_k \rangle).$$

Thus, we can open $\mathbf{u}$ to a matrix M, where $M_k = W'A_k$ is committed to using randomness $\langle \tilde{\mathbf{t}}, A_k \rangle$. We expect M to be a permutation matrix. If it is not, we can find a witness breaking the binding property of the commitment scheme. We extract this witness in two different ways, depending on whether or not $M\mathbf{1} = \mathbf{1}$.

If $M\mathbf{1} \neq \mathbf{1}$, let $\mathbf{w}'' = M\mathbf{1}$. We note that $\mathbf{w}'' \neq \mathbf{1}$ and that $\mathsf{Com}(\mathbf{1}, \bar{t}_j) = \Pi_{i=1}^n u_i = \mathsf{Com}(\mathbf{w}'', \tilde{\mathbf{t}}A)$, meaning that we have found a witness violating the binding property of the commitment scheme.

Now assume that $M\mathbf{1} = \mathbf{1}$. Terelius and Wikström [15] prove that M is a permutation matrix if and only if $M\mathbf{1} = \mathbf{1}$ and $\Pi_{i=1}^n \langle M_i, \mathbf{x} \rangle = \Pi_{i=1}^n x_i$ for a vector $\mathbf{x} \in \mathbb{Z}_q^n$ of independent elements. This fact, along with the Schwartz-Zippel lemma and the assumptions that $M\mathbf{1} = \mathbf{1}$ and that M is not a permutation matrix, implies that there exists, with overwhelming probability, some $j \in \{1, ..., n\}$ such that $\Pi_{i=1}^n \langle M_{i,*}, W_j \rangle - \Pi_{i=1}^n W_{i,j} \neq 0$. As this is true with overwhelming probability, we assume that it is true and rewind if not. Now let $\mathbf{w}'' = MW_j$. Note that $\Pi_{i=1}^n W_{i,j}' = \Pi_{i=1}^n W_{i,j}$ and that $\Pi_{i=1}^n W_{i,j} \neq \Pi_{i=1}^n w_i''$. The equality follows from the base statements, and the inequality follows from the Schwartz-Zippel lemma and the definition of $\mathbf{w}''$. Together, these facts imply that $\mathbf{w}'' \neq W_j'$.

We also see that $\mathsf{Com}(W_j', \tilde{t}_j) = \Pi_{i=1}^n u_i^{W_{i,j}} = \mathsf{Com}(\mathbf{w}'', \langle \tilde{\mathbf{t}}A, W_j \rangle)$. Since $\mathbf{w}'' \neq W_j'$, this means that we have found a witness violating the binding property of the commitment scheme. We conclude that either M is a permutation matrix, or the binding property of the commitment scheme does not hold. We conclude further that we either violate the binding property of the commitment scheme, or we have that $\mathbf{w}'' = W_j$, meaning that $W_j' = MW_j$, for all $j \in \{0, ..., n\}$.

4.3   Proof of Shuffle on the Public Board

A verifiable shuffle for the public board is given in Protocol 2. Note that it is very similar to the shuffle in Protocol 1. The difference is that on the public board, the shuffle is performed on the two last components of each ciphertext, rather than on the full ciphertext. Let $\mathscr{R}_\pi$ and $\mathscr{R}_{com}$ be as in Sect. 4.2. Let $\mathscr{R}_{ReRand}^{shuf}(pk, \mathbf{d}, \mathbf{d}')(\pi, \mathbf{r}')$, where π is a permutation on $\{1, ..., n\}$, be the relation which holds if $d_i' = \mathsf{ReRand}(d_{\pi(i)}; r_{\pi(i)}')$ for all $i \in \{1, ..., n\}$, where $\mathsf{ReRand}(d_i; r_i') = (h^{r_{i,1}+r_{i,1}'} h_1^{r_{i,2}+r_{i,2}'}, mg_1^{r_{i,2}+r_{i,2}'})$ for $d_i = (h^{r_{i,1}} h_1^{r_{i,2}}, mg_1^{r_{i,2}})$ and random $\mathbf{r}, \mathbf{r}' \in (\mathbb{Z}_q \times \mathbb{Z}_q)^n$.

Theorem 2. *Protocol 2 is a perfectly complete, 4-round special soundness, special honest-verifier zero-knowledge proof of knowledge of the relation $\mathscr{R}_{com} \vee (\mathscr{R}_\pi \wedge \mathscr{R}_{ReRand}^{shuf})$.*

The proof is very similar to the proof of Theorem 1 and will be omitted.

4.4   Applying the Fiat-Shamir Heuristic

We now describe how we can make the shuffle non-interactive, by applying the Fiat-Shamir heuristic [5]. The main idea is to replace the challenges sent by the verifier (in step 1 and 3) by a call to some hash function, making the challenges look random. This is straight-forward, but we do not want to run the argument twice, once for the public board and once for the private board. We want to have only one computation. It is easy to see that the interactive public board argument can be extracted from the interactive private board argument, but applying Fiat-Shamir is not straight-forward now, since different knowledge is available in the two cases.

The idea is to use a nested hash function for the private board argument, and then provide the inner hash value as part of the public board argument. This allows us to extract the public board argument from the private board argument by replacing the knowledge that is not present on the public board by their hash value. In order to ensure that no knowledge leaks, we actually commit to the hash of the private values, so that we can prove that the hash value does not contain any information about the private values. This is safe, since commitments are binding.

To obtain $\mathbf{w}$, we first hash the parts of the common input on the private board that is not part of the common input on the public board, i.e. the first three components of the CCE ciphertexts. We then commit to this hash, and hash the commitment along with the part of the common input that is also present on the public board. The challenge $\mathbf{w}$ is set to be this second hash value. The commitment is posted on the public board and opened on the private board.

The challenge β is obtained in a similar manner. We first hash the information on the private board that is not present on the public board, commit to this hash, post the commitment on the public board and then open the commitment on the private board. Further, the commitment is hashed along with the information on the private board that is also present on the public board. This hash is set to be the challenge value β.

5 Machine Checked Proof

Having given a paper proof of the mixnet we now turn our attention to the machine checked proof. One approach would be to codify the above paper proof in an interactive theorem prover. However, codifying such proofs is a complex process, so instead we reuse previous work. The idea is that our variant of the mixnet has a machine checked proof. The gap is that the mixnet is not proved for our particular encryption scheme. But the existing proof applies to a large class of encryption schemes. We need only prove that our scheme is in this class, after which we know that the general results also applies to our concrete mixnet.

For the machine checked proof we will make use of the interactive theorem prover Coq. Our work expands upon Haines et al. [10]; who demonstrated how interactive theorem provers and code extraction can be used to gain much higher confidence in the outcome of elections; they achieved this by using the interactive theorem prover Coq and its code extraction facility to produce verifiers, for verifiable voting schemes, with the verifiers proven to be cryptographically correct. They also showed that it was possible to verify the correctness (completeness, soundness and zero-knowledge) of a proof of correct shuffle. Their work

Protocol 2. Interactive ZK-Proof of Shuffle on Public Board

Common Input: A public key pk, a matrix commitment $\mathbf{u}$, commitment parameters $\gamma, \gamma_1, ..., \gamma_n$ and vectors $\mathbf{d}, \mathbf{d'} \in (\mathbb{G}_2 \times \mathbb{G}_1)^n$.

Private Input: Permutation matrix $M \in \mathbb{Z}_q^{n \times n}$ and randomness $\mathbf{t} \in \mathbb{Z}_q^n$ such that $\mathbf{u} = \mathsf{Com}(M, \mathbf{t})$. Randomness $\mathbf{r} \in (\mathbb{Z}_q \times \mathbb{Z}_q)^n$ such that $d_i' = \mathsf{ReRand}(d_{\pi(i)}, r_{\pi(i)})$ for $i = 1, ..., n$.

1: $\mathcal{V}$ chooses a random $\mathbf{w} \in \mathbb{Z}_q^n$ and sends $\mathbf{w}$ to $\mathcal{P}$.

2: $\mathcal{P}$ computes $\mathbf{w'} = (w_1', ..., w_n') = M\mathbf{w}$, and randomly chooses $\hat{\mathbf{t}} = (\hat{t}_1, ..., \hat{t}_n)$, $\hat{\mathbf{z}} = (\hat{z}_1, ..., \hat{z}_n)$, $\mathbf{z'} = (z_1', ..., z_n') \in \mathbb{Z}_q^n$, $z_1, z_2, z_3 \in \mathbb{Z}_q$ and $\tilde{\mathbf{z}} = (\tilde{z}_1, \tilde{z}_2) \in \mathbb{Z}_q^2$. $\mathcal{P}$ defines

$$\bar{t} = \langle \mathbf{1}, \mathbf{t} \rangle, \quad \tilde{t} = \langle \mathbf{t}, \mathbf{w} \rangle, \quad \hat{t} = \hat{t}_n + \sum_{i=1}^{n-1} \left(\hat{t}_i \prod_{j=i+1}^{n} w_j' \right) \text{ and}$$

$$\mathbf{r'} = \left(\sum_{i=1}^{n} r_{i,1} w_i, \sum_{i=1}^{n} r_{i,2} w_i \right),$$

and sends the following elements to $\mathcal{V}$ (for $i = 1, ..., n$):

$$\hat{u}_0 = \gamma_1 \qquad \hat{u}_i = \gamma^{\hat{t}_i} (\hat{u}_{i-1})^{w_i'} \qquad a_1 = \gamma^{z_1} \qquad a_2 = \gamma^{z_2}$$

$$a_3 = \gamma^{z_3} \Pi_{i=1}^n \gamma_i^{z_i'} \qquad a_4 = (h^{\tilde{z}_1} h_1^{\tilde{z}_2}, g_1^{\tilde{z}_2}) \Pi_{i=1}^n (d_i')^{z_i'}$$

$$\hat{a}_i = \gamma^{\hat{z}_i} (\hat{u}_{i-1})^{z_i'}.$$

3: $\mathcal{V}$ chooses a random challenge $\beta \in \mathbb{Z}_q$ and sends β to $\mathcal{P}$.

4: For $i \in \{1, ..., n\}$, $\mathcal{P}$ responds with

$$b_1 = z_1 + \beta \cdot \bar{t} \qquad b_2 = z_2 + \beta \cdot \hat{t} \qquad b_3 = z_3 + \beta \cdot \tilde{t}$$

$$\tilde{\mathbf{b}} = \tilde{\mathbf{z}} - \beta \cdot \mathbf{r'} \qquad \hat{b}_i = \hat{z}_i + \beta \cdot \hat{t}_i \qquad b_i' = z_i' + \beta \cdot w_i'.$$

5: $\mathcal{V}$ accepts if and only if, for $i \in \{1, ..., n\}$

$$a_1 = (\Pi_{i=1}^n u_i / \Pi_{i=1}^n \gamma_i)^{-\beta} \cdot \gamma^{b_1} \qquad a_2 = (\hat{u}_n / \gamma_1^{\Pi_{i=1}^n w_i})^{-\beta} \cdot \gamma^{b_2}$$

$$a_3 = (\Pi_{i=1}^n u_i^{w_i})^{-\beta} \cdot \gamma^{b_3} \cdot \Pi_{i=1}^n \gamma_i^{b_i'}$$

$$a_4 = (\Pi_{i=1}^n d_i^{w_i})^{-\beta} \cdot (h^{\tilde{b}_1} h_1^{\tilde{b}_2}, g_1^{\tilde{b}_2}) \cdot \Pi_{i=1}^n (d_i')^{b_i'}$$

$$\hat{a}_i = (\hat{u}_i)^{-\beta} \cdot \gamma^{\hat{b}_i} \cdot (\hat{u}_{i-1})^{b_i'}$$

was subsequently expanded upon by [9] who removed a number of limitations in the original work and expanded the result. Specifically they proved that for any encryption scheme that falls within a class, which they formally defined, it can be securely mixed in the optimised variant of Wikström's mixnet. We exploit this result by proving that PPATC falls within this class and hence can be verifiably mixed by Wikström's mixnet. Note that the mixnet generated in the Coq code is equivalent to Protocol 1.

In the rest of this section we will present our work in standard notation. Interested readers can find the Coq code at https://github.com/gerlion/secure-e-voting-with-coq. We begin by proving that the ciphertext space is a group. Let $\mathbb{G}_1$ and $\mathbb{G}_2$ represent the elements of the two groups of the bilinear pairing both of which are of prime order p. We let the set S of the ciphertext space equal $\mathbb{G}_1 \times \mathbb{G}_1 \times \mathbb{G}_1 \times \mathbb{G}_2 \times \mathbb{G}_1$. All operations are performed pairwise and the group axioms are satisfied trivially.

We then show that the ciphertext group is isomorphic to a vector space over the field of integers modulo p. This follows directly from the fact that two groups of the same order are themselves isomorphic to vector spaces over the field of integers modulo p. We are now ready to define the encryption scheme. Beyond the groups already mentioned we denote the field of integers modulo p as $\mathbb{F}$.

Key generation space $:= \mathbb{G}_1 \times \mathbb{G}_2 \times \mathbb{G}_2 \times \mathbb{F} \times \mathbb{F}$.
Public key space $:= \mathbb{G}_1 \times \mathbb{G}_2 \times \mathbb{G}_2 \times \mathbb{G}_1 \times \mathbb{G}_1$.
Secret key space $:= \mathbb{F} \times \mathbb{F}$.
Message space $:= \mathbb{G}_1$.
Randomness space $:= \mathbb{F} \times \mathbb{F} \times \mathbb{F}$.
Key generation $:=$ On input (g, h, h_1, x_1, x_2) from key generation space output public key $(g, h, h_1, g^{x_1}, g^{x_2})$ and secret key (x_1, x_2)
Encryption $:=$ On input public key (g, h, h_1, y_1, y_2), message m, and randomness (r_1, r_2, r_3) and output ciphertext $(g^{r_1}, g^{r_2}, y_2^{r_2} g^{r_3}, h^{r_3} h_1^{r_1}, y_1^{r_1} m)$.
Decryption $:=$ Given secret key (x_1, x_2) and ciphertext $(c_1, c_2, c_3, c_4, c_5)$ and return $c_5 / c_1^{x_1}$.

To show that the encryption scheme can be correctly mixed we need to prove the three theorems stated below. We also require the vector space properties for the spaces defined above, see the Coq code for a formal definition of these properties.

```
Lemma correct : forall (kgr : KGR)(m : M)(r : Ring.F),
let (pk,sk) := keygen kgr in
dec sk (enc pk m r) = m.
```

Theorem 3. *Correctness:* $\forall kgr \in$ *Key generation space*, $m \in$ *Message space*, $r \in$ *Randomness space*, $(pk, sk) =$ *Key generation*(kgr), *Decryption*$(sk$ *Encryption*$(pk\ m\ r)) = m$.

The correctness of PPATC follows directly from the correctness of ElGamal.

```
Lemma homomorphism : forall (pk : PK)(m m' : M)(r r' : Ring.F),
C.Gdot (enc pk m' r')(enc pk m r) =
enc pk (Mop m m') (Ring.Fadd r r').
```

Theorem 4. *Homomorphism:* $\forall pk \in$ *Public key space*, $m\ m' \in$ *Message space*, $r\ r' \in$ *Randomness space*, *Encryption*$(pk\ m\ r) \times$ *Encryption*$(pk\ m'\ r') =$ *Encryption*$(pk\ (m \cdot m')\ (r * r'))$

The homomorphic property of PPATC follows from the homomorphic properties of ElGamal and Abe *et al.*'s commitments.

```
Lemma encOfOnePrec : forall (pk : PK)(a : Ring.F)(b: F),
(VS.op (enc pk Mzero a) b) = enc pk Mzero (MVS.op3 a b).
```

Theorem 5. *Encryption of one preserved:* $\forall pk \in$ *Public key space,* r $r' \in$ *Randomness space, Encryption(pk 1 a)^b = Encryption(pk 1 (a * b)).*

To see that this property holds, first consider a PPATC ciphertext encrypting zero $(g^{r_1}, g^{r_2}, y_2^{r_2} g^{r_3}, h^{r_3} h_1^{r_1}, y_1^{r_1})$. Now observe that raising it to any power a is an encryption of one with randomness $(r_1 a, r_2 a, r_3 a)$, $(g^{r_1}, g^{r_2}, y_2^{r_2} g^{r_3}, h^{r_3} h_1^{r_1}, y_1^{r_1})^a = (g^{r_1 a}, g^{r_2 a}, y_2^{r_2 a} g^{r_3 a}, h^{r_3 a} h_1^{r_1 a}, y_1^{r_1 a})$.

This suffices for a proof that the PPATC scheme can be safely mixed by the optimised variant of the Wikström's mixnet. Readers will have noted that we proved the scheme for any pair of groups with the same prime order. Technically, we didn't even require that there exists a bilinear pairing between them, though this would be required to get the verifiable component of the Abe *et al.* commitments to work. The current work could be extracted into OCaml code and appropriate groups provided to check election transcripts. However, further work is ongoing in Coq to allow these groups to be instantiated within Coq.

6   Conclusion

We have given a paper proof for a variant of the optimised Wikström's mixnet for the PPATC encryption scheme. This is a useful result for anyone wanting to build an efficient e-voting scheme with everlasting privacy which can handle arbitrary ballots. In addition we provide a machine checked proof of the mixnet.

Acknowledgments. This work was supported by the Luxembourg National Research Fund (FNR) and the Research Council of Norway for the joint project SURCVS.

References

1. Abe, M., Haralambiev, K., Ohkubo, M.: Group to group commitments do not shrink. In: Pointcheval, D., Johansson, T. (eds.) EUROCRYPT 2012. LNCS, vol. 7237, pp. 301–317. Springer, Heidelberg (2012). https://doi.org/10.1007/978-3-642-29011-4_19
2. Chaum, D.: Untraceable electronic mail, return addresses, and digital pseudonyms. Commun. ACM **24**(2), 84–88 (1981)
3. Cramer, R., Franklin, M., Schoenmakers, B., Yung, M.: Multi-authority secret-ballot elections with linear work. In: Maurer, U. (ed.) EUROCRYPT 1996. LNCS, vol. 1070, pp. 72–83. Springer, Heidelberg (1996). https://doi.org/10.1007/3-540-68339-9_7
4. Cuvelier, É., Pereira, O., Peters, T.: Election verifiability or ballot privacy: do we need to choose? In: Crampton, J., Jajodia, S., Mayes, K. (eds.) ESORICS 2013. LNCS, vol. 8134, pp. 481–498. Springer, Heidelberg (2013). https://doi.org/10.1007/978-3-642-40203-6_27

5. Fiat, A., Shamir, A.: How to prove yourself: practical solutions to identification and signature problems. In: Odlyzko, A.M. (ed.) CRYPTO 1986. LNCS, vol. 263, pp. 186–194. Springer, Heidelberg (1987). https://doi.org/10.1007/3-540-47721-7_12

6. Fujisaki, E., Okamoto, T.: Statistical zero knowledge protocols to prove modular polynomial relations. In: Kaliski, B.S. (ed.) CRYPTO 1997. LNCS, vol. 1294, pp. 16–30. Springer, Heidelberg (1997). https://doi.org/10.1007/BFb0052225

7. Gjøsteen, K., Haines, T., Solberg, M.R.: Efficient mixing of arbitrary ballots with everlasting privacy: how to verifiably mix the PPATC scheme (full version). Cryptology ePrint Archive, Report 2020/1331 (2020). https://eprint.iacr.org/2020/1331

8. Haenni, R., Locher, P., Koenig, R., Dubuis, E.: Pseudo-code algorithms for verifiable re-encryption mix-nets. In: Brenner, M., et al. (eds.) FC 2017. LNCS, vol. 10323, pp. 370–384. Springer, Cham (2017). https://doi.org/10.1007/978-3-319-70278-0_23

9. Haines, T., Goré, R., Sharma, B.: Did you mix me? Formally verifying verifiable mix nets in voting. In: 2021 IEEE Symposium on Security and Privacy, SP 2021, San Jose, CA, USA, May 23–27, 2021. IEEE (2021)

10. Haines, T., Goré, R., Tiwari, M.: Verified verifiers for verifying elections. In: Cavallaro, L., Kinder, J., Wang, X., Katz, J. (eds.) Proceedings of the 2019 ACM SIGSAC Conference on Computer and Communications Security, CCS 2019, London, UK, November 11–15, 2019, pp. 685–702. ACM (2019)

11. Haines, T., Gritti, C.: Improvements in everlasting privacy: efficient and secure zero knowledge proofs. In: Krimmer, R., et al. (eds.) E-Vote-ID 2019. LNCS, vol. 11759, pp. 116–133. Springer, Cham (2019). https://doi.org/10.1007/978-3-030-30625-0_8

12. Moran, T., Naor, M.: Split-ballot voting: everlasting privacy with distributed trust. ACM Trans. Inf. Syst. Secur. **13**(2), 16:1–16:43 (2010)

13. Paillier, P.: Public-key cryptosystems based on composite degree residuosity classes. In: Stern, J. (ed.) EUROCRYPT 1999. LNCS, vol. 1592, pp. 223–238. Springer, Heidelberg (1999). https://doi.org/10.1007/3-540-48910-X_16

14. Pedersen, T.P.: Non-interactive and information-theoretic secure verifiable secret sharing. In: Feigenbaum, J. (ed.) CRYPTO 1991. LNCS, vol. 576, pp. 129–140. Springer, Heidelberg (1992). https://doi.org/10.1007/3-540-46766-1_9

15. Terelius, B., Wikström, D.: Proofs of restricted shuffles. In: Bernstein, D.J., Lange, T. (eds.) AFRICACRYPT 2010. LNCS, vol. 6055, pp. 100–113. Springer, Heidelberg (2010). https://doi.org/10.1007/978-3-642-12678-9_7

Applied Cryptography

(F)unctional Sifting: A Privacy-Preserving Reputation System Through Multi-Input Functional Encryption

Alexandros Bakas[1]([⊠]), Antonis Michalas[1], and Amjad Ullah[2]

[1] Tampere University of Technology, Tampere, Finland
{alexandros.bakas,antonios.michalas}@tuni.fi
[2] Univeristy of Westminster, London, UK
A.Ullah@westminster.ac.uk

Abstract. Functional Encryption (FE) allows users who hold a specific secret key (known as the functional key) to learn a specific function of encrypted data whilst learning nothing about the content of the underlying data. Considering this functionality and the fact that the field of FE is still in its infancy, we sought a route to apply this potent tool to solve the existing problem of designing decentralised additive reputation systems. To this end, we first built a symmetric FE scheme for the ℓ_1 norm of a vector space, which allows us to compute the sum of the components of an encrypted vector (i.e. the votes). Then, we utilized our construction, along with functionalities offered by Intel SGX, to design the first FE-based decentralized additive reputation system with Multi-Party Computation. While our reputation system faces certain limitations, this work is amongst the first attempts that seek to utilize FE in the solution of a real-life problem.

Keywords: Functional Encryption · Multi-client · Multi-input · Multi-Party Computation · Reputation system

1 Introduction

Functional Encryption (FE) is an emerging cryptographic technique that allows selective computations over encrypted data. FE schemes provide a key generation algorithm that outputs decryption keys with remarkable capabilities. More precisely, each decryption key FK is associated with a function f. In contrast to traditional cryptographic techniques, using FK on a ciphertext Enc(x) does not recover x but the function $f(x)$ – thus keeping the actual value x private.

This work was funded by the ASCLEPIOS: Advanced Secure Cloud Encrypted Platform for Internationally Orchestrated Solutions in Healthcare Project No. 826093 EU research project.

M. Asplund and S. Nadjm-Tehrani (Eds.): NordSec 2020, LNCS 12556, pp. 111–126, 2021.
https://doi.org/10.1007/978-3-030-70852-8_7

While the first definition of FE allowed the decryption of a single ciphertext per decryption, more recent works [12] introduced the more general notion of multi-input FE (MIFE). In a MIFE scheme, given ciphertexts $\mathsf{Enc}(x_1), \ldots, \mathsf{Enc}(x_n)$, a user can use FK to recover $f(x_1, \ldots, x_n)$. This new definition, seems to make MIFE a perfect fit in many real-life applications.

Having identified the importance of FE and believing that it is a family of modern encryption schemes that can push us into an uncharted technological terrain, we try to make a first attempt to smooth out the identified asymmetries between theory and practice. To do so, we first design a MIFE scheme for the ℓ_1 norm of a vector space based on [1]. Then, using our MIFE scheme we attempt a first approach in embedding FE into the design of a decentralized additive reputation system [10].

In particular, we show how MIFE can be leveraged to construct privacy-preserving decentralized additive reputation systems. A reputation system rates the behaviour of each user, based on the quality of the provided service(s), and gives information to the community in order to decide whether to trust an entity in the network. Furthermore, the absence of schemes that provide privacy in decentralized environments, such as ad-hoc networks, is even greater [10]. Our focus is on how to utilize FE and extend existing techniques in order to use this cryptographic primitive to solve the problem of casting and collecting votes in a privacy-preserving way.

Contribution: The contribution of this paper is twofold:

C1 First, we design a MIFE scheme in the symmetric key setting for the ℓ_1 norm of a vector, based on the single-client MIFE for inner products presented in [1]. Then, we show how our scheme can be transformed from the single-client to the multi-client setting. This transformation requires the users to perform a Multi-Party Computation (MPC). More precisely, each user generates their own symmetric keys independently and then they collaborate to calculate a functional decryption key sk_f that is derived from a combination of all the generated symmetric keys. This result is quite remarkable since users generate their private keys locally and independently. As a result, their symmetric keys are never exposed to unauthorized parties, and thus no private information about the content of the underlying ciphertexts is revealed. At the same time, sufficient information to generate the functional decryption key is provided.

C2 Our second contribution derives from the identified need to create a dialogue between the theoretical concept of FE and real life applications. As a result, we tried to provide a pathway towards new prospects that show the direct and realistic applicability of this promising encryption technique when applied to concrete obstacles. To this end, we showed how our MIFE scheme can be used to provide a solution to the problem of designing an additive reputation system. More specifically, we use our Multi-client MIFE to design a protocol that preserves the privacy of votes in decentralized environments. The protocol allows n participants to securely cast their ratings in a way that preserves the privacy of individual votes. More precisely, we analyze the protocol and prove that it is resistant to collusion even against up to $n - 1$ corrupted insiders.

2   Related Work

Functional Encryption: While numerous studies with general definitions and generic constructions of FE have been proposed [4,8,12–14,18] there is a clear lack of work proposing FE schemes supporting specific functions – a necessary step that would allow FE to transcend its limitations and provide the foundations for reaching its full potential. To the best of our knowledge, the only works that have shown how to efficiently run specific functions on ciphertexts is [1,2] which calculates inner-product and [17] which successfully executes computations with quadratic polynomials. While [1] and [8] are symmetric FE schemes (i.e. efficient), their actual application in real-life scenarios can be considered as limited since both are limited to supporting the single-client model. Our work is heavily influenced by the symmetric key MIFE scheme for inner products presented in [1] where authors designed a scheme that can be regarded as the FE equivalent of the one-time-pad and by [7], where two different FE-based applications are presented. In particular, in [7], authors presented a Functionally Encrypted private database, and an Order Revealing Encryption scheme that can be leveraged to design Symmetric Searchable Encryption schemes with range queries support [5,6]. More precisely, using [1] as a basis, we constructed a symmetric key MIFE scheme for the ℓ_1 norm of an arbitrary vector space. Most importantly, we show that our construction can also support the multi-client model while preserving exactly the same security properties as the MIFE for inner-product in [1]. This is a significant result as it proves that functional encryption can be efficiently applied to solve more complex problems.

Reputation Systems: In [16], authors designed a privacy-preserving reputation system and according to them *"The logic of anonymous feedback to a reputation system is analogous to the logic of anonymous voting in a political system"*. To ensure the confidentiality of the votes, authors use primitives such as the secure sum and verifiable secret sharing. In [15], a new approach was presented based on homomorphic encryption and zero-knowledge proofs. In particular, authors proved that by using their construction, the privacy of a user can be preserved even in the presence of multiple malicious adversaries. In [10] authors presented two protocols with similar architecture as in [15]. However, their constructions were significantly more efficient since they did not rely on homomorphic encryption, while at the same time, they reduced the number of the exchanged messages. Despite the efficiency of these approaches, it is our firm belief that functional encryption is a cryptographic paradigm that squarely fits the field of reputation systems, and it has all the necessary traits to provide more a well-rounded and versatile solution. Having identified this research gap in the field, we present a description of a reputation system based on a MIFE scheme that can efficiently calculate the sum of multiple encrypted numbers.

3 Preliminaries

Notation: If $\mathcal{Y}$ is a set, we use $y \xleftarrow{\$} \mathcal{Y}$ if y is chosen uniformly at random from $\mathcal{Y}$. The cardinality of a set $\mathcal{Y}$ is denoted by $|\mathcal{Y}|$. For a positive integer m, $[m]$ denotes the set $\{1, \ldots, m\}$. If $m \in \mathbb{Z}$, we denote by $m[i]$ the digit in the i-th position of m where $m[0]$ is the rightmost digit. The number of digits of m in base n is $\lfloor log_n m \rfloor + 1$. Vectors are denoted in bold as $\mathbf{x} = [x_1, \ldots, x_n]$. A probabilistic polynomial time (PPT) adversary $\mathcal{ADV}$ is a randomized algorithm for which there exists a polynomial $p(z)$ such that for all input z, the running time of $\mathcal{ADV}(z)$ is bounded by $p(|z|)$. A function $negl(\cdot)$ is called negligible if $\forall c \in \mathbb{N}, \exists \epsilon_0 \in \mathbb{N}$ such that $\forall \epsilon \geq \epsilon_0 : negl(\epsilon) < \epsilon^{-c}$. A probabilistic polynomial time (PPT) adversary $\mathcal{ADV}$ is a randomized algorithm for which there exists a polynomial $p(z)$ such that for all input z, the running time of $\mathcal{ADV}(z)$ is bounded by $p(|z|)$. A function $negl(\cdot)$ is called negligible if $\forall c \in \mathbb{N}, \exists \epsilon_0 \in \mathbb{N}$ such that $\forall \epsilon \geq \epsilon_0 : negl(\epsilon) < \epsilon^{-c}$.

Users, which in our scenario will be voters, are denoted by $\mathcal{U} = \{u_1, \ldots u_\ell\}$. The universe of votes is $\mathcal{V} = \{v_1, \ldots, v_\ell\}$. We assume a star-based system in the likes of well-known applications such as AirBnb and ebay. However, we let the number of stars be an a set $\mathcal{ST} = \{n^1, \ldots, n^k\}$ of arbitrary cardinality. Hence, if a user wishes u_i wishes to rate another user with j stars, then u_i's vote is $v_i = n^j$. We now proceed with the definition of a decentralized additive reputation system, as described in [16]

Definition 1. *A reputation system R is said to be a Decentralized Additive Reputation System, if it satisfies the following two requirements:*

1. *Feedback collection, combination and propagation are implemented in a decentralized way.*
2. *Combination of feedbacks provided by the users is calculated in an additive manner.*

Definition 2 (Inner Product). *The inner product (or dot product) of $\mathbb{Z}^n$ is a function $\langle , \rangle$ defined by:*

$$f(\mathbf{x}, \mathbf{y}) = \langle \mathbf{x}, \mathbf{y} \rangle = x_1 y_1 + \cdots + x_n y_n, \text{ for } \mathbf{x} = [x_1, \ldots, x_n], \mathbf{y} = [y_1, \ldots, y_n] \in \mathbb{Z}^n$$

Definition 3. (ℓ_1 norm). *The ℓ_1 norm of $\mathbb{Z}^n$ is a function $\|\cdot\|_1$ defined by:*

$$f(x) = \|\mathbf{x}\|_1 = \sum_{i=1}^{i=n} x_i = x_1 + \cdots + x_n, \text{ for } \mathbf{x} = [x_1, \ldots, x_n] \in \mathbb{Z}^n$$

From Definitions 2 and 3, it follows directly that if $\mathbf{x} = [x_1, \ldots, x_n] \in \mathbb{Z}^n$ and $\mathbf{y} = [1, \ldots, 1] \in \mathbb{Z}^n$ then $\langle \mathbf{x}, \mathbf{y} \rangle = x_1 \cdot 1 + \cdots + x_n \cdot 1 = \sum_{i=1}^{n} x_i = \|\mathbf{x}\|_1$.

Below, we define MIFE in the symmetric key setting. Note that while this definition suits the single-client model, it is inadequate for a multi-client setup.

Definition 4 (Multi-Input Functional Encryption in the Symmetric Key Setting). *Let $\mathcal{F} = \{f_1, \ldots, f_n\}$ be a family of n-ary functions where each f_i is defined as follows: $f_i : \mathbb{Z}^n \to \mathbb{Z}$. A multi-input functional encryption scheme for $\mathcal{F}$ consists of the following algorithms:*

- $\mathsf{Setup}(1^\lambda)$*: Takes as input a security parameter λ and outputs a secret key* $\mathbf{K} = [\mathsf{k}_1, \ldots, \mathsf{k}_n] \in \mathbb{Z}^n$.
- $\mathsf{Enc}(\mathsf{K}, i, x_i)$ *: Takes as input $\mathbf{K}$, an index $i \in [n]$ and a message $x_i \in \mathcal{X}$ and outputs a ciphertext ct_i.*
- $\mathsf{KeyGen}(\mathbf{K})$*: Takes as input $\mathbf{K}$ and outputs a functional decryption key FK*[1].
- $\mathsf{Dec}(\mathsf{FK}, ct_1, \ldots, ct_n)$*: Takes as input a decryption key FK for a function f_i and n ciphertexts and outputs a value $y \in \mathcal{Y}$.*

For the needs of our work, we borrow the one-adaptive (one-AD) and one-selective (one-SEL) security definitions from [1] that were first formalized in [3]. Informally, in the one-AD-IND security game, the adversary $\mathcal{ADV}$ receives the encryption key of the MIFE scheme and then adaptively queries the corresponding oracle for functional decryption keys of her choice. Furthermore, $\mathcal{ADV}$ outputs two messages x_0 and x_1 to the encryption oracle, who flips a random coin and outputs an encryption of $x_\beta, \beta \in \{0, 1\}$. If the functional keys are associated with functions that do not distinguish between the messages (*i.e.*$f(x_0) = f(x_1)$) then $\mathcal{ADV}$ should *not* be able to distinguish between the encryption of x_0 and x_1. In the case of the one-SEL-IND security, the game is identical to the one-AD-IND case, with the only difference being that $\mathcal{ADV}$ needs to decide on the x_0 and x_1 messages *before* seeing the encryption key. The *"one"* in both security games determines that the encryption oracle can only be queried once for each slot i (i.e. the adversary is not allowed to issue multiple queries to the encryption oracle for the same x_i).

Definition 5 (one-AD-IND-secure MIFE). *For every MIFE scheme for $\mathcal{F}$, every PPT adversary $\mathcal{ADV}$, and every security parameter $\lambda \in \mathbb{N}$ we define the following experiment for $\beta \in \{0, 1\}$:*

Adaptive Security

$one\text{-}AD\text{-}IND_\beta^{MIFE}(1^\lambda, \mathcal{ADV})$:

$\mathbf{K} \leftarrow \mathsf{Setup}(1^\lambda)$
$\alpha \leftarrow \mathcal{ADV}^{\mathsf{KeyGen}(\mathbf{K}), \mathsf{Enc}(\cdot, \cdot, \cdot)}$
Output α

Where $\mathsf{Enc}(\cdot, \cdot, \cdot)$ is an oracle that on input (i, x_i^0, x_i^1), flips a random coin β and outputs $\mathsf{Enc}(\mathsf{K}, i, x_i^\beta), \beta \in \{0, 1\}$. Moreover, $\mathcal{ADV}$ is restricted to only make queries to the KeyGen oracle satisfying $f(x_1^0, \ldots, x_n^0) = f(x_1^1, \ldots, x_n^1)$. A MIFE

---

[1] In the literature, this algorithm can often be found as $\mathsf{KeyGen}(\mathbf{K}, f)$ where it outputs an FK for a specific function f. This is the case, with the MIFE scheme from [1] presented in Sect. 4. In our case, we only work with one function, so we can omit the f term in the definition of the algorithm.

scheme is said to be one-AD-IND secure if for all PPT adversaries $\mathcal{ADV}$, their advantage is negligible in λ where the advantage is defined as:

$$Adv^{one-AD-IND}(\lambda, \mathcal{ADV}) =$$

$$|Pr[one\text{-}AD\text{-}IND_0^{MIFE}(1^\lambda, \mathcal{ADV}) = 1] - Pr[one\text{-}AD\text{-}IND_1^{MIFE}(1^\lambda, \mathcal{ADV}) = 1]|$$

Definition 6 (one-SEL-IND-secure MIFE). *For every MIFE scheme for $\mathcal{F}$, every PPT adversary $\mathcal{ADV}$, and every security parameter $\lambda \in \mathbb{N}$ we define the following experiment for $\beta \in \{0,1\}$:*

___ Selective Security ___

> $one\text{-}SEL\text{-}IND_\beta^{MIFE}(1^\lambda, \mathcal{ADV})$:
> $\{x_i^b\}_{i \in [n], b \in \{0,1\}} \leftarrow \mathcal{ADV}(1^\lambda, f_i)$
> $\mathbf{K} \leftarrow \mathsf{Setup}(1^\lambda)$
> $ct_i = \mathsf{Enc}(\mathbf{K}, x_i^\beta)$
> $\alpha \leftarrow \mathcal{ADV}^{\mathsf{KeyGen}(\mathbf{K})}(\{ct_i\})$
> $Output\ \alpha$

$\mathcal{ADV}$ is restricted to only make queries to the KeyGen oracle satisfying $f(x_1^0, \ldots, x_n^0) = f(x_1^1, \ldots, x_n^1)$. A MIFE scheme is said to be one-SEL-IND secure if for all PPT adversaries $\mathcal{ADV}$, their advantage is negligible in λ where the advantage is defined as:

$$Adv^{one-SEL-IND}(\lambda, \mathcal{ADV}) =$$

$$|Pr[one\text{-}SEL\text{-}IND_0^{MIFE}(1^\lambda, \mathcal{ADV}) = 1] - Pr[one\text{-}SEL\text{-}IND_1^{MIFE}(1^\lambda, \mathcal{ADV}) = 1]|$$

Trusted Execution Environments: A Trusted Execution Environment (TEE) is a secure, integrity-protected environment, with processing, memory and storage capabilities, isolated from an untrusted, Rich Execution Environment that comprises the OS and installed applications. While there are several different TEEs in our work we rely on the use Intel SGX whose main functionalities are *(1)* Isolation, *(2)* Sealing and *(3)* Attestation. Due to space constraints, we ommit their formal description (more details can be found in [9]).

4   Multi-Input Functional Encryption for the ℓ_1 Norm

In this section, we present the first result and an important contribution of our work. In particular, in the first part of this section, we design a MIFE scheme for the ℓ_1 norm based on the construction presented in [1], while preserving exactly the same security properties. Then, we show how we can transform our construction from the single-client model to the multi-client one. The security of our MIFE schemes, is derived from the fact that they behave as the functional encryption equivalent of the one-time-pad. Note that, just like in the case of the one-time-pad, to achieve perfect secrecy, we require that $|k_i| \geq |x_i|$, where k_i is the encryption key and x_i, the message to be encrypted. Our construction is illustrated in Fig. 1. Since our construction is a special case of the scheme in Fig. [1], it is straight forward that the security proof of our scheme will be very similar to the one presented in [1].

```
Setup(1^λ) :                           KeyGen(K) :
∀ i ∈ [n], k_i ←$ Z                    Return FK = ||K||_1 = Σ_i^n k_i
Return K = [k_1, ..., k_n] ∈ Z^n
                                       Dec(FK, ct_1, ..., ct_n) :
Enc(K, i, x_i) :                       Return Σ_{i=1}^n ct_i - sk_f
Return ct_i = x_i + k_i
```

Fig. 1. one-AD-IND-secure MIFE for the ℓ_1 norm (MIFE_{ℓ_1}).

Theorem 1. *The MIFE scheme for the ℓ_1 norm (described in Fig. 1) is one-AD-IND-secure. That is, for all PPT adversaries $\mathcal{ADV}$:*

$$Adv_{\mathcal{ADV}}^{one-AD-IND}(\lambda) = 0$$

Proof. The proof consists of two parts. First we construct a selective distinguisher $\mathcal{B}$ whose advantage for the one-SEL-IND experiment is an upper bound for the advantage of any adaptive distinguisher $\mathcal{ADV}$. Then, using the fact that the MIFE for the ℓ_1 norm behaves like the one-time-pad, we prove that the advantage of $\mathcal{B}$ is zero.

For the first part of the proof we will use a complexity argument. In particular, let $\mathcal{B}$ be an adversary that guesses the challenge $\{x_i^b\}$ and then simulates the one-AD-IND experiment of $\mathcal{ADV}$. If $\mathcal{B}$ successfully guesses $\mathcal{ADV}$'s challenge then she can simulate $\mathcal{ADV}$'s view. Otherwise it outputs $\perp$. Hence, $\mathcal{ADV}$'s advantage maximizes when $\mathcal{B}$ guesses correctly the challenge. If the input space is $\mathcal{X}$, then $\mathcal{B}$ can guess successfully with probability exactly $|\mathcal{X}|^{-1}$. Hence:

$$Adv_{\mathcal{ADV}}^{one-AD-IND} \leq |X|^{-1} Adv_{\mathcal{B}}^{one-SEL-IND}$$

From the above, it can be seen that if the input space $\mathcal{X}$ is very large, the advantage of $\mathcal{ADV}$ tends to zero independently of the value of $Adv_{\mathcal{B}}^{one-SEL-IND}$ $\left(i.e.\ |\mathcal{X}| \to \infty \Rightarrow Adv_{\mathcal{ADV}}^{one-AD-IND} \to 0\right)$. However, we will still show that no matter the cardinality of $\mathcal{X}$, $Adv_{\mathcal{ADV}}^{one-AD-IND} = 0$. To do so, we will prove that $Adv_{\mathcal{B}}^{one-SEL-IND} = 0$. This will directly imply that $Adv_{\mathcal{ADV}}^{one-AD-IND} = 0$, since $Adv_{\mathcal{ADV}}^{one-AD-IND} \leq Adv_{\mathcal{B}}^{one-SEL-IND}$. In Fig. 2 we present a hybrid game that is identical to the one-SEL-IND security game. This is derived from the fact that if $u \xleftarrow{\$} Z$, then $\{u_i\}$ and $\{u_i - x_i^\beta\}$ are identical distributions. Finally, it is easy to see that the only information leaking about β, is $||\mathbf{r} - \mathbf{x}^\beta||$, which is independent of β according to the definition of the security game and the restrictions of the adversary.

While we showed how a MIFE scheme for inner products can be transformed into a MIFE scheme for the ℓ_1 norm, our construction is still inadequate for a reputation system. This is due to the fact that it only supports the single-client model. Assuming that such a model can be the right choice for a system that requires input from a large number of users can only be regarded as a fallacious

$$
\begin{array}{ll}
\underline{\text{Hybrid}_\beta(\lambda, \mathcal{B}):} & \underline{\mathcal{O}_{gen}(\mathbf{r}):} \\
\{x_i^b\}_{i \in [n], b \in \{0,1\}} \leftarrow \mathcal{B}(1^\lambda, \mathcal{F}) & \forall i \in [n]: \\
\forall i \in [n]: & \quad \mathsf{sk}_f = \|\mathbf{r} - \mathbf{x}^\beta\|_1 = \sum_{i=1}^n (r_i - x_i^\beta) \\
\quad r_i \xleftarrow{\$} \mathbb{Z} & \text{Return } \mathsf{sk}_f \\
\quad ct_i \leftarrow r_i & \\
\alpha \leftarrow \mathcal{B}^{\mathcal{O}_{gen}(\cdot)}(ct_i) & \\
\text{Output } \alpha &
\end{array}
$$

Fig. 2. Hybrid games for the proof of Theorem 1

conclusion. To this end, in Sect. 4.1, we show how we acutely attune our single client MIFE to support the multi-client model.

4.1 From Single-Client to Multi-Client MIFE

We are now ready to describe how we can transform our single-user MIFE_{ℓ_1} to the multi-user MIFE for the ℓ_1 norm (MUMIFE_{ℓ_1}). The idea is the following: Each user generates a symmetric key $k_i \in \mathbb{Z}$ which uses it to encrypt a plaintext x_i as $ct_i = k_i + x_i$. All the generated symmetric keys, form a vector $\mathbf{K} = [k_1, \ldots, k_n] \in \mathbb{Z}^n$, where n is the number of users. The functional decryption key FK is then $\|\mathbf{K}\|_1$ and decryption works as follows:

$$
\sum_{i=1}^n ct_i - \mathsf{FK} = \sum_1^n (k_i + x_i) - \sum_1^n k_i = \sum_1^n x_i = \|\mathbf{x}\|_1
$$

A third party decryptor who would get access to FK should only learn $\|\mathbf{x}\|_1$ and *not* each individual x_i. In addition to that, the users should never reveal their symmetric keys. To achieve this, we assume the existence of a trusted authority that will allow users to perform an MPC in order to jointly compute a masked version of FK without revealing each distinct k_i. Before we proceed to the actual description of our construction (Fig. 3), we present a high-level overview of our system model that consists of a trusted authority (TA) and an evaluator (EV) that evaluates the value of a function f on a set of given ciphertexts.

Trusted Authority (TA): TA is running in an enclave and is responsible for generating and distributing a unique random number s_i to each user u_i. The users will use the received random values to mask their symmetric keys. By doing so, and considering the fact that TA is running in an enclave and thus it is trusted, they will be able to jointly compute a masked version of the functional decryption key FK which will be used by the evaluator to calculate FK .

Evaluator (EV): EV is responsible for collecting all users' ciphertexts $\{ct_1, \ldots, ct_n\}$, generating the functional decryption key FK based on the masked value that will receive from users and finally, calculate $f(x_1, \ldots, x_n)$ without getting any valuable information about the individual values x_i.

Theorem 2. *The Multi-User Multi-Input Functional Encryption scheme for the ℓ_1 norm (described in Fig. 3) is one-AD-IND-secure. That is, for all PPT adversaries $\mathcal{ADV}$:*

$$Adv_{\mathcal{ADV}}^{one-AD-IND}(\lambda) = 0$$

Proof (Proof Sketch). The proof is omitted since it is a direct result from Theorem 1. This can be seen by the fact that the Encryption and KeyGen oracles are identical to the ones described in Fig. 2. The only difference is that in the case of MUMIFE$_{\ell_1}$, the Setup algorithm is executed by multiple users instead of one, since each user generates a distinct symmetric key. Without loss of generality, we can assume that this is exactly the same procedure since in the case of MIFE$_{\ell_1}$, one user samples n random numbers from $\mathbb{Z}$ resulting to a vector $\mathbf{K} = [k_1, \ldots, k_n]$, and in case of MUMIFE$_{\ell_1}$, n users sample one random number from $\mathbb{Z}$ each, resulting to a vector $\mathbf{K}' = [k_1', \ldots, k_n']$. However, the distributions $\{k_i\}$ and $\{k_i'\}$ are identical and thus we conclude that we can use exactly the same Hybrid game as the one in Fig. 2.

MUMIFE$_{\ell_1}$.Setup(1^λ) :

- $TA : \forall i \in [n], s_i \leftarrow \mathbb{Z}$
- $TA : s_i \to u_i$
- $TA : S = \|\mathbf{s}\|_1 = \sum_1^n s_i \to EV$
- u_i : Generates $k_i \in \mathbb{Z}$

MUMIFE$_{\ell_1}$.Enc(k_i, x_i, s_i)

$T = 0$

for $i = 1$ to n:

- $u_i : ct_i = k_i + x_i$
- $u_i : T = T + k_i + s_i$
- $u_i : ct_i \to EV$
- if $(i == n)$: $u_i : T \to EV$
  else $u_i : T \to u_{i+1}$

MUMIFE$_{\ell_1}$.KeyGen(T, S)

$EV : FK = T - S$

MUMIFE$_{\ell_1}$.Dec(FK, $ct_1, \ldots ct_n$)

$EV : \sum_{i=1}^n ct_i - FK$

Fig. 3. Multi-Input MIFE for the ℓ_1 norm (MUMIFE$_{\ell_1}$)

Correctness: The correctness of the MUMIFE$_{\ell_1}$ scheme presented in Fig. 3 follows directly since:

$$\sum_{i=1}^n ct_i - FK = \sum_{i=1}^n ct_i - T + S = \sum_{i=1}^n k_i + \sum_{i=1}^n x_i - \left(\sum_{i=1}^n (k_i + s_1)\right) + \sum_{i=1}^n s_i$$

$$= \sum_{\cancel{j}=1}^n k_i + \sum_{i=1}^n x_i - \sum_{\cancel{j}=1}^n k_i - \sum_{\cancel{j}=1}^n s_i + \sum_{\cancel{j}=1}^n s_i = \sum_{i=1}^n x_i = \|\mathbf{x}\|_1$$

5   The Reputation System

We begin this section by formalizing the problem that we are trying to solve.

Problem Statement: A user u_i demands feedback for another user u_j. To this end, she requests from other users on the network, to give their votes about u_j. The problem is to find a way that each vote v_i remains private while at the same time an evaluator EV would be in position of understanding what voters, as a whole, believe about u_j, by evaluating the sum of all votes.

Stars, Voters and Votes: As already stated, the stars are represented as a power of an integer n. Hence, for each vote v_i we have that $v_i = n^j$. The reason for representing votes in this way is that we can tell the final reputation score just by looking at the sum of the votes. This is because for all β in base n, we can represent β as a sum of powers of n. In other words:

$$\forall \beta \in \mathbb{Z}, \exists \beta_j \in \mathbb{Z} : \beta = \beta_0 n^0 + \cdots + \beta_{\lfloor log_n \beta \rfloor} n^{\lfloor log_n \beta \rfloor}$$

Hence, if $\sum_{i=0}^{n-1} v_i = \beta$:

$$\sum_{i=0}^{n-1} v_i = \beta = \sum_{j=0}^{\lfloor log_n \beta \rfloor} \beta_j n^j = \beta_0 n^0 + \beta_1 n^1 + \cdots + \beta_{\lfloor log_n \beta \rfloor} n^{\lfloor log_n \beta \rfloor} \in \mathbb{Z}^+,$$

then the coefficient of each n^j tells us how many voters voted for $v_i = n^j$. Moreover, on each round, we only allow $n - 1$ voters to cast their votes. The reason for allowing only $n - 1$ voters is to avoid multiple representations of the same number. Below we present a toy example to help the reader better understand the idea of our design:

Table 1. Voting Example with five voters and five candidates.

Voter u_i	Vote v_i	Sum
u_1	10^1	$10^1 + 10^3 + 10^0 + 10^1 + 10^4 = 11021$
u_2	10^3	
u_3	10^0	
u_4	10^1	
u_5	10^4	

Toy Example: For reasons of simplicity, let the base $n = 10$. We assume a scenario with a five-star system such as $n_0 = 10^0, n_1 = 10^1, n_2 = 10^2, n_3 = 10^3, n_4 = 10^4$ and five voters. Each voter casts her vote as shown in Table 1. After all voters cast their votes, we simply compute the sum $\sum v_i = 11021$. Hence, we see that the coefficients of the n^js are $\beta_0 = 1, \beta_1 = 2, \beta_2 = 0, \beta_3 = 1$ and $\beta_4 = 1$ and as a result, we conclude that one user gave a rating of 1 star

n^0, 4 stars n^3 and 5 stars n^4 (i.e. $\beta_0 = \beta_3 = \beta_4 = 1$), two gave a rating of two stars n^1 (i.e. $\beta_1 = 2$) and no one gave a rating of three stars. two users voted for n_1, one for n_0, n_3 and n_4 and no one voted for n_2. The reason for allowing only $n - 1$ users vote on each round, is because we want to achieve a unique representation of the sum of the votes. For instance, in this example, if we allowed more than $n - 1 = 10 - 1 = 9$ users to vote, then we could interpret 11021 as $11 \times 10^3 + 21 \times 10^0$ which cloud also mean that eleven users gave a rating of 4 stars and twenty-one users a rating of 1 star. By limiting the number of users to $n - 1$, we overcome this problem by achieving a unique representation of each number.

5.1 Formal Construction

In this section, we present our construction. Our scheme consists of three different phases, namely, Setup, Voting and Count. The topology of our construction is depicted in Fig. 4 and a formal description of our construction is presented in Fig. 5.

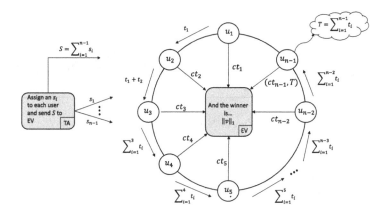

Fig. 4. Topology of the voting scheme

Setup: In the setup phase, TA picks the base n and places the $n - 1$ voters randomly in a circle. Then, generates $n - 1$ random values $\mathbf{s} = [s_1, \ldots, s_{n-1}] \in \mathbb{Z}^{n-1}$ and send an s_i to each u_i. Finally, it computes $\|\mathbf{s}\|_1 = \sum_{i=1}^{n-1} s_i = S$ and sends it to the evaluator EV.

Voting: The voters are voting one by one as follows: At first, u_1 generates an encryption key k_1 such that $\mathsf{k}_1 \in \mathbb{Z}$. Then, she picks her vote v_1 and runs MUMIFE.Enc(k_1, v_1, s_i). In particular, u_1 encrypts v_1 and then masks k_1 by calculating $t_1 = \mathsf{k}_1 + s_1$ where s_1 is the secret value received from the TA during the setup phase. Finally, u_1 sends ct_1 to EV and t_1 to u_2 – the next voter in the ring. The rest of the voters follow exactly the same steps except from the last user (u_{n-1}). In particular, u_{n-1}, apart from sending ct_{n-1} to EV, also sends $T = \sum_{i=1}^{n-1} t_i$. This sum will allow EV to compute the functional decryption key FK that will be used to compute the sum of the votes.

Count: After EV gets $n - 1$ votes, it first computes the function key FK based on the T and S values received during the voting phase. More precisely, EV computes $\mathsf{FK} = T - S = \|\mathsf{K}\|_1 = \sum_{i=1}^{n-1} \mathsf{k}_i$. Then, it simply runs $\mathsf{MUMIFE}_{\ell_1}.\mathsf{Dec}(\mathsf{FK}, ct_1, \ldots ct_n) \rightarrow \|v_i\|_1 = \sum_{i=1}^{n-1} v_i \in \mathbb{Z}^+$. Finally, by looking at the coefficients of the result, it can tell which candidate gathered the most votes.

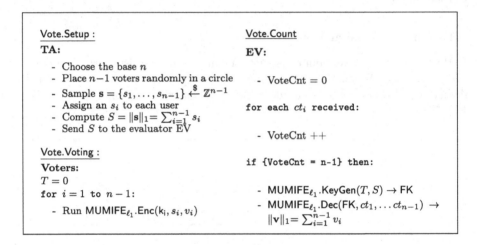

Fig. 5. Voting scheme

6   Security Analysis

In this section, we prove the security of our construction in the presence of an *honest-but-curious* adversary $\mathcal{ADV}$. In particular, we will prove that even if $\mathcal{ADV}$ corrupts $n-3$ of the total $n-1$ voters and EV, she will still not be able to deduce the votes of the uncorrupted voters.

Theorem 3. *Assume an honest-but-curious adversary $\mathcal{ADV}$ corrupts at most $d < n-2$ voters out of those who participate in an election round. Moreover, $\mathcal{ADV}$ corrupts the evaluator EV. Then $\mathcal{ADV}$ cannot deduce the votes of the legitimate voters.*

Proof. We are considering the most extreme case where $d = n - 3$. In this case, $\mathcal{ADV}$ has corrupted all but two voters, u_l and u_ℓ, and the evaluator EV. We start by looking exactly what information $\mathcal{ADV}$ possesses.

 – Since EV is corrupted, $\mathcal{ADV}$ knows $S = \|\mathsf{s}\| = \sum_{1}^{n-1} s_i$.

- For each corrupted voter u_{c_i}, $\mathcal{ADV}$ knows: Her vote, v_{c_i}, Her key k_{c_i} and Her share of the secret $\mathbf{s}$, s_{c_i}.
- For the legitimate voters u_l and u_ℓ, $\mathcal{ADV}$ knows: Their ciphertexts, $ct_l = v_l + r_l$ and $ct_\ell = v_\ell + r_\ell$ and The masked values of their keys k_l and k_ℓ as $t_l = k_l + s_l$ and $t_\ell = k_\ell + s_\ell$.

Note that for $\mathcal{ADV}$ to deduce the votes of u_l and u_ℓ, she must find the keys k_l and k_ℓ. To do so, she has to unmask the masked values $t_l = k_l + s_l$ and $t_\ell = k_\ell + m_\ell$. In other words, to learn the votes v_l and v_ℓ she either needs to find s_l and s_ℓ or k_l and ℓ. We present the above information in the form of equations. The circled terms are the ones $\mathcal{ADV}$ has not been able to compromise.

$$\|v\|_1 = \sum_{i \in [n-1] \setminus \{l, \ell\}} v_i + \textcircled{v_l} + \textcircled{v_ℓ} \qquad \|ct\|_1 = \sum_{i \in [n-1] \setminus \{l, \ell\}} ct_i + \underbrace{\textcircled{k_l} + \textcircled{v_l}}_{ct_l} + \underbrace{\textcircled{k_ℓ} + \textcircled{v_ℓ}}_{ct_\ell}$$

$$S = \sum_{i \in [n-1] \setminus \{l, \ell\}} s_i + \textcircled{s_l} + \textcircled{s_ℓ} \qquad T = \sum_{i \in [n-1] \setminus \{l, \ell\}} m_i + \underbrace{\textcircled{k_l} + \textcircled{s_l}}_{t_l} + \underbrace{\textcircled{k_ℓ} + \textcircled{s_ℓ}}_{t_\ell}$$

From the above equations, we see that for $\mathcal{ADV}$ to deduce the votes of u_l and u_ℓ, she needs to solve a system of four equations and six unknown variables. We thus conclude, that the protocol remains secure even in the extreme case where the evaluator, along with all but two voters are compromised.

7   Limitations

While this work is amongst the first that seeks to utilize FE to address real-life problems, we acknowledge that it faces certain limitations. However, it is our firm belief that our proposed schemes can serve as the basis for more advanced applications. In particular, we plan to extend our application in order to design a more sophisticated solutions to important and complex problem of designing a decentralized additive reputation system.

- **Threat Model:** The most important limitation of our construction directly affecting its security is the considered adversarial model. Our construction is secure under the not so realistic *honest-but-curious* threat model – a model that undoubtedly is inadequate for an e-voting protocol. This is due to the fact that it allows us to overlook important features that need to be appropriately addressed (e.g. double voting and validity of casted votes.).
- **Topology:** The ring topology we presented can be susceptible to various attacks, such as breaking the link between two voters. Additionally, the failure of a single node can cause the entire network to fail (ring down effect).
- **MPC Implies Synchronization:** Another limitation, also related to the adapted topology, is that since the voters need to participate in an MPC, we need to define a time interval where voters will be able to cast their votes.

Additionally, due to the fact that voters are jointly calculating the masked value T that will be sent to EV, we need to make sure that all voters will be online for a certain amount of time. Otherwise, this will lead to changes in the ring and will affect the entire performance of our construction.

8   Experimental Setup and Results

Our experiments mainly focused on analyzing the performance of our scheme. In contrast to similar works in the area, we wanted our measurements to be taken under realistic conditions and not just be conducted as lab-based experiments. It is worth mentioning that while this can substantially weaken the overall measurements and subsequently the performance of our scheme, we decided to adopt the stance that by following this course we would ensure the conclusions of our work are not built on optimal premises but rather on the realistic ones. Based on that, we created a distributed architecture where the TA was running on an Azure cloud with SGX support (VM with 1 vcpu, 4 GB RAM and `Standard DC1s_v2` instance type). The implementation of the TA was based on the Intel SGX SDK[2]. The Evaluator was implemented on a different Azure instance without SGX support (VM with 1 vcpu, 2 GB RAM and `Standard B1ms` instance type). Finally, the voters were running on an Amazon S3 cloud (a VM with 1 vcpu, 2 GB RAM and `t2.micro` instance type). The communication between these three entities was done over the Internet. Furthermore, the TA and the Voters were implemented using C++, whereas EV in C++ and Python 3.

To test the performance of our scheme, we gradually increased the number of voters starting from a set of 1,000 and moving up to 100,000 voters. We evaluated two different scenarios regarding the number of candidates – the first uses 3 and the second 15 candidates. In both scenarios, we ran each experiment ten times and calculated the average processing time. If the attestation is successful, the voters run our scheme by calculating their unique encryption keys locally and communicating with the TA to receive the corresponding shares s_i (i.e. secret values). Subsequently, they perform the multiparty computation through which they compute the sum of all masked keys. At the end of this round, they send their encrypted votes along with the sum of the masked keys to EV. Upon reception, EV attests the TA and receives the sum of all shares sent to the voters in the previous round. Finally, EV uses FK along with the value received by the TA and calculates the total votes. Figure 6a illustrates the communication and the processes run between the three components of our scheme.

By using the described test-bed and evaluating the aforementioned scenarios, we measured the processing time of the following processes: *(1)* Enclave Creation: The average required time to initialize the enclave for the TA was 0.011 s; *(2)* Remote attestation: The average time required for a specific enclave (the TA) to remotely attest itself to a remote party was 1.24 s; *(3)* Voting Processing Time: The average time required to complete the voting for single group of voters was 2.65 s (this includes a complete run of our scheme).

---

[2] https://software.intel.com/en-us/sgx/sdk.

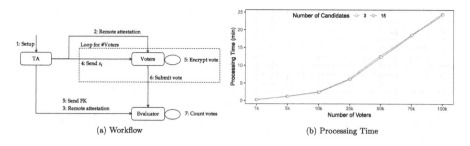

(a) Workflow   (b) Processing Time

Fig. 6. Implementation architecture and performance evaluation

Figure 6b illustrates the results of running the two aforementioned scenarios with up to 100,000 voters. It is important to note that our scheme allows the implementation of the voting procedure in parallel. However, during our experiments, we aimed to demonstrate and evaluate the performance of the scheme without having any support of parallelism and/or scalability.

9   Conclusion

While our approach has certain limitations, and thus may not seem particularly earth-shattering, we believe it should be seen as a valuable contribution to both the field of cryptography and secure and private e-voting. This is due to the fact that we showed how to utilize FE and extend existing techniques to solve the important and difficult problem of casting and collecting votes in a privacy-preserving way. Hence, our work can be seen as the first thoroughfare into the creation of privacy-preserving e-voting schemes with the use of FE.

References

1. Abdalla, M., Catalano, D., Fiore, D., Gay, R., Ursu, B.: Multi-input functional encryption for inner products: function-hiding realizations and constructions without pairings. In: Shacham, H., Boldyreva, A. (eds.) CRYPTO 2018. LNCS, vol. 10991, pp. 597–627. Springer, Cham (2018). https://doi.org/10.1007/978-3-319-96884-1_20
2. Abdalla, M., Gay, R., Raykova, M., Wee, H.: Multi-input inner-product functional encryption from pairings. In: Coron, J.-S., Nielsen, J.B. (eds.) EUROCRYPT 2017. LNCS, vol. 10210, pp. 601–626. Springer, Cham (2017). https://doi.org/10.1007/978-3-319-56620-7_21
3. Ananth, P., Brakerski, Z., Segev, G., Vaikuntanathan, V.: From selective to adaptive security in functional encryption. In: Gennaro, R., Robshaw, M. (eds.) CRYPTO 2015. LNCS, vol. 9216, pp. 657–677. Springer, Heidelberg (2015). https://doi.org/10.1007/978-3-662-48000-7_32
4. Badrinarayanan, S., Goyal, V., Jain, A., Sahai, A.: Verifiable functional encryption. In: Cheon, J.H., Takagi, T. (eds.) ASIACRYPT 2016. LNCS, vol. 10032, pp. 557–587. Springer, Heidelberg (2016). https://doi.org/10.1007/978-3-662-53890-6_19

5. Bakas, A., Michalas, A.: Power range: forward private multi-client symmetric searchable encryption with range queries support. In: 2020 IEEE Symposium on Computers and Communications (ISCC), pp. 1–7 (2020)

6. Bakas, A., Michalas, A.: Multi-client symmetric searchable encryption with forward privacy. Cryptology ePrint Archive, Report 2019/813 (2019)

7. Bakas, A., Michalas, A.: Multi-input functional encryption: efficient applications from symmetric primitives. In: Proceedings of the 19th IEEE International Conference on Trust, Security and Privacy in Computing and Communications (TrustCom 2020) (2020)

8. Brakerski, Z., Komargodski, I., Segev, G.: Multi-input functional encryption in the private-key setting: stronger security from weaker assumptions. J. Cryptol. **31**(2), 434–520 (2018)

9. Costan, V., Devadas, S.: Intel SGX explained. IACR Cryptol. ePrint Arch. **2016**(086), 1–118 (2016)

10. Dimitriou, T., Michalas, A.: Multi-party trust computation in decentralized environments in the presence of malicious adversaries. Ad Hoc Netw. **15**, 53–66 (2014)

11. Dolev, D., Yao, A.C.: On the security of public key protocols. IEEE Trans. Inf. Theory **29**(2), 198–208 (1983)

12. Goldwasser, S., et al.: Multi-input functional encryption. In: Nguyen, P.Q., Oswald, E. (eds.) EUROCRYPT 2014. LNCS, vol. 8441, pp. 578–602. Springer, Heidelberg (2014). https://doi.org/10.1007/978-3-642-55220-5_32

13. Goldwasser, S., Kalai, Y.T., Popa, R.A., Vaikuntanathan, V., Zeldovich, N.: How to run turing machines on encrypted data. In: Canetti, R., Garay, J.A. (eds.) CRYPTO 2013. LNCS, vol. 8043, pp. 536–553. Springer, Heidelberg (2013). https://doi.org/10.1007/978-3-642-40084-1_30

14. Gorbunov, S., Vaikuntanathan, V., Wee, H.: Functional encryption with bounded collusions via multi-party computation. In: Safavi-Naini, R., Canetti, R. (eds.) CRYPTO 2012. LNCS, vol. 7417, pp. 162–179. Springer, Heidelberg (2012). https://doi.org/10.1007/978-3-642-32009-5_11

15. Hasan, O., Brunie, L., Bertino, E., Shang, N.: A decentralized privacy preserving reputation protocol for the malicious adversarial model. IEEE Trans. Inf. Forensics Secur. **8**(6), 949–962 (2013)

16. Pavlov, E., Rosenschein, J.S., Topol, Z.: Supporting privacy in decentralized additive reputation systems. In: Jensen, C., Poslad, S., Dimitrakos, T. (eds.) iTrust 2004. LNCS, vol. 2995, pp. 108–119. Springer, Heidelberg (2004). https://doi.org/10.1007/978-3-540-24747-0_9

17. Sans, E.D., Gay, R., Pointcheval, D.: Reading in the dark: classifying encrypted digits with functional encryption. IACR Cryptology ePrint Archive 2018

18. Waters, B.: A punctured programming approach to adaptively secure functional encryption. In: Gennaro, R., Robshaw, M. (eds.) CRYPTO 2015. LNCS, vol. 9216, pp. 678–697. Springer, Heidelberg (2015). https://doi.org/10.1007/978-3-662-48000-7_33

TLV-to-MUC Express: Post-quantum MACsec in VXLAN

Joo Yeon Cho[1]($\boxtimes$) and Andrew Sergeev[2]

[1] ADVA Optical Networking SE, Fraunhoferstrasse 9a, 82152 Martinsried, Germany
JCho@adva.com
[2] ADVA Optical Networking Israel Ltd., 2 Hatidhar Street, 4366105 Ra'anana, Israel
ASergeev@adva.com

Abstract. MACsec in VXLAN is an end-to-end security protocol for protecting Ethernet frames traveling over IP networks. It can provide a high-speed Ethernet encryption while supporting the virtualization of a large network such as data center network. Although MACsec addresses most of security threats, it is not immune against quantum attacks which are a future, yet disastrous threat against public-key cryptography in use. In this paper, we demonstrate a new solution for a MACsec protocol over VXLAN in a post-quantum setting. Instead of a standard MACsec key agreement protocol, we use an ephemeral key exchange protocol and an end-to-end authentication scheme, both of which are based on post-quantum cryptography. To measure the impact on the performance, we established a quantum-secure link between Germany and Israel using MACsec in VXLAN over public IP networks. We verified that the impact on the latency and throughput is minimal. Our experiment confirms that quantum-secure virtualized links can be already established in a long-distance without changing their infrastructure.

Keywords: MACsec · Ethernet · VXLAN · VPN · Quantum security · Authentication

1 Introduction

Due to ever-increasing risk of cyber attacks, data protection is as important as its speed and performance assurance in modern networks. Wide Area Network (WAN) has been driving the industry to innovate to increase security as well as transport speeds. MACsec (Media Access Control Security) is an IEEE 802.1AE standard protocol for secure communication on Ethernet links to ensure confidentiality, integrity and origin authenticity of user data in transit.

While the standard MACsec protocol was developed for Local Area Network (LAN) security, it can be also used for WAN security with additional frame overhead. A common approach is to add a Virtual LAN (VLAN) tag to the MACsec frame [15]. This tag allows MACsec frames to travel multiple hops and enables the end-to-end network encryption over carrier Ethernet. However, it

© Springer Nature Switzerland AG 2021
M. Asplund and S. Nadjm-Tehrani (Eds.): NordSec 2020, LNCS 12556, pp. 127–141, 2021.
https://doi.org/10.1007/978-3-030-70852-8_8

requires MACsec-aware intermediate switches and bridges in the middle. Hence, MACsec frames often do not cross over IP networks, leaving the deployment of VLAN limited in practice.

VXLAN (Virtual Extensible Local Area Network) technology can extend VLAN and overcome the limited capability and scalability posed by VLAN. VXLAN creates a layer 2 tunnel on top of layer 3 by encapsulating Ethernet frames in UDP frames, enabling large-scale virtualized and multitenant data center designs over a shared common physical infrastructure. Hence, VXLAN is commonly used for a site-to-site VPN such as data center networks. VXLAN allows Ethernet frames to travel over IP networks as long as the terminal device is able to decapsulate the VXLAN into MACsec frames.

1.1 Our Contribution

Attacks using quantum computers are a future, yet critical threat against cyber security. Although quantum attacks should not be overstated, it is sensible to prepare new crypto schemes relying on the quantum-resistant mathematical hardness for a long term security.

A MACsec key agreement protocol in a post-quantum setting is investigated in [8]. We extend this approach to a MACsec in VXLAN tunneling. We demonstrated by experiments that a quantum-secure MACsec in VXLAN can be applied in a long distance network without any modification of infrastructure.

The core primitives of the protocol are a key encapsulation mechanism (KEM) and a digital signature scheme, both of which are adapted from the 3rd round finalists of NIST PQC project [2]. We compare their performance in terms of latency and throughput. In order to achieve a forward security, an end-to-end ephemeral key exchange protocol is established, meaning that each session key is independently generated and there is no way to restore the previous keys even though a current key is disclosed. In fact, this approach has been already widely adopted in the industry, especially for WAN or MAN security although this does not comply with a standard MACsec key agreement protocol.

The rest of this paper is structured as follows: first, we briefly describe the background on MACsec in VXLAN and post-quantum cryptography. Then, we propose a framework of the MACsec in VXLAN in a post-quantum setting. Next, we describe our test platform and experimental results. Finally, we conclude the paper.

2 Background

In this section, the MACsec protocol is briefly described in terms of encryption, authentication and key management. Then, the benefits of VXLAN are discussed. Later, a brief introduction on the post-quantum crypto algorithms is given.

Table 1. PQC primitives: the 3rd round finalists of NIST PQC project [2] and hash-based signatures from IETF [9]

SDO	Family	KEM	Signature
NIST	Lattice-based	CRYSTALS-KYBER [28]	CRYSTALS-DILITHIUM [23]
		NTRU [6]	FALCON [26]
		SABER [10]	
	Code-based	Classic McEliece [5]	–
	Multivariate	–	Rainbow [11]
IETF	Hash-based	–	XMSS [14]
		–	LMS [24]

2.1 MACsec

MACsec is an IEEE standard protocol for Layer-2 security [17]. A MACsec packet is formed with an Ethernet frame by adding a SecTAG (Security TAG) and an ICV (Integrity Check Value). A SecTAG conveys information on the protocol, the cipher suites, as well as the PN (packet number) for replay protection. An ICV is a compressed value of the MAC address, SecTAG, and secure data to ensure the integrity of a packet. Note that payload encryption is optional. If a packet-authentication-only mode is configured, MACsec can verify only the integrity of a transmitted packet.

MACsec supports a limited number of symmetric-key cipher suites: AES-GCM-128 and AES-GCM-256 with a usage of XPN (eXtended PN) as an option [17]. AES-GCM-128 is a default cipher suite. IEEE 802.1AEbn-2011 [18] adds GCM-AES-256 as an optional cipher suite to allow a 256-bit key. IEEE 802.1AEbw-2013 [19] adds GCM-AES-XPN-128 and GCM-AES-XPN-256 for further optional cipher suites that make use of a 64-bit (PN) to allow more than 2^{32} MACsec protected frames to be sent with a single SAK (Secure Association Key). MACsec is now part of the Linux kernel from the version 4.6 [20]. Note that the National Security Agency (NSA) designed the Ethernet Security Specification (ESS) on top of MACsec for providing a hardened layer 2 encryption scheme [25].

Although MACsec was developed for LAN security, a MACsec frame can transverse across local networks by applying VLAN tags defined in IEEE 802.1Q [15]. This technique allows MACsec to be used for WAN (wide area network) security and provide the end-to-end network encryption over carrier Ethernet.

2.2 Virtual Extensible LAN

There are common ways to virtualize Layer 2 networks; VLAN and VXLAN. VLAN is widely used for traffic separation and network segmentation in the enterprise environment. According to the IEEE 802.1Q standard, traditional VLAN identifiers are 12 bits long. This limits network segments to 4094 VLANs.

The VXLAN protocol overcomes this limitation by using a longer logical network identifier that allows more VLANs. The VXLAN protocol uses a 24-bit logical network identifier that allows 2^{24} network virtualizations in total. In addition, VxLAN frames are encapsulated with UDP thus can be transported across IP networks. Hence, VXLANs become dominant for large networks such as cloud environments that typically include many virtual machines. In data centers, VXLAN is commonly used to create overlay networks on top of the physical network, enabling the use of a virtual network of devices. The VXLAN protocol supports the virtualization of the data center network and addresses the needs of multi-tenant data centers by providing the necessary segmentation on a large scale. Note that VXLAN encapsulation by itself does not provide any security features, hence, networks must be protected by other means e.g. as introduced in [21].

2.3   Post-quantum Cryptography

The goal of post-quantum cryptography is to develop cryptographic systems that are secure against both quantum and classical computers, and can interoperate with existing communications protocols and networks [7]. Post-quantum cryptography is usually classified into five families: code-based, lattice-based, multivariate, symmetric-based, and supersingular isogeny-based. Each family is based on a different mathematical problem that is not feasible so far to solve both with traditional computers as well as quantum computers. Recently, post-quantum cryptography has drawn lots of attention from the community mainly due to the NIST PQC project [7]. Code-based crypto has strength on KEM. It has been studied for a long time and, the theory is well developed and understood. However, the key size is usually quite large, compared to other families. It seems not suitable for signature schemes. Lattice-based crypto is the most popular among other families. It is applicable to both KEM and signature. However, selecting security parameters is challenging since their security is still not

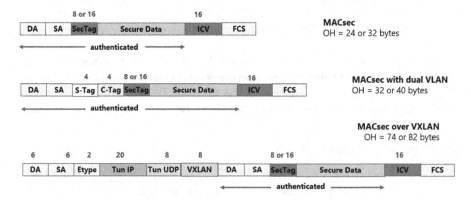

Fig. 1. Comparison of overhead: MACsec encapsulation in VXLAN

well-understood. Multivariate crypto is suitable for signature but not for KEM. Isogeny-based crypto is relatively new but very promising for KEM in terms of the key size. The NIST announced the third round finalists in July 2020 [2]. We sorted out the finalists in Table 1. In addition, NIST supports hash-based signatures that have been already published in IETF [9]. Based on another document from NIST, it is likely that future post-quantum cryptographic standards will specify multiple algorithms for different applications because of differing implementation constraints (e.g., sensitivity to large signature size or large keys) [4].

3 Protocols

In this section, we describe a frame format of MACsec in VXLAN. Then, we present an authenticated post-quantum key exchange protocol in details, together with several aspects of practical considerations.

3.1 Encapsulating MACsec in VXLAN

Due to the minimal requirement of overhead and simple configuration, MACsec is often used for high-speed connectivity at low power and low cost. The disadvantage of MACsec is that all traffic traversing the link requires matching and verifying secret keys at each node. In reality, this downside is avoided by adding a VLAN tag defined in IEEE 802.1Q [15] and re-locating some header fields. However, most of public nodes do not accept the VLAN tag, leaving the MACsec with VLAN tag suitable for a dedicated private link requiring high security. In VXLAN, a UDP header is placed in front of the frame, as shown in Fig. 1. Hence, if a MACsec packet is encapsulated in VXLAN, it can travel over public nodes as long as UDP is accepted. The downside is of course the increased size of overhead. The comparison of frame format is given in Fig. 1.

3.2 Authenticated PQ Key Exchange

Limits on Data Usage. There are cryptographic limits on the amount of data which can be safely encrypted under a single key. For example, TLS 1.3 specifies limits on the number of data to be encrypted by AES-GCM up to $2^{24.5}$ full-size records with a safety margin of approximately 2^{-57} [27]. A new IETF RFC is initiated for the detailed formulation [13]. For this reason, an authenticated key exchange (AKE) protocol is periodically executed and a session key is refreshed before such data limit is reached.

Let us remind that a payload of MACsec frame is encrypted using AES-GCM. A limit on the amount of data that are encrypted by MACsec without needing a key change is determined on the volume of data transmission. Here is an example. Suppose the transmission rate of MACsec packets is 1 Gbps (= 0.125 Gbps). According to [22], the amount of data that can be safely encrypted with a single key is around 0.3887 terabytes with 2^{-60} success probability, which leads us to calculate its re-key rate as

$$\frac{0.3887 \text{ TB/key}}{0.125 \text{ GB/s}} = 31096 \text{ sec/key} \approx 51.8 \text{ min/key}.$$

This means that a key exchange protocol should be executed every 52 min or less to achieve such error probability. More information are given in Table 2.

Table 2. Max data vs. Re-key rate for an 1 Gbps link

Attack success prob.	Max data (terabytes) [22]	Re-key rate
2^{-60}	0.3887	52 min
2^{-50}	12.44	28 h
2^{-40}	398.1	37 days
2^{-30}	12,738	3.2 years

Ephemeral PQ AKE Protocol. The standard MACsec key agreement (MKA) protocol is a centralized key derivation mechanism based on a hierarchical key structure [16]. Even though MKA is efficient and suitable for LAN, it has a non-negligible risk of being hacked by a root key disclosure, which may lead a severe security breach in entire networks. Especially this risk become high if MACsec is used for WAN and MAN security. Hence, as stated earlier, an ephemeral key exchange has been widely adopted in the industry. That is, each session key is derived independently from the previous session keys so that the disclose of current session key does not reveal any data encrypted in the past. This is called forward secrecy.

Suppose Initiator and Responder perform an AKE protocol. Both peers are assumed to have generated a pair of public and secret key. To agree upon a new session key, two peers execute an AKE protocol using PQ crypto primitives listed in Table 1. The detailed protocol is depicted in Fig. 2.

Hybrid AKE Protocol. A hybrid AKE protocol is a combination of post-quantum authenticated key exchange with classical standard crypto schemes. For instance, McEliece KEM with Falcon signature can be combined with DH (Diffie-Hellman) key exchange protocol with RSA signature. In this way, keys derived by a hybrid AKE scheme remain secure if at least one of the component schemes is secure. This is called crypto agility. Note that post-quantum crypto protocols are added independently on top of the standard protocol, rather than being merged together because the security proof of each protocol should be preserved. Recently NIST revised SP 800-56C to permit the use of a hybrid key establishment construction in FIPS 140 validation [3]. The use of hybrid key exchange and dual signature scheme is an on-going research topic e.g. [29].

$Initiator(I)$		$Responder(R)$
Required: pk_I, sk_I		Required: pk_R, sk_R
Initiate AKE		Respond AKE
	$\xleftrightarrow{Start}$	
Choose random number r_I, k_I		Choose random number r_R, k_J
$X_I = \{pk_I, \text{PQSIGN}_{sk_I}(pk_I, r_I)\}$		$X_R = \{pk_R, \text{PQSIGN}_{sk_R}(pk_R, r_R)\}$
	$\xleftrightarrow{X_I, X_R}$	
Verify X_R		Verify X_I
$Y_I = \text{PQENC}_{pk_R}(k_I)$		$Y_R = \text{PQENC}_{pk_I}(k_R)$
	$\xleftrightarrow{Y_I, Y_R}$	
$k_R = \text{PQDEC}_{sk_I}(Y_R)$		$k_I = \text{PQENC}_{sk_R}(Y_I)$
$K = k_I \| k_R \| r_I \| r_R$		$K = k_I \| k_R \| r_I \| r_R$
$M_I = MAC(K)$		$M_R = MAC(K)$
	$\xleftrightarrow{M_I, M_R}$	
Verify M_R		Verify M_I
Accept / Reject K		Accept / Reject K

Fig. 2. A PQ authenticated key exchange protocol

Practical Considerations. During a PQ key exchange protocol, public keys need to be fragmented in multiple Ethernet packets because the maximum size of an Ethernet packet is much smaller than that of a PQ public-key. For instance, Classical McEliece needs more than 1M bytes of a public-key for the security of category 5, while maximum transmission unit (MTU) of Ethernet pack is around 1500 bytes. Note that a single MTU fits well for classical crypto schemes such as RSA or Elliptic Curve Diffie-Hellman (ECDH).

For transferring a large PQ public-key, we used the simplest method – secured file copy (SCP) over IP networks. The public key transfer could be done via a plain RCP Linux command, but the RCP port 512 is disgraced by the security policy and it is usually blocked by firewalls. So SCP is our preferable solution, although security here is not necessary since the protocol is assumed to be executed in an insecure channel. Another argument in favor of SCP is the presence of management network. Most of deployed network elements have a separate management channel over IP network. Hence, SCP can be run over this channel for an out-of-band key exchange protocol.

SCP can be configured in a password-less mode; peers generate a standard SSH key pairs and share their public keys each other. SSH pubic keys can be easily distributed between peers with the help of network management system. SCP uses the standard Linux IP stack, so it can handle a packet loss, which is very handy for general internet. SCP can be used for either out-of-band or in-band communication.

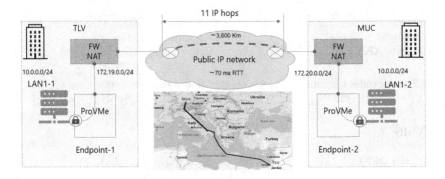

Fig. 3. A site-to-site VPN between TLV and MUC over public IP networks

For a large key transfer, we also considered using a "fragmentation-over-VXLAN" option. However, this requires more implementation efforts and the potential benefit is not so clear. Also, while SCP is suitable for every case, VXLAN-specific implementation would not work for the regular MACsec use case.

4   Experiments

In [8], a post-quantum MACSec key agreement scheme was proposed. For experiments, the authors performed a post-quantum key exchange protocol between two MACsec nodes connected back-to-back in the lab. However, this technique is not directly applicable to a site-to-site VPN where the distance is large and the bandwidth is limited. The reason is that MACsec packets (even with VLAN tag) cannot pass through the nodes in the middle which accept only IP packets. To overcome this limit, MACsec packets are encapsulated in UDP frames. Only end nodes need to decapsulate an ingress packet and retrieve a MACsec frame.

We established a VPN link between Tel Aviv (TLV) in Israel and Munich (MUC) in Germany. A overview of the link is drawn in Fig. 3. The VPN link between TLV and MUC is about 3600 km. The largest part of the path is the JONAH link which is a submarine optical cable spanning 2,300 km. There are 11 traceable IP hops on the way; ICMP ping reports a round-trip delay of around 70 ms. Assuming that a round-trip fiber propagation delay is $2 \times 3600 \times 5\,\mu s = 36$ ms, we can estimate an average delay introduced by a single IP hop: $(70-36)/2/11 = 1.54$ ms.

4.1   System Setup

We set up a FSP 150 ProVMe edge device [1] on both TLV and MUC sites. They are connected to the public internet through corresponding firewall and NAT on site. A FSP 150 ProVMe is composed of a FPGA and a Linux host. The FPGA facilitates an embedded traffic generator and a packet analyzer, allowing the

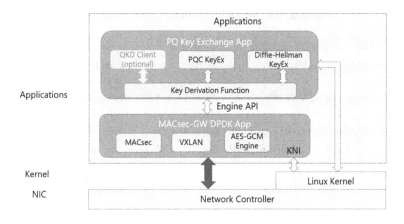

Fig. 4. A block diagram of software architecture on FSP 150 ProVMe

latency measurement with resolution of 50 ns. The Linux host runs a macsec-gw application for tunneling MACsec in VXLAN.

In our experiment, two transmission channels have been established: one is for tunneling MACsec in VXLAN and the other is for performing a PQ key exchange protocol. For this purpose, firewalls on the path must allow the following flows:

- VXLAN for MACsec traffic (UDP port 4789)
- SCP for key exchange (TCP port 22)
- ICMP for a connectivity test
- iperf3 (TCP/UDP port 5200) for a basic IP forwarding test.

Software Design. To achieve the best performance from x86 CPU, we implemented DPDK [12] with the aes-ni-gcm driver for symmetrical encryption. As a result, our macsec-gw DPDK application can process MACsec-in-VXLAN packets up to 9 Gbps on single CPU core. The measurement has been done using a packet size of 1420 bytes and AES-GCM-256 encryption. Our software also includes a DPDK KNI (Kernel NIC Interface) feature, so any application can send and receive IP packets through the port which are used for the VXLAN traffic. An overview of software architecture is given in Fig. 4.

A PQ key exchange engine is implemented in a separated application. It periodically derives a new session key and provides it to the macsec-gw application via an engine API. In fact, a PQ AKE protocol can be performed over either out-of-band or in-band channel through regular kernel interfaces or a dedicated DPDK KNI. This allows users to choose the best suitable communication path for their key exchange protocols. In our experiment, we chose an out-of-band key exchange using DPDK KNI.

Tunneling over IP Networks. Nowadays UDP is widely used for encapsulating Ethernet packets which need to travel over IP network. The reason is that

Table 3. Encapsulation options for PQ MACsec

Encapsulation methods	Overhead (bytes)	Feature
MACsec in VLAN	28	Can't pass IP network
MACsec in VXLAN	24 + 54 = 74	Stripped VLAN
MASsec over GRE in UDP	66 + 8 = 74	Kept VLAN
VXLAN over ESP in UDP	88	Stripped VLAN and duplicated UDP

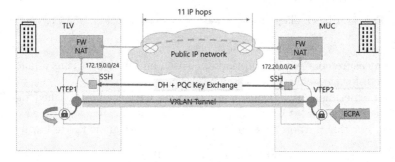

Fig. 5. Site-to-Site VPN setup using post-quantum MACsec over VXLAN

the UDP traffic can take full advantage of equal-cost multi-path (ECMP) routing. UDP is used in VXLAN as well as GRE (or NV-GRE). However, VXLAN gained some popularity over GRE because it is slightly better to be integrated with modern networks e.g. in cloud environment.

Table 3 shows several options for encapsulating MACsec packets in UDP. Among those, MACsec in VXLAN is chosen for our experiments since encapsulation can be done efficiently and the overhead size is acceptable for a limited bandwidth. Alternatively, it is possible to encapsulate VXLAN in ESP-in-UDP tunnel, but in this case the encapsulation includes two UDP headers, which is not necessarily required.

4.2   Test Results

Baseline IP Connectivity. We run an iperf3 application over Linux Kernel IP stack. The test results show that bandwidth allocations are not symmetrical, depending on their traffic directions. See Table 4 for details. It is not clear why the throughput of TLV to MUC link is much worse than that of MUC to TLV link. This is also in line with a packet loss rate which will be presented later.

Table 4. Throughput measured by an iperf3 application

Link	*iperf3 throughput*
MUC to a public iperf3 Server	574 Mbits/s
MUC to TLV	89.5 Mbits/s
TLV to MUC	6.15 Mbits/s

VXLAN Throughput. To measure a VXLAN throughput and a round-trip latency we used the following setup shown in Fig. 5. A traffic generator sends a test stream to a protected port at MUC site. Packets are encrypted by MACsec, encapsulated in VXLAN (VTEP2) and sent towards TLV site. On TLV site the VXLAN traffic is decapsulated by VTEP1, decrypted by MACsec and transmitted via a protected port. We configured a terminal loopback on the protected port, so the traffic is looped back, encrypted by MACsec, encapsulated in VXLAN and sent back to MUC site. On MUC site the decrypted traffic is transmitted via the protected port back to the traffic analyser.

VXLAN Configuration. On TLV and MUC sites the VXLAN endpoint configuration is as follows:

```
#TLV
vxlan vni 5005 src 172.19.252.107 dst 192.0.2.1
#MUC
vxlan vni 5005 src 172.20.140.8 dst 198.51.100.1
```

To allow an in-band SCP file transfer over DPDK KNI interface (vEth0), we need to add the following routes to our nodes:

```
#TLV
ip route add 192.0.2.1 via 172.19.252.1 dev vEth0
#MUC
ip route add 198.51.100.1 via 172.20.140.1 dev vEth0
```

We measured the throughput and latency of traffic with 60 s interval repeatedly. The tested packet size was either 64 or 1412 bytes. Test results show that the packet loss is different depending on the packet sizes. However, the round trip delay does not depend on packet size – average value is approximately 71 ms for either short (64 byte) packets or long (1412 byte) packets. See Table 5 for details.

Packet Loss. A packet loss over public Internet is well expected due to a long distance connection. This is not observable in the lab setup with a back-to-back connection. In Fig. 6, a packet loss in the direction of TLV → MUC link is

Table 5. Latency and packet loss using 64 and 1412 bytes packets

Item	*Long packets (1412 bytes)*	*Short packets (64 bytes)*
Min. delay	70,628 μs	69,912 μs
Max. delay	70,658 μs	78,810 μs
Avg. delay	71,170 μs	70,471 μs
Tx frames	26,470	448,236
Rx frames	26,466	448,159
Rx avg. bit rate	5,055,325 bps	5,055,209 bps
Rx frame success prob	99.98	99.98

compared with a round-trip packet loss, depending on the usage of short and long packets. We observed that the packet loss mainly occurs in the TLV → MUC direction, especially when running a test using large packets. We guess it is due to the channel characteristics but could not find a root cause of this unbalanced packet loss. Note that all IP flows were set by a default DSCP value (0) in order to make the configuration as simple as possible. Hence, no special QoS setting is done.

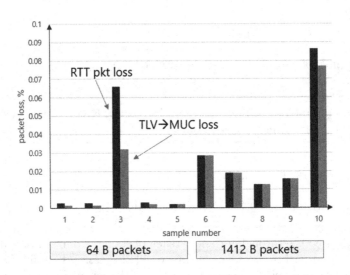

Fig. 6. Comparison of packet loss: round-trip vs. TUV-MUC link

Impact of PQ AKE Protocol. We tested a PQ key exchange protocol with multiple PQ crypto primitives listed in Table 1. Among various parameter sets, we chose those of the category 5; mceliece6960119 (Classic McEliece), ntruhps4096821 (NTRU), kyber1024 (Crystal-Kyber) and FireSaber (Saber) for

KEM, Crystal-Dilithium (Dilithium IV) and Falcon1024 (Falcon) for digital signature. The most challenging primitive is Classic McEliece KEM due to its large key size. Our experiments show that the completion of key exchange protocol takes 17 to 22 s assuming there is no background traffic. If there exists a VXLAN traffic with bidirectional 5 Gbps and a packet size of 1412 bytes, the maximum value increases to 24 s.

To evaluate the impact of the packet loss caused by a PQ key exchange protocol, we monitored Linux kernel TCP counters using *netstat* command once each key exchange is completed. On every key exchange sequence tcp re-transmission counters increased in a range from 2 to 14, regardless of the presence of a background MACsec-in-VXLAN traffic.

```
# netstat -s — grep retrans
269 segments retransmited
235 fast retransmits
```

5   Conclusion

The post-quantum crypto standard by NIST is in the final stage, leaving the final candidates only 7 primitives (4 for KEM and 3 for signature). We implemented those finalists on a commercial product and measured their impacts on the performance over a field trial link. We established a MACsec in VXLAN tunnel between TLV and MUC and performed a PQ AKE protocol over the link. Our test results show that MACsec in VXLAN using post-quantum crypto primitives can be applied to existing networks without significant impact on their performance. For instance, we did not observe any performance degradation on a bidirectional MACsec-in-VXLAN traffic with a range from 5 to 6 Mbps throughput. Therefore, we conclude that PQ MACsec in VXLAN is a practical solution for establishing a quantum-secure site-to-site VPN on existing networks.

For future work, we plan to analyze the security of a PQ AKE protocol by several attack methods, in particular, by timing attacks. Also, we plan to apply our solution to some use cases where a quantum-secure VPN needs to be deployed at a low cost.

Acknowledgment. This research is co-funded by the Federal Ministry of Education and Research of Germany under the QuaSiModO project (Grant agreement No 16KIS1051).

References

1. ADVA Optical Networking. FSP 150 ProVMe Series. https://www.adva.com/en/products/packet-edge-and-aggregation/edge-computing/fsp-150-provme-series
2. Alagic, G., et al.: Status Report on the Second Round of the NIST Post-Quantum Cryptography Standardization Process, July 2020

3. Barker, E., Chen, L., Davis, R.: Recommendation for key-derivation methods in key-establishment schemes. NIST Special Publication 800–56C Revision 2, August 2020. https://csrc.nist.gov/publications/detail/sp/800-56c/rev-2/final
4. Barker, W., Polk, W., Souppaya M.: Getting Ready for Post-Quantum Cryptography: Explore Challenges Associated with Adoption and Use of Post-Quantum Cryptographic Algorithms, May 2020
5. Bernstein, D., et al.: Classic McEliece: conservative code-based cryptography (2019). https://classic.mceliece.org/nist/mceliece-20190331.pdf
6. Chen, C., et al.: NTRU 2019. https://ntru.org/
7. Chen, L., et al.: Report on post-quantum cryptography, NISTIR 8105 (2016)
8. Cho, J., Sergeev, A.: Post-quantum MACsec key agreement for ethernet networks. In: Proceedings of the 15th International Conference on Availability, Reliability and Security, ARES (2020)
9. Cooper, D., Apon, D., Dang, Q., Davidson, M., Dworkin, M., Miller, C.: Recommendation for stateful hash-based signature schemes. Draft NIST Special Publication 800–208, December 2019. NIST.SP.800-208-draft.pdf
10. D'Anvers, J., Karmakar, A., Roy, S., Vercauteren, F.: SABER: Mod-LWR based KEM (2019). https://www.esat.kuleuven.be/cosic/pqcrypto/saber/index.html
11. Ding, J., Chen, M., Petzoldt, A., Schmidt, D., Yang., B.: Rainbow (2019)
12. DPDK: Data plane development kit. https://www.dpdk.org
13. Günther, F., Thomson, M., Wood, C.A.: Usage limits on AEAD algorithms, August 2020. https://www.ietf.org/id/draft-irtf-cfrg-aead-limits-00.txt
14. Huelsing, A., Butin, D., Gazdag, S., Rijneveld, J., Mohaisen, A.: XMSS: Extended Hash-Based Signatures. Internet-Draft draft-irtf-cfrg-xmss-hash-based-signatures-12, Internet Engineering Task Force, January 2018. Work in Progress
15. IEEE: IEEE standard for local and metropolitan area network-bridges and bridged networks. IEEE Std 802.1Q-2018 (Revision of IEEE Std 802.1Q-2014), pp. 1–1993, July 2018
16. IEEE. Local and metropolitan area networks-port-based network access control. IEEE Std 802.1X-2010 (Revision of IE EE Std 802.1X-2004), pp. 1–205, February 2010
17. IEEE: Local and metropolitan area networks-media access control (MAC) security. 802.1AE: MAC Security (MACsec). https://1.ieee802.org/security/802-1ae/
18. IEEE: Media access control (MAC) security amendment 1: Galois counter mode-advanced encryption standard- 256 (GCM-AES-256) cipher suite. 802.1AEbn-2011. https://1.ieee802.org/security/802-1aebn/
19. IEEE: Media access control (MAC) security amendment 2: Extended packet numbering. 802.1AEBW-2013. https://1.ieee802.org/security/802-1aebw/
20. KernelNewbies: 802.1AE MAC-level encryption (MACsec), Linux 4.6, May 2016
21. Liu, Y., Li, W.: VXLAN Security Option, May 2015. https://tools.ietf.org/html/draft-liu-nvo3-vxlan-security-option-01
22. Luykx, A., Paterson, K.: Limits on authenticated encryption use in TLS. www.isg.rhul.ac.uk/~kp/TLS-AEbounds.pdf
23. Lyubashevsky, V., et al.: Crystals-dilithium (2019). https://pq-crystals.org/dilithium/index.shtml
24. McGrew, D., Curcio, M., Fluhrer, S.: Leighton-Micali Hash-Based Signatures. RFC 8554, April 2019. https://rfc-editor.org/rfc/rfc8554.txt
25. National Security Agency: Ethernet security specification, version 0.5, October 2011
26. Prest, T., et al.: Falcon: Fast-Fourier lattice-based compact signatures over NTRU (2019). https://falcon-sign.info/

27. Rescorla, E.: The transport layer security (TLS) protocol version 1.3, March 2016. Internet-Draft draft-ietf-tls-tls13-12
28. Schwabe, P., et al.: Crystals-kyber (2019). https://pq-crystals.org/kyber/index.shtml
29. Steblia, D., Fluhrer, S., Gueron, S.: Hybrid key exchange in TLS 1.3, February 2020

On the Certificate Revocation Problem in the Maritime Sector

Guillaume Bour$^{(\boxtimes)}$, Karin Bernsmed, Ravishankar Borgaonkar, and Per Håkon Meland

SINTEF Digital, Trondheim, Norway
{Guillaume.Bour,Karin.Bernsmed,Ravi.Borgaonkar,
Per.H.Meland}@sintef.no

Abstract. Maritime shipping is currently undergoing rapid digitaliza-tion, but with increasing exposure to cyber threats, there is a need to improve the security of the ship communication technology used during operations across international waters, as well as close to local shores and in ports. To this aid, there are ongoing standardization efforts for an international maritime Public Key Infrastructure, but the inherent prop-erties of limited connectivity and bandwidth make certificate revocation a problematic affair compared to traditional Internet systems. The main contribution of this paper is an analysis of certificate revocation tech-niques based on how they fulfil fundamental maritime requirements and simulated usage over time. Our results identify CRLs (with Delta CRLs) and CRLite as the two most promising candidates. Finally, we outline the pros and cons with these two different solutions.

Keywords: Cyber security · Public key infrastructure · Certificate revocation · Maritime · Shipping

1 Introduction

Maritime shipping is currently undergoing rapid digitalization. The introduc-tion of new communication technologies onboard ships, such as the upcoming VHF Data Exchange System (VDES) [21], enables a wide variety of new dig-ital services, such as digital ship reporting, electronic port clearance, search and rescue communications, vessel traffic services and broadcast of maritime safety information. These services will all require information security, and a prevalent solution to establish and deploy a Public Key Infrastructure (PKI) for distributing digital certificates and securing the integrity and confidentiality of the information exchange. Several different research groups have in parallel worked to define, implement and test the characteristics of a PKI for the mar-itime domain [7,12,13,23], and the concept has now been acknowledged by IMO[1] and brought into the ongoing standardization by IALA[2] [5]. However, there is

---

[1] International Maritime Organization (IMO). http://www.imo.org.

[2] International Association of Marine Aids to Navigation and Lighthouse Authorities (IALA), https://www.iala-aism.org/.

© The Author(s) 2021
M. Asplund and S. Nadjm-Tehrani (Eds.): NordSec 2020, LNCS 12556, pp. 142–157, 2021.
https://doi.org/10.1007/978-3-030-70852-8_9

a significant challenge related to certificate revocation yet to be solved. This is a crucial part of any PKI, and unlike typical Internet applications that can be constantly online, ships tend to be offline for long periods of time or sailing in the open sea where connectivity and bandwidth can be both poor and expensive. The consequences could be delayed awareness of revocations and less trust in the PKI itself. Even though some previous work has evaluated and compared different revocation mechanisms [15,27,28,30], there are no previous studies that address the specific maritime challenges.

The main contribution of this paper is an analysis of certificate revocation techniques based on requirements fulfilment and simulated use in a maritime setting over time. The paper is organised as follows. Section 2 provides the background to our work, including a description of the envisioned maritime PKI as well as an overview of existing solutions for certificate revocation. Section 3 presents the fundamental requirements and Sect. 4 gives an analysis of and simulation benchmarks for the solution candidates. Section 5 discusses these results and Sect. 6 concludes the paper.

2 Background

2.1 The Maritime PKI

A normal PKI depends on a hierarchy of trust, e.g. as depicted in Fig. 1. There are three layers in this model:

1. A Trusted International Root Certificate Authority (CA) that issues certificates to its subordinates. The root CA is envisioned to be operated by IMO, since they are a trusted entity by the majority of maritime stakeholders around the world.
2. A number of (intermediate) Issuing National CAs, that would typically be the Flag State administrations associated with each country.[3]
3. End entities, which are the ships, ports and coastal services that need to communicate securely.

In addition, an entity called "Revocation issuer" responsible for issuing information about invalid certificates, will be needed. This role could also be handled by the root CA.

2.2 Existing Revocation Solutions

Revocation of certificates in a PKI ecosystem can happen for a number of reasons, such as change of ship name, change of association between the end entity and the issuing CA, or compromise of the corresponding private key [10]. Affected entities should be informed as fast as possible after a revocation, and we have described existing revocation mechanisms that we have considered for the maritime sector.

---

[3] Every merchant ship has to be registered under a jurisdiction, called the flag state, which has the responsibility to enforce regulations over vessels registered under its flag.

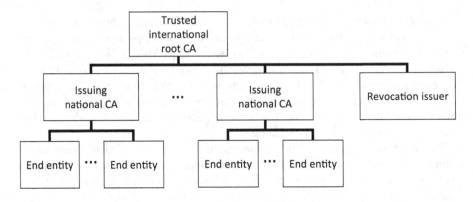

Fig. 1. The PKI trust hierarchy.

Certificate Revocation List (CRL). (RFC 5280 [10]) are issued at regular time intervals. When a user wants to check the validity of a certificate, he needs to have a local copy of the CRL installed. This is usually be achieved by pulling the CRL from the CA's CRL distribution endpoint. While this method works well for PKIs with relatively few end entities, the solution does not scale well, since a full and complete CRL will list all (unexpired) certificates that have been revoked. To counter this problem, delta-CRLs can be used, which only include certificates whose revocation status has changed since last update. A drawback with CRLs (and delta-CRLs) is that the validity check is done "offline" and there is a risk that end entities accept certificates that have been revoked.

The use of CRLs to revoke certificates in the Maritime PKI has been proposed by Froystad et al. [13] and the Maritime Cloud Development Forum [12]. Figure 2 presents the principle: a CRL issuer collects CRLs from all entities entitled to issue such lists, and creates a joint CRL that is distributed to all the end entities in the PKI. However, neither [13] nor [12] specify the use of delta-CRLs or discuss the risk of using obsolete CRLs.

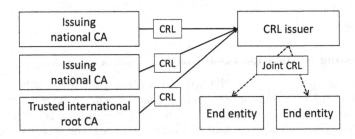

Fig. 2. CRLs from multiple sources are collected and distributed to end entities through a CRL issuer [13].

Online Certificate Status Protocol (OCSP). (RFC 6960 [26]), was designed to provide more timely revocation information compared to CRLs. The protocol is "online"; to verify a certificate's validity, the user sends an OCSP request to the CA, asking for the status of one or more given certificate(s). The CA will respond with the certificate(s)'s status (good/revoked/unknown), along with a response validity interval. However, the solution comes with some drawbacks:

- If the CA is unavailable, the validity of certificates cannot be confirmed.
- Increased latency since the OCSP request needs to be confirmed before the certificate can be used. If the CA is unreachable, it can take several seconds before the request times out,[4] which will be a no-go for time critical applications.
- While the OCSP response is signed, error messages are not. This may open up to interception attacks [18].
- The identity of the user is revealed to the CA each time the user sends an OCSP request, possibly creating privacy issues.

To counter OCSP bandwidth issues, RFC 5019 [11] defines a lightweight profile that minimises the communication bandwidth and client-side processing.

OCSP Stapling/OCSP Must Staple. To solve some of OCSP's problems, RFC 6961 [24] and RFC 7633 [25] (commonly referred to as "OCSP Stapling" and "OCSP Must Staple", respectively) define a method where a server makes a request to the OCSP service and get a signed message with its certificate status that it can then "staple" to its certificate during the Transport Layer Security (TLS) handshake. This method is more efficient than the original OCSP because the server can cache OCSP messages, thus reducing the latency. This also partially solves the privacy issue with OCSP, as the user does not need to reveal its identity each time. Still, OCSP Stapling suffers from being an "online" solution, which is not suitable for all maritime applications.

CRLSet [3]/OneCRL. [1] are currently used by Google and Firefox to revoke CA certificates stored in their web browsers. Revocation lists are built internally by the respective companies and pushed to the clients daily. The lists only include a subset of the most critical revoked certificates. The main benefit is that bandwidth is minimised. In contrast to OCSP, these solutions do not reveal communication patterns, as all end entities receive the same lists. The common downside of CRLSet and OneCRL is that end entities must be online on a daily basis.

CRLite. allows to push all TLS certificate revocations to all browsers. Initially described in a research paper by Larisch et al. [19], it has since 2019 been tested by Mozilla Firefox as its new certificates revocation method [8]. CRLite relies

---

[4] Telemetry from Internet browsing with Firefox shows that OCSP requests "time out about 15% of the time, and take in average 350 ms even when they succeed" [4].

on cascading *bloom filters* to efficiently push out the revocation information, which is "a simple space-efficient randomized data structure for representing set to support membership queries" [22]. The answer to a membership query is probabilistic; if the answer is negative, we know the element is not in the set, but if the answer is positive then chances are that this is a false positive. To remove false positives, CRLite takes advantage of Certificate Transparency (CT), which aims to fix several flaws in the SSL certificate system by "providing an open framework for monitoring and auditing SSL certificates in nearly real time" [2]. In practice, certificate logs are built by collecting all certificates issued by trusted CA [2,20]. In the context of CRLite, a first bloom filter is b.uilt using the revoked certificates data and then, using the CT log, a new bloom filter (smaller than the first one) containing all false positives of the first bloom filter is built. This operation can be repeated until there is no more false positive, thus the name of cascading bloom filters.

Larisch et al. [19] emphasize the following advantages of CRLite over CRLs and OCSP:

– Small Size: About 10 MB is needed to represent the status of *all Web certificates*, and 560 kB in average for daily updates. While OCSP also covers all certificates, it is online. CRL on the other hand is not efficient to handle so many certificates.
– Update Frequency: An OCSP response is valid for 4 days in average for the Web, and a CRL has usually a lifetime of 7 days. CRLite is believed to be more up-to-date because it involves daily update.
– Failure Mode: CRLite covers all certificates and allows end entities to operate in a hard fail mode.
– Privacy: The privacy issues caused by OCSP are avoided as CRLite caches the information locally.
– Deployment and Auditing: CRLite is easily deployed and can be audited.
– Speed: Telemetric data shows that CRLite is faster than OCSP in 99% of the cases [16].

There is also some criticism towards the Bloom filter cascades. Holzhauser [14] shows that CRLite will suffer a scalability problem when the number of certificates increase. She also shows faults in the CRLite design that can lead to higher than expected number of false positives.

Short-Lived Certificates. Which are valid from a few hours up to 2–3 days, represent an alternative strategy. Firefox for instance, does not check such short-lived certificate for revocation if they are valid for less than 10 days [8]. This will efficiently remove the need to revoke certificates, given an acceptable risk that illegitimate keys will probably not be used before the certificates expire. The obvious downside is the need for frequent certificate renewal and distribution, which does not go hand in hand with maritime operations.

Table 1. Data capacity, cost and availability of different data bearers

Communication link	Shared capacity	Cost	Availability
VDES	153.6 kbps	Free	Near shore, between nearby ships
GSM/LTE	100 Mbps	0.006 USD/MB	Near shore
Low Frequency SATCOM	100–500 kbps	5–10 USD/MB	Globally
High Frequency SATCOM	100 kbps–8 Mbps	1–2 USD/MB	Globally, dependent on service provider
WiMAX/Wi-Fi	10–100 Mbps	Free	In port

3 Fundamental Requirements for Revocation

We perform an initial filtering of suitable revocation mechanisms by identifying the fundamental requirements imposed by the maritime sector. These are presented below.

While some ships call at port on a regular basis, others might be out at sea for several weeks or even months [13]. They usually rely on different technologies to get connectivity depending on their position: VDES, SatCom, GSM/LTE or even Wi-Fi when at shore. Table 1 developed by Frøystad et al. [13] gives an overview of their properties. Some will in many cases be too expensive or not available at all while at sea. It should therefore be possible to use a cache of revocation information, e.g. when vessels encounter each other on open sea.

> **Requirement 1 - Offline support:** The revocation mechanism should be able to operate when the vessel has no internet connectivity.

Chrome and Firefox currently push incomplete CRLs with only high value certificates in them, but this is not acceptable in the maritime context. The solution needs to be complete, meaning that revocations must be shared between intermediate CAs and eventually known to all end entities. Of course, with a solution that operates offline from time to time, there will be some delay before a revocation information is available to the end entities. The update frequency of the revocation information is left for discussion.

> **Requirement 2 - Completeness:** The revocation mechanism should inform about all revoked vessels in a timely manner.

While the revocation mechanism should not be dependent on the communication link, its bandwidth usage should be as low as possible to ensure acceptance affordability in the wider maritime community. In practice, this means within the capacities given by Table 1.

> **Requirement 3 - Bandwidth:** The bandwidth usage of the revocation mechanism should be within the capacity of the available communication link.

4   Analysis of the Revocation Candidates

4.1   Requirements-Based Selection of the Revocation Mechanism

We now use the requirements identified in Sect. 3 to do an initial filtering of the candidate solutions.

R1 - Offline support: Amongst the previously presented revocation mechanisms, only CRL, DeltaCRL, CRLSet/OneCRL and CRLite are truly offline mechanisms, meaning that the ships can stay off-line for a long period of time and the mechanism will still work, even though it will be on outdated data. On the contrary, OCSP Stapling, OCSP Must Staple and Short-Lived Certificate all rely on periodic connection to update their staple or certificate in order to work. They are therefore not considered viable solutions for the maritime sector.

R2 - Completeness: All revocation mechanisms but CRLSet and OneCRL are complete or can be. CRLSet and OneCRL by definition only include high value revocation information to allow a quick reaction to critical events like of a CA compromise.

R3 - Bandwidth: This parameter is difficult to evaluate. A known problem with CRL is their growing size when the number of certificates in the system growths. However, the deltaCRL is less dependent on this parameter, and more on the system revocation ratio. CRLite was conceived with low-bandwidth usage in mind, but it has only been applied to the web by Mozilla, and the web has very different parameters than the maritime sector.

Table 2 shows which mechanisms fit our requirements the best. As can be seen, CRL/DeltaCRL and CRLite meet al.l three requirements, but there is an uncertainty on their respective bandwidth usage, which we analyse further below.

Table 2. Requirements vs revocation mechanisms

	CRL/Delta-CRL	OCSP	OCSP Stapling	OCSP Must Staple	CRLSet/OneCRL	CRLite	Short-Lived Certificate
R1 Offline support	✓		~	~	✓	✓	~
R2 Completeness	✓	✓	✓	✓		✓	✓
R3 Bandwidth	?					?	

LEGEND: ✓: OK   ~: Partially OK
?: Unknown   Nothing: Not OK

4.2   Bandwidth Analysis for CRL/DeltaCRL and CRLite

In order to estimate bandwidth requirements for the different revocation solutions, we need to estimate some parameters for the PKI. This includes the expected number of certificates in the system and the expected revocation frequency.

The number of merchant ships in the world is varying, but as of January 2019, there were 96,295 registered ships in the total fleet world wide, whereof 51,684 were commercial ships of 1000 gt and above [6]. In addition there will be shore users communicating with the ships (ports, VTS, applications human users etc.), but this number is lower than 1000. To simplify, we approximate that **the total number of end entities that will be enrolled in the maritime PKI will be around 100 000.** Based on the simulation, we observed that the result remains the same with more entities in the PKI, which covers the case of several certificates per ship.

Revocation of the digital certificates from the end entities in a PKI can happen for a number of reasons, but in the maritime domain, change of flag is expected to be the main driver for revocation. We foresee that the frequency of other reasons are negligible in comparison. All commercial ships must be registered with a country, which is known as its Flag State. Ships normally change their flags in connection with sale and purchase transactions. However, ship owners may also do this to avoid the stricter marine regulations imposed by their own countries. In practice, many ships are therefore registered under a flag that does not match the nationality of the vessel owner ("flag of convenience"). The Flag State with the largest number of registered ships is Panama (6465 ship as of January 2019), followed by China (4039 ships), Liberia (3456) and the Marshall Island (3454) [6]. Even though the total number of Flag States is fairly large (117 as of January 2019), we do not foresee that all of these will operate their own Intermediate CA. However, a ship will still need to obtain a new digital certificate when it changes its flag. A study from 2008 [9] provides an indication of the frequency of flag changes. The study uses data collected from 35,261 port state control inspections on 7,547 vessels, carried out between 2002 and 2008. The data shows that 25.3% of all the inspected ships have had at least one change of flag during this time period. Further, 9.5% of all the ships have had at least one change in flag since their previous inspection, where the average number of inspections per ship in this time period was 4.05. Unfortunately, the paper does not include information on how many times the ships have re-flagged, when they have changed their flags "more than once," but we can use an approximation of the **yearly revocation ratio of around 5%.**

We also need to know how long the certificates will be valid. This will impact our analysis, because when revoked certificates expire, they will not be included in the transmitted revocation information anymore. The validity period of end entity certificates in a maritime PKI was studied by several independent research groups [12,13] who proposed to set it to 3 years. We thus chose to fix this parameters to **3 years** for our simulation.

Theoretical Approach[5]

Size of the CRL: In order to evaluate the size of the CRL, we will consider the scenario in which the CRL contains the most certificates. Given that the certificates have a 3-year validity period, they are removed from the CRL once they are not valid anymore. Thus the maximum number of certificates in the CRL is 15 000 (3 × 100000 × 0.05). After doing some tests, we calculated that in average the size (in bytes) of a CRL is given by $S(n) = 277 + 50 \times n$, where n is the number of certificates to be included in the CRL (with a reason code), 277 the size of an empty CRL in bytes and 50 the average size added by the addition of a certificate to the CRL (empirically determined). So, for the maritime sector we end up with a maximum CRL size of 750 kB.

Size of the DeltaCRL. We need to have an idea of the number of certificates that will be included in it, both newly revoked certificates and those that need to be removed from the CRL. If we make the assumption that the CRL and DeltaCRL are issued on a weekly basis, then there is around 100 newly revoked certificates for each DeltaCRL. In addition, we will assume that there is about the same number of certificates removed from the CRL. Following the same formula as above, the size of the DeltaCRL should be around 10 kB.

Size of the CRLite Filter: We need to find an estimation of the size of the filter that needs to be downloaded by the end entities in order to check for the revocation status of a certificate. In their original paper on CRLite [19], the authors present a way to set the parameters of the different filters to have the smallest possible size of the overall bloom filter cascade. We followed that methodology and chose the filters' parameters to minimise the overall size of the bloom filter cascade. For those condition, the overall size of the filter is given by: $S_{bfc} = 4.92 * |R|$, where R is the set of revoked certificates. In our case, the result yields 73 800 bits, or 9.2 kB.

Size of the Delta CRLite Filter: There is no easy way to theoretically estimate the size of the delta filter for CRLite. This needs to be determined in an empirical manner.

As it can be observed from the estimated sizes of the different "payload" for each mechanism, these sizes are smaller than what is normally found and used on the Internet. However, there is still a 75-factor between the size of the CRL and the size of the optimised CRLite filter. The DeltaCRL is about the size of the optimised CRLite filter.

Empirical Approach

In order to get a better idea of the sizes for the different revocation mechanisms, we developed a PKI simulator, consisting of a Root CA, Intermediate CAs, End entities and a CRL issuer. The parameters of the simulator are its duration in time, the revocation ratio and frequency, along with the PKI (number of

---

[5] All the calculations below are based on x509 certificates in DER format.

intermediate CA and end entities). The simulator can also determine the growth of the PKI, as we can assume that not all ships will be part of it from day one, and thus get a better idea of what will happen when a real PKI is be deployed. The following steps are taken for each iteration:

1. Renew certificates that are about to expire.
2. Revoke random certificates based on the revocation ratio parameter.
3. Generate revocation data:
   (a) Generate new CRL.
   (b) Generate DeltaCRL.
   (c) Generate Optimised (minimum) CRLite filter.
   (d) Update CRLite filter.
   (e) Generate Delta Filter (using the updated filter).
4. Enrol new entities (if any, when growth enabled).

Our implementation of the CRLite bloom filter cascade follows Mozilla's implementation available on Github [17] and the implementation of the delta filter follows what is described in the CRLite paper [19].

For the parameters, we used 100 000 end entities and a revocation ratio of 5% as above. The revocation frequency was set to 7 days, which is the common revocation frequency for a CRL. We also estimated that the PKI will start with 1000 entities and then grow to 100 000 over a 5 year period. However, this was only to get an idea of the system evolution when integrating new components. What we really care about is the system in its "steady" state, which is why ran the simulation over a period of 20 years. Figures 3 and 4 along with Table 3 present the results of the simulation.

CRLite Vs CRL: The results presented in Fig. 3 show that the size of the CRL is much bigger than the size of any other mechanism, with an average size of 356 kB for the simulation. Even if this is much smaller than CRLs from the Internet world, this is still too big to be downloaded over a low-speed network. As presented in Table 3, even if the size of the DeltaCRL remains small (with an average of 8.6 kB), the delta filter is even smaller with an average size of 2 kB. It is also interesting to note that the size of the delta filter is almost constant once the system has reached its equilibrium (no more ship being added), and is not much influenced by big changes in the end entities certificates. Indeed, the certificates having a 3-years validity, large amount of already revoked certificates expire every 3-years, leading to substantial changes in CRL (and thus deltaCRL as well). The "waves" pattern that can be observed is the direct consequence of the initial certificates' expiration. The size of the filter is in average 39.5 kB, but like the CRL, it is based as a reference to get the delta filter, and is not sent over low-speed communication channels. The size of the optimised filter, calculated every day for comparison, is close to the size of the DeltaCRL, with an average size of 10.1 kB. Based on the analysis of the simulation, it seems like CRLite is indeed well suited for low-bandwidth usage, not only for the Internet world, but also for the maritime sector, with a payload being five times smaller than the DeltaCRL.

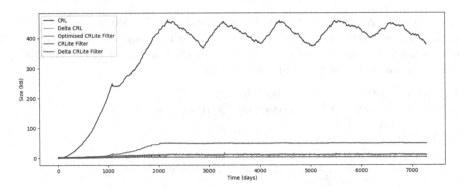

Fig. 3. Results of the PKI revocation simulation, comparing the size of the payload for CRL/DeltaCRL and CRLite filter/Delta filter, over a period of 20 years.

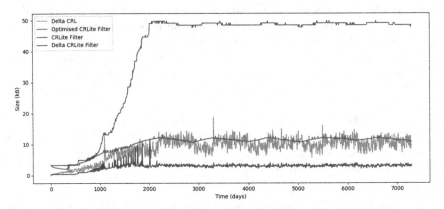

Fig. 4. Zoom on the results of the PKI revocation simulation, comparing the size of the payload for CRL/DeltaCRL and CRLite filter/Delta filter, over a period of 20 years.

Table 3. Size of the payload for different revocation mechanisms

	Theory (Max)	Simulation (Avg.)
CRL Size	750 kB	356 kB
DeltaCRL Size	10 kB	8.6 kB
Optimised filter Size	9.2 kB	10.1 kB
Filter Size	?	39.5 kB
Delta Filter Size	?	2.74 kB

5   Discussion

5.1   CRL and DeltaCRL

Using solely CRL as the revocation mechanism for the maritime PKI is not possible as shown by the simulation: the size of the PKI grows fast and does not meet the low-bandwidth usage requirements. It must be coupled with the use of DeltaCRL.

The main advantage of using CRL/DeltaCRL is that it is a well-known and standardised revocation mechanism. It is also already implemented in commercial PKI solution and is thus more easily acceptable. However, ships can stay at sea for long periods of time, and might have to download several DeltaCRL (or the full CRL) to catch up. Moreover, it is known that CRL/DeltaCRL does not scale well for the Internet. This is true as well for the maritime sector where the constraints are even more strict regarding the internet access and the bandwidth usage. Finally, the CRLs must be collected from all CAs to create a joint CRL by the CRL issuer. This CRL is then transmitted to the end entities. That means that different states might have to trust not only the Root CA but also the CRL issuer.

5.2   CRLite for the Maritime Sector

The second solution is to adapt CRLite to the maritime sector. To the best of our knowledge, this has not been proposed before. A web browser and a ship are very different in nature, and while the main concept can remain the same, the update frequency along with the push/pull model might have to be adapted to fit the need of the maritime sector.

The first advantage of CRLite over CRL is the smaller size of the payload that needs to be delivered to the end-entities. Based on our simulation, the size of the CRLite payload is five times smaller than the equivalent payload for the DeltaCRL. As explained in the background section, CRLite relies on having both the revocation information and the valid certificates information in order to create the filter. To achieve that, CRLite relies on Certificate Transparency, which, even if it is out of the scope for this paper, harden the security of the PKI as a whole. Finally, the authors of the original CRLite paper proposed a way to create the filter in a distributive manner and not involving only the issuer. This is an interesting property for the maritime sector where different states have to collaborate but do not necessarily trust each other.

On the other hand, CRLite is a recent technology (at least compared to CRL), and is neither standardised nor field-tested, which can be an issue to be accepted by the maritime organisations. There is also a lack of formal security analysis and research done. A bachelor thesis from ETH Zurich analysed CRLite and more specifically the usage of Bloom Filter Cascade and concluded that the mechanism presents some weaknesses [14]. In particular, Bloom Filter Cascades do not adapt and scale well with the market growth. This argument does not hold for the maritime sector however, as the amount of certificates is much lower than in the Internet world, where CRLite has been proven to work with around 36M certificates (which is more certificates than the maritime PKI will ever have). Finally, another negative point compared to CRL is that the end entities will get no information on the revoked certificate. When checking for the status of a certificate with CRLite, the answer is either "valid" or "revoked." Depending on how applications plan to handle revocation information, this can be a problem.

5.3   Common Topics to both Solutions

No matter which solution is chosen, the frequency of the updates needs to be determined. CRL and DeltaCRL are usually issued on a weekly basis. For CRLite it is on a daily basis. In our simulation however, we used a weekly basis for both methods as a mean for comparison. Choosing the update frequency comes down to answering the question: "How long do we want the ships to accept revoked certificates." The answer to this question might vary between different ship owners and flag states.

Related to this, the importance of the revocation information may vary depending on the reason why a certificate is revoked. For instance, a certificate being revoked because the ship has changed its flag state is not a security threat by itself, but a certificate revoked because CA compromise is. Different priority could thus be given to different revocation information. The notion of "scopes" is described in RFC 5280 [10], and CRLs (and DeltaCRLs) can be issued with a scope. For instance, it is possible to have a CRL for certificate revoked with the reason code "keys compromised" and another one with all the remaining reasons. It is also possible to implement different frequencies for the different scopes, thus allowing reducing the bandwidth costs as well. Splitting the revocation information in scopes is also feasible in CRLite, but as there are very few cases of key compromises compared to other reasons, creating a filter for those might not be justifiable.

How applications handle the revocation information is also another important issue. Currently, in the Internet world, browsers tend to apply a "soft-fail" techniques, meaning that if it can't verify the certificate validity, it will consider it valid, creating a feeling of false security for the user. In the maritime world, it will be important to think about the failure scenarios, how the information is communicated to the user and what are the process to respond to those failures.

5.4   Looking Elsewhere

Something that has been out of our research scope is to analyse solutions that are still on a conceptual level. For instance, a blockchain-based certificate transparency and revocation mechanism for the web has been proposed by Wang et al. [29] The idea is to remove the trust from the CA, and to transfer it to the end-entities which are in this case the browsers. Servers can then publish their certificates to a public blockchain, and a browser will accept the certificate received during the SSL/TLS negotiations if and only if it matches the ones in the public blockchain and if it is not revoked. It is very much likely that this and similar solutions will require a degree of connectivity that could be difficult to obtain in a maritime setting.

6   Conclusion

In this paper we have identified two potential candidate solutions for revocation of certificates in the maritime sector: 1) CRLs (with DeltaCRLs) and 2) CRLite (with Delta filters). Both these solutions can operate when vessels are offline and they both inform about all revoked vessels in a timely manner. However, our results from simulating the behaviour of these two different solutions over time show that will be significant changes in terms of required bandwidth. While the size of the CRLs itself will have an average size of 365 kB, the size of the DeltaCRLs is expected to be relative small (8.6 kB). Still, CRLite is a much better solution in this respect, with 39.5 kB filter size and 2.74 kB Delta filter size. However, as explained in the discussion, there are pros and cons with both solutions and the final choice will be a trade-off between selecting a more well-known and mature technology (CRL), or going for a potentially more efficient, but less tested, solution (CRLite).

Acknowledgements. This work has been supported by the Research Council of Norway through the "Cyber Security in Merchant Shipping - Service Evolution" project with contract number 295969.

References

1. CA:RevocationPlan. https://wiki.mozilla.org/CA:RevocationPlan#OneCRL. Accessed on 08 Jun 2020
2. Certificate transparency. http://www.certificate-transparency.org/. Accessed on 08 Jun 2020
3. CRL Sets. https://dev.chromium.org/Home/chromium-security/crlsets. Accessed on 08 Jun 2020
4. Improving revocation: OCSP must-staple and short-lived certificates. https://blog.mozilla.org/security/2015/11/23/improving-revocation-ocsp-must-staple-and-short-lived-certificates/. Accessed on 08 Jun 2020
5. The technical specification of VDES. IALA Guideline G1139, Edition 3.0, June 2019
6. UNCTAD Handbook of Statistics 2019 - Merchant Fleet. https://stats.unctad.org/handbook/MaritimeTransport/MerchantFleet.html
7. CySiMS Deliverable D2.2 Using digital signatures in the maritime domain (2017)
8. Revocation Checking in Firefox (2019). https://wiki.mozilla.org/CA/Revocation_Checking_in_Firefox. Accessed on 08 Jun 2020
9. Cariou, P., Wolff, F.C.: Do port state control inspections influence flag- and class-hopping phenomena in shipping? Working Papers hal-00455155, HAL, February 2010. https://ideas.repec.org/p/hal/wpaper/hal-00455155.html
10. Cooper, D., Santesson, S., Farrell, S., Boeyen, S., Housley, R., Polk, W.: Internet X.509 public key infrastructure certificate and certificate revocation list (CRL) Profile. RFC 5280, May 2008. https://tools.ietf.org/html/rfc5280
11. Deacon, A., Hurst, R.: The lightweight online certificate status protocol (OCSP) profile for high-volume environments. RFC 5019 September 2007. https://tools.ietf.org/html/rfc5019
12. Forum, M.C.D.: Identity Management and Cyber Security. IALA Input paper: ENAV19-n.n.n
13. Frøystad, C., Bernsmed, K., Meland, P.H.: Protecting future maritime communication. In: Proceedings of the 12th International Conference on Availability, Reliability and Security, pp. 1–10 (2017)

14. Holzhauser, K.: An Analysis of Bloom Filter Cascades-CRLite (2020)
15. Jain, G.: Certificate revocation: a survey (2000). http://citeseerx.ist.psu.edu/viewdoc/download?doi=10.1.1.17.587&rep=rep1&type=pdf
16. Jones, J.: CRLite: speeding up secure browsing (2020). https://blog.mozilla.org/security/2020/01/21/crlite-part-3-speeding-up-secure-browsing/. Accessed on 08 Jun 2020
17. Jones, J.: filter-cascade (2020). https://github.com/mozilla/filter-cascade/blob/master/filtercascade/. Accessed on 08 Jun 2020
18. Langley, A.: Revocation checking and Chrome's CRL (2012). https://www.imperialviolet.org/2012/02/05/crlsets.html. Accessed on 08 Jun 2020
19. Larisch, J., Choffnes, D., Levin, D., Maggs, B.M., Mislove, A., Wilson, C.: Crlite: a scalable system for pushing all TLS revocations to all browsers. In: 2017 IEEE Symposium on Security and Privacy (SP), pp. 539–556. IEEE (2017)
20. Laurie, B.: Certificate transparency. Commun. ACM **57**(10), 40–46 (2014)
21. Lázaro, F., Raulefs, R., Wang, W., Clazzer, F., Plass, S.: VHF data exchange system (VDES): an enabling technology for maritime communications. CEAS Space **11**, 55–63 (2019). https://doi.org/10.1007/s12567-018-0214-8
22. Mitzenmacher, M.: Compressed bloom filters. IEEE/ACM Trans. Netw. **10**(5), 604–612 (2002)
23. Peiponen, H., Kukkonen, A.: Integrity monitoring and authentication for VDES pre-distributed public keys. IALA Committee Working Document. Input paper: ENAV18-11.10
24. Pettersen, Y.: The transport layer security (TLS) multiple certificate status request extension. RFC 6961, June 2013. https://www.ietf.org/rfc/rfc6961.txt
25. Pettersen, Y.: X.509v3 Transport layer security (TLS) feature extension. RFC 7633, October 2015. https://tools.ietf.org/html/rfc7633
26. Santesson, S., Myers, M., Ankney, R., Malpani, A., Galperin, S., Adams, C.: X.509 internet public key infrastructure online certificate status protocol - OCSP. RFC 6960, June 2013. https://tools.ietf.org/html/rfc6960
27. Smith, T., Dickinson, L., Seamons, K.: Let's revoke: scalable global certificate revocation. In: Proceedings 2020 Network and Distributed System Security Symposium, Internet Society, San Diego, CA (2020)
28. Wang, Q., Gao, D., Chen, D.: Certificate revocation schemes in vehicular networks: a survey. IEEE Access **8**, 26223–26234 (2020)
29. Wang, Z., Lin, J., Cai, Q., Wang, Q., Zha, D., Jing, J.: Blockchain-based certificate transparency and revocation transparency. IEEE Trans. Dependable Secure Comput. 1 (2020)
30. Wohlmacher, P.: Digital certificates: a survey of revocation methods. In: Proceedings of the 2000 ACM workshops on Multimedia, pp. 111–114 (2000)

Security Mechanisms and Training

HoneyHash: Honeyword Generation Based on Transformed Hashes

Canyang Shi and Huiping Sun[✉]

Peking University, Beijing, China
shigle@pku.edu.cn, sunhp@ss.pku.edu.cn

Abstract. Since systems using honeywords store a set of decoy passwords together with real passwords of users to confuse adversaries, they are strongly dependent on the algorithm for generating honeywords. However, all of the existing honeyword generating algorithms are based on raw passwords of users and they either need lots of storage space or show weaknesses in flatness or usability. This paper proposes HoneyHash, a new direction of generating honeywords - generating by transforming password hashes. Analyses show that our algorithm attains expected levels of flatness, security, performance and usability.

Keywords: Password · Honeyword · HoneyHash · Transformed hash · Flatness

1 Introduction

A large number of password disclosures were reported in recent years which have been a big threat to password security. For instance, the hashed passwords of 50 million users of Evernote were exposed [1] and similar leakages of password databases also happened in LinkedIn, eHarmony, Yahoo and Adobe [2]. There are several existing mechanisms against password-related attacks including SAuth [3], PolyPassHash [4], ErsatzPassword [5] and Honeyword [6]. Among those existing mechanisms, the honeyword mechanism, which is influenced by the honeypot technique [7] and Kamouflage [8], stands out for its ability to detect attacks against hashed password databases. In a honeyword system, a set of fake passwords are stored together with real passwords in order to confuse adversaries. When an adversary attempts to log in with a fake password, the system can identify this illegal submission and an alarm may be triggered, marking a possible leakage of the password database.

The honeyword generating algorithm is important since the ability of detecting password database leakages is strongly dependent on the quality of honeywords. Until now, all existing algorithms generate honeywords based on raw passwords of users, which need to find a balance point among several factors such as flatness, performance and usability. For instance, Juels and Rivest [6] proposed *chaffing by tweaking* and *take-a-tail* when they first proposed the honeyword mechanism. *Chaffing by tweaking* brings no burden on the memorability of users and has lower time and space complexity, but it cannot generate flat honeywords. *Take-a-tail* can achieve flatness but it puts more stresses on memorability of users.

M. Asplund and S. Nadjm-Tehrani (Eds.): NordSec 2020, LNCS 12556, pp. 161–173, 2021.
https://doi.org/10.1007/978-3-030-70852-8_10

In this paper, we propose a new honeyword generating algorithm in which honeywords are generated by transforming hashes of original passwords. Comparing with existing algorithms, our algorithm attains higher levels of flatness, security, performance and usability. All the honeywords are transformed hashes which achieve great flatness; the algorithm shows a strong resistance to different password-related attacks including brute-force attacks, dictionary attacks, denial-of-service (DoS) attacks, targeted password guessing and multiple system attacks; the generating process is simple and only one transformed hash is stored in the password database, leading to lower time complexity and storage cost; no extra burden is put on the memorability of users.

The rest of this paper is organized as follows – in Sect. 2 we describe some other mechanisms against password-related attacks followed by the honeyword mechanism. We list existing generating methods of honeywords and analyze them from four aspects including flatness, security, performance and usability. Our new method is presented in Sect. 3 with technical descriptions and basic routines. Then analyses of the proposed method are elaborated from those four aspects thereafter in Sect. 4.

2 Related Works

2.1 Existing Mechanisms Against Password-Related Attacks

There are already several solutions to password-related threats including SAuth [3], PolyPassHash [4], ErsatzPassword [5] and Honeyword [6]. SAuth employs authentication synergy among different services and requires users to log in other servers when visiting a certain server. PolyPassHash employs a threshold cryptosystem to protect password hashes so that they cannot be verified unless a threshold of them have been decoded. ErsatzPassword utilizes a machine-dependent function at the authentication server which can prevent off-site password discovery effectively, and it also employs a deception mechanism to raise an alert if such an action is attempted.

The main idea of the honeyword mechanism is to store a set of passwords (sweetwords) for each account which contains several decoy passwords (honeywords) and the real password (sugarword), so that even if adversaries obtain the password-hash database and recover the original passwords, they cannot discern the real one. When an adversary tries to log in with a honeyword, an alarm may be triggered, informing administrators of a potential leakage of the password database.

2.2 Existing Honeyword Generating Algorithms

Juels and Rivest [6] provided four methods of generating honeywords when they first proposed the honeyword mechanism in 2013. *Chaffing by tweaking* generates honeywords by replacing letters and numbers with other letters and numbers. *Chaffing-with-a-password-model* applies a probabilistic algorithm based on publicly available password databases. *Chaffing with "tough nuts"* generates honeywords which are much harder to crack than the average, e.g., 256-bit, random bit-strings. *Take-a-tail* asks users to add short suffixes to their raw passwords. Then honeywords are generated by changing the suffix of the sugarword.

Imran Erguler [9] proposed another honeyword generating method which maintains a set of integers for each user, corresponding to a set of existing passwords stored in another list. One of the passwords is the sugarword and the others are honeywords. The index of the sugarword is saved in the honeychecker.

Nilesh Chakraborty and Samrat Mondal [11] proposed three new algorithms including *modified-tail, close-number-formation* and *caps-key based approach. Modified-tail* is an extension of *take-a-tail* which allows users to have the freedom to choose tails without diluting the security standards. *Close-number-formation* changes the numbers in original passwords slightly. *Caps-key based approach* changes several letters from lower case to upper case. In another paper, Nilesh Chakraborty and Samrat Mondal [13] proposed *paired distance protocol* approach which not only attains a high detection rate, but also reduces the storage cost to a great extent.

Akshima, etc. [18] proposed two legacy-UI models, *evolving password model* and *user-profile model*, and one modified-UI model, *append-secret model. Evolving password model* utilizes a probabilistic model of real passwords. *User-profile model* generates honeywords by combining details from user profiles. *Append-secret model* generates honeywords by calculating and appending a secret suffix to the passwords.

Several examples of aforementioned algorithms are presented below (Table 1).

Table 1. Examples of existing generating algorithms

Generating algorithm	Sugarword	Possible honeyword(s)
Chaffing by tweaking	BG+7y45	BG+7q03, BG+7m55, BG+7y45
Chaffing-with-a-password-model	mice3blind	gold5rings
Chaffing with "tough nuts"	/	9,50PEe]KV.0?RIOtc&L-:IJ"b + Wol<*[!NWT/pb
Take-a-tail	RedEye2413	RedEye2582, RedEye2766 (413 is the tail generated by the system randomly)
Modified-tail	tea@?|	tea?|@, tea?@|, teal?@, teal@?, tea@|? (@? is the tail chosen by the user from the set of special characters {@, ?, |}.)
Close-number-formation	28May2000	26 May 1999, 25 May 1997, 29 May 2001, 22 May 1998,
Caps-key based approach	aNImal	AnImal, aNimaL, Animal, anImAl
Paired distance protocol	secrettp7	secretk8b, secretekx (tp7 is the tail chosen by the user)
Evolving password model	abcde123%	secret_9
User-profile model	/	Wood = 1995, Alice_19, Jerry#19wood
Append-secret model	abcde1998	abcde4e7j@ (1998 is an extra entry chosen by the user)

2.3 Analysis of Existing Algorithms

The effectiveness of the honeyword mechanism is strongly dependent on the honeyword generating method. In this part, we focus on several factors, including flatness, security, performance and usability, when evaluating existing generating algorithms.

Flatness

Flatness marks the probability of each honeyword to be regarded as the true password from the view of an adversary. A flatter generating method makes it harder for adversaries to discern the sugarword. Among all existing ideas, those algorithms which generate honeywords by changing suffixes achieve better flatness, while tweaking algorithms may not generate flat honeywords in some cases, especially when the sugarword contains a unique pattern and stands out among fake passwords.

Security

The security of an algorithm represents its resistance to password-related attacks such as brute-force attacks, dictionary attacks, denial-of-service (DoS) attacks, targeted password guessing and multiple system attacks. Algorithms like *user-profile model* show lower resistance to targeted password guessing since their honeywords are highly related to personal information. On the other hand, if honeywords are highly predictable, adversaries can use DoS attacks by keeping submitting honeywords deliberately with the help of available true passwords. Some algorithms implement extra mechanisms to defend attacks, but other factors are weakened at the same time.

Performance

Performance measures time and space costs, including time complexity of the generating algorithm and storage space needed by both the password database and the honeychecker. Compared with complex algorithms, those algorithms with simple ideas such as tweaking or changing suffixes have lower time complexity, but nearly all existing algorithms have to store extra k honeywords together with the sugarword, or maintain a huge database of existing passwords which takes a lot of storage space.

Usability

Usability includes some user-related factors. For example, does the system interfere the password choice of the user? Do users need to memorize extra information? What is the possibility of inputting a honeyword by mistake? Among existing methods, generating honeywords by changing suffixes requires users to memorize extra tails, bringing more burdens to users; some other methods, such as the *caps-key based approach*, add extra limits to legal passwords which interferes the password choices of users; for tweaking methods, the typing mistake of a user may be recognized as a submission of honeyword, leading to an alarm which is not expected to be triggered.

3 A New Direction

3.1 Main Ideas

Most of the existing generating algorithms are based on original passwords. They generate honeywords by directly transforming the original password, or by making up a new password according to the original pattern. Thus, existing methods may have a huge storage cost, and the honeywords may not be flat enough so that adversaries can easily discern the real passwords.

Our algorithm – "transformed-hash", generates a honeyword from the hash of the raw password, and actually, the honeyword is just a transformed hash. The information of the transformation is stored in the honeychecker. The comparison between concerns of existing models and our algorithm is showed below (Fig. 1). There are two main improvements of our algorithm. Firstly, we only store one password hash for each user in the password database, which reduces the storage cost to a large degree. Secondly, instead of generating honeywords based on raw passwords, we focus on hashes and use a transformed hash as a honeyword. Therefore, our method attains expected levels of flatness, security, performance and usability.

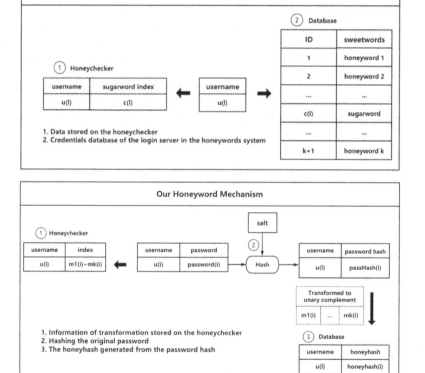

Fig. 1. Comparison between concerns of existing models and our algorithm

3.2 Transforming Methods

Transforming methods are applied to turn the hash of the real password to a fake hash. In this paper, we propose a relatively simple strategy to illustrate our idea. We suppose that the password hashes are 256-bit long. The algorithm transforms a hash by flipping k bits, namely, it selects k bits of the password hash randomly, and then changes them to their unary complements.

It is noteworthy that some transformed hashes may be excluded by adversaries since they do not seem to be hashes of user-generated passwords, so the space of decoy hashes must be huge enough so that enough deceptive keys are incorporated. Let p stand for the ratio of the theoretical key space to the actual key space. For a 256-bit hash, the number of deceptive transformed hashes is

$$\frac{1}{p} \times \binom{256}{k}$$

To find a proper value for k, we should focus on the number of deceptive hashes (Table 2). The values of parameters should be set properly basing on actual situations. In this paper, as an example, we assume $p = 10^8$ and set the value of k to 5, and the number of deceptive hashes is 88 in this case. Therefore, the system generates a transformed hash by flipping 5 different bits of the original hash.

Table 2. The number of deceptive transformed hashes for different values of k and p

k	10^7	10^8	10^9
4	17	2	0
5	881	88	9
6	36853	3685	369

3.3 Technical Descriptions

Symbols

u_i: the ith user of the computer system
p_i: the raw password of u_i
H: the cryptographic hash function used in the computer system
$H(p_i)$: the password hash of u_i
$H'(p_i)$: the transformed password hash of u_i
$m_{i1} \sim m_{i5}$: five integers that mark the indexes of the changed bits.

Password Database

The system maintains a file F storing information of usernames and passwords. File F lists the pairs of usernames and transformed password hashes which have the following form:

$$(u_i, H'(p_i))$$

Thus, file F can be described as $\{(u_i, H'(p_i))\}$.

Honeychecker

Like the original honeyword generation methods proposed by Juels and Rivest, this new method also needs a server called honeychecker to check whether the inputted password is a sugarword. For each user u_i, the honeychecker maintains $m_{i1} \sim m_{i5}$ which represent the indexes of the changed bits of $H(p_i)$. Records of the honeychecker database have the following form:

$$(u_i, m_{i1} \sim m_{i5}) = (u_i, m_{i1}, m_{i2}, m_{i3}, m_{i4}, m_{i5})$$

And the honeychecker database can be described as $\{(u_i, m_{i1} \sim m_{i5})\}$.
Our honeychecker receives messages of the following two types:

$$Set: i, m_1 \sim m_5$$

Store the indexes of the changed bits for u_i, namely, set the values of $m_{i1} \sim m_{i5}$ to $m_1 \sim m_5$.

$$Check: i, m_1 \sim m_5$$

The honeychecker queries its database to get $m_{i1} \sim m_{i5}$. If $m_{i1} \sim m_{i5}$ equals to $m_1 \sim m_5$, then the check succeeds, otherwise the check fails and the honeychecker may raise an alarm.

3.4 Algorithm Routines

Registration

A new honeyword is generated in the process of registration. When a user u_i inputs the expected password p_i, the computer system calculates the password hash $H(p_i)$ at first. Then five random integers $m_1 \sim m_5$ are generated, marking the indexes of bits that will be changed. Later, the system transforms the password hash and gets $H'(p_i)$. Finally, the honeychecker is informed of this operation and the pair $(u_i, H'(p_i))$ is stored into file F.
    The routine of registration is presented below:

(1) Read u_i and p_i inputted by the user
(2) Calculate the password hash $H(p_i)$
(3) Generate five different random integers $m_1 \sim m_5$ that are greater than or equal to 0 and smaller than 256

(4)   Get $H'(p_i)$ by changing the five bits of $H(p_i)$ to their unary complements
(5)   Send *Set*: $i, m_1 \sim m_5$ to the honeychecker
(6)   Store the pair $(u_i, H'(p_i))$ into file F

Login

When a user tries to login with a username u_i and a password w_i (the password may be incorrect), the computer system calculates the password hash $H(w_i)$. Then the system queries the file F database and get $H'(p_i)$. In order to detect possible leakages of password databases, an alarm will be triggered when a similarly-transformed password (we still call it a honeyword for convenience) is submitted. According to our transforming method, compared with the hash of the sugarword, all those passwords whose hashes have exactly five different bits are regarded as honeywords. Therefore, if $H(w_i)$ and $H'(p_i)$ have exactly five different bits, then the system sends the indexes of the different bits to the honeychecker and waits for it to have a further check.

The routine of login is presented below:

(1)   Read u_i and w_i inputted by the user
(2)   Calculate the password hash $H(w_i)$
(3)   Look for $H'(p_i)$, the transformed password hash of u_i, in file F. Then compare $H(w_i)$ with $H'(p_i)$. If $H'(p_i)$ is not found in F, or $H(w_i)$ and $H'(p_i)$ do not have exactly five different bits, the login routine fails.
(4)   Get the indexes of the different bits $m_1 \sim m_5$
(5)   Send *Check*: $i, m_1 \sim m_5$ to the honeychecker
(6)   If the check succeeds, then the user login successfully, otherwise the login routine fails. Besides, an alarm may be raised when the check fails, informing an administrator or other party of a possible leakage of the password hash database.

Modification

The routine of modifying the password is almost the same as that of registration. When a user u_i inputs the modified password p_i', the computer system calculates the password hash $H(p_i')$ at first, then generates five new random integers $m_1' \sim m_5'$, marking the five bits of $H(p_i')$ that will be changed. Later, the system transforms the password hash and get $H'(p_i')$. After informing the honeychecker of this operation, the system stores the pair $(u_i, H'(p_i'))$ into file F.

The routine of modifying the password is presented below:

(1)   Read u_i and p_i' inputted by the user
(2)   Calculate the password hash $H(p_i')$
(3)   Generate five different random integers $m_1' \sim m_5'$ that are greater than or equal to 0 and smaller than 256
(4)   Get $H'(p_i)$ by changing the five bits of $H(p_i)$ to their unary complements
(5)   Send *Set* : $i, m_1' \sim m_5'$ to the honeychecker
(6)   Store the pair $(u_i, H'(p_i'))$ into file F

4   Analysis

4.1   Flatness and Security Analysis

Flatness

Flatness influences the difficulty of detecting the sugarword from honeywords. As our model is based on transforming hashes, the honeyword and the sugarword only have similar hashes and their original forms are totally different. For each account, adversaries must find how the hash is transformed before looking for the sugarword.

However, it is really difficult to find the transforming way, and detecting the sugarword is nearly impossible. We suppose that the password hash is transformed by flipping k bits. Then there are $256! \div (251! \times 5!) = 8809549056$ possible original password hashes for $k = 5$, each of which can be regarded as a honeyword. Comparing with existing generating algorithms which generally store about 20 sweetwords for each account, our algorithm has a huge decoy-key space. Most importantly, adversaries cannot rely on any pattern to help them discover the real hash of the original password because each sweetword is a 256-bit hash and shows nothing special.

Brute-Force Attacks and Dictionary Attacks

Adversaries need to enumerate all possible passwords for a brute-force attack. Because of the huge number of honeywords which may cause alarms, adversaries can easily be detected while submitting guesses. Therefore, the proposed algorithm has a strong resistance to brute-force attacks. For attackers, the computational expense of cracking the password database is also higher comparing with that of attacking other existing honeyword systems.

An adversary may also carry out a dictionary attack with the help of a dictionary of user-generated passwords. If the adversary knows that the stored hashes have been transformed by tweaking k bits, he can keep calculating hashes of passwords from the dictionary offline until he discovers a password whose hash value has exactly k different bits comparing with the stored hash, and then he may submit the discovered password. However, if we suppose that the dictionary contains 10^{-8} of all theoretically possible passwords, then there are $256! \div (251! \times 5!) \times 10^{-8} \approx 88$ confusing honeywords when 5 bits are changed. Therefore, if k is chosen properly, the adversary can probably find many confusing answers when carrying out a dictionary attack, leading to a high possibility of being detected when logging in. In sum, our algorithm can defend dictionary attacks effectively.

Denial-of-Service Attacks

Denial-of-service (DoS) attacks can be a potential problem and threat for the honeyword mechanism, especially when the generated honeywords are highly predictable. If an adversary has not compromised the password database F but successfully knows the original password of the user in some way, he has a great chance to guess honeywords and submits them to the system deliberately. The system may force a global password reset or blocking the whole web-server in response to the submission of one or more honeywords.

The key point to mitigating DoS attacks is reducing the chance of triggering an alarm maliciously. One way is to increase the difficulty of guessing honeywords with the help of known sugarwords or honeywords. According to our algorithm, the sugarword and honeywords can be totally different since they only have similar hashes. Knowing a sugarword or a honeyword brings no benefit to adversaries when trying to discover other honeywords, so the discovery of each honeyword needs a dictionary attack. Besides, the alarming mechanism can be changed so that alarms cannot be triggered unless an enough number of different honeywords are submitted to the system. For those adversaries who have obtained the original password in some way, they have to use dictionary attacks repeatedly until they have found enough different honeywords, so they almost have no chance to trigger an alarm on purpose. Therefore, comparing with existing generating algorithms, our model can help the system to defend DoS attacks to a large degree.

Targeted Password Guessing

Adversaries may also use targeted password guessing attacks by detecting the sugarword with the help of the personal information of users, which can be easily obtained based on usernames or the social network graphs, especially for those users whose passwords are highly related to their personal information.

The best way to prevent targeted password guessing attacks is using irrelevant honeywords so that personal information brings no benefit to adversaries. In our model, only one honeyword, the transformed password hash, is stored for each account and no personal information is involved because of the transformation, adversaries cannot expect to gain any advantage of detecting the sugarword.

Multiple Systems

Users prefer setting the same password across different systems. In that case, adversaries may get advantages for discovering the sugarword. Juels and Rivest described *intersection attacks* and *sweetword-submission attacks* which are related to multiple systems. If a set of distinct honeywords are stored for each account, an adversary can compromise the password database on several different systems and learn the real password from the intersection of those sweetword sets. On the other hand, if a part of those systems do not use honeywords in order to avoid *intersection attacks*, adversaries can submit sweetwords as password guesses to the honeyword-absent systems without risks of detection.

One way to make the system resistant to such attacks is enlarging the intersection of sweetword sets among different systems. If the intersection has many sweetwords instead of one, then adversaries cannot identify the sugarword from it. In our model, when a user employs the same password on two different systems which both transform original hashes by flipping k bits, then the intersection of the two sets has at least $\binom{2k}{k}$ sweetwords (6 sweetwords when k = 2 and 252 sweetwords when k = 5). Therefore, even if an adversary has compromised both systems and has found the intersection of sweetword sets, he still cannot discover the exact sugarword. Thus, our algorithm has a higher resistance to multiple system attacks.

4.2 Performance and Usability Analyses

Performance

Time Complexity

Our algorithm has a comparatively lower time complexity. The idea and routines of our algorithm are simple and the whole generating process can be divided into two parts, calculating a hash and transforming a hash. Transforming a hash can be done easily and quickly with the use of bit operation. Calculating the hash is the most time-consuming part whose time cost depends on the hash method. Therefore, the time complexity of our algorithm is nearly the same as that of calculating a hash, which is necessary for every generating method.

Storage Cost

The hash-based generating method also has a low storage cost. Nearly all existing methods store k sweetwords for one account. If we suppose that $k = 20$ and sweetwords are 256-bit hashes, then for each account, the sweetwords take $20 \times 256 = 5120$ bits in the password database and the honeychecker needs $\log_2 20 \approx 5$ bits to store the index of the sugarword. The total amount of storage cost is $5120 + 5 = 5125$ bits. However, in our model, the transformed hash takes 256 bits in the password database and the indexes of the changed bits $m_{i1} \sim m_{i5}$ are stored in the honeychecker which take $5 \times \log_2 256 = 40$ bits, so the storage space needed for each account is just $256 + 40 = 296$ bits. Therefore, comparing with other existing mechanisms, the storage cost of our algorithm is reduced to a large degree.

Usability

Stress on Memorability

This algorithm puts negligible burdens on the memorability of users. Users do not need to memorize a tail or other extra information since the final password is the same as the expected one. Users can choose their passwords freely without being limited or interfered by the system. They can even set a relatively simple password or one that is related to their personal information because even for a simple or person-related password, the transformed password hash is still hard to be decoded. In addition, since the algorithm is resistant to multiple-system attacks, a user can use same passwords for different systems, which brings negligible stresses on the memorability of users when setting passwords for a new account.

Typo-Safety

When typing the password, a user may make mistakes and input a wrong one, and a worse case is that the wrong password happens to hit a honeyword which triggers an alarm. This probably happens especially when honeywords are almost the same as the sugarword. In our algorithm, however, comparing with the sugarword, those passwords which can cause an alarm just have similar hashes, and their original forms can be totally different from the true password, so it is impossible for a user to input a honeyword by error. Thus, this method can be considered as typo-safe.

5 Discussions

In this paper, we present a simple algorithm of the transforming method. The way of transforming hashes can be changed but the values of parameters should be set properly basing on actual situations. For instance, if the password hash is transformed by flipping k bits, then k can affect the number of theoretical honeywords. When k is too small, adversaries can easily find the sugarword by carrying out a dictionary attack; when k is too big, adversaries may find it nearly impossible to find the sugarword and do not try submitting any guesses in the end, and hence the system may lose the ability to detect a potential leakage of the password database.

6 Conclusion

In this paper, we propose HoneyHash, a new direction of generating honeywords which overcomes some inherent defects of existing generating algorithms. It turns out that the proposed methodology meets high standards of flatness, security, performance and usability. We hope that the proposed algorithm can encourage more systems to use the honeyword mechanism.

References

1. Gross, D.: 50 million compromised in Evernote hack. In: CNN (2013)
2. Gaylord, C.: LinkedIn, Last.fm, now Yahoo? Don't ignore news of a password breach. In: Christian Science Monitor (2012)
3. Kontaxis, G., Athanasopoulos, E., Portokalidis, G., Keromytis, A.D.: Sauth: protecting user accounts from password database leaks. In: Proceedings of the 2013 ACM SIGSAC Conference on Computer & Communications Security, pp. 187–198. ACM (2013)
4. Cappos, J.: PolyPassHash: protecting passwords in the event of a password file disclosure. In: Password Hashing Competition (PHC) (2014)
5. Almeshekah, M.H., Gutierrez, C.N., Atallah, M.J., Spafford, E.H.: ErsatzPasswords: ending password cracking and detecting password leakage. In: Proceedings of ACSAC, pp. 311–320 (2015)
6. Juels, A., Rivest, R. L.: Honeywords: making password-cracking detectable. In: Proceedings of the 2013 ACM SIGSAC Conference on Computer & Communications Security, pp. 145–160. ACM (2013)
7. Cohen, F.: The use of deception techniques: honeypots and decoys. In: Bidgoli, H. (ed.) Handbook of Information Security, vol. 3, pp. 646–655 (2006)
8. Bojinov, H., Bursztein, E., Boyen, X., Boneh, D.: Kamouflage: loss-resistant password management. In: Gritzalis, D., Preneel, B., Theoharidou, M. (eds.) ESORICS 2010. LNCS, vol. 6345, pp. 286–302. Springer, Heidelberg (2010). https://doi.org/10.1007/978-3-642-15497-3_18
9. Erguler, I.: Achieving flatness: selecting the honeywords from existing user passwords. IEEE Trans. Depend. Secur. Comput. 13(2), 284–295 (2016)
10. Chatterjee, R., Bonneau, J., Juels, A., Ristenpart, T.: Cracking-resistant password vaults using natural language encoders. IEEE Secur. Privacy 481–498 (2016)
11. Chakraborty, N., Mondal, S.: Few notes towards making honeyword system more secure and usable. In: Proceedings of 8th International Conference Security and Information Network, pp. 237–245 (2015)

12. Golla, M., Beuscher, B., Dürmuth, M.: On the security of cracking-resistant password vaults. In: Proceedings of ACM CCS, pp. 1230–1241 (2016)
13. Chakraborty, N., Mondal, S.: On designing a modified-UI based honeyword generation approach for overcoming the existing limitations. Comput. Secur. **66**, 155–168 (2017)
14. Pasquini, C., Schöttle, P., Böhme, R.: Decoy password vaults: at least as hard as steganography? In: De Capitani di Vimercati, S., Martinelli, F. (eds.) SEC 2017. IAICT, vol. 502, pp. 356–370. Springer, Cham (2017). https://doi.org/10.1007/978-3-319-58469-0_24
15. Genç, Z.A., Kardaş, S., Kiraz, M.S.: Examination of a new defense mechanism: honeywords. In: Hancke, G., Damiani, E. (eds.) Information Security Theory and Practice. WISTP 2017. Lecture Notes in Computer Science, vol. 10741. Springer, Cham (2017). https://doi.org/10.1007/978-3-319-93524-9_8
16. Wang, D., Cheng, H., Wang, P., Yan, J., Huang, X.: A security analysis of honeywords. In: NDSS (2018)
17. Gutierrez, C.N., Almeshekah, M.H., Bagchi, S., Spafford, E.H.: A hypergame analysis for Ersatzpasswords. In: Janczewski, L.J., Kutyłowski, M. (eds.) SEC 2018. IAICT, vol. 529, pp. 47–61. Springer, Cham (2018). https://doi.org/10.1007/978-3-319-99828-2_4
18. Akshima, C.D., Goel, A., Mishra, S., Sanadhya, S. K.: Generation of secure and reliable honeywords, preventing false detection. IEEE Trans. Depend. Secure Comput. **16**(5), 757–769, (2019)
19. Wang, D., Cheng, H., Wang, P., Yan, J., Huang, X.: Targeted online password guessing: An underestimated threat. In: Proceedings of ACM SIGSAC Conference on Computing Communication Security, pp. 1242–1254 (2016)
20. Choi, H., Nam, H., Hur, J.: Password typos resilience in honey encryption. In: Proceedings of IEEE 2017 ICOIN, pp. 594–598 (2017)
21. Karuna, P., Purohit, H., Ganesan, R., Jajodia, S.: Generating hard to comprehend fake documents for defensive cyber deception. IEEE Intell. Syst. **33**(5), 16–25 (2018)

Agent-Based File Extraction Using Virtual Machine Introspection

Thomas Dangl$^{(\boxtimes)}$, Benjamin Taubmann, and Hans P. Reiser

University of Passau, Innstr. 43, 94032 Passau, Germany
thomas.dangl@uni-passau.de, {bt,hr}@sec.uni-passau.de

Abstract. Virtual machine introspection (VMI) can be defined as the external monitoring of virtual machines. In previous work, the importance of this technique for malware analysis and digital forensics has become apparent. However, in these domains the problem occurs that some information is not available in the main memory at all times. Specifically, files contained on non-volatile memory are typically not accessible for VMI applications. In this paper, we present a file extraction architecture that uses a dynamically injected in-guest agent to expose the file system for VMI-based analysis. To enable the execution of this in-guest agent, we also introduce a process injection mechanism for ELF binaries through the main memory using VMI.

Keywords: File extraction · Virtual machine introspection · Code injection

1 Introduction

Virtual machine introspection (VMI) is the process of monitoring virtual machines from the outside to gain knowledge of the inner state [7]. Due to this external monitoring of live systems, VMI has become an appealing technique for intrusion detection, malware analysis, virtual machine management, software debugging and memory forensics [11].

When dealing with *virtual machine introspection*-based malware analysis and computer forensics, many situations arise that require efficient access to non-volatile memory such as files that are stored on hard disk [15]. However, practical implementations for this use-case (when only access to main memory is given or the file system is encrypted) are lacking. In automated malware analysis, it is desirable to submit payloads that malware downloads to disk to the monitor for static analysis. For example, updates to malware should automatically be transferred to the monitor to track its evolution. For computer forensics purposes, it can be essential to obtain files contained in virtual machines during run-time without interruption of active services. Because files are typically not loaded into memory unless the user actively accesses them, performing forensics on the main memory is insufficient. Access to virtualized storage of the guest through virtual machine introspection instead of extracting the wanted data from the disk image

M. Asplund and S. Nadjm-Tehrani (Eds.): NordSec 2020, LNCS 12556, pp. 174–191, 2021.
https://doi.org/10.1007/978-3-030-70852-8_11

is required in situations where the target is protected by (full) disk encryption. Another reason could be that the targeted file is not stored on the VM itself, but is instead located on network storage, which is not accessible by the monitor.

In order to extract files from persistent storage, domain-specific solutions such as extracting credentials for *NFS* and *WebDAV*-based network storage or key extraction for encrypted volumes such as *encFS* or *LUKS* have been proposed [21]. However, those techniques only apply in their respective domain, as in many cases the file system type is not known in advance, is proprietary, or the technique relies on user actions.

In this paper, we design and implement a file extraction mechanism for use in VMI environments with the assistance of a dynamically injected in-guest agent that directly uses the file system capabilities of the guest. This proposed architecture is built with the following goals in mind: First, it must work on remote and encrypted file systems, this means the mechanism must operate independently of the underlying file system. Second, it should allow for reasonable transfer speeds so that the mechanism can be used to extract large files. Third, it must solely rely on existing introspection APIs without any modifications to the VMM. Last, it must be built considering stealthiness.

The contributions of this paper are the design, implementation, and evaluation of the following components that can be deployed in production environments on an unmodified Xen hypervisor using primitive VMI operations and events:

- A file extraction mechanism for files that are not loaded to main memory
- A process injection mechanism for VMI applications to execute ELF binaries
- A communication channel between an injected process and a VMI application

The outline of the paper is as follows: In Sect. 2 we present the common techniques of virtual machine introspection for hardware-assisted virtualization. The assumptions of our file extraction architecture and potential mitigation measures for the monitored virtual machine are discussed in Sect. 3. Section 4 introduces the components of the file extraction mechanism and outlines their interactions through VMI methods. In Sect. 5 we discuss the implementation of the VMI application and the in-guest agent that is injected into the monitored system as an ELF binary. Section 6 assesses the architecture based on transfer speed, performance degradation and stealthiness. In Sect. 7 we compare our work to the most related approaches concerning VMI-based code injection and file extraction. Finally, we conclude our findings in Sect. 8.

2   Virtual Machine Introspection

We begin by introducing the relevant terminology and the principles integral to the design and implementation of the file extraction architecture.

VMI and the Semantic Gap: Virtual machine introspection *(VMI)* was first designed to enhance robustness in intrusion detection systems by Garfinkel and Rosenblum in 2003 [7]. They defined VMI as the approach of inspecting a VM to analyze its behavior. Their first attempts at this novel technique involved a modified version of VMW are Workstation, which allowed the use of *direct memory access* (DMA) and access to virtual memory through manual address translation.

Pfoh et al. provide the theoretical foundation by describing a formal model for *virtual machine introspection* [24]. They still discuss this in the context of intrusion detection, but their results remain applicable for all VMI-based security applications. In particular, the research alludes to possible practical applications such as computer forensics and secure logging. One of the main issues identified here is the *semantic gap*, meaning the monitor requires assumptions over the internal state of the virtual machine, e.g., the memory layout, data structure layout, and kernel objects. The semantic gap is the problem of extracting high-level semantic information from low-level data sources [5].

Jain et al. summarize and compare multiple approaches concerning bridging the *semantic gap* [15]. They divide the problem of the *semantic gap* into sub-problems: The *weak semantic gap* refers to the challenge of creating *VMI-based* tools. The *strong semantic gap*, on the other hand, is the open problem of protecting such solutions from attacks interfering with the analysis, e.g., *Direct Kernel Object Manipulation.*

Furthermore, they categorize VMI-based monitoring of virtual machines as either *asynchronous* or *synchronous* [15]. Asynchronous monitoring refers to methods that perform analysis of RAM much like traditional memory forensic techniques, without manipulating the control flow inside the monitored VM. Synchronous monitoring on the other hand interferes with the control flow of the monitored VM, so that monitoring can take place at specific events or predetermined locations in the control flow, thus allowing a much greater level of control. This, however, requires support in the virtualizing hardware to perform context switches between VMs based on the monitored events.

Intel VT-x can perform a *VM-exit* when a software interrupt occurs within the guest virtual machine [14]. *VM-exit* refers to the event of a privileged instruction being executed, which traps to the hypervisor and executes the provided handler. This enables our code injection architecture to use the *int3* instruction to trigger a software breakpoint, which exits the virtual machine and allows the VMI application to intervene. Furthermore, we can perform a *VM-exit* on other events depending on the specific implementation. On Intel processors, this behavior can be configured using the primary and secondary *Processor-Based VM-Execution Controls*. Additionally, the monitoring of writes to certain control registers such as *CR3* is supported [14]. As this register acts as the default page table base register (*PTBR*), it must be updated by the scheduler when performing a context switch to an active process to reflect its page table, which enables synchronization through a *VM-exit* when a process becomes active within the monitored virtual machine. This makes synchronous VMI operations on specific processes possible, which is required for many intrusive VMI operations such as code injection.

In this work, we use the Xen hypervisor and refer to the virtual machines using the terms introduced by Taubmann et al. [27]. The term *monitoring virtual machine* (MVM) is used for the virtual machine that performs the introspection and contains the VMI application. The MVM can either be the Dom0 or a DomU with the privilege to perform VMI operations on another VM. The *production virtual machine* (PVM) is the virtual machine that is monitored by the MVM.

VMI Tool Support: Bryan D. Payne [23] provides a library named *libvmi* based on *XenAccess*. This library aids in the prototyping of VMI applications. Through integrated support of existing *memory forensic* frameworks such as *Volatility* [30] and *Rekall* [25], bridging the *semantic gap* is significantly simpler in production environments as provisioning for different machines can now be automated. The bootstrapping of the in-guest agent via process injection and the resulting data transfer will heavily build upon this work.

Libvmtrace, a tracing library for virtual machines based on *libvmi*, is introduced by Taubmann et al. [28]. The library employs the previously mentioned technique of monitoring the *CR3* register to perform synchronous VMI operations. By doing so, the library can inject shellcode into an active process to perform *process forking* for the Linux operating system [26].

3   Threat Model and Assumptions

In this paper, we make the following assumptions regarding the system under analysis and discuss how a potential attacker that has access to the production virtual machine may potentially undermine our efforts. This aspect is relevant to the aforementioned use-cases when malware aims to prevent automated analysis or when the user of the virtual machine tries to impede an on-going forensic investigation.

First, we assume that the attacker does not compromise the kernel in a way that prevents the introspection from bridging the *semantic gap*. In particular, techniques such as *DKOM* are suitable to complicate or avert the use of virtual machine introspection for the use-case of file extraction [2]. Second, general kernel protection approaches such as (kernel) structure randomization [13] may prevent a successful application of introspection altogether. Given the case of randomization on the *task_struct*, the monitor would operate on the false assumption of a default data layout and would thereby be unable to correctly extract process information from the guest.

Furthermore, we assume that the attacker does not escape or bypass the isolation provided by the hypervisor and attack the file extraction VMI application directly. The hard disk's controller may not be modified or controlled by the attacker. Additionally, the guest virtual machine must allow for the execution of the covert in-guest agent. This means there must be no hypervisor or other mechanism in place that limits code execution on the guest by enforcing code signing for all executables. Finally, the attacker can know about the presence of a hypervisor, but he may not be aware of the on-going introspection or code injection. Otherwise, it seems highly plausible to delete or hide sensitive files.

Moreover, the requested file must be accessible by a running process of the guest operating system. That is to say, the in-guest agent needs to be able to read the file after code injection. For this to be possible, it is expected that the kernel has not been modified, e.g., by placing hooks on relevant filesystem system calls. Also, the file system may not be monitored by relevant event-based callbacks in the kernel such as the *fanotify* API as this can be used to mitigate file access to relevant files. Lastly, the file system itself must not be compromised in a way that the relevant file can no longer be located by the PVM.

4   Methodology

In the following section, we describe the design of the system that is used to extract arbitrary files using virtual machine introspection. The following architecture is crafted with regards to the limitations of introspection APIs in off-the-shelf hypervisors, thereby enabling practical application in existing real-world systems.

As explained earlier, a typical guest OS supports many different kinds of file systems. Because the monitor might not know which file system to target and in the worst-case lacks the required implementation, we choose to directly use the file system capabilities of the guest, which makes our architecture suitable for general purpose file extraction by removing file system dependencies from the monitor.

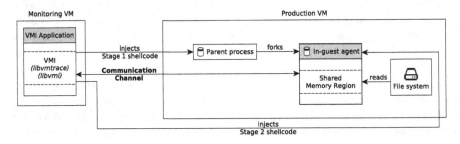

Fig. 1. Our file extraction architecture consists of a VMI application on the MVM and an in-guest agent injected on the PVM via a parent process. The in-guest agent reads the file system and transfers data to the MVM via a shared memory communication channel.

This shall be realized by injecting an agent into the guest system and establishing communication with this in-guest agent via shared main memory. Then, the in-guest agent exposes the file system tree and potential extraction targets through the communication channel, enabling file transfer across virtual machines.

4.1   Components

The primary aim of this paper is to extract files from the guest virtual machine. To achieve this goal, the file extraction architecture consists of two components. These components and their relationships are visualized in Fig. 1.

The first component of this architecture is the *VMI application*. It is executed in the monitoring virtual machine and performs the introspection of the PVM and is responsible for communication with the guest as well as for receiving the targeted file.

As previously mentioned, the extraction mechanism relies on an agent within the PVM. We consider this *in-guest agent* the second component of the file extraction architecture. The in-guest agent is bootstrapped by the VMI application using the technique described in the next section and provides the necessary insight into file systems available to the guest. Its purpose is to load a requested file into memory to make it accessible for VMI.

Because the file may be arbitrarily big, it is unfeasible to load the file into the main memory. Hence, the in-guest agent loads the requested file in chunks into memory. A *chunk* is one part of the file that fits inside the allocated buffer and can thereby be transmitted in one VMI operation. The shared memory region of the in-guest agent contains the file chunk and encodes relevant protocol data. In the context of VMI-based file extraction, shared memory refers to contiguous memory that is shared between VMs.

4.2   Procedure

An overview of the code injection and file extraction process is depicted in Fig. 2. Initially, we need to select a suitable user-mode process, which has the required

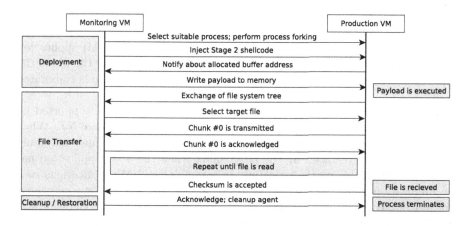

Fig. 2. The sequence of steps to accomplish file extraction consists of three phases: A deployment phase, the actual file transfer, and the restoration phase. The former two are performed using VMI-operations, while the latter is initiated by the agent after file transfer.

permissions to access the targeted file on the file system. We can identify suitable processes by extracting the file permission of the requested file from the file system and comparing them to the list of active processes as already implemented in *libvmi*.

After forking the selected process, the child process is replaced at run-time with the ELF executable in question. For this purpose, shellcode is injected into the child process. The monitor writes the ELF executable to a shared memory region created by the shellcode and resumes execution in the production virtual machine. Finally, the child process is replaced by the ELF executable transmitted from the monitor.

After the in-guest agent has been deployed in the guest machine, the actual process of file extraction begins. As the user of the VMI application possibly does not know where files of interest are stored within the guest virtual machine, the extraction mechanism enables the VMI application to query a full file system tree of the guest virtual machine. The result of this operation is transmitted to the MVM by the same mechanism that is used to transfer the targeted file. This enables the application to query and pick an arbitrary file present on the guest without prior configuration of the in-guest agent.

Once the target has been selected and requested by the VMI application, the in-guest agent determines the size of the file. At this stage, the guest reads the current chunk into memory and signals the monitor that the buffer is clear to read. When the respective chunk has been received by the application, it is stored off to a file on the MVM. Now the only thing left to do is for the VMI application to notify the in-guest agent that it may begin to transfer the next *chunk*. This process repeats until the entire file has been transmitted to the monitor.

4.3   Communication Channel

To establish communication between MVM and PVM, the in-guest agent exposes an interface through shared memory. This interface allows the VMI application to request files and the file system tree. It is also used to transfer the file to the MVM. How the application can interact with this memory region is elaborated on in Sect. 5.2.

This communication channel behaves like shared memory as supported by many operating systems such as *Linux* and *Microsoft Windows NT*. When transferring the targeted file to the monitor via VMI, a file chunk may only be unmapped and replaced by the next chunk when the VMI application has already stored off this particular chunk. In common non-VMI applications such synchronization would be provided by techniques such as *mutexes* or *semaphores*, typically implementations for these procedures are supplied by the operating system. However, this means we cannot rely on them to guarantee mutual exclusion as this makes them unsuitable for use across virtual machines.

Instead of reimplementing these mechanisms for VMI use, we provide synchronization in the presented file extraction architecture through a *spinlock*, which can easily operate independently from both operating systems in the MVM/PVM and is simple to implement.

5   Implementation

This section deals with the implementation of both architectures according to the design principles outlined in the previous Section. All of the following implementations are built upon the *libvmi* introspection library. Because the task of file extraction requires access to kernel structures to perform the code injection and to find relevant user-mode task information, a *Rekall*-profile is necessary to obtain the structure offsets [25]. We implemented our solution for Linux 4.5 and believe that adaptions for other operating systems are possible.

5.1   Code Injection

In the following the characteristics of the code injection procedure for ELF executables across virtual machines are elaborated. The goal of this technique is to inject arbitrary user-mode programs into virtual machines solely through main memory. As alluded to earlier, this process will be performed in two stages: First, an eligible process with suitable rights for file system access must be forked using VMI. Then the child of this process fork is replaced at run-time with the designated ELF executable.

Figure 3 shows the sequence of actions taken without consideration for synchronization. To perform the first step of this procedure—*process forking*—the host must know when and where the vCPU is executing code in the forked user-mode process. For this purpose, we monitor changes to the *CR3*-register, where a pointer to the top-level paging structure is held. By doing so, we can perform synchronous VMI operations when the guest OS scheduler switches to our targeted process. To determine the address at which the program execution will continue, we read the future instruction pointer directly from an offset to the kernel-mode stack pointer. After we injected the *stage 1 shellcode* at this location *(1)*, it will first perform a *vfork* in the parent *(2 & 3)* and then a *execve* in the child. When the *execve* system call in the shellcode is reached, we use the VMI application to store the system call arguments under the user-mode stack pointer. Additionally, the *stage 1 shellcode* must preserve the registers *RAX*, *RCX* and *R11* in the parent process as these are modified by performing a system call.

For the use case of file extraction, the *execve* system call will execute */bin/bash* within the child process, thereby putting it into an infinite loop, which causes frequent context switches to the target process by the Linux scheduler [20]. To inject the ELF executable into this newly created child process in stage 2, we once again employ the technique of monitoring changes to the *CR3*-register to synchronize with the guest system. However, in the use-case of the proposed ELF injection, it must also be taken into consideration that the forked child process might still use the parent's page tables when a CR3 event is first triggered [8].

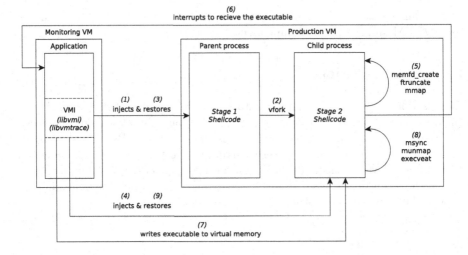

Fig. 3. Our VMI-based ELF injection implementation first forks a process using code injection. Then, we replace the child of this fork at run-time with an executable transmitted by the host.

Because the operating system does not duplicate the page tables of the child process when using *vfork*, both the parent and the child process can refer to the same top-level paging structure until *execveat* is called, thus not allowing any distinction between them. To deal with this issue, it must be ensured that the code injection is delayed until the above procedure is completed[1]. Eventually, we can continue the injection of the *stage 2 shellcode* at the future instruction pointer *(4)*.

In stage 2, initially, a file descriptor to an anonymous file[2] is opened by the shellcode *(5)* using the *memfd_create* system call. This is required because the Linux operating system can execute programs only from files. To reduce the chance of detection, the *MFD_CLOEXEC* flag is used, so that the descriptor closes on program execution. Afterward, the entire file is mapped to virtual memory using the *mmap* system call *(5)*.

At this point the shellcode performs a context switch to the VMI application *(6)*. Now there are two things that must be taken care of: First, the in-guest agent must be written to the buffer *(7)*. Second, measures must be taken to restore the previously backed up memory region that was overwritten by the

---

[1] This is achieved by waiting in the VMI application until the child's top-level paging structure differs from the parent's.

[2] Under Linux operating systems, the term *anonymous file* refers to a file that lives solely in memory. It is not present on any mounted file system and released once it is no longer referenced [12]. The *memfd_create* system call was introduced in version 3.17. For older Linux versions or BSD variants, it is possible to use *shm_open* instead.

shellcode. For this purpose, a breakpoint is placed in kernel-space at $LSTAR^3$ before the *execveat* system call is handled.

Subsequently the shellcode synchronizes the now mapped ELF executable to the file descriptor and cleans up the allocated memory used for the transfer. To finish the injection, *execveat* is invoked with the file descriptor, which discards the anonymous file and replaces the current process with the provided program *(8)*. The only thing remaining is to restore the original instructions from the monitor when the previously placed *execveat*-breakpoint is executed *(9)*.

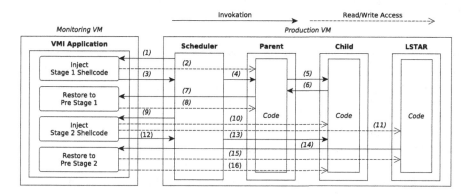

Fig. 4. During the ELF injection, multiple VMX context switches and VMI-based write operations occur between VMI application, scheduler, parent and child process, and system call handlers.

Figure 4 depicts essentially the same process as shown in Fig. 3, however, in this instance, we consider context switches and read/write operations between MVM and PVM instead of control flow. While this architecture for injecting ELF binaries is in theory applicable to any hypervisor, lacking support for event handling in *libvmi* for other hypervisors currently limits the practical applicability to *XEN*.

5.2   File Extraction

After the groundwork has been laid, the details of the file extraction implementation are discussed. As described in Sect. 4.2, the previously introduced code injection mechanism is used to deploy the in-guest agent within the PVM. This in-guest agent will perform all file system related operations and aid in extracting the file. For communication purposes, the in-guest agent exposes a shared memory region as a symbol through its ELF export directory, which can be located in virtual memory by the VMI application.

---

³ $LSTAR$ is a model-specific register that holds the targeted instruction pointer when executing a system call in long mode.

Before any communication is established, the in-guest agent allocates the transmission buffer on the heap. The size and location of this transmission buffer is written to the shared memory region, so that the VMI application knows how many bytes it can read. To prevent the PVM's operating system from paging out the buffer, we lock it into virtual memory using the *mlock* system call for the duration of the in-guest agent's execution.

If the user wishes to skip the transfer of the file system tree, the VMI application signals this decision to the in-guest agent via a bit-flag in the shared memory before any other operation takes place. Otherwise, the in-guest agent pipes the result of *tree*/into an anonymous file, which is then transmitted by the same mechanism as explained below.

After the user has decided on which file to extract, the respective file path is written to the transmission buffer. Before the transmission begins, a *CRC-32* checksum of the entire file and the total file size is stored within the shared memory. Now, the transmission may begin and the targeted file is read chunk by chunk into the transmission buffer by the in-guest agent. After each step, the agent uses a bit-flag to indicate the buffer contents are valid again. As the VMI application is pulling on this specific bit, spinlock alike behavior ensures. On each successful pull, the VMI application extracts the current file chunk and stores it off. In order to signal that the chunk was received correctly, the application flips bit-flag again. If this chunk transfer completes the entire process, the in-guest agent terminates in order to evade potential detection after file extraction.

Eventually this process ends as the entire file has transferred to the VMI application and is stored off on the monitor's file system. Note that the previously mentioned checksum is only intended to detect transmission errors, not to provide any means to prove cryptographic integrity as required in applications for digital forensics. Expanding the protocol, in particular, the in-guest agent for this purpose however seems plausible, yet outside the scope of our current work.

6   Evaluation

In this section, the performance of the file extraction mechanism is measured and evaluated. Additionally, the stealthiness of the architecture is elaborated upon in the context of an attacker within the guest system. All tests are performed on virtual machines equipped with one pinned core of an Intel i7-6700K processor and 2048 MB of RAM, swapping is disabled. Both the MVM and PVM system are virtualized by XEN 4.13 using the *Intel VT-x* processor extension. The PVM is located in DomU, while the Dom0 acts as MVM. The PVM uses the Linux kernel version 4.4.40, and the MVM uses version 4.19.0. The system is installed on a Samsung PM951 128 GB SSD, the DomU is stored within a *qcow2* image. The measurements are performed while *CR3*-monitoring is enabled in *libvmi*.

6.1   Transfer Speed

To evaluate the performance of the protocol and its sample implementation, the first thing to measure is the transfer speed when extracting a file from the guest virtual machine compared to loading the file directly from disk. For this purpose, several files of different sizes are placed in the guest machine as potential extraction targets. We measure the duration of file transmission starting from the request to the agent until the file has been received by the monitor. The following sizes have been selected to represent different classes of files that one may want to extract from the guest: 2 KiB, 1 MiB and 300 MiB.

Then four measurements per file are performed with different buffer sizes:

1. **Native**: Reading the file into a contiguous buffer in the guest without the use of VMI.
2. **One page**: The buffer size is set to one page (4 KiB on the evaluated system) so that the measurement shows the highest possible slowdown due to mutual exclusion.
3. **10 MiB**: The buffer size is set to 10 MiB, a good middle-ground for most applications.
4. **File size**: The buffer size is set to the file size, as this measurement will show potential, inherent slowdowns of the approach that are not caused by mutual exclusion.

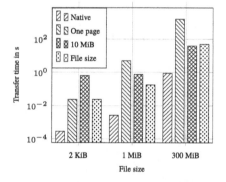

Fig. 5. Transfer time of VMI-aided file extraction Transfer time of VMI-aided file extraction

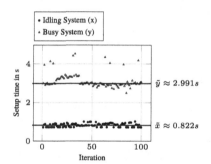

Fig. 6. Scheduler impact on agent deployment

Figure 5 depicts the results of this measurement with a sample size of 10. Given these measurements, we observe a best-case transfer rate of approximately 76 MiB/s with an average of 52 MiB/s. For this estimate, the values of one page buffer size and 2 KiB total file size were not considered. The reason for this decision is that the former is not suitable for general use due to the number of context switches required and only designed to show the worst-case performance of around 1.8 MiB/s. In the latter case however, the run-time is vastly impacted by the setup of the transfer, not by actually exchanging the buffers. The error of these measurements is around 2%, which is not representable in the figure.

While these results can already be considered acceptable, there is still room left for improvement. First, we can disable event handling while the file transfer is in progress. As seen in Sect. 6.3, listening for *CR3* events introduces a huge overhead, which can, therefore, be avoided. Second, the current implementation of the spinlock can be replaced with alternatives that make use of the relevant x86 instructions. Moreover, it seems feasible to use an interrupt for the communication direction PVM to MVM instead.

6.2   Agent Deployment

Additionally, we have to consider the cost of deploying the agent within the production virtual machine in the first place. For this purpose, we measure the duration of ELF injection for our in-guest agent implementation. As this procedure relies on scheduler timing, the results may vary depending on factors such as overall activity in the machine and the specific implementation of the scheduler. We performed these measurements a hundred times on an idling system and a busy system using the default Linux scheduler.

The results of these measurements are depicted in Fig. 6. We find that our assumption of a large fluctuation in the injection time due to scheduler timing is in line with the measured values. The measurements show an expected median setup time of 0.82 s on an idling system, 2.99 s on the busy system. In the worst case, the setup procedure took 1.01 and 4.51 s, respectively. Since the agent can potentially be reused for multiple file transfers, we consider these results to be reasonable.

6.3   Performance Degradation

Furthermore, the execution of the in-guest agent can cause noticeable performance degradation for other applications running in the PVM. To measure potential side effects of the file extraction procedure, a heavy computational load is simulated by executing calculations on the guest. This is done by approximating π with the Chudnovsky algorithm for the first eight iterations [4]. By comparing the computation time under file extraction to normal conditions, any potential slowdowns in the guest system that are not caused by I/O operations become visible. The only way to effectively eliminate the latter problem is to create an artificial bottleneck for the agent's file access. Since this is in direct contrast to the goal of high transfer speeds, I/O throughput is not considered for potential slowdowns. The measurement is repeated 10 times for each instance.

In total, this results in computation time of 2.948 s for normal execution and 3.495 s for file extraction with a respective standard deviation of 0.041 and 0.076 s. Therefore, the use of VMI-based file extraction degrades the guest's performance by approximately 16%. This degradation is mostly caused by the event handling for *CR3* writes. It might be desirable to filter relevant operations in the hypervisor so that the additional context switch for non-monitored processes is no longer required. However, even with this it can be considered unlikely to improve the performance much further as a *VM-exit* is required in all cases to provide the necessary isolation. What is possible nonetheless, is to disable event handling after the code injection.

6.4 Stealthiness

As previously discussed, the approach remains vulnerable to some detection vectors. First of all, the presence of the hypervisor is detectable from the guest by the use of timing attacks [3]. Because instructions like *cpuid* cause a *VM-exit* on Intel CPUs, the elapsed time will be many times greater when a hypervisor is present. However, the presence of the hypervisor itself is common in many environments and does therefore not provide sufficient reason to suspect a maleficent hypervisor abusing the inherent isolation of this technique to extract files. Nevertheless, some known timing attacks allow the detection of virtual machine introspection as employed by the approach at hand [29].

Unlike other inter-VM communication channels such as *ivshmem* and *ZVIM*, our protocol does not introduce a PCI device, but exchanges data directly through the main memory [1,19]. This design choice enhances the stealthiness of the channel as it requires no direct modification of the VM and prevents the detection of suspicious PCI devices.

Additionally, it seems conceivable to monitor the file system for access to sensitive files. Most operating systems allow event-based notifications for certain actions on the file system, on Linux this is provided by the *inotify* API. Using this method, it is possible to detect the in-guest agent as it attempts to read a monitored file into memory. Since the virtual machine introspection approach grants kernel access, it seems plausible to prevent this possibility of detection by placing a hook on the dispatching function from the VMI application. However, access to these sensitive files could also be visible on file systems that are capable of tracking access time separately from modification time, such as *zfs*.

Furthermore, the code injection technique used to both fork and execute the covert in-guest agent is easily detectable from inside the guest. Because the injection mechanism partially overwrites the *.text* section when performing a context switch to the user-mode program, it appears plausible to check the integrity of the program by comparing the *.text* section to the program on disk when the shellcode performs relevant system calls. This technique can detect the injection mechanism even without enforcing strict code singing. To avoid such attempts, the injected shellcode can be dynamically rewritten using *return-oriented-programming*, leaving the entire .text section intact [18].

Finally, the injected in-guest agent itself runs within the guest virtual machine and can, therefore, be detected and potentially attacked. Since the introspection approach allows for kernel access as mentioned above, it is possible to use *DKOM* to hide the forked process and its code from other programs within the guest.

7 Related Work

In the following Section, we evaluate previous work that aims to achieve a similar goal. Table 1 represents an overview over all discussed approaches.

In 2009 Richard Jones introduced a set of tools for accessing and modifying disk images of virtual machines called *libguestfs* [16]. Specifically, the *virt-copy-out* utility enabled file extraction from disk images mounted inside a virtual machine. However, as this tool is not based around introspection, access to encrypted, virtual or network file systems is not possible and applications on live virtual machines are highly limited.

The same year Maartmann et al. demonstrated a technique for extracting cryptographic keys from main memory [17]. One of the use-cases examined for their methods was disk encryption through *TrueCrypt*. By extracting the cryptographic key used in the encryption, the attacker can gain access to sensitive data. Since VMI operations typically operate on the main memory, this approach can easily be adapted for use in VMI environments.

Gu et al. showcased an active introspection framework for narrowing the semantic gap by executing ELF binaries in the context of a production virtual machine in 2011 [9]. This was realized by using the ELF loader on the monitoring virtual machine to load a statically linked program to the main memory. By hooking into the scheduler of the production virtual machine using CR3 monitoring, they implemented context switching on-top of the production operating system. We show that by using the program loader and scheduler inside the PVM instead, we can significantly increase performance and reduce the requirements on the implanted program while decreasing isolation.

Soon after, Hale et al. released the *GEARS* framework for VMI-based services. They argued that such services should place components inside the non-compliant production virtual machine. By doing so, the implementation can be simplified as programs running inside the production virtual machine do not suffer from the semantic gap. This principle is fulfilled in our work through the use of the dynamically injected in-guest agent.

Fu et al. proposed a compatibility layer for non-VMI applications called *HyperShell* in the same year [6]. They introduced the concept of *reverse system calls* that allowed them to selectively forward some system calls to the production virtual machine while executing others on the monitoring virtual machine. This compatibility layer essentially enables the reuse of existing binaries such as *cp*, *ls*, etc. in VMI contexts, thus greatly simplifying VM management. However, the architecture shows weaknesses in terms of compatibility and portability: First, the concept of *reverse system calls* inevitably requires the same (or at least a compatible) set of system calls. This means *HyperShell* cannot be used in situations where the MVM and PVM run different operating systems. Furthermore, the implementation requires modifications to the hypervisor, which presents an obstacle in practical real-world applications where the hypervisor cannot be patched for security and liability reasons.

Morbitzer et al. introduced a technique based on their previously published *SEVered* attack to extract encryption keys for file systems and other applications

Table 1. Comparison with related work

	Arbitrary code execution[4]	ELF injection	Trusted Execution Environment	Hard disk file systems	Encrypted file systems	Other file systems[5]	wo/ VMM modifications	wo/ compatible system calls
LIBGUESTFS [16]	✗	✗	✗	✓	✗	✗	✓	✓
MAARTMANN ET AL. [17]	✗	✗	✗	✓	✓	✗	✓	✓
MORBITZER ET AL. [21]	✗	✗	✓	✗	✓	✗	✓	✓
GEARS [10]	✓	✗	✗	✗	✗	✗	✗	✓
PROCESS IMPLANTING [9]	✓	✓	✗	✗	✗	✗	✗	✓
HYPERSHELL [6]	✓	✗	✗	✓	✓	✓	✗	✗
AGENT-BASED EXTRACTION	✓	✓	✗	✓	✓	✓	✓	✓

[4] Arbitrary code execution means that the application can dynamically inject code into the PVM. However, this does not necessarily indicate that binary formats like ELF can be executed.

[5] For this comparison, we refer to network file systems, virtual file systems and temporary file systems as other file systems.

using virtual machine introspection in 2019 [21, 22]. Their approach enabled the extraction of sensitive data when the virtual machine was protected by *AMD SEV* that encrypts the main memory of the VM with a key unknown to the hypervisor. This enables file extraction, even in areas not covered by our file extraction architecture. However, the presented approach falls short when dealing with file systems that reside purely in RAM such as *tmpfs* or are simply not accessible by the monitor such as *WebDAV*.

8   Conclusion

This paper addresses the adaptation of typical code injection techniques for VMI-based applications and the extraction of files from virtual machines through the use of an introspection-oriented in-guest agent. To address the issue of deploying the in-guest agent in the targeted virtual machine, we show how typically used techniques for inter-process code injection can be adapted for inter-machine applications using introspection. Furthermore, the implementation for Linux MVM/PVM-systems is presented.

For obtaining files that are accessible from within the virtual machine, our approach demonstrates the provisioning and placement of an in-guest agent within the guest. This in-guest agent enables common memory forensic techniques and tools to access non-volatile storage. Additionally, the presented solution is evaluated in terms of transfer speed, performance degradation and stealthiness.

Acknowledgments. This work has been funded by the Deutsche Forschungsgemeinschaft (DFG, German Research Foundation) – 361891819 (ARADIA).

References

1. Armbruster, M.: Device Specification for Inter-VM shared memory device (2016). https://fossies.org/linux/qemu/docs/specs/ivshmem-spec.txt. Accessed 27 July 2020
2. Bahram, S., et al.: DKSM: subverting Virtual Machine Introspection for Fun and Profit. In: 29th IEEE Symposium on Reliable Distributed Systems, pp. 82–91. IEEE (2010)
3. Brengel, M., Backes, M., Rossow, C.: Detecting hardware-assisted virtualization. In: Caballero, J., Zurutuza, U., Rodríguez, R.J. (eds.) DIMVA 2016. LNCS, vol. 9721, pp. 207–227. Springer, Cham (2016). https://doi.org/10.1007/978-3-319-40667-1_11
4. Chudnovsky, D., Chudnovsky, G.: Approximations and complex multiplication according to Ramanujan. In: Pi: A Source Book, pp. 596–622. Springer, New York (2004). https://doi.org/10.1007/978-1-4757-4217-6_63
5. Dolan-Gavitt, B., Leek, T., Zhivich, M., Giffin, J., Lee, W.: Virtuoso: narrowing the semantic gap in virtual machine introspection. In: IEEE Symposium on Security and Privacy, pp. 297–312. IEEE (2011)
6. Fu, Y., Zeng, J., Lin, Z.: HYPERSHELL: a practical hypervisor layer guest OS shell for automated in-VM management. In: Proceedings of the 2014 USENIX Annual Technical Conference, pp. 85–96. USENIX Association, USA (2014)
7. Garfinkel, T., Rosenblum, M.: A virtual machine introspection based architecture for intrusion detection. In: Proceedings of the Network and Distributed System Security Symposium. The Internet Society (2003)
8. Gorman, M.: Understanding the Linux Virtual Memory Manager, vol. 352, 1st edn., pp. 33–38. Prentice Hall, Prentice (2004)
9. Gu, Z., Deng, Z., Xu, D., Jiang, X.: Process implanting: a new active introspection framework for virtualization. In: 2011 IEEE 30th International Symposium on Reliable Distributed Systems, pp. 147–156. IEEE (2011)
10. Hale, K.C., Xia, L., Dinda, P.A.: Shifting GEARS to enable guest-context virtual services. In: Proceedings of the 9th International Conference on Autonomic Computing, New York, NY, USA, pp. 23–32. Association for Computing Machinery (2012)
11. Hebbal, Y., Laniepce, S., Menaud, J.: Virtual machine introspection: techniques and applications. In: 10th International Conference on Availability, Reliability and Security, pp. 676–685. IEEE (2015)
12. Herrmann, D.: memfd_create - create an anonymous file. In Linux Programmer's Manual (2020). http://man7.org/linux/man-pages/man2/memfd_create.2.html. Accessed 09 Feb 2020
13. Hussein, N.: Randomizing structure layout (2017). https://lwn.net/Articles/722293/ (2017). Accessed 01 Jan 2020
14. Intel Corporation: Intel® 64 and IA-32 Architectures Software Developer's Manual, vol. 3D, pp. C1–C3, September 2016
15. Jain, B., Baig, M.B., Zhang, D., Porter, D.E., Sion, R.: SoK: introspections on trust and the semantic gap. In: IEEE Symposium on Security and Privacy, pp. 605–620. IEEE (2014)

16. Jones, R.: libguestfs - tools for accessing and modifying virtual machine disk images (2009). http://libguestfs.org/. Accessed 27 July 2020
17. Maartmann-Moe, C., Thorkildsen, S.E., Årnes, A.: The persistence of memory: forensic identification and extraction of cryptographic keys. In: Digital Investigation, vol. 6, pp. S132–S140. Elsevier (2009)
18. McNamara, R.: Linux based inter-process code injection without ptrace(2) (2017). https://blog.gdssecurity.com/labs/2017/9/5/linux-based-inter-process-code-injection-without-ptrace2.html. Accessed 01 Jan 2020
19. Mohebbi, H., Kashefi, O., Sharifi, M.: ZIVM: a zero-copy inter-VM communication mechanism for cloud computing. In: Computer and Information Science, vol. 4, pp. 18–27. Canadian Center of Science and Education (2011)
20. Molnár, I.: This is the CFS scheduler (2007). http://people.redhat.com/mingo/cfs-scheduler/sched-design-CFS.txt. Accessed 19 Jan 2020
21. Morbitzer, M., Huber, M., Horsch, J.: Extracting secrets from encrypted virtual machines. In: Proceedings of the Ninth ACM Conference on Data and Application Security and Privacy, CODASPY 2019, pp. 221–230. Association for Computing Machinery (2019)
22. Morbitzer, M., Huber, M., Horsch, J., Wessel, S.: SEVered: subverting AMD's virtual machine encryption. In: Proceedings of the 11th European Workshop on Systems Security, EuroSec@EuroSys, pp. 1–6. Association for Computing Machinery (2018)
23. Payne, B.D.: Simplifying virtual machine introspection using libvmi. Technical report, Sandia National Laboratories (2012)
24. Pfoh, J., Schneider, C.A., Eckert, C.: A formal model for virtual machine introspection. In: VMSec 2009. Association for Computing Machinery (2009)
25. Rekall: Rekall memory forensics framework (2012). https://github.com/google/rekall (2012). Accessed 07 Oct 2019
26. Tanenbaum, A.S.: Modern Operating Systems, pp. 74–75. Prentice Hall, Prentice (2004)
27. Taubmann, B., Rakotondravony, N., Reiser, H.P.: Cloudphylactor: harnessing mandatory access control for virtual machine introspection in cloud data centers. In: IEEE Trustcom/BigDataSE/ISPA, pp. 957–964. IEEE (2016)
28. Taubmann, B., Rakotondravony, N., Reiser, H.P.: Libvmtrace: Tracing virtual machines. Winter School on Operating Systems (WSOS) (2016). WiP abstract
29. Tuzel, T., Bridgman, M., Zepf, J., Lengyel, T.K., Temkin, K.J.: Who watches the watcher? Detecting hypervisor introspection from unprivileged guests. In: Digital Investigation, vol. 26, pp. S98–S106. Elsevier (2018)
30. Volatility Foundation: Volatility memory forensics framework (2009). https://github.com/volatilityfoundation/volatility. Accessed 07 Oct 2019

Cyber Range Automation Overview with a Case Study of CRATE

Tommy Gustafsson$^{(\boxtimes)}$ ⓘ and Jonas Almroth ⓘ

Swedish Defence Research Institute (FOI), Linköping, Sweden
{tommy.gustafsson,jonas.almroth}@foi.se
https://www.foi.se

Abstract. Cyber security research is quintessential to secure computerized systems against cyber threats. Likewise, cyber security training and exercises are instrumental in ensuring that the professionals protecting the systems have the right set of skills to do the job. Cyber ranges provide platforms for testing, experimentation and training, but developing and executing experiments and training sessions are labour intensive and require highly skilled personnel. Several cyber range operators are developing automated tools to speed up the creation of emulated environments and scenarios as well as to increase the number and quality of the executed events. In this paper we investigate automated tools used in cyber ranges and research initiatives designated to augment cyber ranges automation. We also investigate the automation features in CRATE (Cyber Range And Training Environment) operated by the Swedish Defence Research Agency (FOI).

Keywords: Cyber range · Cyber range automation · Automated tools · Cyber Range and Training Environment (CRATE)

1 Introduction

A cyber range is a specialized facility dedicated to cyber security where research experiments and training sessions can be executed in a controlled fashion. The basic concept of the cyber range has been used since the beginning of the millennium with early examples being the Emulab [49], DETERLab [39] and U.S. National Cyber Range [15].

In order to better counter threats against computerized systems, there is currently a need for an increased number of experiments and training sessions [1,13,35]. There is a need to shorten the time taken [13,15], and decrease the resources needed [11,13], to setup and execute cyber range events. There is also a need of larger and more complex environments [15,31] and to increase the fidelity of the experiments and the training sessions [11]. Furthermore, there is a need to validate the emulated environments prior to executing events [13,22].

To address these challenges, several cyber range operators are developing automated tools [11,13,35,45,51]. In this paper, we investigate the current status and research trends in automated cyber range tools. We also describe the

M. Asplund and S. Nadjm-Tehrani (Eds.): NordSec 2020, LNCS 12556, pp. 192–209, 2021.
https://doi.org/10.1007/978-3-030-70852-8_12

architecture and tools of the cyber range CRATE, operated by FOI, as an example of a cyber range where automation has been integrated into the design.

The remainder of this paper is organized as follows. In Sect. 2, related work is presented, followed by a presentation of the cyber range CRATE in Sect. 3. In Sect. 4, we describe the automated tools integrated into CRATE. Section 5 describes how these tools have been utilized to perform research and training. Section 6 contains a compilation of the automated tools identified in eleven cyber ranges. The paper is concluded with a discussion of the findings in Sect. 7 and conclusions in Sect. 8.

2   Related Work

In 2013, Davis and Magrath presented 28 cyber ranges and network testbeds [14]. Eight of these were described to include some form of automated features. In 2019, Yamin, Katt and Gkioulos presented a literature review where 100 papers are analyzed [51]. Based on the analysis, the authors of the surveys identify a research trend towards automated cyber ranges starting in 2014. This automation trend is also identified in a survey presented by Karlzén, where a literature review covering 74 cyber ranges is described [25]. Interestingly, the latter actually utilized an automated tool to perform the survey.

In total, fourteen cyber ranges containing different automated tools were identified by the surveys. AIT Cyber Range in Austria incorporate automation to deploy virtual machines during *capture the flag* (CTF) events [16]. The same cyber range also incorporates a tool called *GameMaker* used as a scenario engine to automatically execute injects during cyber range events [27]. Melón, Väisänen, and Pihelgas describe the tool suite *EVE and ADAM*, used to provide situational awareness during exercises hosted in the cyber range used by Nato Cooperative Cyber Defence Centre of Excellence (CCDCOE) [30]. The cyber range used by CCDCOE also incorporate an automated availability scoring system used during exercises such as Locked Shields [34]. Kim, Mæng, and Jang describe multiple automated tools needed in the cyber range used to host a complex exercise called Cyber Conflict Exercise [24]. The described tools automate activities such as system deployment and configuration, flag updates, attack execution and various types of scoring. An automated system which utilize virtualization features to restore the emulated environment after the event is also mentioned. Pham et al. describe an automated tool called *CyRIS (Cyber Range Instantiation System)* used in the cyber range CyTRONE [33]. CyRIS deploys and configures systems and services in the cyber range. In [43], an automated tool capable of executing attacks in CyTRONE is described.

In the cyber range DETERLab, a tool called *MAGI (Montage AGent Infrastructure)* is used to automatically run tests [44]. Davis and Magrath also mention that DETERLab is able to automatically deploy environments based on abstract test definitions [14]. Hibler et al. describe the automated tools used in the cyber range Emulab to allocate hardware, configure networking and execute events [19], and in [8], the tool *Linktest*, used to validate emulated environments in

Emulab, is described. Vykopal et al. describe a tool called *PM Portal* used to automate the setup and control of cyber exercises in the cyber range KYPO in [48]. They also mention automatic scoring of cyber exercises and that attacks can be automatically executed. In the future, a capability to automatically prepare and execute cyber experiments will be developed [48]. Braje describes a tool called *ALIVE (Automatic Live Instantiation of a Virtual Environment)* which is implemented into the cyber range LARIAT [11]. The tool uses configuration files to automatically build and configure virtual machines to create emulated environments. ALIVE is also able to configure many standard network services, including directory services, email servers, websites and file shares.

Urias et al. address the question of how cyber ranges can meet the increasing demand for cyber training and testing, with the U.S. National Cyber Range (NCR) as a use case. One of the solutions proposed is to utilize automated range provisioning and configuration tools to set up the emulated environments [45]. Automation of the NCR is further investigated in [35], where an overview of the tool suite called *FACTR (Flexible, Automated Cyber Technology Range)* is provided. FACTR automates core testing processes and procedures including testbed creation, verification and validation, monitoring, data collection, load and user behavior modeling, testbed reconfiguration, reconstitution, and execution [35]. Another cyber range that is described as partly automated by Davis and Magraph is VSCTC (Virtual Cyber Security Testing Capability). Shu et al. describe the automation features incorporated in VCSTC as capable to deploy emulated environments and to run experiments [38]. Davis and Magrath also describe the cyber ranges SIMTEX, CAAJED and ATC CYDEST as partly automated [14]. However, no further details have been found about the automation features in these cyber ranges, why these will not be further discussed in this paper.

The surveys presented by Yamin, Katt, and Gkioulos [51] and by Karlzén [25] also include several research initiatives where automated concepts and tools, not affiliated to any named cyber range, are presented. Russo, Costa and Armando introduce a scenario definition language used for scenario design and validation in [36]. In [13], the work is carried on with a description of a framework used for automating the definition and deployment of complex cyber range scenarios, based on a scenario definition language called VSDL (Virtual Scenario Description Language). VSDL will be integrated into the future Italian national cyber range [13]. A framework related to VSDL is also presented in [37]. In [12], Burke and van Heerden describe how automated attack capabilities can be developed for use in a cyber challenge environment. Abbott et al. describes how performance assessment can be achieved using automated parsing of log files generated during cyber training exercises [1]. Finally, Yasuda et al. present a tool called Alfons that automates the setup of an emulated environment using definition files and virtualization [52].

3   CRATE - Cyber Range and Training Environment

In this section, we describe the cyber range CRATE operated by the Swedish Defence Research Agency (FOI). The description is based on technical reports released in Swedish by FOI.

3.1   History

The development of CRATE started in 2008 and the cyber range has since been used in numerous research experiments such as [41], multiple training sessions [6], and exercises such as the Baltic Cyber Shield [20] and SAFE Cyber [47].

From the start, CRATE was developed to be a highly flexible and cost-effective cyber range, able to emulate large and complex environments [4]. To achieve this, automation has always been a priority, as exemplified by [17]. In 2016, development of a second generation of CRATE was initiated, where the lessons learnt from operating the cyber range are incorporated [4]. The second generation is scheduled to become fully operational in 2021.

3.2   Architecture

CRATE is a cyber range of the emulation type as categorised by Davis and Magrath [14], using both virtual machines and hardware devices. The research experiments and training sessions are conducted by running scenarios in emulated environments. Both the scenarios and the emulated environments are created and controlled with a set of cyber range tools developed by FOI. CRATE runs on a dedicated hardware platform that is hosted locally, a design choice made to ensure the flexibility and independence of the cyber range as well as the capability to handle sensitive data during research and training [4].

Figure 1 shows a high level architecture of CRATE with the *virtualization servers* that house the emulated environments in the center. The *control plane*, to the left, is utilized for cyber range management and the *event plane*, to the right, for the systems where the experiments and training sessions are executed. The planes represent two security zones and are isolated from each other, which is essential to ensure that the control plane is not affected by the events executed in the event plane.

The virtualization servers house the virtual machines used in the *emulated environments* (Subsect. 3.3). There are currently more than 500 virtualization servers operational in CRATE. The virtualization servers run a tiny, customized Linux-based operating system called CrateOS [5]. To facilitate cyber range maintenance and to ensure server integrity, CrateOS runs in a read-only environment and overlay file systems are used to store the virtual machines and configurations. This enables the operating system of the servers to be replaced without affecting the hosted virtual machines or their configuration, allowing CrateOS to be updated as new software versions and security updates become available. The process to update the servers has been automated using scripts, allowing the cyber range

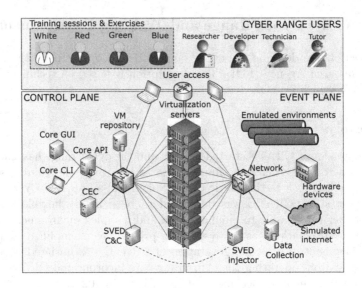

Fig. 1. High level architecture of CRATE showing the principal elements of the cyber range.

administrators to run the desired version of CrateOS on each server. This capability further increases the cyber range stability and security [5].

Integrated in CrateOS is also a system service called NodeAgent. NodeAgent handles communication between the Core API and the virtual machines and automates the deployment and configuration of the emulated environments, as described in Subsects. 4.1 and 4.2.

There is a separate network infrastructure for each plane in CRATE. The LAN in the event plane is described by Almroth in [3] and utilizes software defined networking (SDN) to facilitate automated configuration of the emulated networks. VXLANs, virtual network segments, are used to support a high number of emulated networks. The VXLANs are dynamically assigned to the virtual machines' network cards and the routing protocols OSPF, RIP and BGP are used to share the routing information of each emulated environment within the event plane. Automatic management of the network configuration decreases the work load and skill required to create emulated environments in CRATE. It also decreases the risk of configuration errors [3].

The control plane houses the systems used to configure and control the emulated environments and the scenarios that run in the cyber range. In the second version of CRATE, the *CRATE Core API* (Subsect. 3.5) is used as the primary control channel between the cyber range operators and systems in the event plane. *CRATE Exercise Control (CEC)* (Subsect. 4.3) is a tool used to set up and manage training sessions. *SVED (Scanning, Vulnerabilities, Exploits and Detection)* (Subsect. 4.4) is a tool used to automate experiments and training scenarios.

Depending on the purpose of the cyber range event, the network data in the event plane may be collected along with relevant log files from the virtual machines or hardware devices. The *data collection* capability allows research on events such as training sessions, as exemplified in [18].

3.3 Emulated Environments

The emulated environments in CRATE are set up as organisations. Each organisation contains at least one emulated network and each network contains one or more virtual machines and/or hardware devices. The virtual machines are created using templates defined in the CRATE Core API database.

CRATE is able to run several emulated environments in parallel without them affecting each other. There is no fixed limitation to the number of environments that can be run simultaneously, as this depends on the size and complexity of the organisations being emulated.

Normally, most emulated environments are not operational in the cyber range, but stored as definitions in a configuration database. The database contains more than one hundred different environments that are ready to be deployed in the cyber range. Some of these environments are used to create a *simulated internet*, that contains internet services such as backbone routers, DNS, RIPE Database, search engines and different web services such as social media and newspapers. The simulated internet enables realistic scenarios to be created in the cyber range.

A tool to automatically generate templates for emulated environments by setting some seed parameters is currently in development, and has been successfully tested in CRATE. This tool has the potential to help save time when creating large and complex environments for research and exercises.

3.4 Hardware Devices

One key capability of CRATE is the ability to connect any type of *hardware device* anywhere in the emulated environments. Even though this capability may be used to conduct experiments with hardware-based security solutions, it is mainly used to build replicas of critical infrastructure with industrial control systems (ICS) and SCADA environments, as exemplified by [2]. CRATE hosts replicas of several critical infrastructure environments, including energy production and distribution, a traffic intersection, a railroad, an energy company, and a water purification plant. Several of these environments interact with the physical scale model called CRATE City.

However, using hardware devices make it costly to emulate larger environments due to device cost and the time needed to configure the systems. Few cyber ranges use virtualized industrial control systems as identified by Holm et al. [23]. None of the 30 testbeds included in the survey use virtualized industrial control systems or utilize automated tools to setup or control hardware devices.

To be able to create large and complex ICS environments, CRATE makes use of software based PLCs. The PLCs are based upon a modified version of

OpenPLC [39]. One example of an emulated environment that makes use of this capability is the railroad system in CRATE City, which incorporates more than 70 software-based PLCs.

3.5   CRATE Core API

One of the lessons learned while operating the first generation of CRATE was that the cyber range needs to support continuous development to meet new requirements. Therefore, the second generation is centered around a new API, called CRATE Core API. The API runs as a service and is the central hub that manages all communication between the cyber range infrastructure and the different applications, as depicted in Fig. 2.

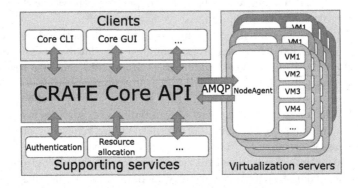

Fig. 2. A high level overview of the role of Core API

The API software is divided into three layers as shown in Fig. 3. In the bottom layer, a database is used to store the configurations of the event environments to be emulated in CRATE. The server module of the API resides in the middle layer, and a series of API clients supply the user interfaces to the cyber range tools in the top layer [40].

CRATE Core API is built upon the Thrift framework [9]. One of the strengths with Thrift is that it can generate clients in several different programming languages [7]. Currently, clients are generated for Python and Java [40]. The Python client is primarily used for scripting purposes and the Java client is used by the graphical user interface called CRATE Core GUI. CRATE Core GUI is a web service that relies on the Vaadin framework [46]. Vaadin generates content in HTML and JavaScript dynamically from server code written in Java [29].

Core API also provides several supporting services such as user authentication via LDAP and a service for cyber range resource reservations.

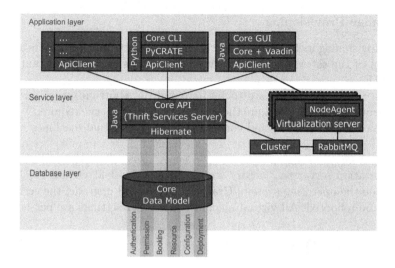

Fig. 3. The architecture of the Core API, showing the central role of the Thrift framework

3.6 Cyber Range Users

The *cyber range users* are exemplified in Fig. 1. Technical staff include the *developers* designing the cyber range tools and the *technicians* who operate the cyber range. The *tutors* use the cyber range for training sessions and exercises, and the *researchers* to conduct experiments.

During training sessions and exercises, users are often assigned to a team designated by a color matching their role, depicted in the top left corner in Fig. 1. The most frequently used colors are blue representing the team being trained or the defending team, red representing counterplay or attacking team, white representing exercise management, and green representing the team managing the technical infrastructure [50]. The *user access* (Subsect. 3.6) takes place via command line or graphical user interfaces (GUIs).

To provide remote access to the cyber range, two solutions are available. Individual users are able to connect via a client-based VPN solution based on OpenVPN [32]. There is also a hardware-based solution where VPN boxes are used to create a site-to-site VPN. The VPN box contains a 48-port network switch and can be remotely administered through a web-based management tool. Each physical switch port can be mapped to a VXLAN (virtual network segment) representing an emulated network in an emulated environment. The automated configuration process takes less time than a manual operation and ensures that the configurations written to the devices are correct [3].

4 Automation Features in CRATE

In the following subsections, we describe where and how the cyber range CRATE makes use of automation features.

4.1   Range Provisioning

Range provisioning includes the preparation of the virtualization servers and configuration of the software-defined networks, processes that are fully automated in CRATE.

When virtual machines are to be deployed on a virtualization server, the NodeAgent service will configure the server's network with the required VXLANs (virtual network segments) and connect them to the virtual machines' network cards.

The automated range provisioning features also include the ability to reset a virtualization server to "factory state", wipe individual virtual machines or to upgrade the operating system, CrateOS. For an OS upgrade, the server only needs to be rebooted. All virtual machines and other settings are persistent.

4.2   System and Service Configuration

The process of configuring virtual machines and their services is fully automated in CRATE, and handled by the NodeAgent service. NodeAgent is a manager that runs on every virtualization server and it is subscribed to an AMQP queue, from where it reads instructions sent from the Core API. When NodeAgent receives the *deploy* command together with a JSON blob containing the virtual machine's configuration parameters, it will copy a virtual machine template to the server, start it and then run configuration commands through the hypervisor's API. NodeAgent will set configuration parameters such as hostname, local users and network settings. Services like DNS, Firewalls, gateways, directory servers and email servers are also configured. To ensure that a deployment was successful, NodeAgent will run a series of validation commands, and report the result back to Core API.

4.3   Exercise Management

CRATE Exercise Control (CEC) is a web-based exercise management and support tool integrated into CRATE [6]. It is used to create and control scenarios, enhance the situational awareness during event execution, and score and evaluate performance of the participants after the training session or exercise. An event is created using a planning view, where injects are chosen from an inject database and scheduled on an event timeline. The database contain information about the inject, information on how the blue team may detect and report the inject, how the response should be scored by the white team and instructions for the red team on how to execute attacks when the inject is played. When exercise planning is ready, CEC generates a timeline view that can be used as a scheduler during the event.

During the event execution, red team activities can be automatically scheduled and launched from CEC if sSVED is used. Scoring is also performed by scoring bots that monitor system and service availability in the event environment. CEC incorporates a view where incidents are reported and managed. Each report is also associated to an inject, which will enhance the situational awareness for the white team during the event.

The foundation for the after-action analysis consists of the event view where the reports are plotted chronologically, the scoreboard view, and information from the inject database [6].

4.4   Inject and Test Execution

SVED (Scanning, Vulnerabilities, Exploits and Detection) provides CRATE with a tool where actions are executed automatically and verbosely logged during an experiment or training session [21]. SVED increases the fidelity of the experiments executed in the cyber range by allowing actions to be executed in a reliable and repeatable manner. It also reduces the effort needed to run training sessions and exercises since the red team actions can be automated.

SVED consists of five components as described in [21]. A *threat intelligence* module collects system and vulnerability data from several different sources, including Core API, U.S. National Vulnerability Database and automatic scans performed with OpenVAS. A *designer* is used to create attack graphs via a GUI or via a script-based REST API. The *executioner* executes the attack graph and *attacker/sensor agents* runs commands or reports alerts in the emulated environments. The latter may be placed on any emulated network in the event plane, enabling SVED to mimic multiple attack patterns. Lastly, a *logger* stores log data generated when executing the attacks in the attack graph.

4.5   User Emulation and Traffic Generation

The ability to emulate realistic user behavior and to generate network traffic is an essential part of a cyber range to enable realistic and relevant experiments, training sessions and exercises.

In CRATE, there are three methods used to automate user behavior. The first option is a bot that runs on the virtualization server and that uses the hypervisor's API to send instructions to the virtual machines. This option works best for command-line actions. The second option relies on the software AutoIt [10] and is used to automate software with graphical user interfaces, such as email clients and web browsers. The third option is integrated in the attack orchestration tool SVED, and is used where user actions are part of an attack. To emulate user behavior, SVED contains several pre-defined user actions that can be invoked, including sending and reading emails, opening files and attachments and visiting web pages. Different user behavior, for example risk-aware users or uneducated users, can be simulated with SVED by setting probabilities on the different user actions such as opening email attachments and clicking on links.

Traffic generation in CRATE relies on the traffic generated by user actions from the methods mentioned above.

4.6   Data Collection

Data is usually collected from several sources during an event in CRATE, but only the traffic monitoring and intrusion detection system has yet been fully automated. Traffic monitoring and intrusion detection is done with system called SNART. SNART consists of several components that are configured to work together: a configuration component in CRATE Core GUI, an infrastructure component to collect network traffic from the network cards of the virtual machines and a dedicated virtual machine running TCPDump and Snort with the web GUI Snorby. The SNART system is configured in CRATE Core GUI and automatically deployed in the event environment.

5   Usage of Automation in CRATE

The automated tools in CRATE are frequently used in the cyber range. In this section, we will exemplify how the automation enables or facilitates research experiments, training sessions and exercises.

5.1   Research Experiments

Holm and Sommestad describe a experiment where SVED is used to investigate if the availability of offensive cyber tools decrease the skill required by an attacker to compromise a system [23]. During the research, SVED was used to automatically execute 1,223 exploits from 45 different exploit modules against 204 virtual machines in the cyber range. Without automation, this experiment would probably have been too labour-intensive to be possible.

[28] describes research performed in an emulated environment hosted in CRATE, where a generated scenario was executed automatically in a SCADA environment. The resulting dataset can also be used for future research. The environment used to perform the experiment is further described in [2].

In [26], Karresand, Axelsson, and Dyrkolbotn describe NTFS cluster allocation behavior. The experiments carried out during the research utilized automated capabilities in CRATE, including the creation of emulated environments as described in Subsect. 3.3 and 3.5 and the management of CrateOS described in Subsect. 4.1.

5.2   Training Sessions and Exercise Events

In [42] and [47], two cyber security exercises in CRATE are described. During both events, CRATE Exercise Control (CEC) was used to automate exercise management and after-action analysis and evaluation, the latter enhancing the learning process of the blue teams. CEC also enabled the situational awareness during the exercises to be achieved without requiring a dedicated observer (often referred to as the yellow team). During repeated exercises and courses run in CRATE, CEC has proven capable of providing a good situational awareness during the events, making this task less labour-intensive, as described in Subsect. 4.3.

Another tool used to automate training sessions and exercises is SVED. During SAFE Cyber [47], SVED was used to perform the tasks normally performed by a red team by executing pre-configured attack graphs.

6 Automated Tools in Cyber Ranges

As described in Sect. 2, numerous cyber ranges incorporate automated tools. However, the terminology used to describe the tools varies and the details available about the tools are sometimes scarce. Table 1 contains a compilation of the automated tools identified in the eleven cyber ranges as described in Sect. 2, 3 and 4. To facilitate comparison, the tools have been grouped into categories as described below.

Table 1. Automated tools used in eleven different cyber ranges.

	AIT CR	CCDCOE	CCE	CRATE	CyTRONE	DETERLab	Emulab	KYPO	LARIAT	U.S. NCR	VSCTC
Range setup											
Range provisioning				X	X	X	X	X	X	X	
Environment setup											
System deployment	X		X	X	X		X	X	X	X	X
System configuration	X		X	X	X		X	X	X	X	
Service configuration				X	X		X	X	X	X	
Hardware configuration											
Environment validation			X	X			X			X	
Event execution											
Environment adaptation				X							
Situational awareness		X	X	X					X		
Traffic generation						X				X	
User emulation				X					X	X	
Inject execution	X		X	X	X			X	X		
Test execution				X						X	X
Performance assessment											
System availability		X	X	X				X	X		
Service availability		X	X	X				X	X		
Data analysis			X								
Post-event actions											
Data collection										X	
System restore			X	X			X			X	

Range provisioning includes tools used to assign and setup cyber range infrastructure. *System deployment* refers to tools used to deploy pre-prepared virtual machines to create emulated environments. *System configuration* and *Service configuration* are used to setup and configure the virtual machines as well as their applications and services. *Hardware configuration* refers to tools used to setup and control hardware devices in the event plane, a capability none of the analyzed cyber ranges currently possess. Once deployed to the cyber range, the emulated environment is tested to ensure that is fulfills the defined requirements with *Environment validation* tools.

Environment adaptation includes tools used to change the environment during event execution and *Situational awareness* include automated tools that provide an overview and visualization of an event. *Traffic generation* refers to tools used to generate traffic in the emulated environments and *User emulation* includes tools used to mimic user behavior on the virtual machines. *Inject execution* is mainly used during training sessions and exercises, and includes automated execution of attacks. *Test execution* is focused on the execution of research experiments and tests in the emulated environments.

Automated performance assessment is mainly used during training sessions and exercises and includes measuring *System availability* as well as *Service availability*. The latter includes more advanced features such as synthetic logon and verifying service functionality. *Data analysis* encompasses tools used to derive the performance assessment based on data produced by the participants or their actions, such as logs or incident reports.

Post-event actions conclude the table. *Data collection* refers to tools that automate the collection of data from multiple sources after an event. *System restore* includes tools used both to release assigned cyber range infrastructure, reset the emulated environments and, when needed, completely erase the event data to prevent data leakage.

Note that Table 1 only includes tools used to automate the cyber range itself and not tools used within the emulated environments, such as scanning tools or analytic tools. Nor does the table include generic IT tools that are manually configured to perform a task, such as sniffers, scanners or monitoring tools.

Figure 4 displays the number of automated tools identified in the eleven cyber ranges included in Table 1.

All but one of the analyzed cyber ranges include automated tools to setup and control emulated environments. During the event execution, a majority of the analyzed cyber ranges utilize automated tools to execute injects. Automated tools used to assess performance is included in five cyber ranges, four of which also include automated tools to enhance the situational awareness. All of these cyber ranges are described as used for training sessions and exercises.

7 Discussion

The information available about the automated tools in cyber ranges has proven to be rather limited. The automation features are often mentioned only in a few sentences, and it is hard to assess the maturity or extent of a certain tool, or even if it is operational or just an identified requirement. The terminology used to describe the tools varies between different papers, and when an evaluation of the automated tools are included, they are normally only compared to performing the same task manually in the same cyber range. All together, these circumstances makes it hard to compare tools in different cyber ranges.

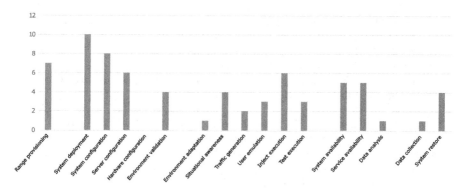

Fig. 4. Number of automated tools in the eleven cyber ranges included in Table 1

The tools in Table 1 are included based on the assessments that could be made based on information available. It is therefore quite possible that tools are incorrectly included, or left out of Table 1. Furthermore, the data in Table 1 should not be seen as a comparison of cyber range capabilities, since the data available is too limited to perform such a comparison.

Two of the surveys, [51] and [25], used as sources in this paper identifies an automation trend in cyber ranges starting around 2014. However, our findings indicate that many cyber ranges have been using automated tools to setup and control emulated environments several years prior to 2014. Even though the reason for this deviation has not been exhaustively analyzed while writing this paper, our theory is that it depends on how cyber range automation tools are described in research papers.

8   Conclusions

In this paper we have presented a compilation of automated tools used in cyber ranges, as well as several research initiatives designated to further increase cyber range automation. We have also presented the cyber range CRATE, operated by the Swedish Defence Research Agency, and described its automation features. We have found that automated tools have been used to setup and control emulated environments in cyber ranges for several years, and that many cyber ranges include such tools today. We have also identified that there is a need to further use automation to be able to increase the number of cyber range events and to increase the fidelity of the experiments executed.

References

1. Abbott, R., Mcclain, J., Anderson, B., Nauer, K., Silva, A., Forsythe, C.: Automated performance assessment in cyber training exercises. In: Interservice/Industry Training, Simulation, and Education Conference (I/ITSEC) (2015)

2. Almgren, M., et al.: RICS-el: building a national testbed for research and training on SCADA security (short paper). In: Luiijf, E., Žutautaitė, I., Hämmerli, B.M. (eds.) CRITIS 2018. LNCS, vol. 11260, pp. 219–225. Springer, Cham (2019). https://doi.org/10.1007/978-3-030-05849-4_17

3. Almroth, J.: Mjukvarudefinierade nätverk i CRATE. Technical report FOI Memo 6386, The Swedish Defence Research Agency (2018)

4. Almroth, J.: Design-, krav- och funktionsspecifikation CRATE 2.0. Technical report. FOI Memo 6666, The Swedish Defence Research Agency (2019)

5. Almroth, J.: Nationell Cyber Range CRATE 2.0 - Virtualiseringsnoder 2.0. Technical report. FOI Memo 6710, The Swedish Defence Research Agency (2019)

6. Almroth, J., Gustafsson, T.: Crate exercise control - a cyber defense exercise management and support tool. In: 2020 IEEE European Symposium on Security and Privacy Workshops (EuroS&PW) (2020)

7. Almroth, J., Härje, T.: Dokumenterat utvecklingsramverk för CRATE 2.0. Technical report FOI Memo 6381, The Swedish Defence Research Agency (2018)

8. Anderson, D.S., Hibler, M., Stoller, L., Stack, T., Lepreau, J.: Automatic online validation of network configuration in the Emulab network testbed. In: 2006 IEEE International Conference on Autonomic Computing, pp. 134–142 (2006). https://doi.org/10.1109/ICAC.2006.1662391

9. Apache Software Foundation: Thrift framework homepage. https://thrift.apache.org/. Accessed 9 Aug 2020

10. AutoIt Consulting Ltd.: Autoit homepage. https://www.autoitscript.com/. Accessed 23 Aug 2020

11. Braje, T.: Advanced tools for cyber ranges. Lincoln Lab. J. **22**(1) (2016)

12. Burke, I., van Heerden, R.: Automating cyber offensive operations for cyber challenges, March 2016

13. Costa, G., Russo, E., Armando, A.: Automating the generation of cyber range virtual scenarios with VSDL. ArXiv (2020)

14. Davis, J., Magrath, S.: A survey of cyber ranges and testbeds. Technical report, Defence science and technology organisation Edinburgh (Australia) Cyber and electronic warfare division (2013)

15. Ferguson, B., Tall, A., Olsen, D.: National cyber range overview. In: 2014 IEEE Military Communications Conference, pp. 123–128 (2014)

16. Frank, M., Leitner, M., Pahi, T.: Design considerations for cyber security testbeds: a case study on a cyber security testbed for education. In: 2017 IEEE 15th International Conference on Dependable, Autonomic and Secure Computing, 15th International Conference on Pervasive Intelligence and Computing, 3rd International Conference on Big Data Intelligence and Computing and Cyber Science and Technology Congress, pp. 38–46 (2017). https://doi.org/10.1109/DASC-PICom-DataCom-CyberSciTec.2017.23

17. Gustafsson, T.: The crate network generator - an automated method for building the dynamic and scalable network architecture of a cyber-range. In: Proceedings: SNCNW 2013–9th Swedish National Computer Networking Workshop (2013)

18. Hammervik, M., Granåsen, D., Hallberg, J.: Capturing a cyber defence exercise. In: TAMSEC - Technology and Methodology for Security and Crisis Management (2010)

19. Hibler, M., et al.: Large-scale virtualization in the Emulab network testbed, pp. 113–128, Jan 2008

20. Holm, H.: Baltic cyber shield - research from a red team versus blue team exercise. PenTest Mag. **9**, 80–86 (2012)

21. Holm, H., Sommestad, T.: SVED: scanning, vulnerabilities, exploits and detection. In: MILCOM 2016–2016 IEEE Military Communications Conference, pp. 976–981, November 2016. https://doi.org/10.1109/MILCOM.2016.7795457
22. Holm, H., Karresand, M., Vidström, A., Westring, E.: A survey of industrial control system testbeds. In: Buchegger, S., Dam, M. (eds.) NordSec 2015. LNCS, vol. 9417, pp. 11–26. Springer, Cham (2015). https://doi.org/10.1007/978-3-319-26502-5_2
23. Holm, H., Sommestad, T.: So long, and thanks for only using readily available scripts. Inf. Comput. Secur. **25**, 47–61 (2017). https://doi.org/10.1108/ICS-08-2016-0069
24. Joonsoo, K., Youngjae, M., Moonsu, J.: Becoming invisible hands of national live-fire attack-defense cyber exercise. In: 2019 IEEE European Symposium on Security and Privacy Workshops (EuroS&PW), pp. 77–84. IEEE (2019)
25. Karlzén, H.: Omvärldsstudie om cyberanläggningar. Technical report FOI Memo 7213, The Swedish Defence Research Agency (2020)
26. Karresand, M., Axelsson, S., Dyrkolbotn, G.: Using NTFs cluster allocation behavior to find the location of user data. Digit. Invest. **29**, S51–S60 (2019). https://doi.org/10.1016/j.diin.2019.04.018
27. Leitner, M., et al.: Ait cyber range: flexible cyber security environment for exercises, training and research. In: European Interdisciplinary Cybersecurity Conference (EICC) (2020). https://pdfs.semanticscholar.org/d4b6/11aee8dcca086e4f473f76dfe996a61149cf.pdf?_ga=2.223971871.580539717.1603710325-1968247500.1591902000. To be presented at EICC 2020, November 18–19
28. Lin, C.Y.: A timing approach to network-based anomaly detection for SCADA systems, June 2020. https://doi.org/10.3384/lic.diva-165155
29. Lundholm, K.: Nationell cyber range CRATE 2.0 - CRATE CORE och CRATE GUI. Technical report, FOI Memo 6711, The Swedish Defence Research Agency (2019)
30. Melón, F., Väisänen, T., Pihelgas, M.: Eve and adam: situation awareness tools for nato ccdcoe cyber exercises. In: Systems Concepts and Integration (SCI) Panel SCI-300 Specialists' Meeting on 'Cyber Physical Security of Defense Systems' (2018)
31. Neville, S., Li, K.: The rational for developing larger-scale 1000+ machine emulation-based research test beds, pp. 1092–1099 (2009). https://doi.org/10.1109/WAINA.2009.183
32. OpenVPN Inc.: Openvpn homepage. https://www.openvpn.net/. Accessed on 19 Aug 2020
33. Pham, C., Tang, D., Chinen, K.i., Beuran, R.: Cyris: a cyber range instantiation system for facilitating security training, pp. 251–258, December 2016. https://doi.org/10.1145/3011077.3011087
34. Pihelgas, M.: Design and implementation of an availability scoring system for cyber defence exercises. In: Proceedings of the 14th International Conference on Cyber Warfare and Security, pp. 329–337 (2019)
35. Pridmore, L., Lardieri, P., Hollister, R.: National cyber range (NCR) automated test tools: implications and application to network-centric support tools. In: 2010 IEEE AUTOTESTCON, pp. 1–4 (2010)
36. Russo, E., Costa, G., Armando, A.: Scenario design and validation for next generation cyber ranges. In: 2018 IEEE 17th International Symposium on Network Computing and Applications (NCA), pp. 1–4 (2018)
37. Russo, E., Costa, G., Armando, A.: Building next generation cyber ranges with crack. Comput. Secur. **95** (2020). https://doi.org/10.1016/j.cose.2020.101837

38. Shu, G., Chen, D., Liu, Z., Li, N., Sang, L., Lee, D.: VCSTC: virtual cyber security testing capability - an application oriented paradigm for network infrastructure protection, pp. 119–134 (2008). https://doi.org/10.1007/978-3-540-68524-1_10
39. Sklower, K., Joseph, A.D.: Very large scale cooperative experiments in Emulab-derived systems. In: Proceedings of the DETER Community Workshop on Cyber Security Experimentation and Test. DETER, USENIX Association, USA (2007)
40. Sohlmér, M.: Utveckling av crate core api och crate core GUI. Technical report FOI Memo 6885, The Swedish Defence Research Agency (2019)
41. Sommestad, T.: Experimentation on operational cyber security in crate. Technical report, NATO STO-MP-IST-133 Specialist meeting (2017)
42. Strålskyddsmyndigheten: It-attack mot kärntekniska anläggningar övas. https://www.stralsakerhetsmyndigheten.se/press/nyheter/2017/it-attack-mot-karntekniska-anlaggningar-ovas/. Accessed 26 May 2020
43. Tang, D., Pham, C., Chinen, K., Beuran, R.: Interactive cybersecurity defense training inspired by web-based learning theory. In: 2017 IEEE 9th International Conference on Engineering Education (ICEED), pp. 90–95 (2017)
44. The Deter Project: Deterlab capabilities. https://deter-project.org/deterlab_capabilities. Accessed 21 Oct 2020
45. Urias, V.E., Stout, W.M.S., Van Leeuwen, B., Lin, H.: Cyber range infrastructure limitations and needs of tomorrow: a position paper. In: 2018 International Carnahan Conference on Security Technology (ICCST), pp. 1–5 (2018)
46. Vaadin Ltd.: Vaadin homepage. https://vaadin.com/. Accessed 19 Aug 2020
47. Valassi, C., Wedlin, M.: Övningsrapport: Safe cyber 2019. planering, utveckling, genomförande och lärdomar av en storskalig cdx-övning. Technical report FOI-R-4885-SE, The Swedish Defence Research Agency (2020)
48. Vykopal, J., Oslejsek, R., Čeleda, P., Vizváry, M., Tovarňák, D.: Kypo cyber range: design and use cases. In: ICSOFT (2017)
49. White, B., et al.: An integrated experimental environment for distributed systems and networks. SIGOPS Oper. Syst. Rev. 36(SI), 255–270 (2003). https://doi.org/10.1145/844128.844152
50. Wilhelmson, H., Svensson, T.: Handbook for planning, running and evaluating information technology and cyber security exercises. Center for Asymmetric Threats Studies, Swedish Defence University, Handbook (2014)
51. Yamin, M., Katt, B., Gkioulos, V.: Cyber ranges and security testbeds: scenarios, functions, tools and architecture, vol. 88 (2019). https://doi.org/10.1016/j.cose.2019.101636
52. Yasuda, S., Miura, R., Satoshi, O., Takano, Y., Miyachi, T.: Alfons: a mimetic network environment construction system, pp. 59–69 (2016). https://doi.org/10.1007/978-3-319-49580-4_6

Applications and Privacy

Privacy Analysis of COVID-19 Contact Tracing Apps in the EU

Samuel Wairimu[1]([envelope])[ID] and Nurul Momen[1,2][ID]

[1] Karlstad University, Universitetsgatan 2, 651 88 Karlstad, Sweden
{samuel.wairimu,nurul.momen}@kau.se
[2] Blekinge Institute of Technology, Karlskrona, Sweden

Abstract. This paper presents results from a privacy analysis of COVID-19 contact tracing apps developed within the EU. Though these apps have been termed advantageous, concerns regarding privacy have become an issue that has led to their slow adoption. In this empirical study, we perform both static and dynamic analysis to judge apps' privacy-preserving behavior together with the analysis of the privacy and data protection goals to deduce their transparency and intervenability. From the results, we discover that while the apps aim to be privacy-preserving, not all adhere to this as we observe one tracks users' location, while the other violates the principle of least privilege, data minimisation and transparency, which puts the users' at risk by invading their privacy.

Keywords: Privacy · COVID-19 · Contact tracing apps

1 Introduction

The global spread of COVID-19 resulted in governments taking extreme measures to prevent further spread of the pandemic within their borders. In the EU, the imposition of these measures, which include partial to total lock-down of cities or the entire country, has seen the restriction of fundamental human rights and freedoms (e.g., liberty), and a significant decline of the economy [23]. For example, EU member states such as Spain, Greece and Portugal whose economies mostly depend on tourism -contributing to over 15% of there respective GDPs- will be highly affected by measures introduced as a way of reducing the spread of COVID-19 [10]. Hence, to ease these restrictions, support manual contact tracing in the context of public health, and allow the return to a new normal, several EU member states have followed suit in the development and rolling-out of contact tracing apps (e.g., France - `StopCovid France` and Spain - `Radar COVID`), while others are on the process of developing one (e.g., Belgium[1] and Luxembourg[2]).

---

[1] https://www.brusselstimes.com/all-news/belgium-all-news/health/120349/belgian-contact-tracing-app-will-be-ready-in-september/, Accessed 07.07.2020.
[2] https://today.rtl.lu/news/luxembourg/a/1514009.html, Accessed 07.07.2020.

© Springer Nature Switzerland AG 2021
M. Asplund and S. Nadjm-Tehrani (Eds.): NordSec 2020, LNCS 12556, pp. 213–228, 2021.
https://doi.org/10.1007/978-3-030-70852-8_13

Nevertheless, with the said advantages that come with the use of contact tracing apps, there have been concerns regarding privacy which slow down their adoption. In the common EU toolbox for member states, the adoption of these apps by users depends on privacy preservation and trustworthiness [8]. Additionally, in the guidelines adopted by the European Data Protection Board (EDPB), contact tracing apps should be compliant with the GDPR and privacy legislation [9]. It is in this regard that we investigate the privacy of contact tracing apps deployed in the EU member states with the aim of determining if they are privacy friendly. As such, we analyse the `AndroidManifest.xml` files of these apps with a focus on permissions declared in relation to their respective frameworks outlined in Table 2. We measure permission usage with and without user interaction to gain an insight into the apps' actual permission access behaviour. Finally, we look into the privacy and data protection goals to assess the privacy aspect of these apps in terms of their transparency and intervenability.

Research Questions: With a number of studies discussing the privacy aspects of contact tracing apps across EU, for instance [18,20]; our interest is driven by critiquing their behaviour and data protection expectations empirically. To accomplish these, we set out to answer the following questions:

1. Do the apps violate the Principle of Least Privilege (PoLP)? According to Saltzer and Schroeder [22], a program needs to function with the least set of privileges in order to avoid any form of malicious interaction. Hence, we assess these apps to identify whether they operate with the least set of privileges (permissions) by measuring their actual permission access in relation to the app's core functionality.

2. How do these apps behave during runtime, i.e., with and without user interaction? While static analysis is used in determining declared permissions and permission levels, we monitor the apps during runtime by measuring permissions access patterns, which provides an insight into how they actually behave.

3. Can a person be identified based on the permissions accessed by these apps during runtime? According to the principles of data minimisation (Art. 5(1)(a)) and purpose limitation (Art. 5(1)(b)) of the GDPR, data collections should be kept at a minimum and for a specific purpose respectively. Violating these principles could lead to the amassing of personal data that potentially allows for linkability and the identification of a person [25]. As such, we identify apps that collect more data than required for their core functionality and assess whether a user could be identified through such data.

4. Is the privacy and data protection goals of transparency and intervenability respected? With the acknowledgement that there are three privacy and data protection goals [16], we identify and assess the goals of transparency and intervenability as they can be inspected from the end-user side. Hence, this bit provides the answer to whether these apps are open in terms of data processing, and if the rights of the data subject are implemented.

To answer the questions, we adapt different assessment metrics that provide an insight and a comparison into the privacy of these apps deployed across the EU member states.

Outline: The rest of the paper is organised as follows: Sect. 2 discusses the background of contact tracing apps. Section 3 discusses the methods, which includes the inclusion criteria for app selection and different analytical approaches for privacy analysis. Section 4 discusses comprehensive results of the analysis while Sect. 5 provides the discussion, limitations, and conclusion of the study.

2   Background

Contact tracing is a key procedure when it comes to preventing the spread of a highly contagious infection. This process requires quick identification of individuals who have come into close contact with an already identified case of the said infection. Conventionally, the process of contact tracing is based on manual tracking where individuals suspected of being in close contact to a confirmed case are identified, and a contact list is constructed for immediate follow-up. However, in certain cases, this process is not only labor intensive and marred with privacy concerns due to direct identification of infected individuals, but is also reliant on human memory, which more than often leads to inaccuracies [1,21]. Manual contact tracing can easily take place where a deadly contagion is contained rather than widely spread to a point of overwhelming the authorities [1,4]. However, with the current global spread of COVID-19, manual contact tracing has become more arduous; hence the need for apps that can construct a digital record of ephemeral proximity identifiers and instantly notify users if they have come into close contact with an individual who has previously tested positive for COVID-19 [11]. While contact tracing apps are not meant to replace manual tracing [9], their uses have been termed as an advantage as they would allow a smooth exit strategy, including the return to normalcy of the fundamental human rights and freedoms that had been restricted to reduce the spread of the disease.

These apps work by building a digital record of identifiers derived from proximity data, which is obtained from either Bluetooth Low Energy (BLE) or location data. The latter, which has already been put in use by certain countries across Asia (e.g., Taiwan and South Korea), uses a comprehensive time-stamped list of GPS locations obtained from users' mobile devices. While this approach seems to work in the mentioned countries, such solutions cannot be embraced by European Citizens as they are regarded invasive in terms of privacy [1]; indeed, the use of location based services could be used to determine both the identity of the person and their surroundings [12]. As such, several contact tracing apps that utilise BLE have been developed as their use has been found to be more effective, or rather suitable, in detecting contacts between people rather than the use location data [3,6]. The BLE technology depends on the exchange of identifiers between nearby devices via a Bluetooth connection. In the context of COVID-19, the proximity and period of exposure between people influences the probability of an infection [1]. It is in the same context that the use of proximity tracing apps has become convenient as the exchange of identifiers between two or more close devices could be used to notify a user if they have been exposed to the infection, without sacrificing their privacy. As a result, in their guidelines, EDPB highlight and support the idea of using apps that do not require access to location data as proximity data is considered sufficient in tracing COVID-19 cases [9].

Hence, several privacy-preserving contact tracing apps that rely on proximity data and are compliant with the GDPR have been proposed and considered within EU member states [8]. These apps leverage a number of frameworks, for example, ROBERT (ROBust and privacy-presERving proximity Tracing), among others [1]. Recently, Google and Apple released the ExposureNotification API framework; a system which facilitates in alerting users of the possibility of having been potentially exposed to COVID-19[3]. These frameworks strive to be privacy-preserving and compliant with the data protection regulation. As a result, these frameworks are currently being leveraged when it comes to developing contact tracing apps across EU member states (see Table 2). Nevertheless, developing contact tracing apps from different frameworks results in apps seeking different goals and having contrasting designs, which could possibly lead to a number of privacy violations. For example, [4] discusses an attacker model where an adversary can violate a user's privacy by deanonymizing their IDs with the intention of tracing new cases. Therefore, we analyse and compare the privacy of contact tracing apps deployed in several EU member states in relation to their respective frameworks, with the aim of investigating whether they are privacy-friendly or privacy invasive.

3   Methods

In this section, we define the inclusion criteria, which is relevant in determining which apps are to be included in the study, followed by the assessment methodology, which we follow to answer the aforementioned questions. We limit our study to the Android platform due to its large user base and open source nature.

3.1   Inclusion Criteria

Several EU member states have already developed and rolled-out contact tracing apps; nonetheless, it is worth knowing that not every app was eligible for inclusion in our study. During the initial app installation phase, it was noted that not all apps could be installed and run on the test device based on a number of reasons, which include but are not limited to: the requirements of citizen's personal data and the unavailability of apps in the official app store, in this case Google Play Store. Following this, we defined inclusion criteria that guided us

---

[3] https://developer.apple.com/documentation/exposurenotification, Accessed 09.07. 2020.

Table 1. Inclusion criteria for app selection

Criteria	Description
Criterion 1	The app should not ask for registration details (e.g., Phone Number)
Criterion 2	The app should be available for installation in the country of study
Criterion 3	The app should be available in official stores, i.e., Google Play Store
Criterion 4	App's functionality - the app should be used for contact tracing purposes

in determining which apps could be included in our study. Table 1 shows the criteria followed in selecting and installing the apps that were deemed eligible for our study. A majority of the released apps were asking for citizen's registration details such as phone numbers with a country code so as to access the app's core functionality (e.g., eRouška - Czechia Republic). As a result, we focused on apps that did not require registration of personal details for its use. Moreover, a number of apps (e.g., ProteGO Safe - Poland) were unavailable within the country where the study was being conducted (i.e., outside of their origin country); hence, such apps were automatically excluded from our study. In addition to this, we targeted official contact tracing apps that had been released by public authorities and published in official app stores. One of the recommendations outlined by EDPB is that public officials should provide links to their respective official contact tracing apps so as to prevent users from installing third-party apps, which might pose significant risks to their privacy [9]. As such, we followed the links provided to download apps as per the criteria provided. Finally, with the apps having different functionalities, for example self-diagnosis as in the case of Greece DOCANDU Covid Checker, we focused only on apps whose core functionality is contact tracing. As a result, we were able to install and run a total of 7 apps, each from a different EU member state as indicated in Table 2.

3.2   Assessment Methodology

The study design followed in order to provide an in depth privacy analysis of the apps has three different assessment metrics: Static Analysis, Dynamic Analysis (with and without user interaction) and, Privacy and Data Protection Goals Analysis.

Static Analysis: During the development of an Android app, it is mandatory for a developer to include an AndroidManifest.xml file within the app's APK. It is in this file that the developer declares, inter alia, the app's package name, build-version code, its principle components, etc., that the app needs for a particular purpose. Of importance is the declaration of the permissions that an app needs in order to access sensitive system resources (e.g., GPS) and user's personal information such as location. By declaring these permissions, the Android Operating System ensures that users' privacy are safeguarded by permitting secure access to sensitive resources [15]. Further, a developer is recommended to declare

Table 2. List of apps collected in conjunction with their respective frameworks

Apps #	Framework	Country
Stopp Corona	Apple/Google - ExposureNotification API	Austria
CovTracer	Safe Paths (MIT-led project)	Cyprus
Smitte—stop	Apple/Google - ExposureNotification API	Denmark
StopCovid France	ROBERT	France
Immuni	Apple/Google - ExposureNotification API	Italy
Apturi Covid	Apple/Google - ExposureNotification API	Latvia
Corona-Warn-App	Apple/Google - ExposureNotification API	Germany

the least privileged set of permissions required for the app's functionality [24]. As such, we extract the manifests from the apps APK files and analyse them with the intention of gaining an insight into the apps' protection levels through the evaluation of the permissions declared. Additionally, we investigate whether the permissions declared correspond to the apps' functionalities in relation to their underlying framework specifications.

Dynamic Analysis: Based on permissions declared, an app is able to request access to required resources during runtime. These permissions, when granted by a user, access resources in a manner and frequency that a user is unaware of. As such, several studies for instance [17,19], shed some light on this by vetting the runtime behaviour of android apps by analysing how often they access sensitive resources and their actual permission access pattern. Hence, we adopt and apply a similar approach on the apps in order to inspect the frequency in which they access resources and if they portray uncalled for behaviour during resource utilisation by analysing their actual permission access patterns. Further, we uncover whether the apps adhere to PoLP, *"that is, each app, by default, has access only to components that it requires to do its work and no more"*[4], by comparing the actual accessed permissions to the apps core functionality. We base this analysis on data gathered from two phases, that is, with and without user interaction; both collected on separate occasions for a period of six days. To accomplish data collection, we use A-Ware, a prototype tool introduced by [19] that runs as a service and uses AppOpsCommand[5] to extract and log in the accessed resources. The tool logs in resource events that the apps previously accessed and records them in a predefined format that is later saved and accessed as a JSON file (see sample log below).

---

[4] https://developer.android.com/guide/components/fundamentals.html, Accessed 28.07.2020.
[5] https://android.googlesource.com/platform/frameworks/base/+/android-6.0.1_r25/cmds/appops/src/com/android/commands/appops/AppOpsCommand.java, Accessed 28.07.2020.

```
{"Package":"com.netcompany.smittestop_exposure_notification
","Permission":"READ_EXTERNAL_STORAGE","Timestamp":"Wed
Jul 08 11:05:41 EDT 2020"}
```

In addition to the aforementioned analysis, we investigate whether the actual permissions accessed and recorded during runtime using A-Ware could be used to identify a user through linkability, that is, *"if too much linkable information is combined"* [25]. For example, if the apps access location data through the ACCESS_COARSE_LOCATION or ACCESS_FINE_LOCATION permissions, one could be able to directly infer the whereabouts, area or address of an app user. To observe this, we adopt a model introduced by [13] that visualises the identity of person by mapping it to permission accessed by a particular app.

Privacy and Data Protection Goals Analysis: In the protection goals for privacy engineering, Hansen et al. [16] describe unlinkability, transparency and intervenability as the three privacy and data protection goals that complement the CIA (confidentiality, integrity and availability) triad. While all these are important aspects, we focus on the transparency and the intervenability goals as they can inspected from the end-user. By analysing the goal of transparency, we assess how open these apps are in terms of data processing. On the other hand, assessing the intervenability goal aims at analysing if the data subject rights have been implemented from the end user perspective [16]. To achieve this, we investigate these goals by relating them to the GDPR and in relation to the apps privacy policies which we extracted and archived.

4 Results

This section presents the main findings of our analysis.

4.1 Manifest Analysis

Essentially, for an app to perform as required, it normally needs access to certain resources from either the user or the system. These resources are conventionally accessed through permissions, and depending on which resources the app requires, the permissions can either be granted automatically or explicitly through user's approval. The permissions requested, which act as protection mechanisms for user privacy, are of three levels[6]: *Normal, Signature* and *Dangerous. Normal* permissions are granted automatically (i.e., during installation of the app) as they access resources that pose little threat to the users privacy. Like normal permissions, *Signature* permissions are automatically granted at install time, however, they only access permissions signed by the same certificate. Finally, *Dangerous* permissions are exclusively granted by the user at run-time as they access sensitive resources that pose a high risk to the user's privacy.

---

[6] https://developer.android.com/guide/topics/permissions/overview#normal-dangerous, Accessed 28.07.2020.

Permissions Declared per App: Table 3 shows the permissions declared in the manifest files of the apps indicated in Table 2. Overall, the apps declare a total of 64 permissions, which are grouped into two permission levels. Of these permissions, 82.81% are Normal and 17.19% are Dangerous. Taking each app in isolation, it can be noted that `CovTracer` requests a large number of permissions (20 in total - with 35% covering dangerous permissions), followed by `StopCovid France`, which requests a total of 11 permissions - with 27.3% covering dangerous permissions. On the other hand, `Corona-Warn-App` requests only one dangerous permission by declaring the use of `CAMERA`.

Table 3. Permissions declared within each app's `AndroidManifest.xml` file. Y is used in this context to indicate the permissions requested per app

Permissions	Stopp corona	Cov tracer	Smitte stop	Stop covid france	Immuni	Apturi covid	Corona-warn-app
BLUETOOTH	Y	Y	Y	Y	Y	Y	Y
BLUETOOTH_ADMIN		Y		Y			
INTERNET	Y	Y	Y	Y	Y	Y	Y
RECEIVE_BOOT_COMPLETED	Y	Y	Y	Y	Y	Y	Y
ACCESS_NETWORK_STATE	Y	Y	Y	Y	Y	Y	Y
WAKE_LOCK	Y	Y	Y	Y	Y	Y	Y
FOREGROUND_SERVICE	Y	Y	Y	Y	Y	Y	Y
ACCESS_LOCATION_EXTRA_COMMANDS		Y					
READ_SYNC_SETTINGS		Y					
WRITE_SYNC_SETTINGS		Y					
ACCESS_WIFI_STATE		Y					
AUTHENTICATE_ACCOUNTS		Y					
REQUEST_IGNORE_BATTERY_OPTIMIZATIONS				Y			
WRITE_EXTERNAL_STORAGE		Y					
ACCESS_COARSE_LOCATION		Y		Y			
ACCESS_BACKGROUND_LOCATION		Y					
ACCESS_FINE_LOCATION		Y		Y			
GPS		Y					
ACTIVITY_RECOGNITION		Y					
CAMERA				Y			Y
RECEIVE		Y				Y	
BIND_GET_INSTALL_REFERRER_SERVICE		Y				Y	

Interesting Observations in Relation to the Frameworks: The frameworks indicated in Table 2 endeavour to preserve users' privacy according to their documentations. Hence, apps that leverage these frameworks use the privacy specifications highlighted within the frameworks' documentations. For example, the ExposureNotification API leveraged by `Stopp Corona`, `Smitte|stop`,

Immuni, Apturi Covid, and Corona-Warn-App specifies the use of a decentralised BLE technology for proximity identification and exchange of identifiers between nearby devices [2], thus alerting users of potential exposure to COVID-19 with minimal privacy risk. Hence, based on its specifications[7] and the Google COVID-19 Exposure Notifications Service Additional Terms [14], these apps are required to declare and use normal permissions only, excluding the use of BLUETOOTH_ADMIN, other permissions such as Signature, Privileged or Special permissions, and any runtime permissions (unless granted their use by Android), for example STORAGE.

Nevertheless, Corona-Warn-App is seen to declare a dangerous permission (i.e., CAMERA), although its usage is explicitly stated in the privacy policy as a feature required for scanning QR codes for test registration. On the other hand, the ROBERT framework specifies the use of a centralised BLE technology for proximity tracing in fighting COVID-19 by measuring risk exposures between users [5]. Hence, StopCovid France, which leverages the framework, should declare the use of BLUETOOTH, among other normal permissions, for the purpose of detecting when users are in close proximity. However, it can be noted that the app requests for dangerous permissions (i.e., CAMERA, ACCESS_FINE_LOCATION and ACCESS_COARSE_LOCATION). While the reason for accessing CAMERA has been pointed out in the privacy policy as a feature needed to scan a QR code to self report whether a user has tested positive for COVID-19, the reason for accessing location is not mentioned.

Contrary to the above-mentioned frameworks that use BLE technology for proximity tracing, Safe Paths leverages the ubiquitous use of mobile devices to trace and reduce the spread of COVID-19 by allowing users to decentrally log in their time-stamped GPS locations [21] and voluntarily share these data with other users in an event where one is tested positive. As seen in Table 3, CovTracer, which utilises the framework, declares not only normal permissions, but dangerous ones such as ACCESS_COARSE_LOCATION and ACCESS_FINE_LOCATION, which when granted accesses the location of the user. While the developers of this app explicitly state the use and advantage of mobile location data for contact tracing[8], this goes against the general legal analysis highlighted by EDPB that states that *"contact tracing apps do not require tracking the location of individual users. Instead, proximity data should be used."* [9]. Furthermore, a number of studies, for example [4,5], show adversarial models on how public health officials or authorities can use the gathered contact tracing information for other purposes. For instance, while the Safe Paths framework enables health officials with ways of redacting location trails of diagnosed carriers[9], such data could be used for other intentions such as re-identification of users with the purpose of inferring their contact graphs. In addition, even though CovTracer targets users whose movements are not restricted at the present time,

---

[7] https://developers.google.com/android/exposure-notifications/exposure-notifications-api, Accessed 16.08.2020.

[8] https://covid-19.rise.org.cy/en/, Accessed 28.07.2020.

[9] https://www.media.mit.edu/projects/safepaths/overview/, Accessed 22.10.2020.

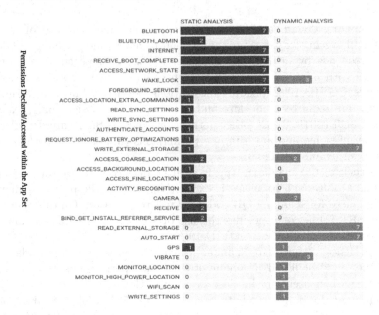

Fig. 1. The chart shows the permissions declared (static analysis) versus the permissions accessed (dynamic analysis) by the apps. The numbers within the bars indicate the number of apps that declare and access that particular permission.

for instance police officers, their data could still be used for other purposes as previously mentioned. As such, this poses a risk in terms of privacy for the users of this app.

4.2   Dynamic Analysis

Figure 1 shows the comparison between what the apps declare in their manifests and what they actually access during runtime. As an assumption, a user would expect the apps to behave in a transparent manner by using permissions that it has actually requested and in a fashion that would not endanger their privacy. However, the actual permission access pattern differs from what has been declared or from what has been mentioned in the apps' privacy policies. Figure 2 shows the visualised results obtained from our app set with and without the user interaction phase respectively. The graphs show the frequency at which the apps accessed the permissions during the period of study. For instance, it can be noted that the frequency at which the apps access permissions without user interaction is slightly less compared to the user interaction phase. Of interest is that apps which leverage the ExposureNotification API tend to access the READ_EXTERNAL_STORAGE and WRITE_EXTERNAL_STORAGE permissions and at a higher frequency in both phases even though these permissions were not requested. According to the Android developers[10], *"Android 4.4 (API level 19) or higher apps do not need to request any storage related permissions to access app-specific directories within external storage"*; hence, this can explain this behaviour of these apps that leverage the ExposureNotification framework. Further, [14] highlights that developers should not request any runtime permissions such as STORAGE expect in a case where Android Developers have authorised their use; this is because the ExposureNotification API accesses the on-device storage for the purposes of storing the ephemeral proximity identifiers required for contact tracing[11]. Regardless of this, it can be noted that two apps, that is, Corona-Warn-App and StopCovid France requested access to the use of CAMERA which was granted during the user interaction phase when we acted like a user who intended to scan a QR code for test registration or wanted to self report a positive case respectively. Having been granted this permission, it was noted that the *camera* feature was constantly accessed by both apps even with the user having ceased to use the QR functionality. Nevertheless, it can be assumed that the use of this runtime permission was exclusively authorised by Android as its use is relevant in reporting and slowing the spread of COVID-19. Further, Corona-Warn-App is shown to access a special permission, that is WRITE_SETTINGS, which [14] prohibits the developers leveraging ExposureNotification API from using, and which the user has to grant exclusively if the app aims for API level 23 or higher[12].

A closer look at both graphs also indicate that one of the app, that is StopCovid France, is violating PoLP as it accesses a permission that it does not require for its core functionality. This is because the privacy policy mentions that the app uses BLE in tracing and notifying users if they have come into close contact with a positive case or are at risk of COVID-19. In spite of this, however, it can be noted that even though the app's core functionality depends on BLE technology, it still accesses location data through the ACCESS_COARSE_LOCATION permission, which provides the approximate location of a user. This does not only violate PoLP, but also contradicts the Commission Nationale de L'informatique et des Libertés (CNIL) opinion, which explicitly states that the app does not track users' location [7] but instead uses BLE functionality for contact tracing. Further, access to location without obvious justification poses a high risk to users privacy as the use of location data could be used to infer the location of a user and their surroundings [12]. As such, one can deduce from the analysis that the use of this app could potentially lead to invasion of privacy. In addition, the issue of under-privilege permissions, that is, the use of permissions that have not been declared in the manifest, arises here. This is because some apps (i.e., CovTracer, StopCovid France and Immuni) fail to declare the use of VIBRATE

---

[10] https://developer.android.com/training/data-storage/app-specific#external, Accessed 23.10.2020.

[11] https://developers.google.com/android/exposure-notifications/exposure-notifications-api, Accessed 16.08.2020.

[12] https://developer.android.com/reference/android/Manifest.permission#WRITE_SETTINGS, Accessed 03.08.2020.

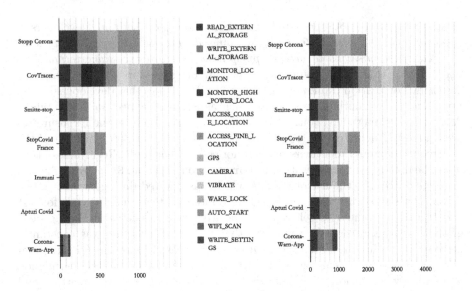

Fig. 2. Permission usage by contact tracing apps for a period of six days: The left bar graph shows permission usage without user interaction while the right bar graph shows the permission usage with user interaction. Of interest, is the access to location by StopCovid France, which supposedly uses BLE technology for contact tracing and CovTracer, which accesses location when the phone rests (without user interaction). The left graph also shows that the apps are (very) active when the phone rests.

permission in their manifests but access it regardless. However, the use of the vibrate permission or its declaration in the manifest file can be omitted by using the performHapticFeedback() function of a View thus vibrating once to deliver response on a user action[13].

Extrapolation of Permission Access Usage: According to Hansen et al. [16], the inability to distinguish a user in a large data set is associated with data minimisation and purpose limitation. As such, it can be argued that when too much information is collected, which goes beyond the app's specified purpose, it could lead to the identifiability of the user. For instance, Fig. 3 shows the user identities derived from the permissions accessed by StopCovid France through the use of the aforementioned partial identity model. As indicated, the app violates PoLP by accessing components that go beyond its core functionality. Through this, the app violates the principle of data minimisation and purpose limitation by collecting location data, which goes against its core functionality as indicated in its privacy policy. Further, with the ROBERT framework allowing the collected data to be stored centrally, the "honest-but-curious" government could be able to infer the whereabouts of the user in question, together with

---

[13] https://stackoverflow.com/questions/56213974/androids-performhapticfeedback-vs-vibrator-documentation-and-use, Accessed 27.10.2020.

their address as shown in Fig. 3, which could further be used to deduce their contact graph [5] or create a hot spot mapping.

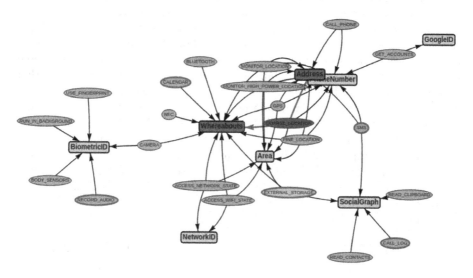

Fig. 3. Derivation of identity attributes from permission accessed by StopCovid France. Identity attributes are highlighted in dark red color (rectangle), with the permissions access contributing to this highlighted in maroon (ellipse) (Color figure online)

4.3   Privacy and Data Protection Goals Analysis:

As highlighted earlier, the property of transparency ensures that the end user is aware of the entire process concerning their personal data, which includes what data is being processed [16]. In the context of the contact tracing apps, it is expected that such information is documented in the apps' privacy policies where users can learn what data is being considered for processing. Considering the principle of data minimisation (Art. 5 (1)(c) GDPR), the apps are required to collect information that are relevant and necessary for their functionality. On the other hand, the principle of purpose limitation (Art. 5 (1)(b) GDPR), limits the collection of data to only specific, definite and lawful purposes. Hence, in terms of transparency, `StopCovid France` is the only app within the app set that violates these two principles as it can be noted in its privacy policy that it does not mention location as a category of data to be processed.

In the context of intervenability, it can be noted that majority of the apps give users control over their personal data via the apps user interface. This promotes users trust towards the use of the app. Art. 6 (1)(a) GDPR mentions consent as a basis for lawful processing of personal data with the conditions specified in Art. 7. From the analysis, it can be noted that 71% of the apps request users consent as the legal basis for processing users data, which includes data collection, use or any form of disclosure. This empowers users with control over their personal data as they have been granted with the right to withdraw their consent at any given time thus preventing further processing. However, two of the apps within the app set, i.e., StopCovid France and Immuni quote Art. 6 (1)(e) - which mentions public interest as the basis for lawful processing. With this being one of the acknowledged basis for lawful processing, Art. 6 (3)(a) permits EU member states to impose such a law, which leaves users with limited control over there personal data. Further analysis of these two apps indicate that users cannot exercise their rights. On one hand, StopCovid France assures users privacy by stating that personal data processed are pseudonymized; hence, Art. 15, 16 and 18 cannot be exercised. However, the user has the right to erasure (Art. 17) as they can delete data on both their device and the central server by uninstalling the app. On the other hand, users using Immuni cannot exercise the rights on Art. 15-20 as the re-identification of users is impossible due to data anonymisation. Notwithstanding, the user, under Art. 21, has the right to object the processing of their data by uninstalling the app, which gradually deletes the data on the central server over a period of fourteen days. Despite these, both apps, like the rest of the other apps, comply with the right for a user to lodge a complaint and contact the Data Protection Officer (DPO) if need be. While this is the case, it can be interpreted that such little control for the users to exercise their rights undermines the respect for user privacy; however, we assume that the user privacy is being backed up by the implementation of security measures. Inspection of the remaining apps indicate that users have the right to exercise Art. 15-20 via the app's interface.

5   Discussion and Conclusion

Having analysed all the apps in Table 2, we present the following findings:

- The EDPB, under the general legal analysis, point out that contact tracing apps need not trace users using location as proximity data is considered sufficient [9]. However, it can be noted that CovTracer tends to use location to track users instead of proximity data, even though the developers of this app specify the use of location data. This can also be noted from StopCovid France - where the app utilises location data by accessing the ACCESS_COARSE_LOCATION.
- StopCovid France not only violates PoLP by accessing more than is required for its core functionality when it accesses location data, but also violates the principle of data minimisation and purpose specification which cause the app to collect more than it requires. This data could be used in ways that the user least expects. For example, developers of the ROBERT framework, which the app leverages, document an adversarial model that indicate how the authority could use centrally gathered data for other purposes, for example, re-identification of users [5].

In regards to our contribution and based on the findings in this research, we note that, the identified contact tracing apps in Table 2 play an important role when it comes to curbing the spread of the pandemic. All apps provide privacy policies that explain clearly to the users what kind of data the apps collect and how they use these data. Further, the apps leverage privacy preserving frameworks that ensure privacy of users. However, while this is the case, it was noted that two apps tend to go against the EDPB recommendations. For example, `StopCovid France`, which leverages a privacy preserving framework that specifies the use of BLE, uses location on top of proximity data without actually being transparent to the users. The use of location data has been shown to be of high risks to users in the context of contact tracing apps, as such, the privacy of users does not need to sacrificed in order to slow the spread of the virus. This applies to `CovTracer` as well, which uses location data for the purposes of contact tracing.

Limitations: Conventionally, apps are dynamic in nature. As such, the reliability of this study would be questionable as the results would lack reproducibility. This would include the results of the apps behaviour with and without user analysis, which would ultimately affect the visualisation of partial identity graphs. In addition, we consider the possibility of false-positives in our data set as we observed instances whether the apps accessed permissions which had not been declared in their `AndroidManifest.xml` files, for example, `VIBRATE`.

Conclusion: In summary, a user would expect apps within the EU Member states to be privacy friendly due to the strong data protection rules. However, while a majority of the apps tend to be privacy friendly, a few are not. For example, `StopCovid France` tends to access course location which gives the approximate location of a user, and goes against PoLP. On the other hand, `CovTracer` does not follow on the EDPB recommendations, which highlight that an app should not track a user using location data, but instead proximity data using BLE. Hence, certain measures need to be taken when developing these apps. For instance, the developers need to follow the guidelines issued by EDPB that highlight the general legal analysis for contact tracing apps. Further, the principles relating to processing of personal data need to be followed.

Acknowledgement. This research is funded by the DigitalWell Research Project from Region Värmlad, Sweden.

References

1. Aisec, F.: Pandemic contact tracing apps: DP-3T, PEPP-PT NTK, and ROBERT from a privacy perspective. IACR Cryptol. ePrint Arch. **2020**, 489 (2020)
2. Apple&Google: Exposure notification: Bluetooth® specification v1.2 (2020)
3. Bell, J., Butler, D., Hicks, C., Crowcroft, J.: Tracesecure: towards privacy preserving contact tracing. arXiv preprint arXiv:2004.04059 (2020)
4. Brack, S., Reichert, L., Scheuermann, B.: Decentralized contact tracing using a DHT and blind signatures. IACR Cryptol. ePrint Arch. **2020**, 398 (2020)
5. Castelluccia, C., et al.: Robert: robust and privacy-preserving proximity tracing (2020)

6. Cho, H., Ippolito, D., Yu, Y.W.: Contact tracing mobile apps for COVID-19: privacy considerations and related trade-offs. arXiv preprint arXiv:2003.11511 (2020)
7. CNIL: Publication of CNIL's opinion on the French "contact tracing" application known as "STOPCovid" (2020)
8. EC: ehealth network: mobile applications to support contact tracing in the EU's fight against COVID-19 - common EU toolbox for member states, version 1.0 (2020)
9. EDPB: Guidelines 04/2020 on the use of location data and contact tracing tools in the context of the COVID-19 outbreak (2020)
10. Fernandes, N.: Economic effects of coronavirus outbreak (COVID-19) on the world economy. Available at SSRN 3557504 (2020)
11. Ferretti, L., et al.: Quantifying SARS-CoV-2 transmission suggests epidemic control with digital contact tracing. Science **368**(6491), eabb6936 (2020)
12. Fritsch, L.: Profiling and location-based services (LBS). In: Hildebrandt, M., Gutwirth, S. (eds.) Profiling the European Citizen, pp. 147–168. Springer, Dordrecht (2008). https://doi.org/10.1007/978-1-4020-6914-7_8
13. Fritsch, L., Momen, N.: Derived partial identities generated from app permissions. Open Identity Summit 2017 (2017)
14. Google: Google COVID-19 exposure notifications service additional terms (2020)
15. Hammad, M., Bagheri, H., Malek, S.: Determination and enforcement of least-privilege architecture in android. In: 2017 IEEE International Conference on Software Architecture (ICSA), pp. 59–68. IEEE (2017)
16. Hansen, M., Jensen, M., Rost, M.: Protection goals for privacy engineering. In: 2015 IEEE Security and Privacy Workshops, pp. 159–166. IEEE (2015)
17. Hatamian, M., Momen, N., Fritsch, L., Rannenberg, K.: A multilateral privacy impact analysis method for android apps. In: Naldi, M., Italiano, G.F., Rannenberg, K., Medina, M., Bourka, A. (eds.) APF 2019. LNCS, vol. 11498, pp. 87–106. Springer, Cham (2019). https://doi.org/10.1007/978-3-030-21752-5_7
18. Klonowska, K.: The COVID-19 pandemic: two waves of technological responses in the European Union (2020)
19. Momen, N., Pulls, T., Fritsch, L., Lindskog, S.: How much privilege does an app need? Investigating resource usage of android apps (short paper). In: 15th Annual Conference on Privacy, Security and Trust (PST), pp. 268–2685. IEEE (2017)
20. Ponce, A.: COVID-19 contact-tracing apps: how to prevent privacy from becoming the next victim. ETUI Research Paper-Policy Brief 5 (2020)
21. Raskar, R., et al.: Apps gone rogue: maintaining personal privacy in an epidemic. arXiv preprint arXiv:2003.08567 (2020)
22. Saltzer, J.H., Schroeder, M.D.: The protection of information in computer systems. Proc. IEEE **63**(9), 1278–1308 (1975)
23. Vaudenay, S.: Centralized or decentralized? The contact tracing dilemma. IACR Cryptol. ePrint Arch. **2020**, 531 (2020)
24. Wang, W., Wang, X., Feng, D., Liu, J., Han, Z., Zhang, X.: Exploring permission-induced risk in android applications for malicious application detection. IEEE Trans. Inf. Forensics Secur. **9**(11), 1869–1882 (2014)
25. Wuyts, K., Scandariato, R., Joosen, W.: LIND(D)UN privacy threat tree catalog. CW Reports (2014)

OnLITE: On-line Label for IoT Transparency Enhancement

Alexandr Railean$^{(\boxtimes)}$ and Delphine Reinhardt

Institute of Computer Science, Georg-August-Universität Göttingen,
Göttingen, Germany
{arailea,reinhardt}@cs.uni-goettingen.de

Abstract. We present a privacy transparency tool, which helps non-expert consumers understand and compare how *Internet of Things* (IoT) devices handle data. The need for such tools arises with the growing number of IoT products and the privacy implications of their use. This research is further motivated by legal acts, such as the *General Data Protection Regulation* (GDPR), which mandates the communication of privacy practices in a clear language. Our solution summarizes key privacy facts and visualizes information flows in a way that facilitates quick assessments, even for large data sets. We followed an interdisciplinary iterative design process that combines input from legal and usability experts, as well as feedback from 15 participants of our think-aloud task analysis study. In addition to explaining the rationale behind the design and evaluation methodology, we compare our solution, implemented as a graphical user interface, with existing ones. The results show that participants consider the interface straightforward and useful. Our solution encourages them to think critically about privacy and question some of the manufacturers' claims. Participants also reported that they would be glad if such tools were widely available, to further improve privacy awareness. Besides, our solution can be a part of an evidence-based standardization process, enabling policy-makers to further promote privacy.

Keywords: Internet of Things · IoT · Privacy · Usability · GDPR

1 Introduction

The number of IoT devices, such as smart appliances, fitness trackers or surveillance cameras, has grown over the last decade [37]. While this brings economic benefits, it also comes with major privacy risks [40]. For example, it has been shown that in some circumstances, individuals can be deanonymized by correlating data sets [6,27]. Another example is the analysis of smart-meter readings to identify media played on a TV [18]. Such privacy issues can be amplified by factors like device ubiquity, sensor diversity, data collection frequency, and the large volume of collected data [21,22]. Moreover, the risks to privacy do not only target users of IoT devices, but also bystanders who are uninformed about the presence of such devices in their surroundings [1,9,23]. Another factor that contributes to loss of privacy is the lack of awareness about the technical

© Springer Nature Switzerland AG 2021
M. Asplund and S. Nadjm-Tehrani (Eds.): NordSec 2020, LNCS 12556, pp. 229–245, 2021.
https://doi.org/10.1007/978-3-030-70852-8_14

Fig. 1. LITE label for a hypothetical IoT device called "Hausio T1000" [32].

capabilities of IoT devices [23,29,33]. Besides that, users are skeptical of the ways algorithms can infer personal facts about them [39].

The GDPR aims to improve privacy, by requiring organizations that control personal data to explain how the data are handled "in a concise, transparent, intelligible and easily accessible form, using clear and plain language" [14]. The regulation creates a context in which privacy tools can gain more traction than in markets that lack enforcement or rely on self-regulation [7].

Despite the introduction of the GDPR, solutions to support IoT transparency have not been sufficiently researched yet. In addition to the legal requirements, demand for such solutions also comes from potential users, who explicitly expressed interest in transparency information or stated that it would influence their purchase decisions [10,19,23]. To address this need, several "privacy facts" labels have been proposed [10,17,31,35], including our own "Label for IoT Transparency Enhancement", LITE (Fig. 1, [32]).

LITE implements the GDPR transparency requirements to inform and help potential buyers protect their privacy, *before* deciding to acquire an IoT device. It provides answers to questions such as "what information is collected?" or "who gets the data?". The answers are presented in a concise way, allowing IoT products to be compared side by side. The results of the usability study conducted in [32] show that participants could interpret the contents of LITE correctly and found it useful. However, they wanted extra details, that did not fit into the label due to size constraints.

In this paper, we present OnLITE, a *Graphical User Interface* (GUI) that extends LITE and addresses its shortcomings. Although LITE was the only user-validated GDPR-based label at the time we started this research, we also considered other designs (see Sect. 8.1, 8.2, 9). We follow ISO-9241, a human-centered, multi-disciplinary, iterative design approach when developing OnLITE. Compared to LITE, the new design shows more information and provides search, sort, and comparison features, as well as visualizations that distill large data sets into concise representations that can be reviewed at a glance. Its goal is to make the ways in which IoT devices handle data more transparent, informing users *before* and *after* the purchase (e.g. when updates are released). Our other contributions are the insights derived from the user validation of OnLITE, based on think-aloud task analysis with 15 participants. We also share evaluation scores that can be used to compare OnLITE with similar interfaces. To foster replicability, we provide the source code of the prototype, our statistical calculations, and other supplementary materials at zenodo.org/record/4126346.

2   The Structure of LITE

The original label is divided into sections that provide information about collected data, destination and frequency of transmission, duration of storage, third-parties that access data, purpose of collection, and received data. The label also contains a "trace view" - a high-level graphical representation of the data flows [16], as well as a *quick-response* (QR) code with actual data samples.

This design has been revised to include a web address with a unique product number, which is also a part of the QR code payload. This change enables users to retrieve the digital version of the label, either by typing the address manually, or by using a specialized program that will scan and interpret the QR code.

3   Requirements and Design Space Analysis

The primary goal of OnLITE is to implement GDPR transparency by assisting consumers in making informed decisions when choosing IoT devices. It uses the same terminology and structure as LITE. Each element of the paper version, can be directly mapped to a section of OnLITE. The second goal is to enhance LITE with search and sort capabilities, and provide details that do not fit on the printed label. Our third goal is to facilitate comparisons, by showing labels side by side, and highlighting differences. This applies not only to different devices, but also to software updates of the same device, released after its purchase. Next, OnLITE must provide practical information to novices, even after brief use. We aim for a design that works on desktops and mobile devices. In addition, accessing OnLITE should take little effort once the physical label is at hand. We also strive for a generic design that can be applied outside of IoT (e.g. smartphone apps).

The information architecture of OnLITE is rooted in the GDPR and is centered around questions about data collection practices [32]:

1. *What* data are collected?
2. *What is the purpose* of collection?
3. *Where* are the data stored?
4. *How long* are they kept?
5. *Who* has access to the data?
6. What do the data look like?
7. How to access the data?
8. How often are the data sent?
9. Which communications are protected?
10. What paths do the data follow?
11. What does the device receive from other sources?

4   OnLITE Design

Based on our analysis, we propose the following design for OnLITE. For brevity, we do not describe the intermediate stages of the prototype, only the last iteration is presented. The interface consists of the following tabs:

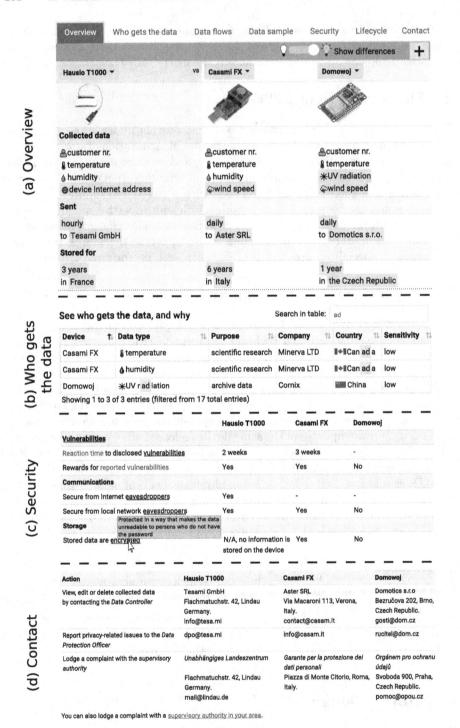

Fig. 2. Collage of screenshots of the tabs of OnLITE. The information is provided by vendors themselves, as the they are obliged to do so under the GDPR.

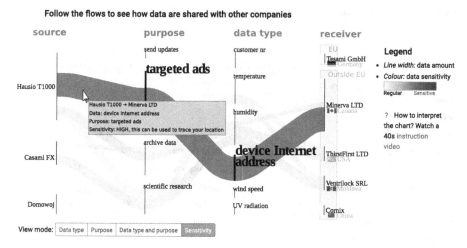

Fig. 3. The "Data flows" tab shows how data are shared with third parties. The "sensitivity" view highlights special categories of data defined by the GDPR.

Overview - the starting page provides the same information as LITE, plus a photo of the device. When several devices are compared, they are shown side by side, and optionally, the differences between devices can be highlighted (Fig. 2a).

Who gets the data - this tab contains a table with the columns: data type, purpose of collection, company, country, and sensitivity. When multiple devices are compared, a "device" column is added. The table can be sorted by each column. A search function is available, it highlights the matching text and only displays rows that contain the searched string, thus reducing the total amount of information shown on the screen.

Data flows are a graphical complement of the previous table, they facilitate a quick comparison of relative data flow sizes, making outliers more prominent. Flow widths are computed as $dataSize \times frequency$. This is a simplified model that is sufficient to test the interpretability of the image; devising a more elaborate formula is outside the scope of this paper. Several visualizations are available, each will group the flows in different ways. Colours are used to differentiate data types or devices, while the view shown in Fig. 3 offers a quantified measure of the sensitivity of each data transfer, highlighting special categories of data defined by the GDPR. The image features a legend and a link to a video that guides the user in interpreting the image. Theofanos et al. found that instruction videos are effective in helping users understand how to use a system [36]. We use Sankey diagrams [24] to distill multidimensional data into a compact view, give a sense of scale of the data flows and reveal the relationships between flow attributes (Fig. 3). Such diagrams can also be interpreted in grayscale.

Data sample - this tab shows actual samples of collected data, revealing aspects that would otherwise go unnoticed. For example, two devices can collect a "customer number", however, one of them can use an email address, while the other could use a more privacy-preserving identifier, such as "481-AHR-1831".

Features grouped by phases of the device lifetime: set-up → usage → maintenance → retiring

	Hausio T1000	Casami FX	Domowoj
Set up – *preparing the device for use*			
Unique factory-set password	Yes	Yes	No
Password change required before remote access for the first time	Yes	No	No
Use – *typical, daily interactions with the device*			
Multiple user accounts	Supported	Supported	No
Separate accounts for children	Supported	Supported	No
Separate account for guests	Supported	No	No
Maintenance – *procedures to increase the device longevity and ensure it works well*			
Automatic updates	Yes	Yes	No
Manual approval of updates	Optional	No	No
Update availability indication	In smartphone app	Mailing list	No
Feature update period	August 2020	March 2020	June 2020
Security update period	December 2023	March 2020	June 2020
Long-term support	January 2024	-	-
Retiring – *when the device is sold, sent for repairs, donated or thrown away*			
Secure data deletion (wiping)	Yes	No	No

Fig. 4. Comparing three IoT devices throughout the phases of their lifecycle.

Security - this tab presents security information (Fig. 2c). We have made sure to use common language. For example, "Secure from Internet eavesdroppers", as opposed to specialized terms [34]. Low-level details, such as encryption algorithms or key lengths can be revealed by clicking on "More technical details".

Lifecycle - this tab structures the attributes of the IoT device around the phases of its lifecycle: set up, use, maintenance, and retiring [33] (Fig. 4). For example, it informs consumers whether unique passwords are factory-set, what the duration of the support period is, or whether automatic updates are available.

Contact - according to the GDPR, a consumer has to be informed about several points of contact: the data controller, the *Data Protection Officer* (DPO), and the *Data Protection Authority* (DPA). This tab groups the contact details based on the action that prompted the need for contact: view, edit or delete data, report a privacy issue to the DPO, or lodge a complaint with the DPA (Fig. 2d). The structure is based on the feedback from a DPA representative, who stated that consumers often contact the DPA right away, expecting that appealing to the highest authority will address a problem faster. This creates unnecessary workload and causes delays, because a DPA can only step in if the DPO was contacted, but did not respond within a certain period of time.

4.1 Usability of Product Codes

These codes enable users to switch from the printed label to OnLITE. To make it a smooth transition, we use the Base58 character set, which excludes look-alike symbols, e.g., 0O Il1, to avoid ambiguities. We split the code in two chunks, to make it easier to keep in short-term memory when writing down or sharing orally [26].

5 Prototype Implementation

We developed a web-based prototype, using standard graphical widgets such as tables, buttons or tabs, to ensure compatibility with accessibility tools and enable users to leverage their experience with GUIs. We refrain from using colour as the sole channel to convey a message, to ensure the interface preserves its efficacy even if viewed in grayscale. We use tables, such as in Fig. 2, as the main way of visualizing information, to make it easier to compare IoT devices side by side.

Non-specialized terms are preferred. When they cannot be avoided, tooltips provide extra details. Text is further simplified by avoiding paragraphs. The information consists of keywords grouped in tables; sentences are an exception, the longest one is 12 words long. While defining a dictionary of terms was outside the scope of our work, we encourage the reuse of terminology from projects such as P3P or SPECIAL [3,7].

To further enhance accessibility, we leverage semantic HTML markup. Interactivity is used to indicate what parts of the interface are clickable, and highlight certain elements when the mouse is above them. The GUI is touch-friendly.

Progressive disclosure is used to show the most important information first. The start page offers a concise privacy facts summary, while exploring other parts of the GUI provides more details.

6 Evaluation Methodology

To test the readability, clarity, and usability of OnLITE, we first applied heuristic evaluation, reviewing early prototypes with usability and legal experts [28]. We presented various elements of the interface to 14 experts, of which 7 had repeated exposure to the complete UI. These sessions prompted us to shorten texts, replace specialized terms with general ones, add more information, and simplify the controls. For brevity, we omit ideas that did not make it into the final version, and the intermediate iterations.

We then conducted a task analysis study with 15 participants, who had to think aloud while carrying out tasks under the observation of a facilitator. The tasks are derived from the GDPR transparency questions listed in Sect. 3 and are aimed at evaluating whether the presented information can be interpreted correctly. After interviewing the first group of five people, the interface was revised and a new iteration was produced for the next group. We iterated until we reached the point of feedback saturation and no new insights were gained.

The incremental nature of the changes between versions means that participants using v2 were looking at a slightly evolved v1, and so on with v3 and v2. Thus, we regard this study as one with a sample of 15 (rather than 3 smaller ones with a sample of 5), which yields a minimum of 90% of usability issues found and a mean of 97% [15]. We further quantified the usability of the GUI using the *System Usability Scale* (SUS) [5], chosen due to its good performance at sample sizes ≥ 12 [38], and because scores of similar interfaces can be compared.

6.1 Experiment Settings

The experiment protocol was approved by our Ethics Committee. After signing an informed consent form, the participant is seated at a laptop equipped with a mouse, touchpad and trackpoint. The GUI is viewed in Firefox v66, running full-screen on a 13.3″ 1366×768 display. We chose a laptop due to availability of tools for debugging and video recording, and because we could hide all toolbars and menus of the operating system, such that participants only see OnLITE. These instructions were given in written form, and then orally summarized, to set the focus on our UI as the primary interaction goal: The aim of this experiment is to evaluate an interface that provides privacy information about devices, enabling you to review their privacy practices and make informed decisions when choosing products. We ask you to analyze the privacy facts of several smart temperature and humidity meters using this interface. Please think aloud and comment your actions and decisions. Remember, that we are testing the interface, not you! There are no wrong actions or incorrect assumptions, do not worry about making mistakes or hurting our feelings, your "raw thoughts" are what we need. An assistant will help if you get stuck, but try to do everything on your own. The participant also gets three 128 mm × 40 mm privacy labels on A6 sheets, each corresponding to a device, as shown in Fig. 1. The labels are centered, such that if they stand side by side, there is spacing between them, as it would be in the case of real product boxes. Audio and screen recordings are made for later analysis. The facilitator sits next to the participant, and gives them a task from Table 1 at a time, observing and taking notes, reminding them to think aloud, if needed. After going through the tasks, the facilitator steps out so the participant can fill out a questionnaire that collects demographic data and includes a SUS form. When the participant is done, they call the facilitator and the evaluation proceeds to the last phase, where several open-ended questions are discussed.

Interviews lasted between 42 and 76 min, the median duration being 57 min.

6.2 Recruitment

We recruited 15 participants from a German language study group at the University of Kiel, Germany, offering an optional 10€ (USD 11) cash reward. The selection criteria were fluency in English and a minimum age of 18 years. The interviews were carried out between April and June 2019.

6.3 Demographics

Among our participants, 53% are male, 40% are female, 7% did not disclose their gender. 67% of the participants are between 27 and 35 years, followed by 18 and

Table 1. The tasks of the experiment. The entries A-F were given sequentially because they depend on one another. Tasks G-N were randomized, to avoid order effects. The entries O-V are open-ended questions that were asked at the end of the session.

Task	Description
A	Retrieve the privacy facts of the device *Hausio T1000*
B	Which partner companies get data collected by this device?
C	What partner company gets the largest amount of data?
D	Compare *Hausio T-1000* with the other two devices
E	Remove the device *Domowoj* from the comparison
F	Add it back to the comparison table
G	Which device shares data that might have the greatest impact on your privacy?
H	What data are used by partner companies for targeted ads?
I	Which device uses a form of customer numbers that protects the owners' identities better?
J	Which device can securely erase all the data before the owner gives the device away?
K	If you suspected that the device *Casami FX* was not protecting your data correctly, whom would you contact?
L	Which collected data is stored outside of the European Union?
M	Who provided the information about each of the devices?
N	In what way are these devices different?
O	Which tab gave you the best assistance in comparing these devices?
P	To what extent did the graphical data flows support you in comparing the devices?
Q	Which of the flow views you found most informative?
R	What conclusions do you draw from the "verified by an independent auditor" marker?
S	What other information or features, if any, would you like this interface to provide?
T	What parts of the interface were not clear to you?
U	Which of the shown devices is the best choice for the given task, in your opinion?
V	What other comments have you got about the system?

26 years (20%), the rest are between 36 and 44 years (13%). Their self-reported technical competence is computed using the method defined in [33]. In our sample, 60% are expert, 27% are intermediate, and 13% are novice (Table 2). The group is diverse in terms of academic fields, and includes economists, mathematicians, computer scientists, environmentalists, and lawyers. Our sample included participants from all of the continents except Australia and Antarctica.

Although we did not collect demographic details about our heuristic evaluators, their ages are between 30 and 65 years. Note that they belong to an older age category than the participants of our study. Since their age is not determi-

Table 2. Demographic data and results.

	Age	Sex	Skill	SUS score	Time (minutes)		
					Tasks	Interv.	Total
P1	27..35	F	expert	92.5	40	13	53
P2	27..35	M	expert	90	43	24	67
P3	18..26	F	expert	60	40	16	56
P4	27..35	F	interm.	67.5	42	15	57
P5	27..35	F	interm.	55	36	19	55
P6	36..44	M	expert	72.5	39	15	54
P7	18..26	M	novice	80	30	12	42
P8	27..35	F	interm.	37.5	42	18	60
P9	18..26	F	expert	65	39	25	64
P10	27..35	M	expert	70	49	11	60
P11	27..35	–	expert	77.5	55	21	76
P12	36..44	M	expert	67.5	27	26	53
P13	27..35	M	expert	65	47	12	59
P14	27..35	M	interm.	47.5	38	20	58
P15	27..35	M	novice	72.5	28	23	51

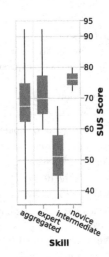

Fig. 5. SUS scores grouped by skill.

nant to their evaluation, we have applied the concept of data minimisation and hence not collected it.

6.4 Data Analysis

To understand the strengths and weaknesses of the prototype, we reviewed the screen recordings, observing the actions and comments of each sample of five participants. The interface was refined, and tested with the next sample.

The interviews were transcribed and processed through thematic analysis, to reveal common interaction patterns and themes [4]. We did not rely on several coders to independently encode transcripts, as the codes are only a step in the process of UI refinement, rather than the end product of our research [25].

7 Results

7.1 Qualitative

The qualitative feedback was used to refine the prototype and is therefore reflected in its latest iteration. We now share the highlights of thematic analysis.

Expectation of clickability was one of the main reasons for design changes. Participants clicked on static UI elements, expecting them to provide tooltips, e.g.: "I wanted it to show me the details of this line, but I cannot, I don't know what is wrong <clicks on flows again>" (P3). The most common click targets were sections of the "Overview" tab and the graphical flows (Fig. 3). This prompted us to make these elements clickable to reduce friction and provide interactivity where users expect it.

Manual comparisons were another common pattern. Some participants counted how often each company occurs in a table, to understand which of them gets the most data: "I counted ... the number of times they appear" (P4). It is more efficient to use the sorting feature, or rely on the graphical flows and look for the widest curve. Though the manual approach is effective, most participants prefer the more efficient methods once they discover them: "I think this one, <points to thickest flow> Minerva from Canada, because of the line width" (P5).

Time to understand how flows work was needed by many participants. They said it was not immediately clear how the graphical flows should be interpreted, and that it took them a while to grasp: "I needed more time to understand them" (P1), "The graphic is also just fine, I just needed a couple more seconds to understand the idea" (P2). In the subsequent prototype iterations, we added a 40s video that explained the logic behind the diagrams, as suggested by P5: "maybe a tutorial on how to interpret the charts of the data flow". The video had a positive impact on user satisfaction and comprehension, e.g., "<watches video> ok, now it's much more clear" (P15), and most participants watched it entirely, without being prompted to do so.

Flows are comprehensive and useful, as stated by many participants: "The data flow gives a lot of information as well, and it's visual" (P6), "It's visual, it has colors and it's easy to use" (P11), "The faster way for me was looking at the data flow, it was more concise" (P12), "I think the graphical representation was really good for making a conclusion about the similarities and dissimilarities between the 3 devices" (P13), and "[flow] is really complete and very dense in information, not too dense" (P15).

Verified information about IoT devices is often referred to as a strong influence on a purchase decision: "it sounds more trustable if there is an independent verification, not just the vendor. They just want to convince you they have the best option, that is not necessarily the case" (P6), another participant said "I'll choose the independently verified one, because things should be verified" (P7).

The authority void came up when we asked participants about an authority, whose independent verification of product information they would trust. Most referred to the government: "anything related to the government" (P6), "I will trust the EU" (P15); and failed to name a specific organization: "I don't know, the international society of web developers, anything similar to that, the board of trust of... I don't know" (P6).

The most useful tab is "Overview", as indicated by most participants: "I could easily see the things written in each column and I saw that [show differences] switch" (P4), "definitely the first one, because it had this option to show differences" (P6), and "It gives information about what parameters are collected and also how long this info is stored. It is the most helpful. If you want more details, you go to other tabs" (P2).

Extra information mentioned by participants, when asked what else they would want to see in OnLITE: price (3 mentions), reviews (3 mentions). Each of the following was referred to twice: how many people bought the device, detailed technical specifications, more device photos and videos, device user guide, and the physical size of the device. P7 wished for telephone numbers, so they could talk to a person in emergency cases. Others would say the interface is complete, for example: "To be honest, I don't know, because it looks very complete" (P6), "I think the interface has a lot of information, I really couldn't think of anything else to add" (P5), "I cannot think of any more to add to this" (P9).

The "Contact" tab is well-structured. Participants understood it and correctly identified the address they would have to write to when solving a particular type of problem: "I think it is this one, because it is just for reporting privacy related issues" (P3).

An educational opportunity arises when reasoning about an IoT device and drawing incorrect conclusions. For example, "I won't be very stressed ... if the information about the temperature in my apartment ... would be read by someone else. I mean, what can they do? ... As long as they don't have the key from my apartment, they can't do anything, I think" (P2). In this case, privacy tools can provide tips like "temperature data can tell whether anyone is at home", which might improve awareness about the privacy implications of sharing seemingly harmless data (e.g. yellow area in Fig. 3).

Data samples are useful, as shown by the participants' ability to reason about different forms of customer numbers: "I think the first one is better, because it is just a sequence of numbers and letters" (P1), "The first one for sure!" (P6). This information prompted some participants to think of workarounds, such as "this could be resolved with an email address that is not important to you" (P2).

Privacy profiles are a personalized formula for computing a sensitivity score, which determines the colour of each data flow in the sensitivity view. Profiles can be created and shared by trusted authorities, or the users themselves. This idea was mentioned during heuristic evaluation and in the interviews: "maybe a multiple choice at the start ... where they can decide which kind of data is sensitive for them ... the data will be presented in that way" (P12). OnLITE determines sensitivity by referring to Art. 9 of the GDPR, which defines "special categories of data", such as religious beliefs or sexual orientation. Note that the flow colours in Fig. 3 are not necessarily aligned with the GDPR, they were hand-tuned for experimental purposes, to see if the participants would notice the difference and how they would interpret it.

Critical thinking is an attitude that OnLITE helps foster, encouraging participants to reflect on the information shown to them. In some cases, they doubt that certain types of data are required for serving the declared purpose: "truth be told, I don't understand why they need to store the device Internet address" (P2), or "why would a temperature measuring device have this feature? This, I don't understand" (P11). In other cases, they would question the data retention period: "6 years, that's a long time for such a small purpose, I can't say it is reasonable" (P15). We consider this an important effect, as it guides participants towards questioning the status quo, as opposed to telling them what to believe.

7.2   Quantitative

The SUS results are given in Table 2 and Fig. 5. The mean score of OnLITE is 68, which matches the industry average for web interfaces [2]. Statistical analysis, by means of a t-test[1], did not reveal any correlation between SUS scores and age or gender. Prototype iterations have no significant difference in scores either, which we attribute to the incremental nature of the changes between versions. We have not found significant differences between expert and non-expert participants' SUS scores. This suggests that the observed variations can be attributed to individual preferences rather than the level of technical skill. While the low power of the t-test with such a sample size cannot rule out differences between groups, it would have revealed major and obvious effects, if they existed.

All participants completed all the tasks, except P1, P3, P4 and P6, who failed task M. Note that the session durations in Table 2 are not an indication of invested effort, because we encouraged participants to explore alternatives and elicited additional feedback, even after a task was done.

8 Discussion

Our results show that participants can understand and use the presented information. The data also reveal a void when it comes to an authority that regulates such labels. All participants agreed they would trust a label that came from "the government" or "a reputable international organization", however none gave a specific name. We believe the EU could be in a unique position to fill this gap, given that it is an international body, and that the GDPR is now in effect.

Sankey diagrams effectively visualize data sharing flows towards partner companies. They appealed to some of our participants and enabled them to make rapid judgments about which IoT device they prefer. However, some found them difficult to read at first. Thus, it is important to ensure that information is also conveyed in another form. Adding an instructional video that explains how the diagrams work had a positive impact on comprehension, and most participants watched the entire video without being nudged to do it. We believe that repeated exposure to OnLITE or the act of observing others reading the diagrams can further decrease the perceived effort.

"Overview" was chosen as the most informative tab by all participants, suggesting that it summarizes well the answers to the transparency questions in Sect. 3. We consider it a good choice for a starting page, as this way OnLITE conveys useful information to users, even if they do not explore other tabs.

Based on participants' positive feedback, we expected higher SUS scores. While this can be explained by two outliers who drove the score down (P8 and P14), it is also possible that OnLITE can be improved, or that a privacy-focused GUI is simply not appealing to users. They may not find the topic of privacy exciting, or the GUI could be perceived as a nuisance that stands in the way of using an IoT device that they are enthusiastic about. According to Bangor et al., the average SUS score varies depending on the type of system [2]. To the best of our knowledge, no SUS scores of similar transparency tools are available at the moment, so we cannot say with confidence whether or not "IoT transparency

---

[1] We chose this test because it is suitable for a sample size of 15, and because we have a normal distribution of scores, verified by means of a Shapiro-Wilk normality test.

tools" constitute a separate UI category with its specific average score. Sankey diagrams may be another reason why some scores were low. Even though the participants completed the tasks by finding answers in other tabs, we always insisted that they interpret the diagrams too. Thus, the diagram could have been seen as an "unnecessary effort".

8.1 Avoiding Scores

Our design only conveys facts and avoids judgment. Instead of telling consumers "what is better", we summarize information, so they can decide for themselves. This is inspired by the concept of *intelligence amplification*, where humans are assisted in various ways, yet remain central in the decision-making process [12]. While comparing device privacy ratings via scores is easy for consumers [11,19], such grading schemes have limitations. (1) Privacy does not map to a linear scale, unlike measurable physical quantities. (2) There is no scoring method that all stakeholders agree with yet. (3) Transparency requires an understanding of the answers to the questions listed in Sect. 3. Some of that information is qualitative in nature and cannot be expressed numerically. (4) Scores can hinder adoption. It is possible that a substantial portion of current IoT devices would get a low privacy score, potentially prompting manufacturers to use their lobbying power to limit a label's standardization. Thus, a gradual introduction of scores could be appropriate. While we have chosen not to use scores, we do not exclude doing so in the future, when the raised issues are addressed.

8.2 The Drawback of Sensor Lists

In contrast to Shen et al., who consider it "critical to enumerate all the sensors that are used by an IoT device" [35], we argue that a better approach is to show what information is *collected*, regardless of whether it was retrieved from sensors, inferred, or obtained through correlation with other data. Sensor lists can (1) obfuscate true intentions, while creating a false sense of security. For example, a device that is equipped with a camera and does *not* have a microphone can reasonably be considered as a "device that cannot record my voice". However, it is possible to extract an audio signal from video [8], thus companies can claim compliance, while engaging in unethical practices. (2) Such lists take valuable space, potentially drawing attention away from other details. (3) Products can contain sensors that are only used internally (e.g., a thermometer is needed to prevent overheating), and listing them could confuse users. (4) Sometimes a sensor can be physically present, but remain unused (e.g., due to economies of scale, keeping it may be cheaper than making a product version without it).

8.3 Limitations

Our tests did not include participants above the age of 44 and we had few novice participants. Although we may have overlooked issues that could occur with some groups, the interface is derived from a design that was evaluated with 31 participants of a wider range of ages and skills [32]. We also believe that heuristic evaluation further compensates this limitation, especially when most of the experts were at least in their forties. Another limitation is that we only tested the GUI on a laptop. We might have missed some issues that arise on touch-only devices with smaller screens. Finally, our evaluation did not explore what happens with repeated exposure to the GUI.

9   Related Work

Several designs were proposed to address IoT privacy and security issues. Some inherit the grid layout and the layered approach of [20]. A taxonomy proposed by [19] places privacy labels into one of three categories: *graded* labels that quantify security or privacy; *seals of approval* which show that a certification was attained, and *informational* labels that communicate facts about a device.

Van Diermen designed a graded and informational label for IoT, accompanied by an electronic interface [31]. The design is inspired by the EU energy efficiency label; it includes details about the support period, a list of processed data types and the available communication technologies, like Wi-Fi or Bluetooth. An extended version of the label provides information about security and the purpose of collection. However, this design has not been subjected to usability tests.

Shen et al. propose two informational labels for IoT [35]. Unlike in the case of LITE, more technical details are provided, e.g., a complete list of sensors and communication interfaces. This label employs a "traffic light" colour-scheme. For example, if encryption is not supported, the corresponding line will have a red marker. The design has not undergone a usability evaluation.

Grace et al. designed an informational privacy label and UI based on the GDPR. The details include a list of collected data, the purpose of collection, contact information and a list or rights that the user has. Although it has been user-validated by means of a focus group, it is not tailored for IoT devices [17].

Emami-Naeini et al. created a user-validated informational privacy and security label for IoT [10]. A difference is the use of scoring to quantify the level of privacy a device provides, while we have avoided using star ratings (see Sect. 8.1). Moreover, their design is not GDPR-centric, so it does not offer some specific information, like the location of the data, or the contact details of a DPA.

Bihr proposes a *trustmark for IoT*, a self-assessed, voluntary seal of approval [30]. Several regulators, e.g., Traficom (Finland) and the National Cyber Security Centre (UK) issue seals for IoT devices that meet a certain standard of security. The seals are derived from ETSI guidelines that dictate what security measures IoT devices should employ [13] (similar to the *security* tab of OnLITE). However, the seals do not convey privacy-related details, nor mandate the way this information ought to be visualized. Thus, they are not directly comparable to OnLITE.

10   Conclusions

We have proposed OnLITE, an on-line label for IoT transparency enhancement. The design has been examined through heuristic evaluation by legal and usability experts, and tested by 15 participants in a think-aloud task analysis study. The results indicate that the prototype conveys privacy facts in a way that can be understood by non-experts and experts alike. The participants find the interface useful, and are in favour of its wider availability. Our findings also suggest that the credibility of such a transparency tool could be higher, if it were regulated by governments or a reputable international organization.

Acknowledgments. We thank the participants of our study and our colleagues at the DPA of Schleswig-Holstein and USECON GmbH, as well as the open source contributors whose software we relied on. This research has received funding from the H2020 Marie Skłodowska-Curie EU project "Privacy&Us" under the grant agreement No 675730.

References

1. Aleisa, N., et al.: Privacy of the Internet of Things: a systematic literature review. In: International Conference on System Sciences (2017)
2. Bangor, A., et al.: An empirical evaluation of the system usability scale. Int. J. HCI **24**, 574–594 (2008)
3. Bos, B.: Data Privacy Vocabulary. W3C Recommendation, July 2019
4. Braun, V., et al.: Using thematic analysis in psychology. Qual. Res. Psychol. **3**, 77–101 (2006)
5. Brooke, J.: SUS - a quick and dirty usability scale. In: Usability Evaluation in Industry (1986)
6. Christin, D.: Privacy in mobile participatory sensing: current trends and future challenges. J. Syst. Softw. **116**, 57–68 (2016)
7. Cranor, L.F.: Necessary but not sufficient: standardized mechanisms for privacy notice and choice. JTHTL **10**, 36 (2012)
8. Davis, A., et al.: The visual microphone: passive recovery of sound from video. ACM Trans. Graph. **33**, 1–10 (2014)
9. De Cremer, D., et al.: The integrity challenge of the IoT. J. Mark. Manag. **33**, 145–158 (2017)
10. Emami-Naeini, P., et al.: Exploring how privacy and security factor into IoT device purchase behavior. In: CHI (2019)
11. Emami-Naeini, P., et al.: The influence of friends and experts on privacy decision making in IoT scenarios. In: ACM on HCI (2018)
12. Engelbart, D.: Augmenting human intellect. Technical report (1962)
13. ETSI: Cyber Security for Consumer IoT: Baseline Requirements. European Standard 303 645 (2020)
14. European Parliament and Council of European Union: Regulation 2016/679 of 27 April 2016. Official Journal of the European Union (2016)
15. Faulkner, L.: Beyond the five-user assumption. Behav. Res. Methods Instrum. Comput. **35**, 379–383 (2003)

16. Fischer-Hübner, S., Angulo, J., Karegar, F., Pulls, T.: Transparency, privacy and trust – technology for tracking and controlling my data disclosures: does this work? In: Habib, S.M.M., Vassileva, J., Mauw, S., Mühlhäuser, M. (eds.) IFIPTM 2016. IAICT, vol. 473, pp. 3–14. Springer, Cham (2016)
17. Fox, G., et al.: Communicating compliance: developing a GDPR privacy label. In: AMCIS (2018)
18. Greveler, U., et al.: Multimedia content identification through smart meter power usage profiles. In: IKE (2012)
19. Johnson, S., et al.: The impact of IoT security labelling on consumer product choice and willingness to pay. PLoS ONE **15**(1), e0227800 (2019)
20. Kelley, P.G., et al.: A nutrition label for privacy. In: SOUPS (2009)
21. Kosinski, M., et al.: Private traits and attributes are predictable from digital records of human behavior. PNAS **110**, 5802–5805 (2013)
22. Lane, N.D., et al.: On the feasibility of user de-anonymization from shared mobile sensor data. In: PhoneSense (2012)
23. Lau, J., et al.: Alexa, are you listening? In: ACM on HCI (2018)
24. Lupton, R., et al.: Hybrid sankey diagrams. In: Resources, Conservation and Recycling (2017)
25. Mcdonald, N., et al.: Reliability and inter-rater reliability in qualitative research. In: ACM on HCI (2019)
26. Miller, G.A.: The magical number 7 ± 2. Psychol. Rev. **63**, 81 (1956)
27. Narayanan, A., et al.: How to Break Anonymity of the Netflix Prize Dataset. arXiv preprint (2006)
28. Nielsen, J., et al.: Heuristic evaluation of user interfaces. In: CHI (1990)
29. Page, X., et al.: The internet of what? IMWUT **2**, 1–22 (2018)
30. Bihr, P.: A trustmark for IoT. Technical report, ThingsCon (2017)
31. van Diermen, R.: A privacy label for IoT products. Ph.D. thesis (2018)
32. Railean, A., et al.: Let there be LITE. In: MobileHCI (2018)
33. Railean, A., et al.: Life-long privacy in the IoT? In: IFIP PIM (2017)
34. Schneier, B.: Click Here to Kill Everybody (2018)
35. Shen, Y., Vervier, P.-A.: IoT security and privacy labels. In: Naldi, M., Italiano, G.F., Rannenberg, K., Medina, M., Bourka, A. (eds.) APF 2019. LNCS, vol. 11498, pp. 136–147. Springer, Cham (2019)
36. Theofanos, M., et al.: Usability testing of ten-print fingerprint capture. Technical report, National Institute of Standards and Technology (2007)
37. Trends-17. Technical report, Globalwebindex (2016)
38. Tullis, T.S., et al.: A comparison of questionnaires for assessing website usability. In Usability Professional Association Conference (2004)
39. Zheng, S., et al.: User perceptions of smart home IoT privacy. In: ACM on HCI (2018)
40. Ziegeldorf, J.H., et al.: Privacy in the IoT. In: Security and Communication Networks (2014)

An Investigation of Comic-Based Permission Requests

Katie Watson(✉) ⓘ, Mike Just ⓘ, and Tessa Berg ⓘ

Department of Computer Science, Heriot-Watt University, Edinburgh, Scotland, UK
{klw1,m.just,t.berg}@hw.ac.uk

Abstract. Research suggests that permission requests do not adequately inform users about the implications of granting or denying such requests. It is important that informed consent is given should users grant the request. This paper reports on the results of a study that examined novel comic-based permission request design in terms of user response and preferences for permission-granting decisions. We conducted co-design workshops to design the comic-based permission requests. We then compared our comic-based designs to current Android text-based permission requests using five common permission request types in an online survey. Our results showed that 52% of participants preferred the comic-based requests, and 24% the text-based requests. While comics were found to be an effective medium to achieve informed consent, some participants reported that the text-based request offered sufficient information to make decisions. Given that a relatively large number of participants preferred the comic-based permissions, we encourage future designers to consider alternative forms of permission requests.

Keywords: Mobile privacy · Comics · App permission requests

1 Introduction

Many smartphone features are provided through applications (apps) that typically require the smartphone user to grant access to resources on their phone by responding to a permission request. However, apps sometimes request access to resources that are not necessarily required, for example a gaming app that requests access to a phone's location. Even when the requested access might be necessary, the permission request descriptions may not be engaging or informative. Previous research showed that users paid little attention to the currently employed, text-based permission requests and displayed low comprehension of what was being asked of them [1]. Almuhimeda et al. [2] and Balebako et al. [3] concluded that users were generally unaware of data collection practices and were not comfortable with the amount of data being gathered and where this data was sent. This suggests that text-based permission requests can leave some smartphone users unaware of potential risks to the privacy of their data.

Previous research has explored the impact of personalized and contextualized versions of text-based permission requests [4, 5]. Kelley et al. [6] found that presenting participants with permission requests in a clear, simple and timely manner increased

© Springer Nature Switzerland AG 2021
M. Asplund and S. Nadjm-Tehrani (Eds.): NordSec 2020, LNCS 12556, pp. 246–261, 2021.
https://doi.org/10.1007/978-3-030-70852-8_15

the likelihood of participants installing applications that requested fewer permissions. Shih et al. [7] similarly found that when participants were presented with information that details the data that an app can access and the reasons why access is required, they were less likely to grant permissions. Despite these measures, researchers have found that many people still do not read permission requests.

Similar to permission requests, research into user acceptance and understanding of app Terms and Conditions (T&C) and Privacy Policies (PP) revealed that such information can be difficult to understand and is often not read [8]. Tabassum et al. [9] and Zhang-Kennedy et al. [10] used comics to teach users about threats to their privacy and security. They established that comics can increase the attention paid to T&C and PP. Researchers in other contexts, such as the medical field, have shown that comics can better educate patients and increase the understanding of, or adherence to medical instructions [11, 12]. As far as we are aware, no research has explored comic-based permission requests compared to their text counterparts.

In this paper, we report on the design of comic-based permission requests which are compared to current text-based permission requests, to investigate the viability of comics as another medium for the current requests. Our approach involves user-centered co-design workshops to inform the creation of the comic-based permission requests, and a survey to assess their effectiveness. In Sect. 2 we discuss related work and our comic-based request design in Sect. 3. In Sects. 4 and 5 we respectively present the survey design and results. In Sect. 6 we discuss some design implications, then our limitations in Sect. 7, followed by our conclusions and future work in Sect. 8.

2 Related Work

2.1 User Awareness

Users have been found to disregard or pay little attention to Terms and Conditions (T&C), Privacy Policies (PP) or privacy permissions [1, 13, 14]. Talib et al. [14] found that participants were not interested in reading the PP of social networking websites as they were too long, difficult to understand and not presented in an appealing manner. They further suggested that the presentation of PPs should be geared towards a multimedia and interactive approach to better engage users. Kelley et al. [6] similarly reported that most of their participants did not consider permissions when downloading apps and actively chose not to check which permissions would be required to install and use the app. Further, Morrison et al. [13], found that only 30% of participants realized a game that the researchers made available on an app store was part of an academic trial despite this being made clear in the T&C, They also found that none of the participants interviewed had read the T&C. Furthermore, even when users do read the T&C they do not necessarily understand them, due to complicated terminology and legalese [14]. Harris et al. [15] discovered that 63% of their participants felt there was often a good reason for apps to request questionable permissions and trusted the Apple app store and Google play markets. Despite this trust Kuehnhausen and Frost [16] have shown that app stores such as Apple app store and Google Play, often contain unsafe apps (e.g. that request unnecessary permissions). Felt et al. [1] found that only 3% of the participants who had read information related to permission requests had a good understanding of them and 42% of participants were unaware of the existence of permissions.

Since the introduction of Android 6.0 (Marshmallow) Android permissions have changed and are now often displayed on an Ask on First Use (AOFU) basis rather than prior to installation [17, 18]. AOFU permissions pop up on the screen when the user tries to use the functionality of an app. The request must be accepted or declined before the user can proceed. This means access is not requested or granted until required, which limits unwanted data collection. The introduction of AOFU permission requests means that whether a user ignores the T&C or PP, or fails to understand them, they will have to interact with permission requests.

2.2 Personalization and Contextualization of Permission Requests

Human Computer Interaction (HCI) research has investigated how personalization and contextualization can affect user receptiveness to permission requests. Personalization refers to information that has been tailored to each user specifically, whilst contextualization refers to the provision of additional information related to how other users have reacted to requests. Tan et al. [19] found that participants were more likely to grant permission requests when they had been allowed to personalize them. Additionally, they found that participants were more likely to grant access to permission requests which contained an explanation of why the app needed access, regardless of whether the explanation contained useful information. Raij et al. [20] likewise, argued the importance of personalization. They reported that participants did not understand the *"sensitive nature"* of the data shown if they had little or no personal stake in it.

Contextualization, unlike personalization is not concerned with the user personally, but with the circumstances surrounding them. Researchers have found that the way information detailing privacy is framed can influence the extent to which users are willing to share their information. Zhang and Xu [5] found that if privacy information is framed socially, such as "91% of people share location", people are more likely to share.

The framing (personalization and contextualization) of the information presented in the request should be designed carefully. Permissions requests should contain a sufficient amount of information to ensure users are informed, not coerced into decisions [7, 21]. This suggests the exploration of alternative, multimedia methods, such as comics, to frame permission requests could encourage users to pay more attention to the requests and in turn make more informed decisions.

2.3 Educational Comics

Comics are an alternative medium that researchers are exploring to successfully convey information more effectively than plain text. A comic is composed of a series of panels in which a story and message are conveyed using imagery and text. Pavio posited that as pictures are coded in two areas of the brain (visual and verbal), and words only one (verbal) that pictures are better remembered and retained for longer than words, which suggests comics could be useful aids in smartphone privacy [21].

Comics have proven to be effective educational tools, with research showing their successful implementation in the healthcare field [11, 22, 23]. Comics have proven similarly effective in online security and privacy contexts [9, 10]. Tabassum et al. [9] explored the use of comic versions of T&Cs as a replacement for text-based T&Cs. They found that comic versions held user attention for longer than text versions but did not improve comprehension. Conversely, Zhang-Kennedy et al. [10, 24] found that the graphical and interactive elements of their comics (Secure Comics) aided reader comprehension. Additionally, they found that Secure Comics improved the understanding of security threats and facilitated readers into more security conscious decisions. Equally, Mekhail et al. [25] explored the use of infographics in a mobile privacy context to determine whether infographics were more beneficial for users than text. They found the infographic information led to 64% of participants reportedly taking additional measures to protect their privacy and approximately two thirds of the users could describe the concepts shown in the infographics. This suggests images alongside text not only help with comprehension but are more likely to be read than their text counterparts and in some cases lead to more privacy conscious decisions.

3   Comic-Based Permission Requests Design

3.1   Co-design Workshops

Over the course of three days we conducted a series of 3 co-design workshops in several UK locations to inform the design of our comic-base permission requests. 13 participants were recruited through a social media and poster campaign (Table 1). The workshops began with a general introduction to comics and comic creation, after which participants in each workshop were spilt into 2 groups and used "big paper" prototyping techniques [26] to create the comics together. Participants were given the descriptions of the permission requests available today on the Android Google Play Store [18] to help guide them. An example of one of the created comics is in Fig. 1. Within their group (intragroup) participants then used the sticky note evaluation technique to answer pre-set evaluation questions, such as *"How could your comic(s) be improved?"*. They then similarly discussed their comics to the other group (intergroup). The intragroup and intergroup discussions were recorded and transcribed. The comics created were analyzed using four design themes inspired by McCloud [27]: (1) tone, (2) characters, (3) content, (4) aesthetic quality. We similarly use these themes to present our final designs in Sect. 4.

Table 1. Co-design workshops demographic information

Workshop	Participants	Mean age	Gender
1	1–4	26.75	2 Male, 2 Female
2	5–8	26.75	4 Male
3	9–13	31	3 Male, 2 Female

Fig. 1. A comic showing the addition of a solution, created during the workshop

For theme one, tone, participants indicated the comics should be light and humorous to some extent, which aligns with people's perceptions of most comics [27]. They were also cautious about the frequency of *"negative"* or *"scare mongering"* aspects of comics. For theme two, characters, participants preferred and drew characters that could exist in the real world, that were likeable, relatable and that reoccur. For theme three, content, participants felt that the comics should have a clear storyline, be easy to follow and that showed negative and positive aspects of permission requests. One group realized that their comic was entirely negative, so they decided to add narrator text to their comic's last slide which informed the reader that they could still make changes to their permissions (Fig. 1). This group wanted comics to show solutions and felt that in doing so they could make comics more positive. For the final theme, aesthetics, participants believed that the amount of text and imagery should be balanced and expressed concern over the quality of their drawings and lack of color. Participants also felt that comics should be large enough for readers to read. We used the information gained from these participatory workshops to support the design of our online survey comic-based permission requests, as discussed below.

3.2   Comic-Based Permission Request Creation

Figure 2 provides examples of the comic-based permission request and sample of the text-based permission request for a generic storage and camera app (respectively) that we used in our survey. Permissions were created for five of the more risky permission types concerning privacy and security (camera, calendar, contacts, location and storage) [28]. The comic-based permission requests are centered around 2 main characters, who encounter permission requests and consider their impact.

For the first design theme, tone, humor has been incorporated into the stories to lighten the mood and to help to create a more enjoyable reading experience. Humor has

Fig. 2. Two comic-based requests shown to participants. For the text-based variants participants saw only the bottom portion, centered vertically (as with current requests).

been found to be a successful tool in gaining and holding attention [29], which is an aspect that the current permission requests are lacking [14], though it is also recognized that humor can be culturally-specific [30]. For the second theme, character, most of the characters created during our workshop were human. Therefore, we focused on creating a relatable human protagonist, designed to have few gender defining characteristics. These choices were made in the hope that readers would identify or relate with the character more if they could interpret the character to be of whichever gender they choose or desire. The literature on character identification has highlighted that people are more likely to have wishful identification with a same-gender character [31]. The secondary character is an anthropomorphic cat, designed to introduce humor into the comic and facilitate dialogue or the progression of the storyline. For the third theme, content, the comic text has been kept relatively informal and simple, as literature has suggested that this helps to increase user understanding [14]. The comics have also been designed to provide the reader with more information about the permission request and has the characters consider what using the app could mean for their privacy. The characters never suggest a correct decision, rather they simply reflect on what granting the permission could mean for them. Additionally, as suggested in our workshops, two of our comics (camera and location) were designed to offer solutions to participants on how they could protect their privacy if they choose to grant the permission, such as by later revoking access or turning off location (e.g., camera request in Fig. 2). Finally, for the fourth theme, the aesthetic of comics are minimized, with simple line drawings for the illustrations. Research has shown that stripping down the comics to their simplest form amplifies the message conveyed by the comics and minimizes distraction [27]. The simplistic style of the comics also helped ensure the comic-based permission requests were more easily read and understood on smaller screens. We decided against the introduction of color, as it could prove problematic with cultural differences and color associations [32].

4   Survey Design

Given our focus on behaviors and perceptions of permission requests an online survey was created to compare the viability of the comics-based requests to the current text-based permission requests [33]. The text-based permission requests were based on Android permission requests, and displayed as they would look on a smartphone, (participation in the survey was open to users of any device or operating system). Participants were not provided any context for the app requesting the permissions in this study, in order to reduce the number of variables influencing their decision and to allow us to focus on a comparison of the two permission request styles. The survey[1] consisted of 3 stages: (1) Demographics and permission statement questions, (2) Permission request responses and (3) Preference and efficacy questions.

In the first stage, demographic information was used to determine any answer patterns for our survey participants. Demographic questions included age, gender, familiarity with comics and permission requests, to gain an understanding of prior knowledge. The permission statement questions sought to evaluate participant knowledge of permissions and privacy risks, and whether this influenced their responses. For these questions, participants were asked whether they agreed or disagreed (or were unsure) with statements such as *"Once a permission requests is accepted you cannot change your mind"*. There were eight statements based on similar statements from related research [24]. In the second (and main) stage, participants were presented with comic and text-based permission requests for each of five permission types: camera, calendar, contacts, location and storage (see examples in Fig. 2). The different permission types were presented to each participant in random order. For each permission request, participants were asked how likely they would be to allow each permission on a 5-point scale (1 = *extremely likely*, 5 = *extremely unlikely*), as well as an open-ended question *"what makes you feel this way?"*. In the third stage, participants were asked which permission requests they preferred, felt taught them more (teachability), and felt they understood better (understandability).

A series of statistical analysis tests were carried out on the quantitative data using SPSS. As the data collected is ordinal data and not normally distributed a series of non-parametric tests were completed. Due to multiple comparisons being made, Bonferroni Corrections were employed, dividing the significance value by the number of tests run. Content analysis was used to analyze the qualitative data from our open-ended questions. Krippendorff's alpha [34] inter-coder reliability test with one other coder (who was not

---

[1] A full copy of the survey can be found here: https://www.macs.hw.ac.uk/~mjust/projects/app Permissions/.

involved in our study) was run to confirm the coding reliability. A sample was randomly selected and alongside the generated categories was sent to the second coder. The chosen sample was approximately 10% (112 units) of the data gathered [35]. Results showed a solid inter-coder reliability score ($\alpha = 0.8928$).

5 Survey Results

We recruited 240 participants, with 204 completing the survey. Considering the stage 1 demographic data, of the 204 participants 83 were male (41%), 120 were female (59%) and 1 preferred not to say. The mean age was 33.5, (med = 29, min = 18, max = 69). The majority of participants were from the UK (38%) and New Zealand (37%) with some from the USA (5%) and the rest from 20 other countries. The majority (71%) were employed, with the remainder being students (22%), self-employed (8%), unemployed (3%), retired (1%), or unable to work (<1%) – some participants chose multiple options. 52% were Android users, with 48% Apple iOS users.

The responses to the permission statement questions suggest that participants did not fully comprehend the potential consequences of granting permission requests, with fewer than half (41%) were unsure or did not know the correct response, and only 8% of participants answered all the statements correctly. We graded the responses using a letter grading system, to help group and compare participants by their levels of understanding. A letter based on the percentage of correct responses was assigned to each participant, spilt into 5 groups, with A = 90–100% and E < 60%. Therefore, for example, those who scored 8/8 were assigned an A, whereas those who scored 4/8 or under were grouped E. We used these grades to examine if participants with different grades responded differently to the permission requests.

5.1 Permission Request Responses and Preferences

For our stage 2 data, Wilcoxon signed ranks test indicated that there was a statistically significant difference between those who would grant access to permissions based on whether the permission request was comic-based or text-based. Overall, participants were less likely to grant access when shown a comic-based permission request (Mdn = 2) than they were when shown a text-based permission request (Mdn = 3), $Z = -7.359, p > 0.001$. Overall, we found that participants aged 18–44 were significantly less likely to grant comic-based permissions and this difference was not significant for those over 44 years. Out of the 5 different permission types investigated (camera, calendar, contacts, location and storage), the comic-based versions for the calendar, contact and storage permissions were all significantly less likely to be granted (Table 2). These were the comic-based requests that did not offer a solution. The two requests which offered a solution, camera and location, were not significantly different when compared to their text-based counterparts. However, when compared against the other permission types, location and camera are significantly more likely to be granted in general than all the other requests (both comic and text-based versions), which suggests that the location and camera permission types might be more likely to be allowed in general. We found no other statistically significant differences in participants responses to comic-based versus text-based permission requests for any other demographic factors, or participant responses to the permission statement questions. A comparison of all permissions is in Fig. 3.

For stage 3, participants were asked which permission request types they preferred: 52% preferred comic requests, 24% text, 17.2% had no preference, and 6.9% would prefer no requests. Additionally, participants were asked which permission request they would rather experience in the future. 52.9% preferred comic requests, 27.9% text, 15.2% said it did not matter, and 3.9% preferred no permissions. Tests were carried out to explore whether demographics or the permission statement questions influenced preference and no such correlations were found.

Table 2. Sig. Wilcoxon Signed-Rank test results comparing comic and text-based permissions

Type of permission	Median	Mean	Std. d	Z	p
Calendar comic	2	2.45	1.34	−6.16	>.001
Calendar text	3	2.96	1.36		
Camera comic	3	2.75	1.36	−0.453	0.651
Camera text	3	2.8	1.36		
Contact comic	2	2.10	1.20	−5.08	>.001
Contact text	2	2.47	1.35		
Location comic	3	2.91	1.30	−0.122	0.903
Location text	3	2.90	1.25		
Storage comic	2	2.35	1.26	−5.12	>.001
Storage text	3	2.81	1.32		

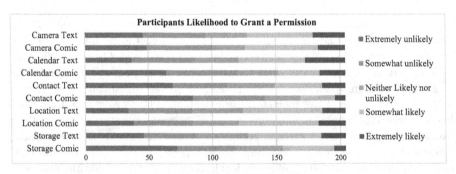

Fig. 3. Graph comparing participants overall likelihood to grant each permission

5.2 Permission Request Understanding & Teachability – Quantitative Results

In stage 3, participants were also asked how understandable they felt the comic and text-based permissions were. Likert scale results showed that 62.3% of participants felt the comic-based requests were *extremely easy* to understand, and 25% felt they were *somewhat easy*. For the text-based 39% of participants felt that they were *extremely easy* to understand and 29% *somewhat easy*. A Wilcoxon Signed-Ranks test showed that there was a significant difference between the perceived understanding of comic and text-based permissions, with comic-based (Mdn = 5) permissions being perceived as more understandable than the text-based (Mdn = 4), Z = −4.298, p > 0.001.

Additionally, participants were asked how effective they felt the comic and text-based requests were at teaching them about what can happen to their data if they allow access. Likert scale results showed that 43% felt the comic requests were *extremely effective* at teaching, and 13% felt the text requests were *extremely effective*. 33.8% felt that comic requests were *somewhat effective*, and 18% felt text requests were *somewhat effective*. A Wilcoxon Signed-Ranks test established a significant difference between how much participants felt that each version of permission request taught them, with the comic-based requests (Mdn = 5) being viewed as more effective at teaching participants than the text-based (Mdn = 2). Z = −8.895, p > 0.001.

5.3   Permission Request Understanding & Teachability – Qualitative Results

Out of the 204 participants, 178 (87.3%) stated they felt that the comic-based permission requests were *somewhat* or *extremely easy* to understand. When asked *"what makes you feel this way?"* 106 participants indicated that this was due to the informative nature of the requests. Participants wrote that they felt the comics were detailed and offered a better explanation. Participants also stated that the comic visuals made it easier to understand the consequences of allowing the permission, and that they grabbed their attention *"You see a picture and you get the words in it. If it was just text I don't think the questions would capture my attention as much as they did with the cartoon"* (P5). Participants responded positively to the characters and humor of the comics *"[The comics are] Really straightforward, the scenarios are great, funny but also raise awareness. Love the cats, especially the lady cat"* (P83).

However, ten participants reported that the additional information in the comic-based permission requests was difficult to understand. In terms of aesthetics, participants remarked that the requests were cluttered, and that comics are an inappropriate medium to convey permission requests. Some participants felt that the comic-based requests were *"unprofessional"*, and even though they were easy to understand, they found the comic-based requests *"a little trivializing"* (P23). Participants also remarked that the comic-based requests were too positive and assumed that they would encourage readers to either ignore them or be too open to accept, *"Comic versions seem too light-hearted for my device. A little too 'right on'"* (P23) despite the results showing evidence of the reverse. Another participant disliked the comic-based permissions as they taught them too much and preferred to be left in the dark *"comic version made me less likely to want to accept, so couldn't use app if wanted to"* (P176). Some participants also felt that more information should be included, such as why access needs to be granted, e.g., *"I only really trust permission popups when they have some context about why the app requires the permission"* (P113).

Out of the 204 participants, 139 participants (68.6%) said they felt the text-based requests were somewhat or extremely easy to understand. 22 participants indicated this was due to the straightforward nature of the requests, as they found the requests, *"Neutral, straight to the point and clear"* (P150) and that there was *"No misleading jargon"* (P156). Other participants indicated that it is what they are used to e.g. *"It's what's always used, so everyone understands it"* (P129. Participants also indicated they preferred the *"clear and concise"* (P110) nature of the text requests, as *"They were simple and not overwhelming with information"* (P184).

Some participants stated their preference for text-based permission requests was due to their prior knowledge, e.g. *"I'm younger and have been using this tech from the beginning"* (P103) and *"They seem straightforward. Maybe because i have a CS background or i'm just familiar with them."* (P83). However, one participant did suggest that people may not be engaged by text-based requests, *"I feel I'm slightly more tech savvy (and paranoid) than the average user. I doubt most people do more than glance and agree"* (P117). Participants also indicated that more information should be included, e.g. *"Easy to understand but lacking context"* (P23), and *"they were pretty straight forward but didnt give much context to someone who doesnt understand"* (P8). Additionally, some participants expressed concern for other user's privacy as the implications are not clear in the text-based requests e.g. *"the permission requests are easily understood. The implications of them are not. They can seem innocuous, but I could be giving away far more than I realise"* (P28) and *"They are written simply and seem clear, but there are unspoken implications of decreased privacy"* (P202).

77% of participants felt that the comic requests were either *"somewhat"* or *"extremely effective"* at teaching people about smartphone permissions and indicated that this was due to the informative nature of the requests. Participants commented on how the comics reminded them of potential consequences of allowing access, e.g., *"[the comics are] much better than text, many users would just hit approve without thinking it through but this step forces a secondary appraisal"* (P69). Participants also regularly commented about the *"succinct"* nature of the requests and the level of convenience offered through the visual aspect of the comic-based permission requests, e.g., *"Visually better at communicating the point than words"* (P79). The addition of a graphic element was said to help visualize what happens when a request is allowed and how to change it. Participants also mentioned how the visual nature of the comic requests may be beneficial to people who have limited knowledge of permission requests.

Some participants (8.3%) felt that the comic requests were *"ineffective"* or *"nether ineffective nor effective"* at teaching users about permissions and stated that they were already knowledgeable in the topic. However, one user who felt this way suggested they could see the value for other users: *"Im very aware of the dangers of cyber threats, so for me this didnt teach me anything new, but for others i see it being quite valuable"* (P1). One participant further felt the comic-based requests taught them the concepts behind the current text-based requests *"They were straightforward.[text-based permissions] But, I didn't really grasp the concepts behind them until I saw the comics"* (P70).

30% of participants indicated that they felt the text requests were *"somewhat"* or *"extremely effective"* at teaching people about smartphone permissions. Participants indicated this was due to the text-based requests being familiar and the simplicity of the requests. Participants specified that they felt that text-based permission requests contained *"Clear information"* (P110) and that *"They asked you simply so it's easy to understand what they want"* (P78). The experience of the participants also had an impact on their perceived teachability, as participants commented, *"I am aware of security and privacy concerns so more openness and transparency is good"* (P127) and *"I can read"* (P32) One participant also felt the lack of information was a positive, *"you are not aware of danger you are more likely to accept the request"* (P196). In addition participants commented that their data is *"worthless"*: *"In my opinion, my data is worthless. I'm not famous, I'm not a wanted criminal. I don't care who knows about me. Privacy is dead anyways so better not to remind people that it's dead."* (P129). A few participants displayed a lack of concern towards their personal privacy on smartphones, with participants indicating they are not bothered by permissions and that they are always going to accept them in the future.

52% of participants felt that the text requests were *"ineffective"* or *"nether ineffective nor effective"* at teaching users about permissions. 72 participants indicated this was due to the uninformative nature of the text-based requests, as *"It is easy to just click yes without fully realising the implications. They did not explain request or any of the consequences of saying yes"* (P7). Additionally, participants also suggested the level of trust between users and app providers could influence responses e.g. *"It is generic and could mean many different things, ultimately it comes down to how much trust you have in the app"* (P90) and *"I felt like I was trusting and blindly accepting just so I could use the app."* (P202). Concern regarding less knowledgeable users was also expressed, with participants suggesting the requests *"assume knowledge"*. E.g., *"those with little technology experience won't understand the implications"* (P52) and *"no other info given. Its just assumed you understand what you're agreeing to"* (P91).

6   Discussion

While some participants continued to prefer the text-based permissions, a large proportion saw some value with the comic-based permission requests. However, there were also some criticisms and suggestions for improvement. We discuss such feedback below with an aim to inform future designs and studies. We structure our discussion based on the four design themes identified previously: (1) tone; (2) characters; (3) content; and, (4) aesthetic quality.

Tone: The results suggest that the tone conveyed by each of the permission requests had an impact on preference. Participants responded positively to humorous comics and negatively to comics perceived as *"A little too 'right on'"* (P23) or that they *"Only tells me about the negative use"* (P15). For some of the participants the somewhat lighthearted and humorous nature of the comics made them seem *"friendlier"* (P74 & P111), and more likely to engage with the permission request as they found them entertaining *"More informative, entertaining, willing to read"* (P201) and *"It's more entertaining than the usual neutral messages."* (P150). Overall, the majority of participants found the comics *"friendlier"*, *"entertaining,"* and more *"engaging"* and the *"light-hearted"* humorous tone of the comics an improvement over the clinical text-based requests. However, some participants felt the comics were a little *"patronizing"* or preachy which led to them favoring the text-based permissions. Participants who favored text-based permissions felt that they were more *"simple"* and *"professional"* which they felt made them more appropriate mediums to request access. Despite this, one participant who was initially wary of comics reported *"At first I thought it was childish but then I realized the importance of what's being said."* (P98). This suggests that whilst a humorous tone shows promise in creating more engaging permission requests [29], not everybody appreciates the same humor. This could be overcome in future designs by offering user choice of whether they receive comic or text-based permission requests, and the tone (e.g., serious or lighthearted).

Characters: An advantage comics have over text is that they make use of characters who inhabit a story to convey the information. The results likewise suggest that the characters in the comics had an impact on participant preference. Participants in general responded positively to the two main characters, as they felt that they were *"relatable"* and made the requests seem personal. For example, *"The comics themselves with the characters going through similar experiences to the user made the request more personal, like the request is talking to me personally. Plain text just seems flat, or dead. It doesn't care about informing me, it just wants access."* (P16), *"The characters hesitation added to my hesitation"* (P118) and *"Consequences are shown explicitly. The character weighs up the pros and cons, showing us what is at stake"* (P70). By encouraging users to empathize with the characters, permission requests can be re-framed as a personal request from character to reader rather than a formal request for access to data. The presence of relatable characters undergoing similar experiences as the reader, and the personal nature of the request could encourage further reflection on what is being asked of the user. Previous research has shown that if participants have a personal stake in a matter it can increase participant understanding of privacy risks [20].

Content: The content of the permissions requests was also found to greatly influence user preference and likelihood of allowing different permissions. This is seen when a solution was proposed within the comic-based permissions, leading to participants being just as likely to allow a permission compared to a text-based permission request. This could be a result of the privacy and control paradox [36], with solutions offering participants a feeling of increased control over their data, helping them justify their current text-based response. In other words, the solution offered in the comic might remind the user that they can change their mind and deny access to the permission at a later time. Solutions additionally offer a rationale for participants to allow access, though it is even unclear whether participants will follow through and later deny access previously allowed. Similar effects have been noted by other researchers [37] and is reflected by participants in our study, for example, *"the actual impact by normalising the tracking behaviour. 'I can always turn it off when I want' is a big lie. Users don't turn things off per use. They set their settings and leave them alone most of the time."* (P30). The inclusion of a solution, providing the impression of increased control, could lead some users to allow access they ordinarily would not, as they know they can revisit such access. In this way our results suggest that the content of the request, in particular the inclusion of a solution, could trigger other decision-making considerations by users. We encourage researchers to study the impact of solutions in permission requests further. The inclusion of solutions in permission requests warrants further study.

Aesthetic quality: In terms of the aesthetic quality of the comic-based permissions requests, the majority of participants responded positively, with participants indicating that the use of visuals contributed to increased understanding. This phenomenon, *"pictorial superiority effect"* [38] was highlighted in numerous participants responses, *"The comics explain in pictures what the permission actually involves"* (P47) and *"Visuals are easier to understand than reading"* (P79). Participants indicated the comics were *"Well drawn, clear and concise"* (P50) and *"Good visual cues"* (P45). However, some felt the addition of comics to permission requests came across as *"unprofessional"*, and *"scaremongering"*. Some participants echoed this sentiment and stated they preferred text-based permission as they are *"used to it"*. This could suggest that personal preference and an individual's opinion on comics as a medium could influence receptiveness of use: *"They were straightforward.* [the text-based permissions] *But, I didn't really grasp the concepts behind them until I saw the comics"* (P70). This implies that even though some users will prefer the current text-based requests, there are users who will benefit from the additional visual cue.

7 Limitations

Our survey was not limited to users on smartphones. Therefore, the effectiveness of the comic-based permission requests may differ between participants using a larger screen. Also, the requests were not experienced by users as they would be in a real-life situation, and as such potential disruption or irritation caused by a permission request is not explored. Finally, the comparison with today's text-based permissions doesn't necessarily reveal which aspects (e.g. the introduction of imagery or text) of the comics affects behavior. Future studies could compare comic-based designs to enhanced text-based designs to confirm the effect of the visual aspects of comics.

8 Conclusion and Future Work

Comic-based permission requests show promise, at least for some users. The results of our survey indicate that many participants preferred the comic-based permissions. Participants also reported that they found the comics easier to understand and that they were more informative. However, a number of participants did continue to prefer current text-based permission requests. Participants also requested that both types of requests (text and comic-based) contain more information about implications behind allowing access, and why the app requires access.

Future work could include investigating further improvements to permission requests, possibly by running co-design workshops with a different set of users, or by including personalized options so that users might choose the type of permission request that they would see. Furthermore, the applicability of humor could be further explored, and comics of another tone (e.g., less lighthearted) created and tested. The level of information presented in permission requests could also be explored, not only in comic-based permission requests but also text-based permission requests. Comic-based permission requests with more or less information could be tested, as could enhanced text-based permission requests. The impact of aesthetics could also be examined, with the creation of more detailed or colored comics. Future studies should consider *"in the wild"* evaluations to investigate the acceptance of new types of permission requests in more realistic contexts.

References

1. Felt, A.P., Ha, E., Egelman, S., et al.: Android permissions: user attention, comprehension, and behavior. In: SOUPS 2012 (2012)
2. Almuhimedi, H., Schaub, F., Sadeh, N., et al.: Your location has been shared 5,398 times!: a field study on mobile app privacy nudging. In: CHI 2015 (2015)
3. Balebako, R., Jung, J., Lu, W., et al.: Little brothers watching you': raising awareness of data leaks on smartphones. In: SOUPS 2013 (2013)
4. Shklovski, I., Mainwaring, S.D., Skúladóttir, H.H., et al.: Leakiness and creepiness in app space: perceptions of privacy and mobile app use. In: CHI 2014 (2014)
5. Zhang, B., Xu, H.: Privacy nudges for mobile applications: effects on the creepiness emotion and privacy attitudes. In: CSCW 2016 (2016)
6. Kelley, P.G., Cranor, L.F., Sadeh, N.: Privacy as part of the app decision-making process. In: CHI 2013 (2013)
7. Shih, F., Liccardi, I., Weitzner, D.: Privacy tipping points in smartphones privacy preferences. In: CHI 2015 (2015)
8. Cranor, L.F., Hoke, C., Leon, P.G., et al.: Are they worth reading? An in-depth analysis of online advertising companies' privacy policies, p. 23 (2014)
9. Tabassum, M., Alqhatani, A., Aldossari, M., et al.: Increasing user attention with a comic-based policy. In: CHI 2018 (2018)
10. Zhang-Kennedy, L., Carleton, R.B., Carleton, S.C.: Secure comics: an interactive comic series for improving cyber security and privacy, pp. 1–3 (2017)
11. Furuno, Y., Sasajima, H.: Medical comics as tools to aid in obtaining informed consent for stroke care. Medicine **94**, 4 (2015)
12. Kraft, S.A., Constantine, M., Magnus, D., et al.: A randomized study of multimedia informational aids for research on medical practices: Implications for informed consent. Clin. Trials J. Soc. Clin. Trials **14**(1), 94–102 (2017)
13. Morrison, A., Brown, O., McMillan, D., et al.: Informed consent and users' attitudes to logging in large scale trials. In: CHI EA 2011 (2011)
14. Talib, S., Razak, S.M.A., Olowolayemo, A., et al.: Perception analysis of social networks' privacy policy: Instagram as a case study. In: ICT4M. IEEE (2014)
15. Harris, M.A., Brookshire, R., Patten, K., et al.: Mobile application installation influences: have mobile device users become desensitized to excessive permission requests. In: AMCIS 2015 (2015)
16. Kuehnhausen, M., Frost, V.S.: Trusting smartphone apps? To install or not to install, that is the question. In: CogSIM 2013. IEEE (2013)
17. Reinfelder, L., Schankin, A., Russ, S., Benenson, Z.: An inquiry into perception and usage of smartphone permission models. In: Furnell, S., Mouratidis, H., Pernul, G. (eds.) TrustBus 2018. LNCS, vol. 11033, pp. 9–22. Springer, Cham (2018). https://doi.org/10.1007/978-3-319-98385-1_2
18. Google. Permissions overview. Documentation, Permissions overview (2019). https://developer.android.com/guide/topics/permissions/overview
19. Tan, J., Nguyen, K., Theodorides, M., et al.: The effect of developer-specified explanations for permission requests on smartphone user behavior. In: CHI 2014 (2014)
20. Raij, A., Ghosh, A., Kumar, S., et al.: Privacy risks emerging from the adoption of innocuous wearable sensors in the mobile environment. In: CHI 2011 (2011)
21. Paivio, A.: Picture superiority in free recall: imagery or dual coding? Cogn. Psychol. **5**, 31 (1973)
22. McNicol, S.: The potential of educational comics as a health information medium. Health Inf. Libr. J. **34**, 20–31 (2017)

23. Delp, C., Jones, J.: Communicating information to patients: the use of cartoon illustrations to improve comprehension of instructions. Acad. Emerg. Med. **3**, 264–270 (1996)
24. Zhang-Kennedy, L., Chiasson, S., Biddle, R.: The role of instructional design in persuasion: a comics approach for improving cybersecurity. Int. J. HCI **32**(3), 215–257 (2016)
25. Mekhail, C., Zhang-Kennedy, L., Chiasson, S.: Visualizations to Teach about Mobile Online Privacy (2014)
26. Guha, M.L., Druin, A., Chipman, G., et al.: Mixing ideas: a new technique for working with young children as design partners. In: IDC 2004 (2004)
27. McCloud, S.: Understanding Comics - The Invisible Art, 1st edn. HarperCollins Publishers, New York (1994)
28. Harris, M.A., Chin, A.G.: Consumer trust in Google's top developers' apps: an exploratory study. Inf. Comput. Secur. **24**, 474–495 (2016)
29. Powell, J.P., Andresen, L.W.: Humour and teaching in higher education. Stud. High. Edu. **10**(1), 79–90 (1985)
30. Laroche, M., Vinhal Nepomuceno, M., Richard, M.-O.: Congruency of humour and cultural values in print ads: cross-cultural differences among the US, France and China. Int. J. Advertising **33**, 681–705 (2014)
31. Hoffner, C., Buchanan, M.: Young adults' wishful identification with television characters: the role of perceived similarity and character attributes. Media Psychol. **7**, 325–351 (2005)
32. Aslam, M.M.: Are you selling the right colour? A cross-cultural review of colour as a marketing cue. J. Mark. Commun. **12**, 15–30 (2006)
33. Müller, H., Sedley, A., Ferrall-Nunge, E.: Survey research in HCI. In: Olson, J.S., Kellogg, W.A. (eds.) Ways of Knowing in HCI, pp. 229–266. Springer, New York (2014). https://doi.org/10.1007/978-1-4939-0378-8_10
34. Hayes, A.F., Krippendorff, K.: Answering the call for a standard reliability measure for coding data. Commun. Methods Meas. **1**, 77–89 (2007)
35. Lombard, M., Snyder-Duch, J., Bracken, C.C.: Practical resources for assessing and reporting intercoder reliability in content analysis research projects (2010)
36. Brandimarte, L., Acquisti, A., Loewenstein, G.: Misplaced confidences: privacy and the control paradox. Soc. Psychol. Pers. Sci. **4**, 340–347 (2013)
37. Patil, S., Schlegel, R., Kapadia, A., et al.: Reflection or action?: how feedback and control affect location sharing decisions. In: CHI 2014 (2014)
38. Winograd, E., Smith, A.D., Simon, E.W.: Aging and the picture superiority effect in recall. J. Gerontol. **37**, 70–75 (1982)

Author Index

Printed in the United States
By Bookmasters